Social Work Evaluation

Related books of interest

Research Methods for Social Workers: A Practice-Based Approach, Second Edition

Samuel S. Faulkner and Cynthia A. Faulkner

Doing Research: The Hows and Whys of Applied Research, Third Edition

Nel Verhoeven

Using Statistical Methods in Social Work Practice with a Complete SPSS Guide, Second Edition

Soleman H. Abu-Bader

A Practical Guide to Social Service Evaluation, Second Edition

Carl F. Brun

Clinical Assessment for Social Workers: Quantitative and Qualitative Methods, Third Edition

Catheleen Jordan and Cynthia Franklin

Navigating Human Service Organizations, Third Edition

Rich Furman and Margaret Gibelman

Social Service Workplace Bullying: A Betrayal of Good Intentions

Kathryn Brohl

Policy, Politics, and Ethics: A Critical Approach

Thomas M. Meenaghan, Keith M. Kilty, Dennis D. Long, and John G. McNutt

Social Work Practice with Families: A Resiliency-Based Approach, Second Edition

Mary Patricia Van Hook

Child and Family Practice: A Relational Approach

Shelley Cohen Konrad

Social Work Evaluation
Enhancing What We Do
Second Edition

JAMES R. DUDLEY
University of North Carolina at Charlotte

LYCEUM
BOOKS, INC.

Chicago, Illinois

© 2014 by Lyceum Books, Inc.

Published by

LYCEUM BOOKS, INC.
5758 S. Blackstone Avenue
Chicago, Illinois 60637
773-643-1903 fax
773-643-1902 phone
lyceum@lyceumbooks.com
www.lyceumbooks.com

6 5 4 3 2   14 15 16 17 18

ISBN 978-1-935871-40-8

Printed in the United States of America.

Library of Congress Cataloging-in-Publication Data

Dudley, James R.
   Social work evaluation : enhancing what we do / James R. Dudley,
University of North Carolina Charlotte. — Second edition.
      pages cm
   Includes bibliographical references and index.
   ISBN 978-1-935871-40-8 (pbk. : alk. paper)
   1. Social service—Evaluation. 2. Evaluation research (Social action programs)
I. Title.
   HV41.D83   2014
   361.3072—dc23
                                                   2013015830

I dedicate this book to my students, who have inspired and encouraged me over many years. I am deeply grateful to them!

Contents

CSWE's Core Competencies Practice Behaviors Covered in This Book

Competency	Chapter
Professional Identity	
Practice behavior examples	
Advocate for client access to the services of social work	2, 4, 6, 7, 8, 11, 12
Practice personal reflection and self-correction to assure continual professional development	3
Attend to professional roles and boundaries	1, 2, 3, 7
Demonstrate professional demeanor in behavior, appearance, and communication	3, 6, 7
Engage in career-long learning	
Use supervision and consultation	1
Ethical Practice	
Practice behavior examples	
Recognize and manage personal values in a way that allows professional values to guide practice	2, 3, 12
Make ethical decisions by applying standards of the National Association of Social Workers' Code of Ethics and, as applicable, of the International Federation of Social Workers/International Association of Schools of Social Work Ethics in Social Work, Statement of Principles	1, 2, 3, 9
Tolerate ambiguity in resolving ethical conflicts	3
Apply strategies of ethical reasoning to arrive at principled decisions	1, 2, 3, 10
Critical Thinking	
Practice behavior examples	
Distinguish, appraise, and integrate multiple sources of knowledge, including research-based knowledge and practice wisdom	1, 2, 4, 6, 10, 12
Analyze models of assessment, prevention, intervention, and evaluation	2, 4, 5, 6, 8, 9, 10, 12
Demonstrate effective oral and written communication in working with individuals, families, groups, organizations, communities, and colleagues	5, 7, 11

Diversity in Practice

Practice behavior examples

Recognize the extent to which a culture's structures and   2, 3
   values may oppress, marginalize, alienate, or create or
   enhance privilege and power

Gain sufficient self-awareness to eliminate the influence of   3, 10
   personal biases and values in working with diverse groups

Recognize and communicate their understanding of the   2, 3, 6
   importance of difference in shaping life experiences

View themselves as learners and engage those with   1, 2, 5, 6, 7, 8, 10, 11
   whom they work as informants

Human Rights and Justice

Practice behavior examples

Understand the forms and mechanism of oppression   2
   and discrimination

Advocate for human rights and social and   1, 2, 3
   economic justice

Engage in practices that advance social and   1, 2, 6, 7, 8, 9, 11
   economic justice

Research-Based Practice

Practice behavior examples

Use practice experience to inform scientific inquiry   1, 2, 5

Use research evidence to inform practice   1, 2, 4, 6, 9, 10, 11, 12

Human Behavior

Practice behavior examples

Utilize conceptual frameworks to guide the processes of   5, 7
   assessment, intervention, and evaluation

Critique and apply knowledge to understand person   10, 12
   and environment

Policy Practice

Practice behavior examples

Analyze, formulate, and advocate for policies that   1, 2, 5, 11
   advance social well-being

Collaborate with colleagues and clients for effective   1, 2, 5, 6, 7, 10
   policy action

Practice Contexts

Practice behavior examples

Continuously discover, appraise, and attend to   1, 2, 6, 12
   changing locales, populations, scientific and
   technological developments, and emerging societal
   trends to provide relevant services

Provide leadership in promoting sustainable changes in   1, 2, 5, 6, 8, 11, 12
   service delivery and practice to improve the quality of
   social services

Engage, Assess, Intervene, Evaluate

Practice behavior examples

   A) Engagement

   Substantively and effectively prepare for action   2, 3, 5, 7, 8, 12
      with individuals, families, groups, organizations,
      and communities

   Use empathy and other interpersonal skills   8

   Develop a mutually agreed-on focus of work and   1, 2, 3, 5, 7, 8
      desired outcomes

   B) Assessment

   Collect, organize, and interpret client data   4, 5, 6, 8, 10, 11

   Assess client strengths and limitations   2, 6, 7

   Develop mutually agreed-on intervention goals   1, 2, 5, 7
      and objectives

   Select appropriate intervention strategies   1, 2, 7, 8

   C) Intervention

   Initiate actions to achieve organizational goals   2, 6, 8, 11

   Implement prevention interventions that enhance   2, 6
      client capacities

   Help clients resolve problems   2, 7, 8

   Negotiate, mediate, and advocate for clients   1, 2, 3, 5, 7, 8

   Facilitate transitions and endings   9, 11, 12

   D) Evaluation

   Critically analyze, monitor, and evaluate interventions   1, 2, 4, 5, 7, 8, 9, 10,
                                                                      11, 12

Preface

Every social worker is expected to know how to conduct an evaluation of his or her practice. Growing numbers of social workers will also be assuming a program evaluator role at some point in their careers because of the increasing demands for program accountability. Ironically, most social workers are still inadequately prepared to design and implement such evaluations. *Social Work Evaluation: Enhancing What We Do* introduces social workers and other human service workers to a broad array of knowledge about evaluations that they can conduct. The book also prepares them with the insights, knowledge, and skills needed to conduct a range of evaluations.

The book is organized around a three-stage model of evaluation. The stages divide evaluation into activities during the planning of an intervention, its implementation, and the measuring of its impact on recipients. In addition, the text describes seven general steps to follow in conducting evaluations. These steps offer a flexible set of guidelines to follow in implementing an evaluation with all of its practicalities. Specific tools in the form of questions to ask, designs, techniques, and practical skills are described for readers to be able to take and use. Both quantitative and qualitative methods as well as mixed research methods are used in the evaluations covered in this book.

This book can be used for several research and practice courses in both bachelor of social work (BSW) and master of social work (MSW) programs. It is designed for primary use in a one-semester evaluation course in MSW programs. It can also be a primary text for a two-course research sequence in BSW programs. The book can also be very useful as a secondary text in BSW and MSW practice courses at all system levels. Further, it is an excellent handbook for professionals of several disciplines to use in conducting evaluations.

MAJOR ADDITIONS IN THE SECOND EDITION

The new edition gives central attention to evidence-based practice. New material is highlighted throughout the book about how evaluations can generate and promote evidence as a central goal. Several recommendations are also given for how the readers can promote evidence-based practice in specific ways. The logic model is given much more attention as a theoretical framework and a tool of evaluators. The logic model is offered as a means of designing and understanding program and practice interventions. The logic model is also viewed as a primary means of promoting evidence-based practice.

The seven steps in conducting an evaluation are emphasized throughout the book and provide a helpful guide for the readers to follow. An emphasis on client-centered change emphasized in the first edition is strengthened and offers new, innovative ways of bringing clients, staff members, and community groups into the evaluation process. A new chapter, "Becoming Critical Consumers of Evaluations," is added to stress the importance of the consumer role in reading and utilizing evaluation studies. The chapter walks the readers through each of the steps in consuming evaluation reports using a recently published evaluation report as an illustration. This chapter and others provide guidelines for how to apply the findings of an evaluation to the readers' field settings. Chapter 8 on implementation processes is considerably expanded to include new material on implementation evaluation, connections to evidence-based practice, more material on evaluating the roles of staff members in programs, and other topics. Other changes in the new edition include new graphs and formatting to make the material easier to read and visualize.

OTHER SPECIAL FEATURES ALSO IN THE FIRST EDITION

Social Work Evaluation: Enhancing What We Do has several distinct features. First, both program and practice evaluation are discussed throughout the book. Evaluations at both levels have much in common. In addition, there is frequently a need to distinguish the two levels of evaluation. In these instances, separate sections are provided on both program and practice evaluations that explain their differences and how each can be implemented.

Both qualitative and quantitative methods of evaluation are also described and highlighted throughout the book. Although quantitative evaluations are especially pertinent to summative evaluations, qualitative methods are presented as especially relevant to many types of formative evaluations. Criteria are offered for when to use qualitative evaluations and when to use quantitative ones, and examples of both are provided. Mixed methods are also often encouraged.

The book presents evaluation material in a form that is easily understandable and especially relevant to social work students. Research is among the most difficult content areas for social work students to comprehend. This is largely because it is difficult to see the applicability of research to social work practice. The statistical and other technical aspects of research content also tend to be alien to students and difficult to comprehend. This book is especially designed to overcome these and other types of barriers more than other social work evaluation texts do because it continually discusses evaluation in the context of social work programs and practice and uses numerous pertinent examples.

Another feature of the text is that it directly addresses all of the current accreditation standards of the Council on Social Work Education (CSWE), the national accrediting organization for social workers. The CSWE promulgates minimum curriculum standards for all BSW and MSW programs, including research and evaluation content. This book devotes an entire chapter to several issues related to evaluation with a special focus on evaluation's links to three other foundational areas: ethics, diversity, and social and economic justice. Because of the importance of these three foundational areas, they are highlighted in numerous examples and exercises throughout the book. In addition, practice, a central foundational area of the social work curriculum, is often highlighted as it relates to evaluation. Evaluation is described throughout the book as a vital and necessary component of practice at both the MSW and the BSW levels.

Although a social work perspective is emphasized that helps in understanding the connections of evaluation with practice, ethics, diversity issues, and social justice, other human service professionals will also find these topics pertinent. Professionals in psychology, family and individual therapy, child welfare, health, mental health, criminal justice, school counseling, special education, substance abuse, and others will find this text to be a very useful handbook.

Another distinguishing aspect of this book is the extensive use of case examples. Specific evaluation studies from professional journals, websites, and books are frequently highlighted to illustrate concepts, findings, data analyses, and other issues. It has been the author's experience that students' learning is enhanced when they can immediately see the application of abstract concepts to human service situations. Exemplary evaluation activities of social work students and practitioners are also generously included. These illustrations reflect what students will often find in the field agencies and social agencies that will hire them. The book also contains a glossary of terms, discussion questions at the end of each chapter, and other visual aids.

In addition, the book is user-friendly for faculty who teach evaluation courses. Sometimes social work educators who do not have the time to conduct their own evaluations teach research courses. Such faculty may often feel less than qualified to teach an evaluation course. This text is understandable to both inexperienced and experienced faculty. Also, discussion questions included at the end of each chapter can serve as a focus for class discussions, quizzes, and tests. In addition, a teacher's guide is available from Lyceum Books that elaborates on how the content of the book can be used and suggests helpful ways to involve students in understanding and using it. Multiple-choice exam questions are also available from Lyceum Books for each chapter.

Moreover, the evaluation process is described, when possible, as a collaborative effort that encourages the participation of the clients and other stakeholders in some of the steps. A periodic focus on the principles of participant action research is highlighted in some sections to emphasize how evaluation can be used to promote client involvement, empowerment, and social change. Also, special emphasis in the new edition is placed on client involvement in consuming evaluation findings and becoming more active gatekeepers.

Finally, knowledge and technology skills are infused throughout the text. Social work practitioners must know how to use various electronic tools like e-mail, electronic discussion lists, the World Wide Web, and data analysis programs like SPSS. The text includes electronic exercises and other assignments that involve the students in using such tools. Emphasis is given to electronic skills that help students obtain access to the latest information on client populations, practice and program interventions, information from professional organizations, relevant articles, and helpful discussion lists.

ORGANIZATION OF THE BOOK

The book is organized into seven parts. Part I, the first chapter, provides an introduction to evaluation and how it is described and defined in the book. The chapter begins with a persuasive rationale for why social workers should be proficient in evaluation. Definitions of program and practice evaluation, their characteristics and aims, and the larger social contexts for evaluations are introduced. The misuses of the term *evaluation* are also pointed out. Evidence-based interventions are introduced as a critical concept in the context of evaluation.

Part II is an orientation to the bigger picture about evaluations. Chapter 2 highlights key historical events that have shaped current ways of conducting evaluations. Also, six different theoretical perspectives on evaluation are introduced to remind readers that evaluation is not a monolithic enterprise; to the contrary, its purposes vary widely depending on who is conducting the evaluation and what he or she is attempting to accomplish. Aspects of almost all of these perspectives contribute to the concept of evaluation covered throughout the book. Chapter 3 focuses on the ethics of evaluation, drawing on the Code of Ethics of the National Association of Social Workers (NASW) and the ethical principles of the American Evaluation Association (AEA). The chapter explains how the accreditation standards of the Council on Social Work Education (CSWE) can be implemented, including the ethics of social work and the importance of diversity and social and economic justice. Chapter 4 introduces readers to several types of program and practice evaluation that are commonly practiced in the settings in which social workers and other human service workers are employed. These types are identified in this chapter to help readers identify and search them out in various field settings. These types range from client satisfaction studies to outcome studies, licensing of professionals and programs, quality assurance, and judicial decisions. Chapter 5 offers guidelines for focusing an evaluation and presents a tool that can be used to craft a focus for a variety of evaluation purposes.

Part III focuses on the first of three stages of evaluation activities, the planning stage, when a program or practice area is being conceptualized. The planning stage is presented as a critical time for evaluation activities, especially to document the need for a new intervention. Chapter 6 is devoted to conducting needs assessments, especially during the planning stage. The chapter explains why needs assessments are so important, describes a variety of assessment tools, and describes the steps involved in conducting a needs assessment. Crafting goals and objectives for a new program or practice intervention are highlighted in chapter 7. Characteristics of goals, limitations of goals, and the importance of measurable objectives are highlighted. A practical approach to crafting measurable objectives is described with several examples and exercises to ensure that readers are able to understand how to craft objectives for their own interventions.

Part IV, consisting of an expanded chapter 8, focuses on the second of three stages, the implementation stage, when numerous evaluation activities can occur. Implementation or process evaluations can address a wide variety of important issues, and this chapter describes the central ones. The chapter explores an array of evaluations, including testing an intervention against the logic model; determining whether the actual intervention is what it was initially intended to be; focusing on staff involvement; and determining quality, accessibility, and client satisfaction at both the program and the practice levels.

Part V, consisting of chapter 9, covers the third of the three stages, the outcome stage, when evaluations are initiated to determine how an intervention has affected the clients. The chapter portrays outcomes as multidimensional and complex. Criteria are offered for choosing outcome measures. Also, the enormous challenge of adequately documenting that an intervention is the cause of any improvement in the clients' lives is explained in some detail. Several outcome designs are introduced for evaluating both program and practice interventions, and the advantages and limitations of each design are highlighted. These designs are presented in a practical way so that readers can easily implement them. Ethical issues in selecting designs are also discussed.

Part VI discusses the final steps in conducting an evaluation. Data analysis is an important step to understand and implement as discussed in chapter 10. The chapter discusses the many options available for analyzing both qualitative and quantitative data. Several statistical tools are described for analyzing data for quantitative evaluations, and three different approaches are offered for analyzing data from qualitative evaluations. Although the principles of data analysis in an evaluation are similar to those used in a research study, several differences are also evident and noted in this chapter.

Most important, analysis of evaluation data begins and ends with questions of who needs to know what, when, and why. Chapter 11 addresses the final steps in conducting an evaluation, preparation and dissemination of the report of the findings. The chapter emphasizes involving stakeholders in the planning of the report. Several options for report formats are explored. Also, several strategies are offered to both prepare a report and disseminate it to stakeholders and others.

Chapter 12, a new chapter in the second edition, is devoted to consuming evaluation reports. How is this done? What do you look for? How can consumers critically consume a report? How can they use it in their own work or lives as administrators, practitioners, students, clients, regulatory entities? All of these questions and others are addressed. Clients of social services, in particular, are likely to have the most at stake in the critical consumption of evaluation reports. They need to know if the interventions they receive are effective and a good fit for what they need. A special section of the chapter discusses how to do more to present evaluation reports in a form that clients can understand and use.

Acknowledgments

Numerous people have graciously assisted in the preparation of this text. Tom Meenaghan and Carl Brun contributed significantly to the organization and conceptualization of the book. I also thank David Moxley, Shweta Singh, Brandon Youker, Michael Cronin, and Robert Fischer for thoughtful and thorough reviews of the manuscript. Scott Wilson, Israel Colon, Cy Rosenthal, Dennis Brunn, and Bill Perry, former colleagues at Temple University, initially introduced me to the complex enterprise of evaluation and its relevance to social work and social change. Several colleagues at the University of North Carolina at Charlotte provided support along the way, particularly at times when it was most needed. Among them, Dennis Long generously assisted with material resources needed to attend conferences and obtain editorial assistance. Frada Mozenter helped retrieve several websites and other resources, always in amazingly supportive ways. Jeff Shears contributed to the writing of one of the chapters. Robert Herman-Smith contributed to the writing of another chapter and Daniel Freedman contributed to the writing of a third chapter. Nohra Núñez and Cynthia Stasiewski helped in countless ways.

My MSW social work students from seven years at UNC Charlotte and another eight years at Temple University gave invaluable feedback and support while I taught program and practice evaluation courses over these years. They consistently assured me that these evaluation courses were useful and valuable to their professional development, and they gave me the initial encouragement to develop a textbook reflecting the multifaceted content areas covered in the courses.

David Follmer, my publisher, was an invaluable catalyst for writing the text and broadening its focus to the larger community of professional evaluators. He supported me throughout the writing period, which often seemed endless. Appreciation also goes to Paul Mendelson, Sarah Butcher, Catherine Dixon, and Anna Jones.

Part I

Introduction

Chapter 1

Evaluation and Social Work
Making the Connection

Let's begin by considering three important questions:

1. Is evaluation an important area of social work?
2. Is the evaluator role an important one for social workers?
3. How can evaluations help improve or enhance social work interventions?

These questions may be your questions as you begin to read this book. They are questions that many social work students and practitioners have pondered.

This book is about evaluation so the responses to the first two questions, in brief, will be no surprise to you. Yes, evaluation is an important area of social work. Further, the evaluator role is an important role for every social worker to prepare to assume. Some social workers will be evaluators of programs, and virtually every social worker will be an evaluator of their own practice. It's like asking whether social workers need to know whether they are doing a good job, or asking them if they know whether their interventions are effective in helping their clients. The third question, asking how evaluation can help improve social work interventions, is the focus of this text.

The underlying theme driving the book is that evaluation is a vital element of any social work approach and is critical for ensuring that social work actually *does* work! A reassuring theme is that evaluation is a practice area that BSW and MSW students and practitioners alike can learn. Social workers and students wanting to maximize their impact in their jobs will find that the perspective, knowledge, ethics, and skills of evaluations covered in this book are a central component of practice and ensure that you will have a much greater impact on your clients' well-being.

This book provides the needed preparation for evaluation in both a comprehensive and a readable format. The primary emphasis is on the various kinds of small and mid-range formative evaluations that are often implemented at the local agency level; less emphasis is placed on the large, complex national and regional studies that may draw the most coverage under the title *evaluation*. These smaller formative evaluations are also the critical ones that social work students and graduates either are assigned or should consider taking on in their field placements and employment agencies. Such evaluations often are instrumental in determining whether the programs in which you are working will continue and possibly expand.

Example of a Small, Formative Evaluation

An agency that provides an anger management program to perpetrators of domestic violence offers a series of ten psychoeducational group sessions to help them manage their anger. The agency also conducts an evaluation of this program that is integral to it. An anger management scale is used to measure changes that occur in the participants' anger after they have completed all ten sessions of a group program. Throughout the series, the specific items of the anger management scale (e.g., being respectful, having self-control, being self-aware, learning alternatives to violent behavior) identify some of the key discussion topics of the group sessions. In this way, the intervention and its evaluation go hand in hand in helping practitioners and clients partner to meet the goals of the program.

Evaluation is a multifaceted approach that addresses some of the most vital questions and issues facing programs and practice, including the following:

- Who are the clients that need the intervention most?
- What kinds of intervention do they need?
- How are the interventions to be implemented?
- What will the intervention achieve?

In other words, evaluations can address important issues at all stages of development of a program or practice area:

- Planning, when a vision is created for an intervention and developed into a proposal or plan
- Implementation, when the plan is actually carried out
- Outcome observation, when the clients' outcomes or affected behaviors are measured during a post-program period

Evaluation is important to consider for both the practice provided by each practitioner and the program itself. At the practice level, an evaluation can investigate inputs such as who will be the client population; the processes the practitioner uses to implement the intervention; and the outcomes or client accomplishments resulting from the practitioner's interventions. At the program level, an evaluation can investigate the same stages (inputs, processes, and outcomes) of interventions typically provided by several practitioners, for example, the case management services of a mental health program.

PRACTICE IS EMBEDDED IN A PROGRAM

Programs and individual practice are closely intertwined. Practice is, at times, a microcosm of a program. For example, a small program can consist of a set of similar interventions of a few practitioners (e.g., a family counseling program). In addition, practice is almost always embedded in a program, and the program is instrumental in informing, shaping, and directing the definition of practice. Practice is not an entity to be developed in a vacuum or at the whim of a practitioner or supervisor, even though this can inadvertently happen in reality.

Social work practitioners, once they graduate, usually have a good beginning sense of an overall practice approach to helping clients. However, it is an approach that is still mostly understood in the abstract, based on practice theories being taught in a professional program along with some opportunities for testing the theories in field practicum experiences.

However, when practitioners begin work at an agency, there are numerous new variables that come into play. The client population is one of them. Who are the clients? What kinds of problems and needs do they have? What kinds of interventions do they need the most? In addition, the agency typically has a practice approach (or approaches) that it uses to help clients, and the agency expects its practitioners to know this approach and become competent in using it. The approach may be explicit and detailed or quite vague and mostly abstract. Practitioners new to an agency need to ask how they can fully understand and implement this practice approach, hopefully with assistance from a supervisor. Later on, new practitioners also face growing challenges as they become aware of the need for subtle variations in the application of the agency approach based on the varied and sometimes unique needs of clients.

Because this book is about both programs and practice, and their relationship, it offers numerous insights into the vital link between professional practice and its program context. In this light, this book offers several objectives for practitioners to consider:

- Realize that your practice is embedded in a program context.
- Recognize how your program works and informs your practice.
- Understand the bigger picture of the agency, its policies, organizational structures, external environment, and stakeholders, and how they affect your practice.
- Know what is important to evaluate in your practice, taking into account the program context.
- Realize that program evaluations usually have valuable implications for improving your practice.
- Consider using some of the strategies of program evaluations when evaluating your practice.

COMMON CHARACTERISTICS OF EVALUATIONS

To fully understand the nature of an evaluation, we need to understand its common characteristics. These characteristics include accountability, use of scientific research methods, the logic model as an analytic tool, stakeholders, political processes, an ethical code, and critical thinking. These characteristics continually interact with and influence one another.

Being Accountable

If there is one overall concept that explains why evaluations are so important, it is accountability. Partially because of past failings of social programs, all governmental and most privately funded agencies are now held accountable for how they use their funds and what they achieve for their clients. Evaluations have become one of the most reliable mechanisms incorporated into program proposals for ensuring such accountability. Agency accountability is now inherent in the jurisdiction of virtually all funding and regulatory agencies, and it has become a key job expectation of agency and program administrators.

These funding, regulatory, and administrative roles require accountability to address questions such as the following:

- Is the intervention focusing on the target population with the greatest need?
- Is the intervention designed to meet the specified needs of the target population?
- Is the intervention being implemented in the way that it was designed and proposed?
- Is the intervention being implemented with high standards?
- How satisfied are clients and their families with the intervention?
- Is the intervention achieving its goals and objectives?
- Is the intervention cost-effective?

Ultimately, it is also important for program sponsors to be accountable to the clients they serve. Because of the power imbalance between an agency and clients, special attention is needed to bring more balance to these two entities in the form of greater power and protection for clients. In addition, agencies need to be accountable to the communities intrinsically connected to clients, such as their family members and the immediate neighbors surrounding residential programs. Accountability to clients and relevant communities often requires the introduction of empowerment strategies, such as client satisfaction surveys and client representation on agency boards. Another strategy is to encourage agencies to involve client groups as participants in program evaluations and to share the results of their evaluations with them. Chapter 2 further elaborates on other empowerment strategies.

Social workers who work in such programs must also be accountable not only to the agency employing them but also to their own professional groups, such as the National Association of Social Workers (NASW), Political Action for Candidate Election (PACE, a political arm of NASW), and their state professional licensing boards. In these instances, accountability refers to abiding by an ethical conduct for social workers, commitments to clients' dignity and well-being, advocating for social justice, and implementation of sound and evidence-based professional practice.

Using Scientific Research Methods

Evaluation activities are scientific and use a wide range of research methodologies (e.g., Dudley, 2011). Scientific research has long-standing values and principles that distinguish it from other types of information gathering. Many of these principles are evident in evaluations, including:

- The search for something that exists rather than something that is desired
- Use of a methodology that minimizes the influence of biases and involves a systematic set of steps or procedures that can be flexibly employed
- Abiding by a special code of ethical conduct that includes a commitment to neutrality in conducting research and a demonstration of concern to protect the people studied
- Assumption of the evaluation having a universal stance, representing the concerns of all society, even though it may focus on a few subgroups of people or a narrow topic
- Accurate reporting of findings despite whether they are consistent with the researcher's viewpoints

Although these principles of scientific research are ideals that should be fulfilled to the greatest extent possible in all scientific studies, in reality they are evident in evaluation studies to varying degrees and along a continuum of quality. The more an evaluation rigorously fulfills these ideals, the more confident one can be that it is considered "good" science.

The Logic Model as an Analytic Tool

The logic model is both an organizing framework and a tool that evaluators use for analyzing a program. The logic model can also be used to analyze a practice approach. The logic model helps highlight how the stages and elements of a program are logically linked. Using this model, it is important to examine the sequence of stages in a program's development, beginning with identifying the problems of prospective clients, followed by developing and implementing an intervention to address these problems, and

FIGURE 1.1   Three-Stage Approach

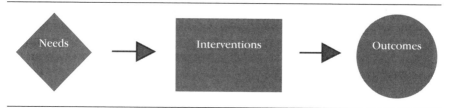

culminating in anticipated client outcomes that reflect a resolution of these client problems. These stages can be visually understood in figure 1.1.

Figure 1.1 is an important framework that helps begin to organize much of the content of the book and thus will be presented periodically in appropriate chapters to highlight the stages and program elements as they are being covered. As mentioned earlier in the chapter, the logic model comprises three stages: planning, implementing, and observing outcomes. During the planning stage, the problems and needs of the client population are defined and documented and an intervention is conceived and developed to address these problems and needs. During the implementation stage, this intervention is implemented. Finally, during the outcome stage, the outcomes for clients who receive the intervention are observed and measured. The logic model helps the evaluator link the documented problems and needs to the intervention that will address them, and the intervention is, in turn, linked to the client outcomes that are anticipated after the intervention has been implemented. The logic model is elaborated on further in later chapters, particularly chapter 6 and 8.

Example of the Use of the Logic Model in Designing a Program

A group of students were asked to design a program that would effectively help clients overcome substance abuse problems. They used the logic model to complete this exercise. They began by identifying some suspected causes of substance abuse, including heredity, peer influence, low self-esteem, social isolation, and inadequate coping skills. Next they decided to design a program to address only the suspected causes that revolved around interpersonal issues, including peer influence, social isolation, low self-esteem, and inadequate coping skills. They decided to offer psychoeducational groups to teach clients the skills needed to manage these and other personal and interpersonal issues. They decided to cover specific topics such as how to find positive peer influences and avoid negative peer influences, how to find and participate in support groups, and some self-esteem-building exercises. They anticipated that once participants had completed the psychoeducational group sessions they would be able to identify the factors that reduced their self-esteem, to identify specific ways to build more positive self-esteem, and to learn three or four new coping skills. By completion of the program, participants would also have made two or more visits to a support group in the community to help them stop using substances.

Involving Stakeholders and a Political Process

While basic research is often considered apolitical, evaluations involve an overtly political process. Historical events and current political considerations need to be considered when discussing, planning, and implementing an evaluation. Indeed, an evaluation is a special type of research that incorporates political considerations into its execution. An evaluation may have several different stakeholders, and each could have special interests that compete with one another. When talking about an evaluation, political issues almost always come into play, whether explicitly or implicitly. For example, political processes might be involved in any of the following types of questions that agency administrators raise:

- How can we help those with the greatest need?
- How can an evaluation help our program survive?
- How can an evaluation improve the chances of obtaining funding to expand our program?
- How can the results of an evaluation be used to enhance our program's identity in the larger network of agencies in our field?
- How can we report negative findings from an evaluation without jeopardizing our program's existence?

Example of a Political Consideration

A graduate student conducted an evaluation of staff morale at her field agency. She gave the staff members a questionnaire to fill out, asking them how important they perceived each of several different issues that affected their morale. The issues included salaries, medical benefits, size of caseloads, hours of work, supervision (its quality and frequency), and openness of administration to staff concerns. The findings revealed that their major concerns about morale related to their problems with supervisors and administration. Because the administration of the agency was taken by surprise and unprepared to seriously address these issues, they decided to ignore them and instructed the graduate student to withhold her findings from the staff members.

Stakeholders of an evaluation have different interests. Stakeholders often include agency administrators, governmental funding and regulatory agencies, foundations, elected officials, board members, staff members, citizens, clients, advocacy groups, accountants and auditors, and the surrounding community. A funding agency, for example, might ask the following questions:

- How can I be sure that this program is fulfilling its responsibilities?
- How can I determine whether this program is more or less important than another program that we fund?
- How can I get the most fiscal value out of this program?
- I like this program and its director, but how can I justify funding them when the proposal falls short of what we want?

Political considerations such as these must be taken into account at all stages of evaluating interventions, including planning, implementation, and outcome. An approach to identify and analyze these contextual forces within and outside an agency is elaborated on later in the chapter. In general, this approach can help evaluators consider the political issues and questions that they may need to address or avert in conducting an evaluation before they become serious problems or ethical dilemmas. The approach identifies a wide range of possible constraints that can create conflicts for an evaluation and considers a range of potential resources that can help in conducting the evaluation. The identification of potential constraints and resources before implementation of an evaluation helps address both its feasibility and its ethical standing.

Abiding by an Ethical Code

Ethical issues are extremely important to identify when addressing political issues. Actually, the way in which decisions are made or not made should be partially based on an ethical code such as the NASW Code of Ethics (www.naswdc.org) or the ethical principles of the American Evaluation Association (AEA; www.eval.org). As social workers and other human service professionals know, those who participate in research and evaluation are obligated to follow an ethical code. The NASW Code of Ethics is a basic code required of all social workers. It obligates an evaluator to be well informed about ethical issues and well versed in how to implement a variety of measures intended to prevent ethical problems from occurring. The ethical principles of the AEA are designed for professional evaluators specifically conducting evaluation studies. These principles are valuable to consult because they are directed toward issues essential for a professional evaluator to address (the AEA ethical principles are located in appendix A).

Ethical problems include such things as physical and psychological harm to research participants, invasion of privacy, and misrepresentation of study findings. Evaluators are obligated to prevent such ethical problems by implementing a variety of ethical safeguards, including an informed consent protocol, confidentiality, and selection of evaluators with appropriate credentials and objectivity. Chapter 3 focuses on an extensive introduction to many of the ethical concerns that are evident in evaluations and how to address these problems. It examines the NASW Code of Ethics and portions of the ethical principles of the AEA, particularly as they pertain to social workers' ethical obligations related to evaluations.

Thinking Critically

Another important characteristic of evaluations is critical thinking. Critical thinkers are natural skeptics about how well an evaluation is conducted, whether it is someone else's evaluation or one's own. Gibbs and Gambrill (1996) identify several types of problems that program providers experience when they fail to be critical thinkers:

- Overlooking the people who may need the services of a program the most
- Not understanding the larger social forces that influence the ways clients behave
- Misclassifying or misdiagnosing clients and their problems
- Focusing on irrelevant factors that are not important in helping clients make progress
- Selecting interventions that are weak or inappropriate
- Arranging for interventions to continue either too long or not long enough
- Being overly preoccupied with financial profit and neglecting the impact of such decisions on the clients' well-being (particularly for-profit agencies)

The Council on Social Work Education (CSWE) views critical thinking as essential to the practice of every social worker. Because of the importance of critical thinking, CSWE mandates that it be one of the basic tenets of the professional foundation of every accredited social work education program at both the BSW and the MSW levels. One of the core program objectives required of the curricula of all programs and to be infused into every course is to "apply critical thinking skills within the context of professional social work."

Distinguishing Evaluations from Social Science Research

As we begin to explore evaluations, a basic question emerges. How is an evaluation different from other types of research, particularly social science research conducted in academic settings? A closer look at the above characteristics provides a helpful way of distinguishing them. An evaluation can be distinguished based on its greater emphases on some of the characteristics of evaluations described above. Evaluations, unlike most social science research, give major emphases to four of the above characteristics. First, evaluations are conducted primarily to provide accountability to a funding agency, clients, and the community that an intervention works effectively and efficiently. Second, an evaluation places major emphasis on the logic model while most social science research does not. The logic model helps evaluators focus on the links among client problems, an intervention, and success in helping clients address these problems. Next, effective evaluations seek the involvement of all of the stakeholders while social science research may not. These stakeholders typically include groups with widely varying perspectives such as clients, regulatory agencies, and the agency providing the intervention. Finally, an evaluation is continually engaged in a political process that attempts to bring together these widely different stakeholders so that ideally all of their views are taken into account and all are participating together.

THE AIMS OF EVALUATION

Overall, evaluations of programs and practice are concerned with many purposes, including efficiency, quality, effectiveness, effort, and relevance. Martin and Kettner (1996), among others, stress the importance of efficiency, quality, and effectiveness. *Efficiency* is concerned with carefully channeling available resources to the target problems. Misdirected and wasted resources are to be avoided or minimized. Efficiency is important because resources for health and human service programs are always likely to be limited or even scarce, and the more efficiently that programs and practices are delivered, the more clients can be helped.

Quality refers to services being delivered as intended and done very well or at a high standard. Sometimes this high standard has been referred to as best practices. Quality is obviously important because a program or practice delivered well will have the greatest positive impact on the recipients; the higher the quality, the greater is the likely impact. For example, a social worker who is not adequately prepared to provide intensive counseling to emancipated adolescents about to be released from foster care will fall short of helping them enough to function on their own.

Also, interventions have to be effective or lead to *effectiveness*. If interventions do not successfully work to bring about the anticipated changes in clients' lives, the interventions should be reevaluated or the social worker will risk losing funding. All three of these areas—efficiency, quality, and effectiveness—are extremely important to evaluations. One cannot be preferred over the other two, as all three are required to ensure that a program or practice intervention works well.

In addition to these three common qualities of programs and practice, two more are also crucial: evidence of effort and relevance to the clients and community. Evidence of effort is important regardless of the achievements of a program. *Effort* refers to what staff members, volunteers, and administrators put into a program and practice. Effort especially refers to what happens when the interventions are implemented. How much time was spent in the helping process? How many visits or sessions occurred? What happened in these sessions? Most important, was the effort commensurate with the expectations of the funding agency, the program director, and clients?

Relevance is another fundamental quality of any intervention. Relevance of the intervention to the clients' needs and the larger social problems that clients experience is the most important aspect of relevance. A program intervention can be carried out in a high-quality way that uses resources efficiently and achieves program goals, but if it is not directly relevant to what the clients need, it is incomplete or misguided. The concept of relevance is related to the seeking of social justice for client populations and determining that the diversity in the client population reflects the larger population that needs the interventions. Both of these efforts, social justice and diversity, as well as other important issues of relevance, are covered extensively in this text.

Both the NASW Code of Ethics and the AEA Code highlight these issues and the responsibilities of evaluators to take into account the diversity of general and public interests and to be mindful of the rights and needs of all pertinent groups.

DEFINING IMPORTANT TERMS

Several important terms need to be defined before going further. They are relevant to answering numerous basic questions like, what is a program and how is it different from services? What distinguishes programs from the practice of individual workers? What are program evaluations and practice evaluations? How are they similar and different? Finally, what are evidence-based interventions? Let's take a look at the basic terms: program, program and practice theory, services, professional practice, intervention, program evaluation, practice evaluation, and evidence-based interventions.

A *program* is a subunit of a social agency that provides a set of goods and/or services with common goals. These goods and services are typically provided to a particular population of clients who either voluntarily seek them or are required to receive them. A program typically employs more than one and usually several staff members to provide goods and services.

Chen (1990) expands on this definition by developing the notion of *program theory*. Program theory is expected to encompass two important sets of documentation. First, it provides a descriptive documentation of the goals, outcomes, and interventions of the program based on the perspectives of various stakeholders. Second, program theory documents the nature of the causal relationship between the program interventions and the desired outcomes for the target group of recipients. It does this by offering research evidence that the proposed program model has been effective in helping, in the past, a group of clients with a particular set of characteristics. *Practice theory* can easily be described in a similar way. Goals, outcomes, and interventions are documented as well as the causal relationship between a practice intervention and the desired outcomes for a particular client.

Services are the activities that programs or one practitioner offer. Services focus mostly on the processes that help clients reach their program goals. They are the means to the ends, not ends in themselves. These helping processes are the major focus of practice courses of professional social work programs and draw from a broad range of practice theories, such as generalist problem solving; locality development; and cognitive behavioral, person-centered, and solution-focused treatments. In addition, in-service training programs periodically provide helpful updates on such knowledge and helping skills.

Example of a Program and Services of a Home Health Agency

A home health agency often sponsors one overall program, the goals of which are to help medically indigent clients remain in their own homes independently and prevent placement in a residential program such as an assisted living facility. Such a program offers several services to clients who are homebound, including counseling and referrals, nursing, physical therapy, and occupational therapy. These services, provided by a team of social workers, nurses, physical and occupational therapists, and others, exist to help the program meet its goals. Home health programs also offer goods, such as medical supplies and incontinence products.

Distinguishing between programs and services is important. For example, if you were to describe a program to someone unfamiliar with what you do, you would likely begin by referring to its goals and what it attempts to accomplish for clients. In contrast, if you begin by describing the services of the program, your explanation may appear incomplete and beg for an explanation of why these services exist or what they intend to accomplish. Note the difference between saying, "Our program is designed to help prevent teenagers from participating in unsafe sex," and "Our services include individual counseling and psychoeducational groups for teenagers."

Professional practices are the interventions of a human service worker in helping a client system. Professional practice can be offered to one individual, a family, a small group of clients, an organization, an institution, a social policy area, or a larger community. It is important to distinguish between the professional practice of one individual and the services of a program, which encompass the practices of all staff members within a program.

Because this book balances emphasis on programs and the practice of an individual practitioner, the term *intervention* is often used to refer either to the services and goods of programs or to an individual worker's practice. As an example, interventions are evident both in the recovery programs of a substance abuse agency and in the clinical practice that one social worker offers to a client's family.

Using working definitions of these key concepts (programs, services, professional practice, and interventions), we can define program evaluations and practice evaluations. A *program evaluation* is a study of a social program that uses the principles and methods of scientific research. It concerns itself with the practical needs of an organization, not theoretical issues, and it abides by a professional ethical code. The primary purposes of a program evaluation are to provide accountability to its various stakeholders and to improve what the program can accomplish.

A *practice evaluation* is a study of a professional practitioner's interventions with a client system, which can be at several different system levels (e.g., individual, group, neighborhood). Like a program evaluation, a practice evaluation uses the principles and methods of scientific research. Unlike a program evaluation, it focuses on only one practitioner's practice at a time. Its primary purposes are to increase the effectiveness of a practitioner's interventions and to determine whether the interventions successfully help clients reach their goals.

Although these definitions of program and practice evaluations are meant to be fairly distinct, at times they are blurred. For example, if we decided to evaluate an agency's group services, would it be a program or practice evaluation? Two issues need to be considered before this question can be answered: (1) does the group service comprise the groups of only one worker or of several different workers? and (2) is the purpose of the evaluation to examine the effectiveness of an individual practitioner's interventions or the group services of the entire program?

In our example, if only one staff member provided the group service, it could be both a program and a practice evaluation. Therefore, it is important to clarify at the outset what kind of evaluation is intended. For example, is it a practice evaluation intended to evaluate the interventions of individual staff members, or is it a program evaluation concerned with agency-wide issues, such as reaching the goals of the group service generally or determining the use of limited resources?

Evidence-based interventions are a central concept of evaluation. We are expected to find out whether an intervention has existing evidence that it works or is effective before we use it. This essentially means that the intervention has been implemented before and found to be effective in helping a particular group(s). The more evidence available that a program has worked, the more confident we can be about its effectiveness in using it again.

Evidence can take many forms and can be used with varying degrees of confidence. The best evidence is based on evaluation studies using all of the characteristics of evaluations described earlier in the chapter. Other forms of evidence are also possible to consider, including the wisdom passed on by another professional who has used the intervention, and policies on practice promulgated by respected professional organizations like NASW. However, these sources are weaker than the results of evaluations unless they are ultimately backed up by evaluations. Evidence-based interventions are discussed in much more depth in the next chapter.

What Program Evaluation Is Not

Considering what a program evaluation is not can also be helpful in understanding these key concepts. *Program evaluations are not evaluations of individual clients;* instead, program evaluations typically aim to provide useful information about cohorts of clients. In this case, the emphasis is on the impact of the entire program on the cohort that it serves. Program evaluations usually have an informed consent protocol that clarifies that the client's personal identity is not to be revealed in association with any of his or her specific responses. However, a program evaluation occasionally could become an evaluation of individual clients under special circumstances. In this case, the ethical thing to do would be to notify the clients as to why the change is occurring before implementation of the policy change. This preparatory step allows clients the opportunity to withdraw from the study if they wish.

Example of a Change from a Program Evaluation to Evaluation of Individual Clients

The state of North Carolina was successfully sued in a federal district court for failing to provide adequate services and physical safety to a selected group of people with mental illness and mental retardation in state mental hospitals (Dudley & Ahlgrim-Delzell, 2002). For four years, a university sponsor of a longitudinal evaluation of the class members reported only to a state agency on the aggregate data, using a set of statewide indicators of client progress or success. Then the state agency's needs shifted and it decided to begin requesting information on individual participants in these programs. The original informed consent letter of the academic sponsor of the evaluation specified that data would be released only in aggregate form without identifying individuals. Therefore, a change in informed consent was needed. As a matter of policy, the longitudinal research team provided each class member and his or her guardian or family member with a letter informing of the change in policy. The letter explained the purpose of the study, outlined the type of data that would be collected, and how the data would be obtained and released to the state on an individual basis. This letter also provided the recipient with the opportunity to withdraw from the study at any time without repercussions. Surprisingly, no one withdrew from the study.

Program evaluations do not evaluate the performance of individual staff members. Although evaluations of staff effort and performance are necessary, it would be confusing and a mistake to mix the purposes of a program evaluation and an evaluation of individual staff members. Such an initiative would not only confuse the participants in a study but also would likely instill distrust in the evaluation and discourage full cooperation of staff members. It may even encourage staff participants to manipulate their response in their favor or sabotage the study by boycotting it.

Program evaluations are not public relations projects. A public relations project could be falsely presented as a program evaluation and used to promote the agency's programs in annual reports and other material disseminated to the public. In this case, the purpose would be misleading and dishonest, as it gives the impression that a genuine evaluation is going on. Although the results or portions of the results of an evaluation may be useful and appropriate to display in public relations materials that promote the agency once an independent evaluation is completed, having a public relations emphasis built into an evaluation could bias the study toward a distorted positive outcome. In this case, some of the dramatic positive findings could end up being used in a report prepared for a funding agency while the neutral or less dramatic findings are disregarded and forgotten.

Example of a Program Evaluation with Potentially Conflicting Purposes

A student was asked to conduct an evaluation for a family agency of two different sets of groups of formerly incarcerated women. In designing the study, the student was told by her supervisor that the agency wanted to use the data in part to determine whether one staff member's group practice was less effective than the others. After some discussion, the supervisor agreed to remove this concern, a personnel matter, as one of the agency's study questions, so as not to confuse the study's intent and to maximize staff cooperation.

What Practice Evaluation Is Not

What practice evaluation is not is similar to the points made about a program evaluation. For example, practice evaluations do not evaluate the performance of the individual staff members; they evaluate whether a staff member's intervention succeeds in helping clients reach their goals. As mentioned previously, evaluations of staff performance are needed, but it would be confusing to mix such evaluations with a practice evaluation. Mixing these two different types of evaluation can easily instill distrust and resistance in staff members. Furthermore, the results of evaluations are likely to be manipulated if success with a client can be translated into a favorable performance review of their work.

Practice evaluations are not measures of the effectiveness of a program; they only evaluate individual practice. Although one practitioner in a program may effectively help his or her clients based on the results of a practice evaluation, it is not logical to conclude that the program is therefore effective. A practice evaluation does not take into account other components of the program, including the services that other staff members offer.

It is also important to note that although it would be unethical to refer to a staff performance evaluation as an evaluation of a program or practice, this can still happen. As mentioned earlier, the politics of evaluations could lead some agencies to considering such things if it could be viewed as beneficial to the agency and its programs. Evaluators always need to be ready to confront any ethical dilemmas that can surface, as their obligation is to do the most ethical thing.

UNDERSTANDING THE LARGER CONTEXT OF A PROGRAM

A program does not exist or operate in a vacuum. It is part of a larger dynamic system of many forces and factors, such as a wide range of policies, administrative leadership styles, staff and administrative communication patterns, varied perceptions of clients, and financial issues, all of which must be taken into consideration when conducting a program evaluation. Figure 1.2 provides a sketch of many of these factors in the agency and its environment.

All of these factors and their dynamic interplay can have a major influence on an evaluation conducted by the agency. Social policies have direct influence on evaluations since they give programs and practice approaches meaning and purpose related to the problem to be addressed and the proposed solution. Governmental policies (local, state, and federal) are important to consider because they dictate what these problems and solutions are that they will fund. Agency policies also have a direct or indirect influence in a wide range of areas such as financial matters, hiring, personnel, client admissions, and programmatic issues. An agency may have a particular policy, for example, about which client groups to prioritize. Or they may take a strong stand supporting evidence-based interventions or client-centered practice. Or they could have a major commitment to strong fiscal policy and an expectation that benefits be in line with costs. Unfortunately, agency policies that explain what programs are about may not be evident to a new staff member, and may need to be identified for them.

FIGURE 1.2   Contexual Factors in Evaluations

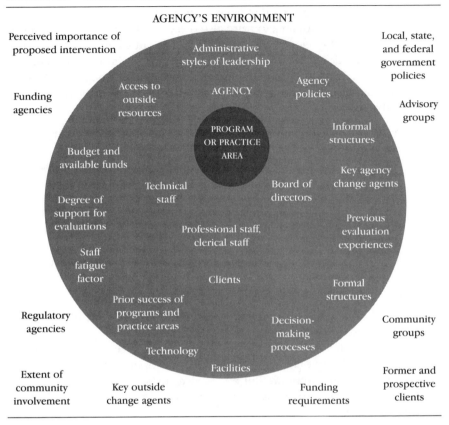

AGENCY'S ENVIRONMENT

Perceived importance of
proposed intervention

Administrative
styles of leadership

Local, state,
and federal
government
policies

Funding
agencies

Access to
outside
resources

AGENCY

Agency
policies

Advisory
groups

PROGRAM
OR PRACTICE
AREA

Informal
structures

Budget and
available funds

Key agency
change agents

Degree of
support for
evaluations

Technical
staff

Board of
directors

Previous
evaluation
experiences

Staff
fatigue
factor

Professional staff,
clerical staff

Regulatory
agencies

Clients

Formal
structures

Prior success of
programs and
practice areas

Decision-
making
processes

Community
groups

Technology

Extent of
community
involvement

Facilities

Key outside
change agents

Funding
requirements

Former and
prospective
clients

Leadership style is another factor of influence. One illustration of this dynamic interplay is the leadership style of the administrators. Administrators can assume many styles, including autocrat, collaborator, and delegator. Administrators who are primarily collaborative, for example, are likely to have a different kind of influence on staff members when conducting an evaluation than those of an autocratic administrator.

Also, organizational structures and processes, both informal and formal, are important factors with respect to their interplay with decision making (Weissman, Epstein, & Savage, 1983). In this case, while it is usually a good idea to consult everyone in an organization who is interested in and affected by an evaluation, some players will be more important to identify, including the administrators who formally oversee the program in question and those who have informal influence regardless of their formal title. These informal players could be instrumental in supporting or undermining an agency's formal structure. They could be, for example, lower-ranked employees, such as a highly invested secretary or a popular and outspoken staff member. All in all, evaluators can commit a serious and possibly fatal error in an evaluation if they overlook stakeholders who may be potentially central to the success of an evaluation but are excluded from evaluation discussions.

Many other contextual factors are also directly relevant to an evaluation. For example, are the agency leaders informed about evaluations, and supporters of evaluations? Or do they comprise novices who may be cautious and reluctant to pursue a study that can be risky? What is the agency's track record in this regard? Some fairly standard questions of this sort could be asked at the outset:

- What kinds of expertise does the agency have for conducting a variety of evaluations?
- How cooperative are staff members, both professional and support staff, in taking on additional responsibilities such as filling out questionnaires or searching for client records?
- What's in it for the administration and direct service staff? Are all of the motives openly known and transparent or do some appear to be covert or hidden?
- Are there reasons staff members may be suspicious of the motives for an evaluation or reluctant to participate for fear of jeopardizing their jobs?

Several contextual factors could also influence the extent to which the agency will disseminate the findings of an evaluation and implement its recommendations, including whether there are adequate resources, degree of desire to bring about a change in direction, and openness to risk the program's future. More attention will be given to these various forces in later chapters within the context of specific topics and the seven steps in conducting an evaluation.

SEVEN STEPS IN CONDUCTING AN EVALUATION

A general approach for conducting an evaluation is introduced here and elaborated on throughout the book. The steps of this approach apply to both program and practice evaluations. The approach involves seven general steps based on a modified version of the steps identified in other evaluation models (e.g., Bamberger, Rugh, & Mabry, 2012; Posavac & Carey, 1997). Since the word *steps* is also used in other contexts in various parts of the book, whenever steps refers to the seven steps in conducting an evaluation it will be identified as the *Seven Evaluation Steps*.

Seven Evaluation Steps

Step 1: Identify the Problem or Concern to Be Evaluated
Step 2: Identify and Explore Ways to Involve Stakeholders
Step 3: Determine the Purpose of the Evaluation

Step 4: Plan the Evaluation
Step 5: Implement the Evaluation
Step 6: Prepare a Written or Oral Report
Step 7: Disseminate the Findings

Step 1: Identify the Problem or Concern to Be Evaluated

During step 1, the evaluator becomes familiar with the problem or concern that an evaluation will examine. Some general questions include the following: What is to be evaluated? Is the program working well or are there some problems that are evident? On the practice level, is my intervention with my client working well? Why or why not?

During this step it is also important to begin gathering information about the program or practice context of the problem. It would be helpful to find out more about some of the pertinent components of the program or practice intervention. A description of the intervention should include identifying the client population that is served, the problems and needs that the intervention addresses, and the goals of the intervention. The services and goods that are provided to reach these goals are also important to identify and understand.

Step 2: Identify and Explore Ways to Involve Stakeholders

A concurrent step with the information gathering of step 1 is to identify and explore ways to involve the stakeholders of the program. Stakeholders are the people who are invested in the intervention in some way, such as representatives of the funding and regulatory groups that finance and set standards for the intervention or the administrators and board members of the agency sponsoring the program and those who direct the program. Some stakeholders, especially program directors, are likely to be evaluated on the basis of the intervention's performance, so they have an obvious stake in what happens.

Staff members who deliver the goods and services have an obvious stake in the intervention as well. Their jobs depend on the program's survival, and their careers, currently and in the future, may also be entwined in the intervention's outcome. In addition, clients who receive the intervention and their family members have a vital stake in what happens to the intervention, as their daily functioning and very survival may depend on how well it performs. Stakeholders are likely to be different for program and practice interventions. Program interventions tend to primarily have macro stakeholders, such as members of a board of directors, community advisory boards, and others in the public sector, while the main stakeholders of practice interventions are often supervisors, practitioners, and client advocates.

Step 3: Determine the Purpose of the Evaluation

Once the evaluator is familiar with the program or practice intervention to be evaluated and the problems or concerns, and has developed a relationship with all stakeholders, more information needs to be gathered about who wants the evaluation and why. These discussions can help the evaluator find out how much the stakeholders know about evaluations, their views and past experiences with them, and whether they have a narrow or broad understanding of what an evaluation can be. These discussions should be used to highlight the potential contributions of an evaluation, such as program improvements, the creation of new opportunities to help or understand clients, or assistance to the agency in making an important decision.

Possible Contributions and Resources to Consider

- Expressed concerns are highly relevant to clients' well-being
- Considerable interest in an evaluation
- Existing policies are supportive
- Financial support
- Awareness of a problem with a program
- Openness to examine a problem further
- Some understanding and respect for evaluation
- Openness to the evaluator as a resource
- Staff support

These discussions should not only uncover any contributions and resources that can support an evaluation, but also any apprehensions or doubts of stakeholders about evaluations generally. For example, could an evaluation be risky for some reason? Too costly? Take too much time? Interfere with program or practice operations? Therefore, during this step, it is also important to help the stakeholders identify any real or potential constraints.

Possible Constraints or Resistant Forces

- Limited time
- Costs too high
- Payoff is risky
- Not relevant to existing policies
- Evaluation focus can be too subjective
- Fears it will open up the need to change
- Limits to what can change
- Politics of the system
- Evaluator lacks expertise

- Problem of access to clients
- No need to justify such an evaluation to funding agency
- Lack of creativity

Step 3 becomes complete when all stakeholders and the evaluator have agreed on the general purpose of an evaluation. If a commonly agreed-on purpose for an evaluation cannot be identified, negotiations would likely discontinue or be delayed until a purpose could be identified. The purpose of a program evaluation could lead to keeping, expanding, or eliminating a program, whereas a practice evaluation may lead to varying an approach with some types of clients.

Step 4: Plan the Evaluation

Once a general purpose for an evaluation is agreed on, a plan for conducting an evaluation follows. As background work, a literature review is often needed to find out more about the problem that is the focus of the evaluation team and to identify reports on research methodologies, pertinent program and practice approaches, and studies on which to base the evaluation. Then several aspects of a research design need to be developed, including a set of study questions and hypotheses to explore or test, a data source (e.g., clients, staff members), a specific data collection method, and a data analysis plan. A plan to protect human participants of the study is also an important task to complete for approval.

All of these aspects of a plan should be discussed and involve the stakeholders so that there is strong support for a specific evaluation plan. When appropriate, the plan should be prepared as a readable written proposal or oral presentation understandable to all stakeholders. With practice evaluations, attention needs to be given to engaging the clients in understanding and participating in the evaluation. For example, a goal attainment scale may be used in a practice evaluation to measure the clients' progress on their outcomes. In this case, the scale should be described to the clients initially, and clients should be encouraged to help define the specific outcome measures that fit their circumstances. Goal attainment scales and the role that clients can play in developing them are described more fully in chapter 9.

Step 5: Implement the Evaluation

The plan that has been developed for an evaluation, often referred to as the evaluation design, is now ready to be implemented. Often its implementation may involve several people in an agency, such as secretaries searching for client case material, staff members who might interview clients individually or in focus groups, and a questionnaire that staff members might need to hand out to clients. In a practice evaluation, staff members are likely to implement one form or another of a single-system design. Along with implementing the data collection effort, collected quantitative data are coded, entered into computer programs, and prepared for analysis. Qualitative data are usually prepared for analysis in narrative form.

Step 6: Prepare a Written or Oral Report

Once the study has been completed, preparation of a report of the results follows. Such reports are designed to address the major questions of stakeholders, usually reflected in the initial purpose worked out in step 3. The report can be oral, written, or both. Report preparation involves several steps, including organizing, analyzing, and interpreting the findings so that they are understandable; developing conclusions and recommendations that are useful and practical; and exploring the use of visual aids, such as tables and graphs, to assist in communication. Reports of program evaluations are usually prepared for different stakeholders (e.g., funding agencies, administrators, boards of directors, community groups) than those of practice evaluations (e.g., supervisors, program coordinators, clients).

Step 7: Disseminate the Findings

The last step of an evaluation is to disseminate the results or findings to stakeholders and others. Unfortunately, this step is often overlooked or its importance minimized. The results are likely to be disseminated to several different types of stakeholders, some of which are obvious, such as the funding and regulatory agencies and agency administration. Other stakeholders may be easily overlooked but are also important, including former and current clients and relevant community groups. A report can be communicated in many forms—including oral or written, comprehensive or brief—and in varied formats, such as a technical report, a public meeting, a staff workshop, a series of discussions, a one-page summary for clients and their families, or other formats.

What's Next?

The chapters in part II focus on the bigger picture of evaluations, including various evaluation perspectives in chapter 2, professional ethics relevant to evaluations in chapter 3, and some common types of evaluations evident in agencies in chapter 4. These chapters are intended to provide a general background of relevant information for the chapters that follow them. Finally, chapter 5 begins to consider how to conduct an evaluation.

KEY TERMS

Accountability
Critical thinking
Efficiency
Effectiveness
Effort
Ethical codes
Evidence-based intervention
Implementation stage
Intervention
Link between policies and
    evaluations
Logic model
Outcome stage

Planning stage
Political process
Practice evaluation
Professional practice
Program
Program evaluation
Quality
Relevance
Scientific research methods
Services
Seven Evaluation Steps
Stages of program development
Stakeholders

DISCUSSION QUESTIONS AND ASSIGNMENTS

1. Prepare an agency information sheet about your field or employment agency. Answer all or some of the following questions to learn more about the agency.
   a. What programs does your agency provide?
   b. What are the agency policies that you are aware of that define these programs?
   c. What have you discovered so far to be the views, attitudes, and experiences of administrators and staff in your agency about program and practice evaluation?
   d. What types of program and practice evaluations are conducted in your agency? & may I have access to previous evals.
   e. Who in your agency, if anyone, is involved and interested in evaluations? Have you been involved in any evaluation activities?
   f. What aspects of programs or professional practice in your field agency need to be evaluated, in your opinion?
   g. List the key funding and regulatory agencies, professional associations, consumer groups, and other organizations that you think your agency should be accountable to.
2. Assume that you are employed at the agency mentioned in the chapter that provides psychoeducational group services to perpetrators of domestic violence. After the study was completed, the executive director of the agency decides to use the results of the study to evaluate the performance of individual staff members who are group leaders. What are the ethical issues that the executive director needs to consider before proceeding? What would you recommend that the

agency do or not do related to evaluating the performance of staff members?

3. Review the factors that make up the larger context of a program in figure 1.2. In your opinion, which factors are essential to consider related to the effective functioning of a program? Which are optional? Give reasons for your answers.

4. Select three different types of stakeholders of interest to you. Then identify the kinds of informational needs of each stakeholder. How are their needs different? How might they result in conflicting views about the purpose of an evaluation?

5. Interview a staff member about an evaluation that he or she was (or currently is) conducting at your agency and read the final report of such an evaluation. In what ways, if at all, do you see the six common characteristics of evaluations (accountability, use of scientific research methods, the logic model as an analytical tool, stakeholders and a political process, an ethical code, and thinking critically) evident in the interview with the staff member or in the final report?

REFERENCES

Bamberger, M., Rugh, J., & Mabry, L. (2012). *Real world evaluation: Working under budget, time, data, and political constraints.* 2nd ed. Los Angeles: Sage.

Chen, H. (1990). *Theory-driven evaluations.* Newbury Park, CA: Sage.

Dudley, J. R. (2011). *Research methods for social work: Being producers and consumers of research* (updated 2nd edition). Boston: Pearson.

Dudley, J., & Ahlgrim-Delzell, L. (2002). From lawsuit to quality improvement. In J. Dudley, M. L. Calhoun, & L. Ahlgrim-Delzell (Eds.), *Lessons learned from a lawsuit: Creating services for people with mental illness and mental retardation* (pp. 99–107). Kingston, NY: National Association for the Dually Diagnosed Press.

Gibbs, L., & Gambrill, E. (1996). *Critical thinking for social workers: A workbook.* Thousand Oaks, CA: Pine Forge Press.

Martin, L. L., & Kettner, P. M. (1996). *Measuring performance of human service programs.* Thousand Oaks, CA: Sage.

Posavac, E. J., & Carey, R. G. (1997). *Program evaluation: Methods and case studies.* Upper Saddle River, NJ: Prentice Hall.

Weissman, H., Epstein, I., & Savage, A. (1983). *Agency-based social work: Neglected aspects of clinical practice.* Philadelphia: Temple University.

Part II

Orientation to the Bigger Picture of Evaluations

Some helpful background information is needed on the "bigger picture" about evaluations before going any further. This background information includes descriptions of the many different philosophies and perspectives that are evident among evaluators, covered in chapter 2. Chapter 3 reviews the ethical issues and principles that must be followed in conducting an evaluation, and the common types of evaluations are introduced in chapter 4. Chapter 5 begins to delve into how evaluations are conducted and provides guidelines for how to focus an evaluation.

Chapter 2

The Context for an Evaluation

What drives the evaluation process?
What motivates evaluators to conduct evaluations the way we do?

The evaluation enterprise is by no means driven by one overall philosophy or standardized approach. It has been influenced by many different philosophies, practical approaches, and some key historical events. Moreover, evaluations have been used to obtain many different kinds of results. In this sense, they are similar to research in general. Evaluation studies can vary from small exploratory case studies to large explanatory studies involving representative samples and well-tested measurement instruments. Evaluation philosophies can range from inductive to deductive, qualitative to quantitative, and local to global.

This chapter provides a better understanding of the widely varied intentions of evaluators operating from several different disciplines, including social work. The chapter addresses several important historical events and many theoretical notions that have influenced what evaluations are all about. The chapter begins by highlighting some pertinent historical events that have greatly influenced the evolution of evaluations in recent decades, followed by a description of several philosophical approaches and perspectives on program evaluation. The chapter closes with a synthesis of the many perspectives and an introduction to how these forces have contributed to the concept of evaluation developed in this text.

RELEVANT EVENTS IN HISTORY

Program Evaluations

Evaluations have emerged through a long and tumultuous history of experimentation with social programs. Several historical events have been instrumental in ensuring that social programs are increasingly accountable to the larger society and to the funding and regulatory agencies that oversee their activities. Social workers function within these programs, and they too have been confronted with increasing responsibility to be accountable for what they do.

Program evaluations have not always been a central concern in the functioning of social programs. However, even administrators of social programs operating during the Settlement Movement and within Charity Organization Societies in the early part of the past century were mindful that their programs must work. However, their costs were relatively low, they often depended on volunteers, and they operated at the local level with little governmental assistance or regulation. Perhaps this local control and management ensured that those who oversaw the early programs kept a close watch on their volunteers and activities. Further, they most likely used common sense to determine that they were making headway in accomplishing their goals.

Since then, social programs have become much more complex and expensive. And they have expanded to serve almost infinitely more people. The New Deal legislation ushered in the beginning of national involvement in social programs by establishing old-age pensions and public assistance. The public assistance program, for example, was intended to provide temporary relief to poor people who could not find employment. The emphasis was on helping limited numbers and only during the Great Depression. Yet, as we know in retrospect, public assistance programs developed into a huge, burgeoning system of programs that provided permanent, not temporary, relief.

Social programs boomed in the 1960s. Historical events of that decade resulted in major changes in public policies, particularly in the areas of civil rights, poverty, and de-institutionalization of people with mental illnesses and mental retardation. President Johnson's Great Society and War on Poverty were instrumental in creating numerous programs, including local Community Action Councils, Job Corps, Neighborhood Youth Corp, Community Legal Services, and Head Start among others. But the War on Poverty promised much more than it could deliver, as it pursued broad goals like eliminating poverty and building community control.

In addition, the 1962 and 1967 Social Security Amendments instituted new initiatives such as services for welfare recipients in addition to financial support. Rehabilitation became the mantra that replaced relief, and training people for useful work became the goal for addressing prolonged dependency. The 1967 Amendments separated eligibility and social services functions in the hope of affecting family disorganization and conflicts. These new social service functions were to be filled by professionals with advanced degrees who would help poor people strengthen their family ties and become employed, educated, and ultimately self-sufficient. All of these initiatives not only promised more than they could even begin to deliver but also required runaway federal funding to pay for them.

All of these and other events moved program evaluation to the top of the list of priorities for legislators, funding agencies, and program providers. The pie-in-the-sky promises and expanding federal budgets devoted to social programs created an environment in which a rising social movement of fiscal conservatives demanded more emphasis on financial cutbacks and fiscal management, program accountability, and evaluations.

After the euphoric reform days of the 1960s, social programs began to face major problems in the 1970s and 1980s. Such programs, particularly those funded by governmental agencies, were no longer popular among many people in positions of power and came under attack. Accountability was still lacking for many of the programs, which left them exposed to growing criticism. Their ambitious agendas sought too much, including overcoming dependency on government and eliminating poverty. Ironically, the opposite seemed to be happening as the number of recipients in public programs soared and costs to the public exploded.

The growing demand for social program accountability culminated in the passage of the Government Performance and Results Act of 1993. The act required strategic planning by all governmental agencies focusing on client outcomes and especially required definitions of how their outcomes would be achieved. The act gave the U.S. Congress tools to hold all governmental programs and those receiving governmental funds accountable. From here on, the federal government intended to base budget decisions on the agencies' reports of performance and success in achieving their intended outcomes. This federal act was so important to social work that it became a focus of an article in the journal *Social Work* (Kautz, Netting, Huber, Borders, & Davis, 1997).

From this point on, programs would be expected to develop annual performance plans with clear goals and objectives for their programs and employees, quantifiable measurements of these goals, strategies for achieving goals and objectives, a description of the program evaluations that they would use, and a presentation of the results demonstrating the extent to which they had reached their identified goals. These new policies were implemented in 1997. By the end of that year, almost one hundred federal agencies delivered their plans to Congress as required. However, the new act helped federal overseers realize that evaluation plans did not offer an easy or quick fix. Performance goals and measures were not as results-oriented as expected, and some goals were found not to be objective or measurable. Further, these goals and objectives were not always linked to the individual programs and day-to-day agency activities intended to affect them. Nevertheless, the Government Performance and Results Act has become a key catalyst in an ongoing social movement aimed to hold social programs accountable for documenting their achievements. Amazingly, virtually every program proposal submitted to a funding agency today requires an evaluation.

Today, the development of program and practice evaluations has become more and more professional. Professions like social work, education, and other disciplines have formed professional associations to promulgate standards for high-quality, acceptable evaluations and a conference context for sharing ideas and experiences in implementing evaluations.

These types of activities occur in professional associations like the National Association of Social Workers and the Council on Social Work Education (CSWE). In particular, the CSWE gives major emphasis to evaluating BSW and MSW social work programs as part of its accreditation standards. Multidisciplinary organizations like the American Evaluation Association are also actively involved in promoting similar purposes, and there are at least eight professional journals that focus exclusively on evaluation (see chapter 6).

Practice Evaluations

Prominent social workers and government officials have challenged the social work profession to be accountable for their practice effectiveness. In 1973, Joel Fischer wrote a landmark article in *Social Work* titled "Is Casework Effective? A Review," in which he examined all of the studies that he could find to determine whether social casework (i.e., practice with individuals) was effective. Fischer assumed that effectiveness could be determined only by using a classic experimental design with a control group that did not receive social casework services. He found seventy studies that he had to discard because they did not have a control group. Only eleven studies met this criterion and were reviewed. Unfortunately, Fischer found no evidence from the eleven studies that social casework worked; in some cases, clients actually deteriorated.

Numerous evaluations and meta-analyses have been published since Fischer's study focusing on the effectiveness of specific interventions in helping a variety of client populations (for an example of such a meta-analysis, see Harding & Higginson, 2003). In brief, this meta-analysis uncovered findings not too dissimilar from Fischer's; of twenty-two evaluations of interventions to help cancer and palliative care patients, few used experimental and quasi-experimental designs to evaluate effectiveness.

The social work profession has been involved in a long, arduous, and impressive search for new ways to examine how to scrutinize social work interventions to ensure that they worked for clients. This examination has continued, sometimes in dramatic ways, up to the present. Many of the efforts have come from social work authors. Gibbs and Gambrill (1996) have made major contributions to the development of critical-thinking principles that practitioners can use. Gibbs (2003), O'Hare (2005), and many others have expanded on the concept and practice of evidence-based practice. O'Hare, in particular, introduces evidence-based concepts that apply to specific client conditions and circumstances like schizophrenia, depression, personality disorders, and child abuse and neglect. Finally, Fischer himself and colleagues (e.g., Bloom, Fischer, & Orme, 2003) have helped develop more sophisticated practice evaluation tools, especially additional ways to apply a single-system design to evaluating practice.

PERSPECTIVES AND APPROACHES FOR EVALUATIONS

Although the various theoretical perspectives and approaches existing in the evaluation field are too many to cover in this short introduction (e.g., Stufflebean, 2001), some are highlighted next. This sampling is intended to acquaint readers with those that are most pertinent to social work and to highlight some useful concepts, principles, and skills for new evaluators to incorporate into their own evolving eclectic approaches to evaluation. It is important to note that these perspectives and approaches sometimes overlap with each other. These theoretical perspectives and approaches include the following:

- Results-oriented model
- Feminist models
- Empowerment models
- Experimental and quasi-experimental models
- Fourth-generation evaluations
- Evaluations evolving within particular fields of practice

Results-Oriented Model

The results-oriented model focuses on performance, outcomes, and accountability. Evidence-based program and practice approaches and outcome evaluations fit here as well. This model has emerged as a public necessity because social programs have often fallen short of meeting their goals or have had difficulty communicating how they were achieving their goals (Wholey, 1999). Advocates of the results-oriented model believe that it is important to convince a variety of stakeholders that the outcomes they achieve are the ultimate reason why they are in business. In this regard, Wholey presents this three-step process: (1) development of agreement from stakeholders on goals and strategies, (2) regular measurement and evaluation of performance goals, and (3) use of performance results to improve programs and enhance accountability to stakeholders and the public. This model gives most of its attention to the ultimate point of a program's existence: socially desirable outcomes for clients.

As mentioned in chapter 1, Martin and Kettner (1996) give primary attention to performance and its measurement based on elements such as the efficiency and effectiveness of a social program. Efficiency involves calculating the amount of service provided and the number of clients who complete the program (program outputs) and comparing the outputs to the costs involved (program inputs). Effectiveness, another element of performance measurement, focuses on outcomes of social programs or results, impact, or accomplishments. Examples could include the number of parents who stop abusing their children as the result of a parenting-skills training program or the number of an adoption agency's successfully placed adoptions. The concepts of program inputs, outputs, and outcomes are developed further in later chapters.

Feminist Models

Feminist evaluations are defined by the substantive areas that such researchers choose to study. Feminist models are likely to aim to conduct evaluations that increase social justice for the oppressed, especially but not exclusively for oppressed women. They are inclined to focus on the relative positions and experiences of women in relation to men and the effects that gender issues have on both sexes (Deem, 2002). Examples in agency organizations include gender discrimination in hiring and promotion, the low representation of women in administrative and other leadership roles, salary inequities based on gender, and family-supportive policies of employers. Other feminist topics could include the roles of men and women in parenting children and assuming household tasks, enforcement of child support, the earning power of single-parent households, and the availability of quality day care for low-income families.

An Example of a Feminist Study: Women's Salaries

Gibelman (2003) examined the issue of men's and women's salaries in the human services by analyzing existing data from the Bureau of Labor Statistics. She found that salary disparities continue to exist. She attributes these disparities to discrimination patterns. Gibelman recommended several strategies to combat such discrimination, including public and professional education and advocacy. She also pointed out that the gender discrimination experienced by social workers is also evident among some client groups.

In addition, feminist evaluations can be partially defined by the research methods that they prefer. Most feminist researchers prefer qualitative over quantitative methods because of the flexibility built into this method and the value that it places on uncovering new knowledge about and insight into interventions at deeper levels of meaning. In addition, some suggest that similar principles guide both feminist studies and qualitative methods (Skeggs, 2001). Both feminist and qualitative methodologists are sensitive to a power differential between evaluators and participants in evaluations and both are concerned that the participants gain something from their involvement in an evaluation. Both feminist and qualitative methodologists are also likely to assume accountability to the wider community as well as to the participants. Many feminist evaluators also attempt to use principles of the participatory action approach, such as involvement of participants in as many of the steps of planning and implementing an evaluation as possible. It should be noted that some evaluators do not perceive feminist evaluation as a model; instead, they view it as a stance taken within a broader evaluation model.

Many authors have covered feminist perspectives in social work practice (e.g., Bricker-Jenkins, Hooyman, & Gottlieb, 1991). Their practice perspectives have focused on person-centered approaches, inclusiveness, collaboration with clients, and empowerment. These qualities would also tend to be highlighted in practice evaluations that encourage clients to become as fully involved as possible in evaluations to benefit clients' welfare.

Empowerment Models

Empowerment is a familiar action word in social work. It refers to promoting increased power for clients and helping equip them to assume greater control over their lives. Empowerment models advocate for both client rights and client responsibilities in their lives. An empowerment philosophy is especially important to evaluation activities, as is evident in the empowerment evaluation approach that Fetterman, Kaftarian, and Wandersman (1996) articulate. The value orientation of their approach is to help people help themselves and to improve their programs using self-evaluation and self-reflection techniques. Fetterman (2003) describes a simple, logical, and systematic approach to facilitating self-evaluation. Program participants are helped to conduct their own evaluations, and they use outside evaluators and other experts as coaches. Evaluation concepts, techniques, and findings are used to help specific oppressed groups or communities develop their self-determining capacity and improve their programs. Such evaluators typically play the roles of coach, facilitator, expert consultant, and critical friend.

Fetterman et al. (1996) distinguish between empowering processes and empowering outcomes. Empowering processes help people develop the skills needed for them to become independent problem solvers and decision makers (Zimmerman, 2000). These processes are critical in providing people with a particular stake in gaining control over their future, obtaining needed resources, and critically understanding their social environment. Macro practice approaches taught in social work programs emphasize these processes. Empowered outcomes, in some contrast, are the consequences that empowerment processes seek. Examples include creating or strengthening organizational networks, creating greater accessibility to community resources, and greater citizen control over community decision making.

Inclusive evaluations, developed by Mertens (2003), are similar to the empowerment approach; she advocates for a deliberate inclusion of groups and communities that have been historically discriminated against on the basis of race, ethnicity, culture, gender, social class, sexual orientation, and disability. This perspective aims to redress power imbalances in society by involving stakeholders and taking seriously and accurately their views and needs. This perspective promotes social justice outcomes and takes issue with deficit models that blame those affected by a problem.

Participatory action research (PAR) is a practical type of empowerment model that can be used in evaluations. Sometimes referred to as participant action research or critical action research, PAR is readily familiar to social work research (DePoy, Hartman, & Haslett, 1999). As its perspective PAR has an interest in actively involving research participants in all or most steps of the process. Some of the key PAR principles are the following:

- Collaborate with those affected by the problem to clearly articulate the social problem, its scope, and all stakeholders.
- Articulate the purpose of the change that the research is designed to accomplish.
- Have both professional and lay researchers on the team.
- Train the lay researchers in how to design, conduct, and use appropriate research methods.
- Report findings in accessible formats for all stakeholder groups.

Implementation of PAR can occur in all or some of the Seven Evaluation Steps. For example, if involving community stakeholders at every step is not realistic, they can be involved in some steps. Client and community stakeholders can be particularly important in the first step (identify the problem to be evaluated) by helping articulate program issues that need to be addressed. Clients can also be involved in the last step (disseminate the results) by assisting in dissemination of evaluation results to various community groups and getting feedback and greater community involvement.

Example of an Evaluation with PAR Principles to Support Social Action

Reese, Ahern, Nair, O'Faire, and Warren (1999) initiated a program evaluation using PAR principles that resulted in improved access to hospice services for African Americans. Collaboration occurred with research participants and practitioners throughout the study. The evaluators' activities began with a small qualitative study with African American pastors. The pilot study was followed by a larger quantitative study of African American hospice patients that documented their access barriers to hospice. Finally a social action effort was initiated to engage local health-care providers in addressing these access barriers. The findings of their studies were used to facilitate this social action effort.

Experimental and Quasi-Experimental Models

Supporters of experimental models believe that experimental and quasi-experimental designs are superior to other designs because they deliver scientifically credible evidence of the impact of programs on clients' welfare (Cook & Campbell, 1979). They argue that experimental designs and randomized samples are feasible and ethical. Further, the features of these designs are the only way to rule out the influence of other factors, such as other means of helping clients and the maturity processes for participants that inevitably occurs over the time of an experiment.

Philosophies deriving from this traditional scientific research paradigm are reviewed only briefly in this section, as readers are expected to be well acquainted with this paradigm from research methods courses in professional degree programs. Also, chapter 9 is partially devoted to experimental and quasi-experimental designs used in program and practice outcome evaluations.

Fourth-Generation Evaluation

Lincoln (2003) advocates for a fourth-generation approach for this millennium that strives to redress power imbalances and expand the repertoire of data-gathering and data analysis methods used in evaluations. She argues that we must move beyond the modernist and Eurocentric philosophies that tend to believe that rational, orderly investigations and deductions in the social sciences will help us arrive at social truth, as in the physical sciences. A postmodernist would argue that no single method or design can produce anything more than a partial truth. A postmodernist distrusts all methods equally and recognizes and admits the situational limitations of the knower, whether based in science, literature, or another vantage point. Lincoln views politics as a major voice of influence in her inquiries, and her perspective takes into account the needs of global society, not just Western society. This global perspective particularly seeks to hear and value the often-unheard indigenous voices of other societies.

Lincoln (2003) also advocates for the use of naturalistic inquiries along with the more traditional quantitative methodologies in evaluations. Her writings offer qualitative methodologies and techniques in many forms for evaluation purposes. In terms of the practical aspects of evaluation, she warns that evaluators who fail to pay attention to the growing number of pluralistic voices in social life will find these voices in a chorus of opposition to any evaluation with a single method of inquiry. Several sections of this book describe qualitative methods for evaluation, including client and staff satisfaction studies in chapter 8 and data analysis in chapter 10.

Evaluations Evolving within Particular Fields of Practice

The various program evaluation texts currently available reveal that many evaluation approaches are tailored to particular fields of practice and specific client populations. Health care is a good example. Evaluation is an integral part of health-care programs, for example, in the special emphasis on health maintenance organizations, diagnostic treatment groups, and the growing importance of managed care. As health-care technologies expand, the costs continue to soar, as growing numbers of people can benefit from these technologies. Thus, cost-benefit analyses are critical. Other special interests in health-care evaluation include risk management, quality improvement, patient and consumer communications, safety and security needs for evaluation in long-term care, AIDS treatment, and other areas (Kavaler & Spiegel, 2003).

Child welfare is another example of a field that has an extensive evaluation literature. Briar-Lawson and Zlotnik (2002), for example, have edited a collection of articles that focus on the necessity of clear and relevant child welfare outcomes in programs for children. They stress recruiting and retaining social workers who have special preparation in child welfare in the public sector.

Other examples of fields of practice that emphasize a particular evaluation approach include teacher and staff performance in school settings, dignity and normalization for people with developmental disabilities, child-custody evaluations in family court, and evaluations using various community organization models.

SYNTHESIS OF THE DIFFERENT EVALUATION PERSPECTIVES

Some authors have provided a fuller understanding of the different perspectives driving evaluations and what each values in their classification. These classifying efforts have been useful in synthesizing several distinct perspectives and in revealing the strengths and limitations of each one.

Patton's Five Distinct Paradigms

First, Patton (2002) offers his understanding of different evaluation perspectives by identifying five distinct paradigms. Each paradigm, in part, captures elements of the types of evaluations that are pertinent to social service agencies, schools, and institutions that employ human service workers:

1. Traditional scientific paradigm: the traditional social science paradigm emphasizes objectivity and the independence of the evaluator from the group studied, and it minimizes investigators' bias. It also pays close attention to validity, reliability, generalizability, and a marked preference for quantitative measurement and experimental

designs. This paradigm is expanded in the work of Rossi, Freeman, and Lipsey (2003).

2. Social construction and constructionist: this paradigm asserts the inevitability of subjectivity, uses multiple perspectives, favors qualitative inquiry, and offers alternative criteria to validity and reliability for judging methodological quality (e.g., trustworthiness, authenticity, and gathering findings that enhance and deepen understanding). Responding to multiple stakeholder perspectives is a hallmark of constructionist evaluation. This paradigm is expanded in the work of Guba and Lincoln (1989) and Greene (2000).

3. Artistic and evocative paradigm: this paradigm, while not yet widely used in evaluations, uses role-playing and dramatic techniques, poetry, and other literary forms to gather and present data, as well as short stories and narrative techniques to report findings. The criteria for judging artistic and evocative evaluations include creativity, aesthetic quality, and interpretive vitality. The findings of such studies can open the program world to the evaluation audience through literary and dramatic devices and offer a deep sense of the lived experience of program participants. Eisner's (1991) work models this paradigm.

4. Pragmatic and utilitarian paradigm: this paradigm emphasizes the specific practical, informative needs of users of an evaluation. Criteria include responsiveness to the needs of stakeholders, situational adaptability, attending to interactive engagement between the evaluator and stakeholders, methodological flexibility, and preparation of findings such that they respond to stakeholders' needs. Utilization-focused evaluations highlight this paradigm (Patton, 2008).

5. Critical change paradigm: in this paradigm, evaluators are involved in evaluations primarily as change agents by bringing a critical change orientation and explicit agenda to uncover political, economic, and social inequalities; to raise people's consciousness; and to strive to change the balance of power in favor of the less powerful. An underlying purpose of such evaluations is to increase social justice, and to increase the ability of the oppressed to represent their own interests through the evaluation and follow-up actions. Critical change criteria undergird empowerment evaluations (Fetterman, 2003), diversity-inclusive evaluations (Mertens, 2003), and those aspects of deliberative democratic evaluation that involve values-based advocacy for democracy (House & Howe, 2000).

Social workers need the objectivity and methodical rigor of the traditional scientific research paradigm described extensively in later chapters. The social constructionist paradigm is also useful, because social work evaluators are increasingly using both qualitative and quantitative methods to describe and define a growing number of unfamiliar concepts and are committed to addressing the concerns of multiple stakeholders, especially program recipients. In addition, social work, a very practical profession, stresses a utilitarian perspective similar to the pragmatic and utilitarian paradigm, as social work evaluations must be relevant, practical, and responsive to the evolving program needs in social agencies. Also among the ethical priorities of a social work evaluator is the persistent concern for social justice; therefore, social work evaluators gravitate toward evaluations that focus on macro practice interventions that can bring about social change beneficial to clients, in keeping with the critical change paradigm. As noted previously, the evaluation enterprise is by no means monolithic or uniform in its theoretical perspective. It has been driven by many different perspectives and can generate many different benefits for social program development and program recipients.

Brun's Typology

Carl Brun (2005), a social work educator and experienced program evaluator, offers another helpful way to look at the various evaluation perspectives. He conceptualizes evaluation as driven by five overall factors: (1) decisions that have to be made, (2) the involvement of stakeholders, (3) the following of values, (4) application of theory, and (5) use of appropriate data-collection methods. Although he states that all five factors are evident in all evaluations, one of these five factors usually has the greatest influence. Decision-making evaluations emphasize the gathering of data to address specific decisions that have to be made about a program. Involvement of stakeholders gives the most attention to the processes of identifying stakeholders critical to the evaluation and how they can become involved as fully as possible. Values-driven evaluations give greatest emphasis to the underlying values of the evaluation. For example, social work values stress the importance of the strengths of participants, their cultural context, and empowerment of oppressed client groups. Theory-driven evaluations begin with theoretical explorations and commitments and a desire to link the causes of the participants' problems with how the interventions can address such causes. Data-driven evaluations emphasize the types of data needed and the preferred methodologies to obtain them, such as a preference for a qualitative or quantitative method, with all decisions revolving around the methodological commitment. According to Brun, all five factors, and their emphases, are important.

All five of Brun's emphases—making decisions, involving stakeholders, following values, applying theory, and choosing research methods—are important in evaluations. They all compete for resources and influence in most evaluations, so Brun's framework is helpful in sorting out all of their contributions and the frequent need to set priorities. For example, an evaluation that pays extensive attention to identifying and involving a range of stakeholders, including client groups, has the potential to be in tension with theory-driven evaluations. In theory-driven evaluations, all of the stakeholders would need to be adequately trained in the theories undergirding a program, which could require considerable time, collaboration, and cost.

Formative and Summative Evaluations

Finally, an important way to distinguish evaluations is to ask whether they are formative or summative. This is the traditional way in which evaluations are distinguished in many program evaluation texts. Formative evaluations focus on planning for a program and improving its delivery of services. Program processes are important to examine, correct, and enhance because of the direct impact they have on the outcomes for program recipients. These evaluations tend to be exploratory and utilitarian in that their findings can be immediately channeled back into enhancing a program, solving a problem, or filling an obvious omission in a program. The agency sponsoring the program usually initiates and conducts such evaluations; the agency staff or outside consultants internally drive the evaluation.

Summative evaluations focus on the outcomes of programs and attempt to answer the ultimate question: did the intervention reach its goals or make a real difference in the lives of recipients? These evaluations have a finality to them in that they attempt to measure whether a program was effective. An external agent, such as an independent evaluator or governmental agency, typically conducts such evaluations to ensure that they are objective. They primarily use a narrower set of research design options, such as experimental and single system. The results of these studies can be decisive in determining whether a program continues, expands, or terminates. Funding and regulatory agencies are most interested in summative evaluations because they provide the kinds of information that they need to make major decisions about future funding.

These two distinct types of evaluations, formative and summative, are somewhat similar to the distinction in research between exploratory and explanatory studies. Exploratory studies are conducted to learn more about a phenomenon when not much is currently known. Exploratory studies identify general research questions to answer. Explanatory studies are conducted to find support for theoretical explanations that the researcher has already crafted. Explanatory studies usually identify hypotheses to confirm or refute. Formative evaluations are like exploratory studies in that they are exploratory in nature and not intended to provide results that can help make major decisions about a program. Summative evaluations are like explanatory studies in that they are used to bring finality to a program's future; either it did or it did not have a significant impact on recipients (see table 2.1).

TABLE 2.1   Characteristics of Formative and Summative Studies

Formative studies	*Summative studies*
Intent: How is the program or practice intervention functioning?	Intent: Is the program or practice intervention reaching its goals?
Focus provided by general research questions	Focus provided by hypotheses: How much does the intervention have an impact on the recipients' lives?
Use of both qualitative and quantitative methods	Use of quantitative methods
Audience: Stakeholders are mostly affiliated with the agency sponsoring the intervention	Audience: Stakeholders include the funding and regulatory agencies

In formative studies, the intent is to learn more about how the program is functioning and to consider whether the program is instrumental in helping clients meet their predetermined goals. Such studies mostly involve the asking of general study questions that will produce more information about the program so that it can be improved or enhanced. Formative studies often have up to four or five general study questions. The audience for such studies is usually affiliated with the agency sponsor, such as administrators, board members, advisory board members, staff, clients, and others. In contrast, in summative studies, the intent is to determine whether the program is actually effective in reaching its goals. Instead of study questions, explanatory evaluations usually test hypotheses to determine whether the intervention had a positive influence on client outcome measures. Summative studies may have as many as three or four explanatory statements or hypotheses to be tested.

However, these two types of evaluations, formative and summative, are helpful only to a limited extent. Most evaluations conducted by social workers will be formative. Summative evaluations are less likely to be initiated by a social agency. Nevertheless, the purposes of summative evaluations are important to understand, as they have a vital role in decisions about a program's future. Research designs used in summative evaluations are a focus of chapter 9 and are illustrated in other parts of the book.

Evidence-Based Interventions

Evidence-based interventions are not a philosophy or perspective as much as they are a pledge or assurance that programs and practice approaches are effective and ultimately accountable to our clients. Regardless of the specific perspective that an evaluator selects to conduct an evaluation, it should attempt to be as evidence-based as possible. Evidence-based interventions have been defined in medicine as the "integration of the best research evidence with clinical expertise and patient values" (Sackett,

Richardson, Rosenburg, & Haynes, 2000, p. 1). Gambrill, a social worker, states that "it involves integrating individual practice expertise with the best available external evidence from systematic research as well as considering the values and expectations of clients" (1999, p. 346). In this text, evidence-based interventions are those that use the best available external evidence that the interventions are effective. Evidence comes mostly from practice experience and research studies with quasi-experimental or experimental designs. It is also important that evidence-based sources are consistent with the values and expectations of the clients who receive such interventions.

The words *evidence* and *evidence-based* are often used throughout this book. Evidence is something observed firsthand with some or all of the senses (sight, hearing, taste, touch, smell). Evidence documenting the effectiveness of a program or practice area needs to be empirical or reflect some form of reality in the world. When evidence of a phenomenon is not directly observable, then a secondhand source needs to be found that is reliable and valid. Agency case records and questionnaire responses are examples of secondhand sources of evidence.

Evidence can take many forms and can be used with varying degrees of confidence. The best evidence is based on evaluation studies using the scientific method. Yet, the results they produce provide evidence at differing levels of confidence. For example, a pre/post-test design only measures how a client functions before and after an intervention, which is much weaker evidence than a pre/post-test experiment using a control group.

Another important aspect of evidence pertains to the clients that benefited from the intervention. Evidence may be available indicating a particular intervention works with a group of white mothers in a suburban area of a large city, but we must be cautious not to necessarily assume that this evidence is also relevant to mothers of different ethnic groups or mothers living in large cities, small towns, or rural environments. An evaluation focuses on a particular group that received the services of an intervention to determine whether they were helped. They could be predominately African American, Euro-American, or Mexican, high income or poor. Whatever the characteristics of the clients, they need to be known so we can assume that the evidence is more likely applicable to people representing this group than people of different characteristics or circumstances. Generalizing is an important concept in this respect. If we are to consider evidence that a program works, we should first consider that it may work for others with similar characteristics before we consider its benefits for people with different characteristics. Generalizing has to be done carefully and the sampling approach used in an evaluation largely determines how confident we can be that the intervention that works for one group allows us to draw conclusions for another group.

The NASW Code of Ethics stresses the importance of evidence as an ethical issue: "social workers should . . . use evaluation and research evidence in their professional practice." Evidence also has a wider range of implications beyond evaluations. For example, a participant's signature on an informed consent form provides evidence of consent; needs assessments provide evidence of clients' specific problems, clinical diagnoses, or medical conditions; evidence is required for outcome studies to document outcome measures.

Example of Evidence-Based Interventions

Harding and Higginson (2003) systematically reviewed articles from several relevant professional journals to identify interventions for helping non-institutionalized cancer and palliative care patients and their caregivers. They found twenty-two relevant interventions. Overall, they concluded from their review that one-to-one interventions are a means of providing support, education, and building problem-solving and coping skills. However, they are time-consuming, costly, and may be unacceptable to many caregivers. Group work interventions, in contrast, were reported to be widely used for support and education for both caregivers and patients.

Empirical evidence of a phenomenon could be illustrated in an outcome study in which the frequency of contact between a client with mental illness and other people is an outcome measure of social adaptation. How can this be determined empirically? Theoretically, it can be observed first-hand if someone were available to observe the interactions of a client all day long without interfering with the contacts in any way. However, it is not realistic or ethically sound to obtain such information in this way. A secondhand source of such information, such as a relative, friend, or the self-reporting of the client, is subjective and likely inaccurate. Moreover, secondhand sources could be biased, so the challenge is to make sure that such reports are as accurate as possible. One way to increase this possibility is to obtain multiple sources, such as reports from two or more people and compare them.

A Unique International Source of Evidence-Based Information

The Collaboration or C2 (www.campbellcollaboration.org) is an international source of evidence-based information for programs and practice. It is "an independent, international, non-profit organization that provides decision-makers with evidence-based information to empower them to make well-informed decisions about the effects of interventions in the social, behavioral and educational arenas." C2 has a strategic network of renowned scholars and practitioners worldwide that can provide evidence-based information in two ways: (1) by preparing, maintaining, and disseminating systematic reviews of existing social science evidence, and (2) by random controlled trials using their own databases. C2's vision is to promote positive social change and to improve programs and services across the world.

Best practices is a frequently heard term in agencies these days, and is also relevant to the discussion of evidenced-based interventions. Best practices are the best or most effective programs or practices known to work in helping people overcome their problems. For this reason, evidence-based practices, in many ways, are strongly correlated with best practices. For example, best practices could be the best evidence-based practices known to exist for a particular client group.

KEY PERSPECTIVES FOR THE BOOK

This review of several types of perspectives and approaches in conducting evaluations reveals some fairly common and overlapping elements. Those that seem most compatible with the evaluation approach described herein include the following:

- Importance of science, neutrality, and objective methods
- Use of critical-thinking skills
- Recognition that achieving socially acceptable outcomes is an essential program expectation
- Recognition that the purposes of evaluations vary widely and dictate what is to be done
- Importance of working closely with stakeholders and accountability to them
- Following a professional ethical code
- Flexibility in the use of various methodologies, including considering the use of qualitative and artistic ones
- Affirmation and promotion of diversity
- Commitment to social and economic justice

INTRODUCTION OF THE THREE-STAGE APPROACH

When discussing all of these evaluation perspectives and approaches, it is important to remember that a social program or a practice area is the focal point of an evaluation. Programs and professional practice are dynamic and, in some ways, similar to human beings: they are conceived, evolve in an embryo-like form, are birthed, grow up, mature, and ultimately decline and end. For programs and practice approaches, these stages are referred to as follows:

- Planning stage, when a program or practice area is conceived and developed into an initial proposal or plan
- Implementation stage, when the program or practice area is implemented
- Outcome stage, when the impact of the program or practice area on client outcomes is the major focus

The book is organized around these three developmental stages of programs and practice and is referred to as the three-stage approach. This approach is central to the book because evaluations address important issues at all three stages. However, it is noteworthy that these stages may not always occur in sequential order. To the contrary, they often overlap. For example, during the planning of an intervention, the same intervention may also be implemented as a pilot project for a small group of clients, to explore its potential on a larger scale and to identify the necessary resources. Or after the implementation of an intervention, a process evaluation may be initiated to determine whether the intervention is moving in the right direction toward its goals. The results of such a study could lead to a decision to start over, make major corrections, or move ahead with few or no changes.

Programs

Important elements of a program that are pertinent to an evaluation need to be identified at each stage. Input elements, such as the potential population of clients and client needs, the theoretical underpinnings of the program, the technologies to be used, and hiring needs are identified during the planning stage. During the implementation stage, such elements are referred to as process elements. Examples include testing out the intervention, training and supervising the staff, and ongoing monitoring of the implementation of the intervention. The outcome stage elements are referred to as output and outcome elements. They include, for example, the number of clients who complete the program (an output element) and outcome elements such as measures of client progress in reaching their goals. Figure 2.1 reminds us that the assessment of client needs is addressed as an input element during the planning stage, interventions are addressed as process elements during the implementation stage, and outcomes are addressed during the outcome stage.

Practice

Let's look more closely at how these stages are evident in practice evaluations. At the practice level, an evaluation can investigate the input elements before the implementation of practice interventions. Some important

FIGURE 2.1   Three-Stage Approach

input elements in practice are the credentials that practitioners would need to have to qualify for their positions, such as a professional degree, work experience, and other special skills. Other input elements are the criteria used to select prospective clients and the characteristics of those clients (e.g., ethnicity, age, gender). Identifying and developing the chosen practice approaches to be used are another example of an input element.

During the implementation of a practice intervention, important process elements can include how the practice approach and its specific techniques are actually being implemented. The outcome stage takes into account other sets of elements, such as the total number of sessions provided to a client (output element) and measures of client progress (outcome element).

Client Satisfaction with Various Practice Approaches

Client satisfaction studies are sometimes used to evaluate how well a practice approach is being implemented based on the clients' perceptions. A client satisfaction study by Baker, Zucker, and Gross (1998) sought, among other things, to determine the perceptions of five groups of inpatient mental health clients who were receiving different treatment modalities and services in five different facilities. The evaluator assumed that the clients with severe mental illness "know what's good for them[selves]." Practice approaches varied across facilities. For example, one facility offered extensive assistance with daily activities, while another offered training groups in psychosocial skills and a third emphasized case management, family services, and individual counseling. No overall pattern of client satisfaction was found across the widely varied approaches, though some approaches received lower ratings.

In conclusion, the stages of program and practice development and the elements important to consider in each stage provide a major organizational framework for the book. This organizational framework is helpful in informing you about how to focus an evaluation before you proceed to implement it.

KEY TERMS

Empowerment models
Evaluations evolving within particular fields of practice
Evidence-based interventions
Experimental models
Feminist models
Formative and summative evaluations
Fourth-generation evaluation
Participatory action approach
Results-oriented models

DISCUSSION QUESTIONS AND ASSIGNMENTS

1. In small groups, choose one of the historical events listed below, review what is summarized about the event in the chapter, and find an additional source of information related to evaluation. Discuss within your small groups what you learned about the event and its importance in shaping evaluations. Then share what you have learned with the class.
   - President Johnson's Great Society and War on Poverty, which were instrumental in creating programs such as local Community Action Councils, Job Corps, Neighborhood Youth Corp, Community Legal Services, and Head Start.
   - The 1962 Social Security amendments, which instituted initiatives such as services for welfare recipients, rehabilitation, and training for useful work to overcome prolonged dependency.
   - The passage of the Government Performance and Results Act of 1993, which requires all governmental agencies to focus on client outcomes and define how they are to be achieved.
   - Joel Fischer's article "Is Casework Effective? A Review."
2. Select one of the six evaluation perspectives. Find out more about this perspective by reading about it in an evaluation text. Then find one evaluation study in a professional journal that is an example of this perspective.
3. What is your view of the role of empowerment in evaluation? How can an evaluator promote empowerment through an evaluation? What are your views about the limits of empowerment in evaluation, if any?

4. Develop a program evaluation that could be conducted at your agency. What is the overall purpose of the evaluation? What could be accomplished by conducting this evaluation? Which perspectives described in the chapter would have the most impact on how you would conduct this evaluation? Why?
5. Why is it important to know the philosophical orientation of an evaluator? Pick one of the six perspectives described in the chapter and discuss how it can affect, both positively and negatively, how an evaluator conducts a study.

REFERENCES

Baker, L., Zucker, P., & Gross, M. (1998). Using client satisfaction surveys to evaluate and improve services in locked and unlocked adult inpatient facilities. *Journal of Behavioral Health Services Research, 25*(1), 51–68.

Bloom, M., Fischer, J., & Orme, J. G. (2003). *Evaluating practice: Guidelines for the accountable professional*. Boston: Allyn & Bacon.

Briar-Lawson, K., & Zlotnik, J. L. (Eds.). (2002). *Evaluation research in child welfare: Improving outcomes through university-public agency partnerships*. Binghamton, NY: Haworth Press.

Bricker-Jenkins, M., Hooyman, N. R., & Gottlieb, N. (Eds.). (1991). *Feminist social work practice in clinical settings*. Thousand Oaks, CA: Sage.

Brun, C. F. (2005). *A practical guide to social service evaluation*. Chicago: Lyceum Books.

Cook, T. D., & Campbell, D. T. (1979). *Quasi-experimentation: Design and analysis issues for field settings*. Skokie, IL: Rand McNally.

Deem, R. (2002). Talking to manager-academics: Methodological dilemmas and feminist research strategies. *Sociology, 36*(4), 835–856.

DePoy, E., Hartman, A., & Haslett, D. (1999). Critical action research: A model for social work knowing. *Social Work, 44*(6), 560–569.

Eisner, E. (1991). *The enlightened eye*. New York: Macmillan.

Fetterman, D. (2003). Empowerment evaluation strikes a responsive chord. In S. I. Donaldson & M. Scriven (Eds.), *Evaluating social programs and problems: Visions for the new millennium* (pp. 63–76). Mahwah, NJ: Lawrence Erlbaum Associates.

Fetterman, D. M., Kaftarian, S. J., & Wandersman, A. (Eds.). (1996). *Empowerment evaluation: Knowledge and tools for self-assessment and accountability*. Thousand Oaks, CA: Sage.

Fischer, J. (1973). Is casework effective? A review. *Social Work, 18*(1), 5–20.

Gambrill, E. (1999). Evidence-based practice: An alternative to authority-based practice. *Families in Society, 80*(4), 341–350.

Gibbs, L. (2003). *Evidence-based practice for the helping professions: A practical guide with integrated multimedia*. Pacific Grove, CA: Thomson.

Gibbs, L., & Gambrill, E. (1996). *Critical thinking for social workers: A workbook*. Thousand Oaks, CA: Pine Forge Press.

Gibelman, M. (2003). So how far have we come? Pestilent and persistent gender gap in pay. *Social Work, 48*(1), 22–32.

Greene, J. C. (2000). Understanding social programs through evaluation. In N. K. Denzin & Y. S. Lincoln (Eds.), *Handbook of qualitative research* (2nd ed., pp. 981–999). Thousand Oaks, CA: Sage.

Guba, E., & Lincoln, Y. (1989). *Fourth generation evaluation*. Thousand Oaks, CA: Sage.

Harding, R., & Higginson, I. J. (2003). What is the best way to help caregivers in cancer and palliative care? A systematic literature review of interventions and their effectiveness. *Palliative Medicine, 17*, 63–74.

House, E. R., & Howe, K. R. (2000). Deliberative democratic evaluation. *New Directions for Evaluation, 85*, 3–12.

Kautz, J. R., Netting, F. E., Huber, R., Borders, K., & Davis, T. S. (1997). The Government Performance and Results Act of 1993: Implications for social work practice. *Social Work, 42*(4), 364–373.

Kavaler, F., & Spiegel, A. (2003). *Risk management in health care institutions: A strategic approach*. Sudbury, MA: Jones & Bartlett Publishers.

Lincoln, Y. S. (2003). Fourth generation evaluation in the new millennium. In S. I. Donaldson & M. Scriven (Eds.), *Evaluating social programs and problems: Visions for the new millennium* (pp. 77–90). Mahwah, NJ: Lawrence Erlbaum Associates.

Martin, L. L., & Kettner, P. M. (1996). *Measuring the performance of human service programs*. Thousand Oaks, CA: Sage.

Mertens, D. M. (2003). The inclusive view of evaluation: Visions for the new millennium. In S. I. Donaldson & M. Scriven (Eds.), *Evaluating social programs and problems: Visions for the new millennium* (pp. 91–107). Mahwah, NJ: Lawrence Erlbaum Associates.

O'Hare, T. (2005). *Evidence-based practices for social workers: An interdisciplinary approach*. Chicago: Lyceum Books.

Patton, M. Q. (2002). Feminist, yes, but is it evaluation? *New Directions for Evaluation, 96*(Winter), 97–108.

Patton, M. Q. (2008). *Utilization-focused evaluation* (4th ed.). Thousand Oaks, CA: Sage.

Reese, D., Ahern, R., Nair, S., O'Faire, J., & Warren, C. (1999). Hospice access and use by African Americans: Addressing cultural and institutional barriers through participatory action research. *Social Work, 44*(6), 549–559.

Rossi, P., Freeman, H., & Lipsey, M. (2003). *Evaluation: A systematic approach* (7th ed.). Thousand Oaks, CA: Sage.

Sackett, D. L., Richardson, W. S., Rosenburg, W., & Haynes, R. R. (2000). *Evidence-based medicine: How to practice and teach E.M.* (2nd ed.). New York: Churchill-Livingstone.

Skeggs, B. (2001). Feminist ethnography. In P. Atkinson, A. Coffey, & S. Delamont (Eds.), *Encyclopaedia of ethnography* (pp. 426–442). London: Sage.

Stufflebean, D. L. (2001). Evaluation models. *New Directions for Evaluation, 89*, 7–98.

Wholey, J. S. (1999). Quality control: Assessing the accuracy and usefulness of performance measurement systems. In H. P. Hatry (Ed.), *Performance measurement: Getting results* (pp. 217–239). Washington, DC: Urban Institute.

Zimmerman, M. A. (2000). Empowerment theory: Psychological, organizational, and community levels of analysis. In J. Rappaport & E. Seldman (Eds.), *Handbook of community psychology* (pp. 43–63). New York: Plenum.

Chapter 3

The Role of Ethics in Evaluations

What are our ethical obligations as evaluators?

Ethics plays a crucial role in both program and practice evaluations. This chapter describes the most important ethical issues to be considered when conducting evaluations. Because much of this material is largely a review of the ethics material covered in a basic research methods course, it is condensed here. A research methods text can be a helpful supplement to this chapter for those who want more information on ethics (e.g., Dudley, 2011; Marlow, 2011).

This chapter primarily reviews the ethical standards of three professional associations: the National Association of Social Workers, the American Evaluation Association (AEA), and the Council on Social Work Education.

Ethical concerns for evaluations are similar to those for research studies generally. They are so important to social work evaluations that the section "Evaluation and Research Standards" of the NASW's (2008) Code of Ethics covers ethical concerns specifically for research.

Because social work has many functions, and evaluation is only one of them, it is valuable to consult an ethical code of a group such as the AEA, which focuses exclusively on evaluation activities. The five major principles of AEA evaluators are the following:

1. *Systematic inquiry*: A commitment to systematic inquiries that use the highest technical standards and a commitment to communicate the inquiries as clearly as possible to all stakeholders and other parties.
2. *Competence*: Evaluators are expected to provide competent performance to stakeholders, which includes an appropriate educational background, skills, and experiences, as well as cultural competence to conduct an evaluation effectively in terms of race, ethnicity, gender, religion, socioeconomic factors, and others.
3. *Integrity and honesty*: Evaluators are to display honesty and integrity in their own behavior and attempt to ensure honesty and integrity throughout the entire evaluation process, including disclosing conflicts of interest and not misrepresenting their procedures, findings, or interpretations.

4. *Respect for all people*: Evaluators are to respect the security, dignity, and self-worth of evaluation participants, clients, and other evaluation stakeholders. They are to prevent risks of harm and invasion of privacy for participants and assure participants of any benefits they can accrue from an evaluation.

5. *Responsibilities for general and public welfare*: Evaluators are to articulate and take into account the diversity of general and public interests and values that may be related to the evaluation, and to be mindful of the rights and needs of all pertinent groups.

Ethics important to conducting evaluations are also promulgated in the accreditation standards of the CSWE, including recognizing the importance of diversity, promoting social and economic justice, and abiding by the values and ethics of professional social work.

ETHICS FOR CONDUCTING EVALUATIONS

Having an entire section of the NASW Code of Ethics devoted exclusively to social workers' ethical obligations to research and evaluation clearly indicates the importance of ethics. Section 5.02, titled "Evaluation and Research," can be found at the NASW's website (www.naswdc.org). Some of the section's specific principles are reviewed below along with selected AEA principles.

Promote and Facilitate Evaluations and Research

This introductory statement of Section 5.02[b] of the NASW Code of Ethics reminds social workers that they have an ethical obligation to promote and facilitate evaluation studies and other types of research. This suggests that social workers should be supportive of others who conduct evaluations in their employment agencies. However, to do this, they need to be familiar with the ethical standards of research and other ethical standards of social work so that they can become gatekeepers, both to encourage new evaluations that meet the ethical standards of the profession and to discourage evaluations that do not.

Consult Appropriate Institutional Review Boards

Institutional review boards (IRBs) are groups of people at an institution who have been designated to promulgate ethical standards and to approve and monitor the ethical provisions of all studies sponsored by the institution. Virtually all universities and governmental agencies have an IRB. Evaluators and other researchers are required to submit a formal statement to the IRB that describes their study, its procedures, its benefits, and how it protects research participants from risks of harm and invasion of privacy

(Section 5.02[d] of the NASW Code of Ethics). In addition, IRBs can serve as training centers to inform researchers of specific requirements of informed consent.

Many social agencies also have an IRB, ethics committee, or they create a similar ad hoc group when it is needed. Social agencies that sponsor research and do not have such a group should institute a formal way to establish ethical standards and procedures, to protect research participants, and to prevent ethical problems. Using the guidelines herein, you can create a new structure for your agency to carefully review any new studies before they are approved.

Create Your Own IRB or Ethics Committee

1. Select a group of five to seven agency staff members who represent different programs, disciplines, and positions in the agency.
2. Orient the staff representatives to the ethical problems and safeguards that an IRB typically considers. Introduce them to the various functions of an IRB. Ask experts on these subjects from other agencies and institutions to speak about them to your new IRB members.
3. Role-play three or four typical scenarios involving evaluation studies that have ethical omissions or problems.
4. When reviewing the first two or three cases, step back and examine the process that you used in arriving at your decisions as well as the decisions themselves. You may also want to ask a more experienced IRB or ethics committee to review your deliberations and decisions.
5. Consider combining your IRB with a human rights committee if you have one. However, be sure to distinguish how the review process for approving an evaluation and the process of reviewing a client human rights case are different.
6. Make sure that the IRB or ethics committee is formally accountable to someone in the agency in an authority position, such as the executive director or an assistant director. Make sure this person is assigned with the responsibility for overseeing the training and operation of the committee and has a budget necessary to meet its resource needs.

Conduct Your Own Evaluations

The NASW Code also encourages social workers to conduct their own evaluations within agencies or to assist others in doing so (Sections 5.02[a] and [c]). Social workers are encouraged to "monitor and evaluate policies, the implementation of programs, and our practice interventions."

At this point, you may have questions, such as, "What if I don't have an interest in conducting evaluation studies?" The Code of Ethics encourages everyone to participate in evaluation studies. Despite whether or not someone wants to conduct an evaluation, as a professional, social workers are obligated to do so. If they do not, evaluations conducted without their input and leadership will likely overlook the particular perspectives and experiences they have as a result of direct contact with clients. The NASW Code also states, "Social workers should critically examine and keep current with emerging knowledge relevant to social work and fully use evaluation and research evidence in their professional practice." This is the ultimate reason for us to both support and facilitate evaluation studies by others and to conduct them ourselves. We have an ethical obligation to learn about the most up-to-date knowledge and skills available in our specific fields of practice.

Protect Participants of Evaluation Studies

The NASW Code indicates that it is essential that we protect the research participants, who are usually our clients, from any adverse consequences of an evaluation study (Section 5.02[d] and [j]). Such problems often occur inadvertently because the evaluator has not given enough forethought to consequences or may have decided that the potential contributions from a study outweigh the potential problems that participants experience.

Several types of ethical problems could adversely affect participants of a study, including physical harm, psychological harm, invasion of privacy, or deception. There have been many studies known to harm participants. The Tuskegee Institute study, conducted in the 1930s to determine the adverse effects of untreated syphilis, is a classic example. In that study, African American men were deliberately deceived and effective treatment was deliberately withheld. By the time the study's ethical violations were exposed, twenty-eight men had died from syphilis, one hundred others had died of related complications, at least forty of the men's wives were infected, and nineteen of their children had contracted the disease at birth.

Although such studies are no longer conducted in the United States (thanks to regulations enacted by governmental agencies, universities, and other groups), evaluation studies can still result in physical harm today, even if that harm is not as horrific as in the Tuskegee Institute study. Examples of harm include asking vulnerable people unnecessary sensitive questions or withholding essential services from a client assigned to a control group.

Some evaluation studies also have the potential to cause psychological harm. Although psychological harm is likely to be less tangible and more difficult to detect than physical harm, it can have an equally damaging impact on participants. Evaluations can cause psychological harm, for example, in investigations of sexually abusive experiences of children or adolescents or the dreams of someone with psychosis. The issue of psychological harm is complicated because the harm can manifest immediately after participation in a study or several months or years later.

Evaluation studies can also unnecessarily invade participants' privacy, and they are considered unethical if the possibility of such an invasion of privacy is not pointed out to participants beforehand. It is best to avoid such evaluations unless there is a strong justification to the contrary. People who have difficulty saying no to requests to participate in studies are among the most likely to be susceptible to invasion of privacy. Examples of evaluation study topics likely to invade some people's privacy are those that ask about alcohol or drug practices, sexual orientation, or clinical diagnoses. These evaluation topics are still legitimate if participants provide informed consent, if support is made available to them, and if there is adequate justification to explore these topics.

Deceiving a person into participating in an evaluation can also be harmful. Evaluators can have good reasons to deceive participants, such as minimizing a reactive effect from sharing too many details about the study's purpose or hypotheses. Nevertheless, such deception still can have ethical implications. The *60 Minutes II* undercover episode described subsequently is an example of the administration and staff of a psychiatric facility being deceived. Yet the investigation led to the reform of a facility that was harming its patients. The dilemma embedded in the example is obvious. Although the use of deception in an investigation is wrong, so are unsound professional practices. A decision had to be made about whether the intent of the study and the deception involved outweighed the professional agency's right to privacy. What do you think?

Example of Deception

The former television news-magazine program *60 Minutes II* hired a social worker as an undercover investigator to observe life in a psychiatric facility (O'Neill, 1999). The social worker concealed a videotape recorder in his shirt and a camera in his unusually thick eyeglasses while working as a mental health technician at a private psychiatric hospital. The CBS network was motivated to initiate the story after hearing of the death of a sixteen-year-old boy who had been restrained at a facility owned by the same company. The investigation documented many appalling conditions at the institution, including fraudulent and sometimes bogus case reporting, an understaffed facility, neglect in giving potentially dangerous drugs, and the restraint of juveniles by staff without training. Two facilities owned by the company were closed after the airing of the episode. The episode also led to renewed activities by Congress and mental health advocates to monitor and reform options available for using restraints.

Obtain Voluntary Informed Consent from Evaluation Participants

An informed consent protocol can be designed to address many of the concerns raised about potential ethical problems of studies, including physical and psychological harm, invasion of privacy, and deception. Informed consent means that the participants of a study are thoroughly informed about the study before they agree to participate (American Evaluation Association, 2007; NASW, 2008). Evaluation participants should give informed consent before they are encouraged to participate in any study. The information provided with informed consent is to be clearly communicated and presented at the level of the participants' understanding. It has been suggested that informed consent documentation be written at no higher than a sixth-grade reading level to ensure that it is simple enough to understand. Several types of information should be explicitly covered in an informed consent protocol, including (Dudley, 2011):

- The general purpose of the evaluation
- The evaluator's qualifications and agency affiliation
- The expectations of the participant (e.g., number and length of interviews, location and time of interviews, types of questions)
- Assurance of confidentiality; when participants cannot be assured of confidentiality, participants must be told about how their identities will be revealed and to whom
- Identification of any potential negative effects of the evaluation on participants
- Identification of any potential benefits to participants as a result of their participation
- A reminder that participants can leave the study at any time without negative consequences, such as loss of client services (NASW, 2008, Section 5.02[h])
- A name and phone number of someone at the agency who can respond to participants' questions or concerns

An Ethics Exercise

Assume that you work for a family services agency that provides various services. In discussing your caseload with other social workers, you discover that many of your cases include children whose father is not present in their primary household. You want to conduct a needs assessment to find out whether the children have any contact with their father and how the absence affects them. You decide to ask the children several personal questions and want to consider any possible negative effects of the questions. Answer the following exercise questions:

- What ethical issues are evident as you prepare for the study?
- How will you address these issues?

- What types of questions, if any, would you decide not to ask the children to protect them?
- Would you ask questions of children of all ages or just some age groups? How would your questions be different depending on the child's age?

It is also important to consider the ethical principles of the AEA (2007) for informed consent protocol. For example, while the purpose of the evaluation needs to be explained, a balance of information is recommended. Giving too much information about the evaluation could create a reactive effect in which the participants respond with what they perceive the evaluator wants to hear. Yet, giving too little information could be perceived as being deceptive and unethical.

Preferably, informed consent is provided to participants in written form. The advantages of written informed consent are important; for example, participants can easily review the forms, which make them easier to understand, and participants can keep a copy of the form for their records. Also, information provided by the evaluator in writing cannot be easily questioned at a later time, particularly if any legal issues arise. A participant's signature on the informed consent form is clear evidence of consent. Most universities and social agencies require written consent for many of these reasons.

There are some limitations to written informed consent. For example, it is still possible that participants misunderstand some aspects of the evaluation. Therefore, a written explanation of the study should also be provided to participants and discussed with them to make sure that they fully understand. Such a discussion is particularly helpful with people who have limited cognitive skills or distorted thinking processes as a result of mental retardation or mental illness. It is also important to fully inform involuntary clients, who may need to hear more than once that participation is voluntary.

Evaluation studies with questionnaires involve special circumstances. The informed consent information can be included in a cover letter or in the introductory paragraphs of the questionnaire. In this case, no one is usually available to answer any questions, so the informed consent must be fully self-explanatory. Participants usually are not asked to sign their names for consent in order to keep the questionnaire anonymous. Instead, the evaluator assumes that participants who voluntarily fill out the questionnaire and return it accept the informed consent provisions.

Steps to Follow in Constructing and Using an Informed Consent Form

1. Check to see what your agency requires to protect evaluation participants.
2. Find out whether the agency has an IRB to approve studies; if not, propose that an ad hoc IRB be set up for this purpose.

3. Consider all of the following information in your efforts to inform the participants about the study:

- Purpose of the study
- How the results will be used
- What will be expected of the participant
- Your affiliation with a social agency
- Any possible harmful effects from participating in the study
- Possible benefits of participation
- Confidentiality
- Optional participation and ability to withdraw at any time
- Contact information for someone who can answer questions and concerns

4. Find out if there are any mechanisms in place to assist participants if they experience any harmful effects (e.g., dealing with difficult emotions).
5. If children are participants, decide how you will inform and involve their parents. If other clients have guardians, decide how you will involve them as well.
6. With all the information that you have collected so far, prepare a draft of the informed consent forms or statements.
7. Get feedback from your IRB or ad hoc committee on the adequacy of the informed consent form.
8. Decide how you will protect the privacy and confidentiality of participants during data collection and the presentation of findings.
9. Describe your plans to store and protect the data, including informed consent forms. Also indicate when you will destroy the data if the agency has no further use for it.
10. Seek agency approval of your study.

Address Participants Who Are Incapable of Giving Informed Consent

In the special case of evaluation studies that involve children or clients with legal guardians, the parents or guardians must give informed consent in their place (NASW, 2008, Standard 5.02[f]). Although this extra step may seem a complication or inconvenience, legal guardians must make the decision on participation. In addition, even though the children and other clients without guardianship are not legally responsible, they should be treated with equal respect and given a thorough explanation of the study and the option to not participate. An "assent form" with all the information about the study, the same as is covered in the informed consent form, should be prepared for the children and others with guardians to sign. Thus, two informed consent procedures are needed.

Protect the Confidentiality of Participants

The NASW Code mentions several ways to protect the confidentiality of the participants (Sections 5.02[k]–[m]). As indicated earlier, participants' confidentiality or anonymity should be protected, and participants should be informed of the specific measures taken to ensure confidentiality and of when their responses will be destroyed. Exceptions to confidentiality should also be explained, such as if participants respond in a way that indicates that they or another person is at risk of harm.

Participants should be informed that their responses will not be associated in any way with their name or any other identifying information. Sometimes a funding agency, such as a state agency, may require identifying information in connection with responses. In such instances, it is important to explain to participants why they will be identified and to whom they will be identified (e.g., specific groups or officials). Such an exception should be stated in the initial informed consent with an explanation of why it is required. At that time, participants should also be told that they can voluntarily withdraw from the evaluation without penalization.

Finally, measures must be taken to ensure that the information that participants share in an evaluation will only be discussed for professional purposes and only with people professionally concerned with this information. Such results are not to be shared casually or as an outlet for casual conversation or entertainment.

Participants' Access to Support Services

Evaluators also have a responsibility to protect participants by providing access to support services when negative effects of participation in the evaluation do occur (NASW 2008, Section 5.02[i]). This is particularly important if participants are vulnerable in some way or if their participation could result in any physical or psychological harm. Support services could be offered by the agency sponsoring the evaluation or by a referral agency that can provide treatment or other assistance.

In the case of the needs assessment of the children of an absent father cited earlier, the social workers or counselors assigned to serve these children can be alerted to the sensitivity of the questions so that they can explore any troubling feelings that the children reveal (e.g., hurt, abandonment, guilt). The social workers counseling the children could also take the initiative to ask the residential parent to fill out a questionnaire periodically to uncover any problems in adjustment. Once the study is over, the agency could even consider offering a program of older males as mentors or friends with whom the children can spend time.

Evaluations and Evaluators without a Conflict of Interest

Professionals chosen to conduct evaluations should be free of any conflicts of relationships (AEA, 2007; NASW, 2008). They should avoid and be alert to dual relationships with study participants and other stakeholders. For example, evaluators should not oversee programs or client services at the same time that they conduct an evaluation of the programs and clients because of the possible role conflicts.

One way for the evaluator to avoid conflicts of interest is to hire qualified outside evaluators who have no stake in the study results. If agency-based evaluators, for example, obtain results that are negative or potentially damaging to the agency, they should not be pressured to minimize or ignore such results in their presentations.

Misrepresentation of the findings of a study and other actions that compromise the study's integrity and safety of the participants must also be addressed (NASW, 20089, Section 5.02[n]). For similar reasons, agency staff members who conduct evaluations may be inclined to manipulate findings, such as omitting certain results or falsifying findings that could be counterproductive to an agency and its programs. The hiring of qualified outside evaluators ensures that they have the autonomy and freedom to report all significant findings, similar in some ways to a journal's peer-review panel of experienced professionals, which is a valuable safeguard in preventing the publication of misrepresented findings.

Checklist of Questions to Consider in Hiring an Outside Evaluator (Fitzpatrick, Sanders, & Worthen, 2004)

1. Does the evaluator have the ability to use the methodologies and techniques that may be required in the study?
2. Does the evaluator have the ability to help articulate the appropriate focus for the study?
3. Does the evaluator have the management skills to carry out the study?
4. Will the evaluator maintain appropriate ethical standards?
5. Will the evaluator be interested in and able to communicate results to desired stakeholders in such a way that they will be used?

DIVERSITY AND SOCIAL JUSTICE

The CSWE mandates that every BSW and MSW program prepare its students with understanding, respect, and methods to help people from diverse backgrounds, those experiencing social and economic injustice, populations that are at risk, and people whose human rights are violated. Because social workers typically work with a diverse population of clients that are often oppressed and at risk, this mandate is critical to meet the needs of people in a culturally competent way (CSWE, 2012). This, of course, means being responsive to these issues when conducting program and practice evaluations.

Diversity and Its Importance to Evaluations

When we fully consider the term *diversity,* we are talking about an almost unlimited number of characteristics that distinguish people. The NASW Code of Ethics (2008) highlights several characteristics of diversity that are particularly important in preparing social workers with cultural competence and sensitivity to social diversity: "Social workers should obtain education about and seek to understand the nature of social diversity and oppression with respect to race, ethnicity, national origin, color, sex, sexual orientation, age, marital status, political belief, religion, and mental or physical disability."

Although the code has helped narrow the list of characteristics of diversity considerably, the list is still rather long. We know that often these areas of diversity comprise minority groups or groups that are more vulnerable than others, such as people with extremely serious needs, hardships, and diseases and people experiencing various forms of oppression.

So what does it mean to give special attention to diversity in evaluation? Fortunately, diversity has become a normative aspect of social work research in recent years. Evaluations conducted by social workers typically include participants who are women; people of color; and people of different social classes, sexual orientations, disabilities, and age. Also, theoretical perspectives in social work have expanded to include feminism and Afrocentrism, and to a lesser extent perspectives emphasizing the cultural needs of Latinos, Asian Americans, and recent immigrant groups; gays and lesbians; disability groups; and others (Anderson & Carter, 2003). International issues are also becoming more important as we increasingly realize that we live in a global community and depend on a global economy. However, many of these exciting developments are in an early formative stage and need to be expanded.

Diversity issues are important to consider in evaluations during all stages: planning, implementation, and outcome. For example, some possible diversity issues to consider when conducting a needs assessment during the planning stage include the following:

- Are the participants able to read?
- Are there any language barriers?
- Are face-to-face interviews conducted in a location that feels safe and is easily accessible for the interviewee?

- Will some important groups be inadvertently excluded in a phone interview study?
- Will any group have discomfort or difficulty participating in an interview study?
- Will some groups choose to be excluded if an observational approach is used?
- How will difficult-to-reach groups such as racial minorities, people with very low incomes, undocumented workers, and those who do not speak English be recruited and involved?

A growing number of journals have recently sprung up that focus on issues of diversity and international issues. Many of their articles report on evaluations of some type. The journals include *Affilia: The Journal of Women and Social Work, Ethnic and Racial Studies, Indian Journal of Social Work, Journal of Gay and Lesbian Social Services, Journal of Gerontological Social Work, Hispanic Journal of Behavioral Sciences, Human Services in the Rural Environment, Journal of Multicultural Social Work, International Social Work, Journal of Immigrant and Refugee Services*, and *European Journal of Social Work*.

Example of Chinese Hospice Patients

Mak (2002) interviewed thirty-three Chinese patients in a hospice program to investigate how they perceived features of a "good death." The qualitative study uncovered seven elements or themes that can be helpful to hospice interventions: being aware of dying, maintaining hope, being free from pain and suffering, experiencing personal control, maintaining connectedness to others, preparing to depart, and accepting the timing of one's death. Acceptance of the timing of death was reported to be easier in four circumstances: if the person had completed his or her social roles (e.g., parenting), if the person had reached an old age, if the person had a religious faith to help facilitate a hope in a better life after death, and if the person had experienced a meaningful life.

While the general diversity characteristics proposed by CSWE (e.g., race, ethnicity, social class, gender) are vitally important in conducting evaluations, additional types of diversity are also important within specific client groups (Dudley, 2011). For example, if an evaluator is investigating the impact of mental health, substance abuse, or developmental disabilities programs, some aspects of those clients' diversity could be overlooked. Programs for people with developmental disabilities could have varying degrees of impact given the different levels of disability (mild, moderate, severe, and profound) or the different causal or etiological factors (e.g., Down's syndrome, cerebral palsy, environmental factors). Evaluations of programs for people with mental illness should consider the wide range of diagnoses of mental illnesses as well as whether they are acute or chronic. Programs for people who have survived physical and psychological abuse can have varying impact given current family arrangements, who the perpetrators were, environmental circumstances, and a history of abuse in family members' own family of origin. In summary, evaluations must consider the impact of programs with respect to the various characteristics of diversity that affect clients. Ultimately, it is up to the evaluator to be sensitive to and identify the various effects of interventions as a result of clients' diversity.

Example of a Needs Assessment That Addresses Diversity in Homelessness

Two social workers conducted a needs assessment of homeless people in St. Louis (North & Smith, 1994) to investigate and document the varied ways that white and minority men and women were thought to experience homelessness. The sensitivity of the authors to diversity issues was commendable in that they broke down all of their results by race and gender. Essentially, they compared the circumstances of four subgroups (i.e., nonwhite men, white men, nonwhite women, white women). On the negative side, they grouped all people of color together under the category of "nonwhite" and neglected to differentiate among African Americans, Latinos, and Native Americans.

Relevance of Human Rights and Social and Economic Justice

Another special mandate promulgated by the CSWE is that social work programs give special emphasis to issues of social and economic justice. One section of the CSWE (2012) educational policy describes three objectives for graduates in fulfilling this mandate. Social workers are expected to

- understand the forms and mechanisms of oppression and discrimination
- advocate for human rights and social and economic justice
- engage in practices that advance social and economic justice

These mandates are important to address in program and practice evaluation activities as well as in social work practice. According to the values and ethics of the profession, social workers are encouraged to develop knowledge that promotes the welfare of all people and especially of disadvantaged groups. In other words, evaluations can be an empowering process for social work clients.

There are several ways to conduct program evaluations with a social justice dimension or emphasis. Some of the subsequent examples suggest that the entire focus of a program evaluation can be on a social justice issue, while others may include only a social justice component.

- Evaluating the effectiveness of job-training and employment pro-grams for people with disabilities on the basis of whether they gain better employment in the competitive job market
- Documenting the ways that people with disabilities are discriminated against in hiring practices
- Evaluating programs for homeless people by investigating how the programs help them obtain improved jobs, jobs with longevity, and higher incomes that can sustain them
- Executing a needs assessment of homeless people that documents the extent to which those who are employed cannot afford decent housing
- Eliciting the viewpoints of client groups such as those with AIDS or schizophrenia, gays or lesbians, teenage parents, or former inmates to explore the extent to which the programs they use perpetuate their problems with stigma
- Any evaluation that interviews difficult-to-reach clients rather than relies on more accessible secondary sources, such as a family mem-ber or someone in a social support network

Thinking Outside of the Box by a Practitioner

A social worker, Sharon Galusky, naturally reveals her under-standing of the connections between evaluation and social justice when she describes the various ways she evaluates her practice as a case manager helping people with developmental disabilities. First, she describes the regulations that Medicaid, the funding agency, requires that she address in her agency documentation to receive reimbursement for her services. She then explains that she has addi-tional criteria that she feels compelled to use to evaluate the effec-tiveness of her work as a case manager. She knows that one of her major goals with her clients is to help them reach a higher quality of life, so she and her clients have devised additional individualized criteria for each client, such as helping one find a higher-paying job and finding another a volunteer position in which he can offer advice about saving money while grocery shopping (Sharon Galusky, MSW social worker at Open Doors Inc., Charlotte, NC, per-sonal communication, July 2007).

Incorporating Diversity, Human Rights, and Social and Economic Justice into Evaluations

There are numerous specific ways to incorporate perspectives on diver-sity and promotion of social and economic justice into evaluations. First, it is important to identify and invite involvement from a diverse group of stakeholders, including people who represent the clients that the agency serves. Second, several initiatives can be considered at each of the Seven Evaluation Steps.

During step 1 (identify a problem to be evaluated) and step 2 (identify and explore ways to involve stakeholders), several potential stakeholders from the client population, former clients, and the local community can be asked along with other stakeholders to offer their views about a program-related problem or concern that requires evaluation. Because they will not know the perspectives of the agency administrators and staff members, they will likely benefit from an orientation to such information. However, their unique perspectives as clients and family members of clients need to be explored with questions such as the following:

- What programs have you or your family members used?
- How would you describe the agency and its programs and services based on your experiences?
- What stands out to you as particularly helpful? What stands out as weak or problematic?

Having discussions with some of these stakeholders in step 1 will be helpful in revealing who they are, their particular positions, how their views vary, and their skills and confidence in effectively communicating what they think. Among such a group of potential stakeholders, a few can be selected to assist in an evaluation. One approach to working with stakeholders is to create an advisory committee or collaborative team of stakeholders, including clients and community members, to assist and support the evaluators in the subsequent steps of the evaluation. Another approach is to periodically consult various stakeholders on an individual basis at a time and place convenient to them.

Step 3 (determine the purpose of the evaluation) focuses the evaluation on a particular problem or concern. This step is a critical one for considering diversity and social justice issues. All stakeholder groups, particularly those representing the client population, can be encouraged to give input on the purpose of the evaluation and the social change that the evaluation could accomplish. Some of the questions that could be posed to the client stakeholders include the following:

- What interventions have been particularly useful to you and others that you know? Which ones have not helped?
- In your opinion, what seem to be the most important ingredients in an effective approach to helping clients like yourself?
- How have the interventions assisted you in reaching your personal goals over time?
- What would you like for the interventions to do differently to help bring positive change into your life?
- What difficulties have you or your family members experienced, if any, in receiving services from these programs and practice areas?

Step 4 (plan the evaluation) can raise many design issues, such as which single-system design to use, who to interview, what questions to ask, and how large a sample should be. Both professionals and lay stakeholders will need some training to participate, in an informed way, in such decisions. Some of the design questions have a diversity or social justice component; for example:

- Have we considered all important demographic characteristics in selecting the sample?
- What are some of the ways to reach a former client when we do not have a forwarding address or phone number?
- How can we formulate specific questions to encourage accurate answers?
- How does a program intervention further social justice for clients?
- How does an intervention strengthen clients' rights and responsibilities?

Example of an Evaluation Exploring Diversity

An evaluation (Dudley, 1986) investigated the interventions of a community organization located in a multiethnic community in a large city; its primary goal was to lessen interracial strife. Approximately one hundred Southeast Asian (Hmong and Cambodian) people had been relocated from their native countries to this neighborhood. The neighborhood had mostly comprised African Americans and Puerto Ricans before the relocation. The organization initiated several programs over two years to address the multiethnic strife, including a series of cultural events in which each group shared its customs, food, arts, and leisure activities with the larger community. Two years later, seventeen of the Southeast Asian residents were interviewed to explore the impact of events on their attitudes and intergroup exchanges. The respondents recalled fairly accurately the events that they had attended, and fourteen admitted having learned something from the events. Five volunteered that the events improved their multiethnic understanding. When asked if they had developed any intergroup friendships, eleven of the seventeen indicated having made friends of a different nationality. Although most relationships were rather limited, almost all were with African American or Puerto Rican neighbors.

Step 5 (implement the evaluation) involves carrying out the plans and procedures worked out in step 4. Orientation could be provided to assist stakeholders in becoming involved in contributing to this step in an informed way. Stakeholders could be useful in carrying out many aspects of this step, such as by suggesting strategies to find and engage participants who are difficult to contact or interview, contacting community and civic organizations to help identify participants for the study and offer a site for data collection, and assisting in data collection.

Step 6 (prepare a written or oral report) is one of the most important steps in which to involve stakeholders, as the findings are intended to inform them and help them take action. Report findings should be in a format accessible to all stakeholder groups. Client and community stakeholders in particular are often overlooked when preparing an evaluation report. To overcome this omission, evaluators would be remiss if they did not prepare a report that was relevant to clients and made available to them in some form. Formats that may be most helpful to these stakeholders may be fliers on a bulletin board, brief reports in agency and community newsletters, and informal presentations during client sessions.

Finally, step 7 (disseminate the results) is another critical step for stakeholders because they know a lot about how and when to disseminate evaluation findings in a manner that is relevant and useful to constituents. Evaluation findings can be disseminated in numerous creative ways. For example, evaluation findings intended to inform people and elicit feedback include community forums, regular civic and other neighborhood meetings, church gatherings, and community fairs. Further, stakeholders are valuable as resources in disseminating the results of an evaluation and receiving feedback on proposed next steps for an agency.

Example of an Evaluation Focusing on Empowerment Issues in Practice

Linhorst, Hamilton, Young, and Eckert (2002) reviewed existing documents and conducted focus groups with clients and staff of a public psychiatric hospital to identify barriers to client empowerment. They attempted to identify the conditions necessary for empowerment to occur, especially in getting clients to participate in their own treatment planning. The results revealed several empowerment issues, including the need to prepare clients with decision-making skills, to provide a range of treatment options, to ensure enough time for client participation in the planning process, and to promote staff attitudes that are respectful of clients' ability and potential to participate in treatment planning.

Overall, diversity and social justice concerns can be infused in all or most of the Seven Evaluation Steps. The suggestions herein are flexible and apply to numerous types of evaluations. The main point of the discussion in this section has been to make serious efforts to involve stakeholders most likely to be affected by the problem being addressed in the evaluation.

KEY TERMS

Confidentiality
Diversity issues
Ethical principles of the AEA
Human rights issues
Informed consent
Informed consent form
Institutional review board (IRB)
Section 5.02 of the NASW Code of Ethics
Social and economic justice

DISCUSSION QUESTIONS AND ASSIGNMENTS

1. Have groups of three to five people to work on each of the following scenarios of ethical issues in evaluation.

   Scenario 1: You have been assigned to conduct an assessment of the needs of older adults in a community surrounding your agency, a senior center. You want to know whether the older adults would use some of your center's existing services and new services that you are considering, including exercise groups, conversation groups, lunches, and nutritional workshops. You plan to conduct a phone interview and will call a representative sample of households in the community.

   Questions:
   a. What will you say/do to provide informed consent? What will you do if someone does not want to respond to phone interviews or wants to know more about your legitimacy?
   b. What will you do if the person who answers the phone only speaks Spanish or another non-English language?
   c. If the person who answers the phone is not an older adult but the household has older adults living there, how will you proceed? For example, what if the older adult is hesitant to speak, or the person answering the phone is determined to respond for her or him? What can you do to ensure that the older adult's voice is heard?

   Scenario 2: You are a supervisor and you want to evaluate the impact of counseling groups on their members or clients. You want a non-involved social worker to observe the group, but you are concerned that this evaluation could disrupt the group leader or inhibit participation of group members.

Questions:

a. What ethical issues may need to be considered in this observational study? How would you address them?

b. What will you say or do with the group leader and group members to gain informed consent?

c. How can you minimize disruptions in the group process during an observation?

2. A social worker informs you that she is providing a unique sexual counseling program to several clients with cognitive challenges. No one else in her agency or any other agency that she knows about is offering such a program. In addition, her agency administrator is not asking her to evaluate her program; the administrator is just pleased that she is offering her services. This social worker consults you to ask what she should do. Should she continue providing her services without an evaluation plan? Or should she devise an evaluation? What specific suggestions would you have for her in conducting an evaluation?

3. Assume that you conducted a study three months ago in which you asked a group of clients to complete a questionnaire that measured their progress in improving communication skills since they had first received services from the agency. They were told that the findings would be kept strictly confidential and their names would not be included with any responses. However, now the agency wants to use the findings to evaluate the individual progress of each client. You have the original data and information on who filled out each questionnaire. What ethical issues are involved in this situation? What should you do?

4. What are two advantages and disadvantages of using an outside evaluator (instead of a staff member) to conduct an evaluation in your agency? What are some criteria you might use to select an outside evaluator?

5. Assume you are an evaluator who has been asked to assist in preparing pretest and posttest instruments for an evaluation of a premarital workshop for couples. The evaluation is intended to measure the extent to which the participants improved in their communication with each other in several areas, including their sexual needs. You are asked to come to a board meeting to explain what the evaluation is all about. During the board meeting, an officer of the board states that he would like to add a "newly effective method of natural birth control" as a topic to add to the premarital workshops. He points out that he knows of a study that found that the divorce rate was significantly

lower for a group of couples practicing this new form of natural birth control. He doesn't give the board members a specific reference for this study. Up to this point, no material had been offered in previous workshops on specific forms of birth control or family planning. As the evaluator you are concerned that this seems like it may be an effort to emphasize one form of birth control over other forms based on the religious preference of this board member. As the evaluator you are not a member of the board and do not attend board meetings on a regular basis. What would you do?

REFERENCES

American Evaluation Association. (2007). *The principles of the American Evaluation Association*. Fairhaven, MA: American Evaluation Association. (Available from http://www.eval.org).

Anderson, J., & Carter, R. (Eds.). (2003). *Diversity perspectives for social work practice*. Boston: Allyn & Bacon.

Council on Social Work Education. (2012). Educational policy and accreditation standards. (Revised March 27, 2010/Updated August 2012). Alexandria, VA: Author.

Dudley, J. R. (1986). Program evaluation of Logan Community Development Assistance Project and Logan Community Development Corporation (Philadelphia). Unpublished manuscript.

Dudley, J. R. (2011). *Research methods for social work: Being producers and consumers of research* (updated 2nd ed.). Boston: Pearson.

Fitzpatrick, J. L., Sanders, J. R., & Worthen, B. R. (2004). *Program evaluation: Alternative approaches and practical guidelines*. Boston: Pearson.

Linhorst, D., Hamilton, G., Young, E., & Eckert, A. (2002). Opportunities and barriers to empowering people with severe mental illness through participation in treatment planning. *Social Work, 47*(4), 425–434.

Mak, M. H. J. (2002). Accepting the timing of one's death: An experience of Chinese hospice patients. *Omega, 45*(3), 245–260.

Marlow, C. (2011). *Research methods for generalist social work* (5th ed.). Stamford, CT: Thomson Learning.

National Association of Social Workers. (2008). Code of ethics of the National Association of Social Workers (approved by the 1996 NASW Delegate Assembly and revised by the 2008 NASW Delegate Assembly). Washington, DC: Author.

North, C., & Smith, E. (1994). Comparison of white and non-white homeless men and women. *Social Work, 39*(6), 637–649.

O'Neill, J. (1999). Advocacy takes a new tack. *NASW News, 44*(8), 4.

Chapter 4

Common Types of Evaluations

What types of evaluations are readily practiced in the everyday world of social agencies?

Anyone wanting to conduct an evaluation in today's world has many types from which to choose. One overall consideration, of course, is to decide whether you want to conduct a program or a practice evaluation, an important distinction. A further way to differentiate evaluations is to consider variations in methodology, especially whether you wish to use quantitative, qualitative, or mixed methods. There are many other ways to distinguish evaluations, and both experienced and novice evaluators are encouraged to become familiar with them. They are referred to as types in this chapter because they are practical approaches that are readily evident in numerous settings in which social workers and other human service workers are employed. Each type can be implemented in a variety of ways. They are different from the perspectives and approaches described in chapter 2, which are largely theoretical.

The purpose of the chapter is to acquaint readers with most of the types of evaluations commonly used in social agencies. After reading this chapter, you should be able to identify them in your agency, attach names to them, and have a general understanding of their respective purposes. These types of evaluations are commonly practiced in most social agencies, hospitals, health departments, schools, and residential and institutional programs across the country and most are elaborated on in later chapters when we get further into the implementation of an evaluation. Let's first look at common types of program evaluation followed by types of practice evaluation.

COMMON TYPES OF PROGRAM EVALUATIONS

The types of program evaluation presented herein vary considerably in terms of the extent that they are research-oriented and use systematic and rigorous research methods. Some of them are naturally viewed as research models. Outcome studies are a good example; their research designs have to be rigorous to accurately determine whether an intervention has a positive impact on clients' outcomes. Other types such as quality assurance studies may be designed to be less rigorous. However, the research rigor that is evident in any of these evaluations depends largely on the evaluators and their commitment to the methodology.

The types of evaluations to be presented in this chapter include needs assessments, program monitoring, client satisfaction studies, outcome studies, efficiency and cost-benefit analysis studies, licensing of programs serving clients, licensing of professionals, auditing and other accounting investigations, accreditation of social programs, quality assurance studies, court decisions, and newspaper and other media reports.

Needs Assessments

Needs assessments are a type of evaluation that usually occurs in the planning stage prior to implementing a program. These assessments are used to determine whether there is enough documentation of the need for a new or expanded program to justify it. Needs assessments often use questionnaires disseminated to the potential users of proposed programs. Other methods of data collection include informant interviewing, focus groups, public forums, and use of existing data from such documents as the Current Population Surveys, conducted periodically by the U.S. Census. Needs assessments are more fully described in chapter 6.

Example of a Needs Assessment

Two social workers (Muehlbauer & Runnberg, 2006) conducted a basic needs assessment of immigrants and refugees who were students of English as a second language program in Duluth, Minnesota. They conducted face-to-face interviews with twenty-three students using both forced response and open-ended questions. The students were from several countries in Asia (China, Laos, Thailand, and Vietnam), Poland, Bosnia, Ecuador, Russia, Germany, and Somalia. Among the questions that the authors asked were the reasons they were living in the Duluth area, the amount of time they had spent in the United States and in Duluth, their employment status, and the extent to which they spoke English. They were also asked whether they had health and dental insurance. In addition, they were asked simple questions about their mental status (e.g., "Do you often feel sad or cry easily?") and their worries, joys, and dreams. The results revealed a variety of needs, ranging from medical and dental care to qualitative comments about joys and worries.

Program Monitoring

A wide variety of evaluations are used to monitor how an existing program is functioning. Program-monitoring evaluations are also referred to as evaluations of program processes. They may be initiated voluntarily by an agency sponsoring the program or required by funding or regulatory agencies. These evaluations ask such questions as the following:

- Is the program reaching its intended target population?
- Is the program being implemented as it was proposed?
- Do current staff members reflect expectations of equal employment and affirmative action policies?
- How do employees spend their time on the job?
- Are clients satisfied with the program?
- Are agency facilities safe and accessible (e.g., are elevators to upper floors available for clients in wheelchairs)?

Program monitoring typically uses many different types of data-collection strategies, such as questionnaires given out to clients or staff members, individual and group interviewing of staff and clients, observations of programs and specific interactions between staff members and clients, reviews of existing documents such as client files and personnel documents, and consulting experts.

Client Satisfaction Studies

Client satisfaction studies are especially important when evaluating the implementation of an intervention. The purpose of client satisfaction studies is to find out how the clients are feeling and perceiving the services that they are receiving. These evaluations usually elicit the views of a fairly large number of clients, perhaps all those receiving the services of a program or all who have completed a program. These studies use either questionnaires or interview strategies to ask clients a series of questions about the various dimensions of a program.

The results of client satisfaction studies can provide helpful insights and other ideas about improving a program or even clearing up clients' misperceptions of programs. The results also offer numerous opportunities for service providers to engage in informal conversations with clients on topics for which they have different views. These conversations can be conducted without violating confidentiality if they are simply introduced as general topics deriving from the responses to client satisfaction evaluations.

How Much Do Clients and Staff Agree about Client Satisfaction?

A client satisfaction interview was conducted with people with a dual diagnosis of mental illness and mental retardation. There were twenty-one forced-response questions, such as "Do you like living here?" "Do staff listen to you or ignore you?" and "Do the staff treat you like a child or an adult?" (Dudley, 2002). The same questions were asked of the staff member who knew each client best, but staff were asked to guess the clients' answers to each question. The results revealed agreement 60 percent or more of the time on seventeen of the twenty-one questions. However, there were some discrepancies, such as a question on whether the clients wanted to continue to live at their current residence (more clients said they wanted to leave than staff guessed) and whether they felt afraid rather than safe (more clients felt afraid than staff guessed).

The clients' responses to satisfaction questions are undoubtedly subjective and may be biased as a result of their status as recipients of services. Clients may not be able to be objective about those providing them services, and they could easily blame providers for problems that could be more their own. Regardless of the confidentiality promised by the evaluator, clients may also report being more positive about services than they actually are. This can happen for numerous reasons, such as a fear of jeopardizing their client status or desire for the approval of staff members. The accuracy of their responses also depends on whether they have adequate knowledge about what is being asked and whether they have the same understanding of what is being asked as the interviewer does. Other possibilities for error are that they may have little recall of the time frame of the questions or they may not understand the specific wording used in a question.

Outcome Evaluations

Outcome evaluations are conducted to determine whether the recipients of a program are reaching the goals set for them when they began the program. These outcomes can take many forms and are typically socially desirable goals intended to help them. Outcome evaluations mostly use quasi-experimental and experimental group designs to control for, to varying degrees, other factors that could influence clients' progress on their goals. A program can usually take no more than partial responsibility for any progress that clients make. Chapter 9 is largely devoted to outcome evaluations and the various types of quasi-experimental and experimental research designs available for outcome evaluations. The results-oriented model described in chapter 2 can be considered a theoretical version of outcome evaluations.

Efficiency and Cost-Benefit Analysis Studies

Efficiency evaluations are conducted to find out whether the resources allocated to a program are being used as efficiently as possible. These studies examine the ratio of inputs to outputs, and measure the amount of a specific output (e.g., number of clients served, number of clients completing a program) against the costs. In this example, the higher the number of clients served at a fixed cost, the better. These studies usually want to get the maximum amount of output for the money spent to help clients. A major limitation of efficiency studies is that they do not assume that program goals are being fully accomplished; evaluating outcomes is not part of their purpose.

In contrast, *cost-benefit analysis studies* are designed to determine whether programs are reaching their goals in a cost-effective way. In other words, are the incurred costs reasonable? Cost-benefit studies look at the ratio of inputs to outcomes. These studies typically aim to find out how much a program costs and whether the program is less costly than another program that has been found to be equally effective. Often cost-benefit analyses are conducted by comparing two or more programs using, for example, different approaches or different combinations of staff members and other resources. The program that meets its goals with the least amount of cost is usually the most desirable one. Examples of questions asked in cost-benefit studies that compare one program to another are the following:

- Is the per capita cost of an institutional program more or less than a community program for people with mental illness or developmental disabilities?
- Are outpatient rehabilitation programs for offenders serving time for victimless crimes less expensive per capita than are similar programs for such offenders in federal prison?
- Are the public health costs of preventing cigarette smoking among teenagers more cost-effective than the public health care cost of treating cigarette smokers for lung cancer?

Licensing of Programs

Licensing of the programs serving clients is an important form of evaluation. Licensing is usually concerned with basic health and safety standards and related concerns. Licensing is particularly relevant for residential programs, such as group homes for adolescents, people with developmental disabilities, or older adults. Licensing is also likely to be required for health-care agencies and agencies that provide meals to clients. Licensing inspections and renewals may occur annually or more often and they may be conducted to detect unsanitary conditions in food preparation, the adequacy of safety in bathrooms, and safety in use of floors and stairs. Licensing activities are also conducted to find out whether there are such things as fire doors, sprinkler systems, alarms, extinguishers, and adequate fire exits.

Either local or state governmental agencies usually assume responsibility for licensing programs, and the policies defining the parameters of licensing regulations are usually enacted as laws passed by legislative bodies and further developed into regulations by licensing agencies. Usually, licensing evaluations require that only minimal, not maximum, standards be met. Licensing sometimes functions as an external influence that may push agencies to pursue additional evaluation activities of their own.

Licensing of Professionals

Licensing of professionals in social work and other helping professional areas is another type of evaluation. This type of licensing is becoming increasingly evident as human services become more complex and professionalized, and as expectations about client outcomes are raised to higher levels. Licensing laws exist to protect the use of a professional title, like clinical social worker, psychologist, or family therapist so that the public can be assured that qualified people provide them with services.

State governments license professional titles, including the title of professional social worker. Many states use the acronym LCSW, which stands for licensed clinical social worker, as a standard social work title. Other titles are also often used and are viewed more as certifications than licenses. These certificates are not usually required titles for hiring; nevertheless, they provide a status that can distinguish the holder from those with fewer or different credentials. Such certification titles include certified bachelor of social work, certified master of social work, and social work manager. Although state licensing of social workers is a recent development, primarily having occurred in the past two decades, all fifty states now have some form of professional licensing for social workers.

To be professionally licensed, a person is usually required to have an advanced degree in the professional area of licensing. Additional professional employment, such as two years of post-degree practice under the supervision of a licensed supervisor, and passing an exam on the knowledge and skill areas of the profession are also usually required.

Auditing and Other Accounting Investigations

Auditing of an agency's financial affairs and other accounting measures are another form of program evaluation. In this case, the evaluation involves an independent review of the financial policies, procedures, and records of an agency to make sure that they are accurate and meet existing legal codes and procedures. Auditing is important to ensure that tax codes are followed and to detect and prevent misuse of funds by agency personnel and others. Trained accountants and tax experts who represent private firms independent of the agency being audited usually conduct audits. Obviously, audits are carried out by accountants, who have very different training from social workers. Nevertheless, social workers in administrative positions should know the basics of auditing and other accounting procedures, their varied purposes, and the appropriate procedures to follow in hiring qualified auditors and overseeing their work.

Accreditation of Social and Educational Programs

Program accreditation is another important form of evaluation. Agencies that accredit programs are concerned with programs meeting specific standards rather than the qualifications of individual professionals. Accreditation is a form of quality control that program sponsors recognize and seek out to ensure that a program meets professional standards. Because the standards of a professional accrediting organization and the policies of their member agencies are likely to differ, it is almost inevitable that the accrediting body and the agencies being accredited experience some tension and possible conflict over priorities. For example, while the member agencies are likely to base many priorities on their access to funding and the demands of their board members, accreditation groups may stress value-oriented areas, such as promoting client dignity and greater client independence. Accreditation groups are likely to expect programs to maintain relatively low ratios between the number of direct-care staff members and the recipients of services, while a member agency may feel less compelled to follow such ratios, particularly if it has a shortage of funds or wants more independence to freely transfer resources from one program to another.

What makes accreditation so unusual is that it is run by nonprofit professional organizations rather than governmental agencies. Accrediting agencies essentially propagate specific professional standards or requirements that university and agency members are expected to follow. At times, member agencies may perceive that the accreditation standards interfere with their internal decision making; they may also complain about the relatively high fees required for accreditation. Yet accreditation processes are a remarkable example of a decades-long cooperative partnership among professionally sponsored accreditation agencies, accredited member agencies, and governmental agencies that allow an independent group to enforce professional standards. Accreditation organizations are very familiar to most agencies that employ social workers (see table 4.1).

TABLE 4.1 Accreditation Organizations and Their Member Agencies

Accrediting organization	Website	Member agencies
Child Welfare League	www.cwl.org	Child protection agencies, adoptions, foster care
Council on Social Work Education	www.cswe.org	BSW & MSW programs
Family Service Association of America	www.fsa.org	Family service agencies
Joint Commission on the Accreditation of Health Organizations	www.jcaho.org	Hospitals, home health
Commission on Accreditation of Rehabilitation Facilities	www.carf.org	Developmental disabilities facilities and community agencies

Accreditation is usually a voluntary process, but programs are strongly persuaded to obtain it for status and program legitimacy. Social work education accreditation, for example, is essential for both BSW and MSW degree programs that expect to succeed in admitting a critical mass of students to their programs and to gain support from their university sponsor. Furthermore, when graduates of a non-accredited program look for jobs as professional social workers, it will not be long before they receive questions about their program's legitimacy. The benefits of graduating from an accredited program include eligibility to apply for a state social work license, ability to receive third-party payments as reimbursement for work with clients, and ability to enjoy many of the benefits of membership in NASW and other professional associations.

Quality Assurance

Quality assurance is a rather distinct collection of evaluation activities implemented in many agencies to monitor how well their programs work. The quality of the program's functioning is the obvious intent of such evaluations. Quality assurance (QA) is also sometimes referred to as quality improvement (QI) or quality control. The QA activities are implemented to gather information about the processes of programs and to determine whether they function the way they are supposed to. Such activities have their earliest origins in health care settings and are likely to be implemented most easily in these settings. However, with some minor modifications, QA activities are also relevant to evaluation of programs in other social welfare settings, such as child welfare and aging.

Example of Quality Assurance or Quality Improvement

Youth Homes is an agency that provides specialized foster care, residential group homes, and family-strengthening services for abused, neglected, and other at-risk children. The agency works closely with the local Department of Social Services and Office of Justice. Youth Homes has a full-time staff member, an experienced social worker with an MSW degree, assigned to oversee its QA services. The staff member works with three staff committees to conduct reviews. The Clinical Care Committee meets every eight weeks to review a random sample of client cases and another sample of high-risk cases to determine whether four types of documentation are evident in each case file and whether recommendations have been implemented. The Client Rights Committee meets quarterly and reviews client incident reports (e.g., accidents, administrative errors), client grievances, feedback from the suggestions box, results of client focus groups, and results of a client satisfaction survey (administered annually) to investigate whether the rights of the clients have been violated. The Staffing and Facilities Committee meets quarterly to review staff turnover reports, staff training reports, employee satisfaction survey results, annual staff exit interviews, and a variety of facility issues (e.g., new facility needs; assessment of vehicles; maintenance needs; fire, safety, health, and accident reports). The QA social worker convenes the committees, reviews and coordinates the committees' corrective action requests, and prepares evaluation reports quarterly and annually. The annual report is then incorporated into an annual plan that provides projected agency goals and plans for the next year (B. Lackey, quality improvement coordinator with Youth Homes, Charlotte, NC, personal communication, January 2005).

Quality assurance activities can be most easily distinguished from other program-monitoring approaches by the specific methods and techniques that are used. These methods and techniques include peer-conducted reviews, heavy reliance on client records, observation of small samples of the services, ensuring that minimal standards are met, and immediate incorporation of useful results into program improvements. These special characteristics are elaborated on next.

Peer reviews.   First, the methods of QA involve peer reviews rather than the more typical administrative reviews. A QA approach empowers staff members to conduct their own evaluations instead of relying on administrators to conduct the reviews. Peer review teams usually include representatives of the different specializations and disciplines of the agency's staff. It should be noted that peer assessments will likely have a natural tendency to be biased in favor of the staff members' attitudes, needs, and practices over administrative perspectives. To bring some balance to this tendency and to maintain as much objectivity as possible, peer-review teams often use special methods, such as representation from all staff groups and reports to administrative staff.

Many administrators actually prefer QA activities because they are delegated to the staff members involved most directly in a program. Many administrators like this approach because it places staff members in charge of evaluating their own programs, which can instill in them a mind-set of self-evaluation. Also, delegation of QA activities can free up administrative time and energy for other important matters. From an ethical perspective,

QA promotes the social work value of self-determination, as it empowers staff members to continually evaluate themselves and how they can improve.

Use of client records.   The QA approach typically relies on appraisals of staff revealed in client records rather than direct observation of services. Such a data source makes it much easier to conduct a review in a short period of time because records already exist and are easily accessible, whereas direct observations take considerably more time and could inconvenience or interfere with the delivery of services to clients. Also, a focus on record-keeping reveals a secondary characteristic of QA; it monitors the quality of the record-keeping system, which in itself is an important means of accountability.

Reviewing small samples of services.   Another methodological aspect of a QA approach is that it serves only as a spot check on how the program is functioning. Typically a small sample of program recipients is selected, and sometimes a sampling of only a few components of a program. In contrast, many other program evaluation approaches tend to examine all components of a program and virtually the entire client population that they serve. Quality assurance typically uses random sampling to avoid selection bias, and the evaluators usually do not notify the direct service staff of when the evaluation will occur and which clients will be involved until the evaluation actually happens. Theoretically, this approach ensures that virtually every client and component of service can be included in an evaluation, thereby precluding any attempt on the part of direct service staff to select specific records to review or to prevent the review of other records.

Minimal standards.   Another characteristic of QA is its limited goal of meeting minimal standards. On the one hand, a staff review team could easily decide that it is not important to meet exceptionally high standards. Yet lower expectations from external sources could also give a QA team more freedom and flexibility to strive for higher standards on their own with the application of self-imposed standards. A disadvantage of emphasizing minimal standards is that a QA team may not be able to focus on the more dysfunctional aspects of a program.

Immediately implemented results.   A final characteristic of QA is that if its findings suggest the need for program improvements, the changes can be implemented immediately. This benefit has obvious advantages over an approach that expects a study to be completed before any results are considered for implementation. In the case of QA, an administrator can take immediate steps to correct a program component or add a new procedure when an omission is discovered in program operation.

Court or Judicial Decisions

Judicial decisions are often an overlooked form of program evaluation even though they are most likely to focus on policies, not programs. Our judicial system at the local, state, and federal levels is a form of checks and balances on the executive and legislative branches of government. Class action suits in particular are pursued when all other attempts to seek justice for a group of people may have failed. A class action suit brings together a large number of people who have similar circumstances and conditions and have been treated unjustly according to an existing law. Such a lawsuit, if successful, can lead to the propagation of new or corrective policies that must be implemented as long as the suit is in existence. In this case, a special master and staff are set up to oversee implementation of the lawsuit and report to the ruling judge. The judge temporarily removes from legal responsibility the governmental agency that has been found negligent and replaces it with the judge and a special master who oversees the implementation of court-mandated corrective measures and monitors their implementation.

Although the initial focus of a class action suit is on government policies, an evaluation often is implemented to determine whether new or modified programs address the needs and problems of the class of people who are the plaintiffs. An example is a lawsuit conducted in North Carolina for more than ten years on behalf of more than 1,200 people with a dual diagnosis of mental illness and mental retardation. These class members had all been misplaced in state hospitals because there was no other reasonable alternative available (Dudley, Calhoun, & Ahlgrim-Delzell, 2002). However, by admitting them to state hospitals for a decade or more, the federal district court order specified that the plaintiff class members had their constitutional rights violated in several basic areas, including safety, protection from harm, treatment under safe conditions, freedom from undue restraint, minimally adequate habilitation or treatment, and treatment necessary to remedy any injuries caused by the class members' stay in the hospitals. A longitudinal evaluation was established to monitor how the implementation of the court order affected the class members, and it primarily focused on existing and new programs that were expected to remedy the violations incurred.

Newspaper and Other Media Reports

Television and newspaper journalistic accounts often focus on the inadequate and sometimes scandalous conditions of social programs that purport to serve a neglected group of people. Reporters' accounts may not be considered evaluation per se, but they are typically investigations that are thorough, are based on the specific conditions of the people who are investigated, and provide valuable information to the public and those who are expected to protect them. Sometimes these reports are case studies that vividly portray one person's conditions as excerpts.

Could the State Have Saved Lynnette?

Another patient dies in mental health care. . . . The girl in the hospital bed looked nothing like Lynnette. Purple bruises covered her face, arms, chest, and legs. Her mouth was swollen. Blood dripped from her nose. She had a rug burn on her shoulder. She was unconscious, and a ventilator helped her breathe. Donald Morris threw himself across her bed and cried. Ileine Morris whispered, "Mommy's here. Mommy's here." Twenty-four-year-old Lynnette Martin, who was mentally ill and mildly retarded, had suffered a head injury about eight hours earlier in a Moore County home operated by a company called Preferred Alternatives. Police believe she and her caregiver may have struggled, and Lynnette hit her head on the floor. Her caregiver waited about seven hours before calling an ambulance, police say. On December 19, Lynnette died after seven weeks in a coma. She is one of the most recent mental health patients to die under questionable circumstances while in the care of group homes, psychiatric hospitals, and other mental health facilities.

The Morrises and a growing group of supporters are launching a push to change North Carolina's mental health laws, particularly for a group of 2,500 of the state's most vulnerable patients. They are adults like Lynnette, known as Thomas S. clients, who have both developmental disabilities and mental illness (Cenziper, 2000).

Newspaper and television series have covered numerous stories of massive program dysfunction and have often provided the first report that educates the public on such outrages. One could say that these reports are one-sided, in favor of the people who are alleged to be exploited, but otherwise they seem to be objective in reporting what actually happens in local communities throughout the country. They can be viewed as program evaluations in the broadest sense of the term, and they are an important community tool for exposing many types of inadequate existing policies and programs provided to the public. They have been instrumental in exposing such problems as inadequate housing, the hiring of untrained workers, misuse of medications, inadequate staff supervision, safety concerns, clients' exposure to inappropriate hardships and harm, and the overlooking of groups of people who need access to a program's services.

Table 4.2 summarizes examples of questions that could be asked for each of the types of program evaluation described above.

TABLE 4.2 Examples of Questions Suitable for Each Type of Program Evaluation

Type of evaluation	Types of questions	Example
Needs assessment	Assessing the needs of prospective clients	Would you attend a group on exercise if we offered it?
Program monitoring	Finding out if a program is being implemented as proposed	How do employees spend their time?
Efficiency evaluation	Measure the ratio of inputs to outputs	What is the maximum number of clients that we can serve for $10,000?
Client satisfaction study	How clients perceive the services they are receiving	Are you satisfied with the services you are receiving?
Licensing a program	Finding out if a program is meeting explicit standards, usually set by the government	Are the bathrooms accessible for people with disabilities?
Licensing a professional	Determining if professionals are meeting specific standards, set usually by a professional organization	Are LCSW social workers completing the required 40 hours of continuing education every two years?
Auditing investigation	An independent review determining if the financial affairs of an agency meet existing legal codes	Are any of the funds of an agency being misused?
Accreditation of program	Determining whether a program is meeting professional standards, usually promulgated by a professional association	How does this MSW program fulfill the accreditation standard of promoting social and economic justice?
Quality assurance	Determining the quality of a program or how well a program is working	Is this client receiving all of the services that she is supposed to receive?
Court or judicial decisions	A class action suit that requires that an agency redress any wrongful actions it has committed toward its clients	Did the clients of the class receive services that are relevant to their diagnosis of mental retardation?
Newspaper and media reports	Newspaper or media accounts of how a specific client problem has been neglected by the existing human service system	Documenting how some home health agencies are motivated more by the revenue they received than the needs of their clients
Outcome study	Determining whether the recipients of a program are reaching their goals	To what extent do substance abuse clients stop using substances after completing a counseling program?
Cost-benefit analysis study	Determining whether a program is reaching its goals in a cost-effective way	Is the cost of program A in finding clients a job more or less costly than program B?

COMMON TYPES OF PRACTICE EVALUATIONS

Just as there are common and well-known ways of evaluating programs, there are also common ways of evaluating professional practice that are popular across agency settings. They fall under four broad categories: (1) assessing client needs, (2) monitoring the quality of practice, (3) client satisfaction, and (4) client outcomes.

Assessing Clients' Needs

Based on the problem-solving approach, an assessment of clients' problems logically precedes the taking of any steps to help them. Assessing clients' problems and related circumstances is a common practice that is needed to determine what the next steps should be, that is, the interventions that will effectively help them. Familiar assessment tools include family genograms, ecomaps, a variety of biopsychosocial assessment tools, and assessments of client strengths and weaknesses. *Family genograms* provide a visual display of a family across two or more generations and offer insights into and understanding of the patterns evident in families. *Ecomaps* are a visual tool that identify the person-in-environment constellation of a client, including relationships with friends and family members, agencies and schools, jobs, and other social supports. *Biopsychosocial assessment tools* are available in most agencies and identify questions and topical areas to be explored in all three areas of a client's life: biological, psychological, and social. Sometimes these tools include assessment questions about the spiritual, mental, and cultural dimensions of a client as well. Assessments of client strengths and weaknesses, especially assessment questions about a client's strengths, are an area that is often overlooked in assessments. Cowger, Anderson, and Snively (2006), for example, have constructed an elaborate qualitative assessment tool of client strengths for use with clients.

Monitoring Practice

Process recordings.   Social work practitioners often use various means to monitor their practice. In many cases, these monitoring efforts may not even be considered evaluations. Process recordings are one well-known practice. Supervisors and practice teachers often ask new practitioners or students to complete a process recording of a sampling of their client contacts. These recordings are then carefully reviewed in a supervisory session to explore how the social worker responded to the client's comments and conducted the session overall. Often these recordings help reveal missed opportunities to respond to a subtle message of the client that a worker may have ignored or misread. In these instances, the supervisor can help the worker explore how to address such client behaviors differently in future interviews. Such supervisory discussions have been known to help new workers consider alternative responses and to be more disciplined in future interviews.

Direct observations.   Direct observations of practice through a two-way mirror or videotaping have helped supervisors and workers critique practice to make improvements. Audiotaped interviews should not be overlooked, as much can be learned from listening to how one sounds and about what one says in an interview.

Case summaries, journals, and logs.   Other devices such as case summaries and personal journals or logs have been known to help monitor practice. A case summary of one individual or group session, or a summary of work with a client over a period of time along with questions and plans for future interviews, can be very helpful to review. Having clients keep a log of some aspect of their behavior that they wish to change (e.g., circumstances when they are depressed, desire to use alcohol, or to partake in negative self-talk) and discussing the results with their social worker is another form of monitoring practice.

Case management.   Case management is a formal employment title often held by a social worker (e.g., Frankel & Gelman, 2011). In this position, the employee often monitors the individual practice of other human service workers and the programs that are provided to a client. Case managers typically find services for their clients, negotiate or facilitate contracts with the agencies offering services, monitor them to ensure that they actually deliver the contracted services, and advocate when necessary on behalf of clients. Case managers continually monitor the range of services that are provided to their clients to ensure their quality and continued appropriateness.

Client Satisfaction

Client satisfaction not only is important to introduce in monitoring programs but also has important value for practice. Client satisfaction is usually conducted at the time when a client is terminating services. However, inquiring about client satisfaction while services are being delivered adds the possibility that changes can occur in practice interventions for future sessions. It is wise for social workers to periodically hold informal client satisfaction discussions with their clients. The workers can ask clients whether they are satisfied with the services that they are receiving. When clients are not fully satisfied, they can be asked how the services could be provided differently or in a more helpful way. Also, such inquiries often help empower the client and increase the bond between a worker and client. Typical client satisfaction questions that can periodically be asked of a client include the following:

- What am I doing that is helpful to you? How is it helpful?
- What do you like about what I am doing to help you?
- What would you like for me to do that I am not doing that could be helpful?
- What am I doing that is not helpful to you?
- How am I helping you reach your goals?

Client Outcomes

Practitioners are expected to adequately document that their interventions are effective in improving outcomes for clients, that is, in meeting their clients' goals. Basic questions that all practitioners need to frequently ask themselves are the following:

- Are my interventions helping clients reach their goals?
- Are my interventions responsible for bringing about positive or constructive changes in my clients' lives?
- How are my interventions helping?
- In what ways could my interventions be more effective in helping my clients reach their goals?

Several evaluation tools are available to help practitioners evaluate whether their clients are reaching their goals. These tools include *single-system designs*, which plot the changes that a client makes in an observed behavior over time and observe whether the interventions are responsible for changes in behavior when they occur. Single-system designs focus on the impact of one or more worker-introduced interventions on a client system. A *goal attainment scale* (GAS) is another helpful tool that can be used to evaluate the extent to which the worker's interventions affect the clients' goals in a favorable way. It is an incremental scale that can be used to measure the degree of progress. A *target problem scale* (TPS) is another outcome scale that can be used particularly when client goals are difficult to identify. A TPS is helpful, for example, if clients remain focused on their problems and are not prepared to pursue goals beyond the problems. More information is provided about all three of these evaluation tools in chapter 9.

Table 4.3 summarizes examples of questions that could be asked for each of the types of practice evaluation described above.

TABLE 4.3   Examples of Questions Suitable for Each Type of Practice Evaluation

Type of evaluation	Types of questions	Example
Needs assessment	Assessing the needs of a client	How often have you experienced this problem in the past year?
Tools for monitoring practice	Finding out if a practice approach is being implemented in a helpful manner	Is there another way that you could have handled this client's outburst?
Client satisfaction	How this client perceives the services he is receiving	What am I doing as your social worker that is helpful to you?
Single-system design	Finding out if the intervention of the worker is responsible for a client reaching her goal	Did the introduction of this intervention result in an improvement in a mother's discipline of her child?
Goal Attainment Scale	Finding out the extent to which a client achieves his/her goals	After 3 months, did this client achieve the expected level of success—learning one new parenting skill?
Target Problem Scale	Finding out whether clients' problems are becoming less severe after an intervention is introduced	Did the parents' problem of getting their child to bed late get better or worse after the intervention was introduced?

TYPES OF EVALUATIONS AND THE THREE-STAGE APPROACH

The three-stage approach introduced in chapter 2 is an important organizational framework. Using this framework, the types of evaluations described in this chapter can be further classified on the basis of whether they focus on the planning, implementation, or outcome stage. It seems notable that most of the types of evaluations introduced in this chapter are process evaluations conducted during the implementation stage. These types primarily focus on how well program or practice interventions function and evolve to help clients. These types of evaluations are more abundant and varied than evaluations evident in the planning and outcome stages, largely because there are so many interacting elements during the implementation stage. Can you identify the types of evaluations in tables 4.2 and 4.3 that are process evaluations occurring during the implementation stage? Which ones occur during the planning stage? The outcome stage?

Now that you have a grasp of several commonly used evaluations and how they can be classified using the three-stage approach, we turn to the next section on topics important to the planning stage.

KEY TERMS

Accreditation of social and educational programs
Auditing investigations
Biopsychosocial assessment tools
Case management
Case summaries
Client outcomes
Client satisfaction studies
Cost-benefit analysis study
Court or judicial decisions
Efficiency evaluations
Goal attainment scales
Journals and logs
Licensing professionals
Licensing programs
Needs assessment
Newspaper and media reports
Outcome study
Peer reviews
Process recordings
Program and practice monitoring
Quality assurance
Single-system designs
Target problem scales

DISCUSSION QUESTIONS AND ASSIGNMENTS

1. Select a program evaluation approach from one of the types described in the chapter that gives emphasis to research methods. It could be, for example, a needs assessment, a program-monitoring study, a client satisfaction study, an outcome study, or a cost-benefit analysis. Try to find an actual evaluation that uses this approach conducted at your agency or another agency with which you are familiar. If such a study is unavailable, look for an example of this approach in a professional journal. Carefully review the evaluation, look closely at how it was conducted, and report to your class on what you learned.

2. Several other types of evaluations tending to emphasize research methods less are also described in this chapter. They include quality assurance, licensing, and court decisions. Find out if your agency has conducted any of these evaluations in the past two to three years. Find out what the agency learned from the study and how the findings were used to improve the program.

3. Select one of the accreditation agencies listed in table 4.1. Visit the agency's website and find out what specific kinds of agencies are members. Also identify two standards that the accreditation organization requires of member agencies. List one compelling reason to require these standards and one reason why some member agencies may find it difficult to implement these standards.

REFERENCES

Cenziper, D. (2000, February 12). Could the state have saved Lynnette? *The Charlotte Observer*, 1A.

Cowger, C. D., Anderson, K. M., & Snively, C. A. (2006). Assessing strengths: The political context of individual, family, and community empowerment. In D. Saleebey (Ed.), *The strengths perspective in social work practice* (pp. 93–115). Boston: Pearson.

Dudley, J. (2002). When staff and consumers disagree about consumer satisfaction. In J. Dudley, M. Calhoun, & L. Ahlgrim-Delzell (Eds.), *Lessons learned from a lawsuit: Creating services for people with mental illness and mental retardation* (pp. 117–122). Kingston, NY: National Association for the Dually Diagnosed Press.

Dudley, J., Calhoun, M., & Ahlgrim-Delzell, L. (Eds.). (2002). *Lessons learned from a lawsuit: Creating services for people with mental illness and mental retardation*. Kingston, NY: National Association for the Dually Diagnosed Press.

Frankel, A. J., & Gelman, S. R. (2011). *Case management: An introduction to concepts and skills*. 3rd ed. Chicago: Lyceum Books.

Muehlbauer, N. A., & Runnberg, M. (2006). *A needs assessment of immigrants and refugees attending the English as a second language program at an adult learning center*. Duluth, MN: College of St. Scholastica.

Chapter 5

Focusing an Evaluation

How do you focus an evaluation?

How does an evaluator decide how to focus an evaluation? This is primarily step 3 of the Seven Evaluation Steps. Step 3 is to determine the purpose of the evaluation. This is an important step that has several ramifications and no simple answers. As was discussed in previous chapters, social programs and practice areas tend to be complex and multifaceted. Furthermore, they cannot be fully understood in a vacuum. The agency sponsoring the program and its social and political context must also be taken into account.

The first two of the Seven Evaluation Steps are important to explore prior to moving ahead to focus an evaluation. These steps include (step 1) identifying the problem to be evaluated, and (step 2) exploring ways to involve the stakeholders. This chapter elaborates on many of the tasks involved in conducting these two steps and recommends several questions to ask initially to gain a fuller understanding of the stakeholders, clients, and the larger agency context. Once these two questions are explored and have been largely answered, a set of specific guidelines are offered that can assist an evaluator in articulating a focus for an evaluation (step 3).

IMPORTANT INITIAL QUESTIONS

Some initial questions should be directed to all of the stakeholders, including the following:

- What do they believe are the problems and issues that are most important to address in an evaluation?
- Why are these issues important to them?
- What are their perceptions of the intervention or proposed intervention generally?
- What do they perceive to be its goals?
- To what extent do they understand the intervention or proposed intervention, how it is supposed to be implemented, and how it actually is implemented?
- What would each of them hope to accomplish by conducting an evaluation?
- How would they like to use the results of such an evaluation?

Let's assume that there is more than one stakeholder. As was discussed in chapter 1, stakeholders of a social program can include the administrators of the agency sponsoring the program, relevant funding and regulatory agencies, agency staff members, clients, family members of clients, members of the geographic community surrounding the agency, and others.

If we ask each of these stakeholders many of the preceding questions, we are likely to hear a multitude of perspectives and concerns. For example, an agency administrator may want to determine why there is so much staff turnover, a funding agency may want to know whether the program recipients are reaching their designated goals, and staff members may want to explore whether their caseloads are too large. In this instance, all of the stakeholders' responses would need to be reviewed individually and in conjunction with one another. Concerns of stakeholders may be not only very different from one another but also, in some cases, in conflict with one another. In such cases, decisions would need to be made about which concerns are given priority and how conflicts are addressed.

The Input of Clients during the Planning Phase

Ultimately, a more in-depth set of questions needs to be asked of a special group of stakeholders: clients and their families. These questions can offer insights into some of the central reasons for conducting an evaluation, such as the following:

- How can clients benefit from an evaluation of an intervention?
- How can an evaluation contribute to clients' well-being?
- How will the results of an evaluation be used to more fully promote the clients' quality of life?

Most evaluations are not likely to involve the program recipients in planning, even though the evaluation may focus directly on them. In some ways this is logical, as clients may wonder whether the personnel of the agency know what they are doing if they have to ask for client input. Also, many client populations have cognitive limitations, psychiatric and substance abuse diagnoses, and other challenging attributes that may prevent them from offering substantially useful input. Other clients have involuntary status with the agency; they do not choose to be there. Such clients may have difficulty thinking about how they can help the providers because of their adversarial relationships with them. In addition to all of these points, one could argue that the demands on clients' time need to be protected and reserved for work on their own problems.

Nevertheless, consulting clients, former clients, prospective clients, and other program recipients in the planning of an evaluation can be especially positive and useful for a program. Indeed, social work ethics expect such involvement. Ultimately, a program or practice area exists because of clients, who likely know the most about their personal problems and the help they need. They may also have views and suggestions that are pertinent to the methodology to be selected for the evaluation. For example, they may be able to advise an evaluator on whether clients would be more responsive to observations, interviews, or questionnaires.

The participatory action approach, introduced in chapter 2, assumes that the people studied or evaluated can be involved in implementing any or all stages of an evaluation. Such involvement largely depends on the perspective of the evaluators and other stakeholders. In the case of planning an evaluation, clients, for example, could be consulted to help in the following areas:

- They can be asked how important the program/practice concerns already identified are to them.
- They can become involved in several ways, such as being interviewed on a relevant topic, sitting on an advisory committee, assisting a collaborative team of stakeholders, or informal consulting.
- They can be encouraged to react to the views expressed by other stakeholders.

The Social and Political Context of the Agency Sponsor

Once the concerns of all stakeholders are identified, clearly understood, and prioritized, further questions will need to be asked about the agency context of the program. As was discussed in chapter 1, several contextual factors are likely relevant and need to be taken into account in preparing an evaluation plan. For example, how do agency and governmental policies inform the need for an evaluation? How do decisions get made in the agency and who will participate in decisions and advisory processes involving the evaluation? Will the executive director be the sole decider or will several key staff members and possibly an advisory group be primary decision makers? Also, if staff members are expected to participate in an evaluation (e.g., by filling out forms, by preparing clients for participation), such demands on their time and a possible fatigue factor should be explored.

An Exercise: Example of Decision Making as a Factor

In an earlier example in chapter 1, a graduate student planned an evaluation of the morale of staff members with her supervisor. The supervisor seemed quite interested in such a study because she was concerned with occasional complaints of staff, a tendency among some to resist following administrative policies, and more staff turnover than usual in recent years. The student proceeded to construct a questionnaire for staff members to fill out that asked them to comment on the extent to which several work-related issues were a concern. These concerns included salaries, medical and pension benefits, caseloads, supervision, staff meetings, opportunities for staff training and educational advances, and relationships with administrators. When the questionnaire was completed, returned to the student, and tallied, the results revealed that supervisory and administrative relationship issues were most frequently cited as a problem for most staff. Other concerns were also mentioned but much less frequently. When the student shared the results with her supervisor, who then shared them with her supervisor, concerns emerged about the results, and the student discovered that the study was never fully understood or formally approved by the administration. She was instructed to write up her report for her social work course assignment but to do nothing more with the results. She was forbidden to share the results in any form with the staff members, who had anticipated hearing about them. Unfortunately, she had not adequately explored the focus of the evaluation initially with key administrative stakeholders before conducting the study. What do you think the student should have done at this point? If staff members asked her to share the findings with them, what should she have said that would be both ethical and consistent with the administrator's decision? How could this conflict of interest possibly be prevented at the time of the study's initial planning and negotiation? What do staff members, administrators, clients, and the student potentially lose from this experience?

The degree to which the agency sponsor understands what evaluations entail, in general, and the degree to which it values and respects what an evaluation can provide are important issues to explore initially. Evaluators will be more likely to succeed in conducting their evaluations if they are respected and understood. Another contextual issue to explore is to determine the essential material resources required for the evaluation. For example, evaluators will need to be paid if they are not employed by the agency, and considerable release time will need to be provided if the evaluators are staff members of the agency overseeing the evaluation. Also, a budget is inevitable to pay for such things as electronic equipment and statistical software, supplies like postage and paper, the purchase of scales, costs of typing a report, and extra phone use.

CRAFTING GOOD STUDY QUESTIONS FOR AN EVALUATION

Before embarking on a specific program or practice investigation, a general focus is needed to guide the evaluator so that he or she knows what is to be investigated. General study questions provide that focus or determine the purpose of an evaluation (step 3). General study questions are broad in nature and open-ended. They serve two purposes. First, they provide parameters for an evaluation, limiting the topic of investigation. Second, they provide enough specificity for an evaluator to know what is to be explored in a specific sense. In other words, they are not too broad to be unrealistic and not too specific to be too restrictive.

These general research questions are not to be confused with the specific questions that may be asked of participants or the specific behaviors to be observed in a study. A general study question is likely too broad if the number of specific questions it generates seems endless. Similarly, a general study question is likely too narrow if it generates only one or two specific questions. Each general study question when further delineated should generate a manageable number of specific questions to ask participants.

In brief, the best study questions to ask in an evaluation have several notable characteristics:

1. Importance: They identify a program concern that is important to address.
2. Not too broad or specific: Each general study question is broad enough to generate several specific questions to be asked (or behaviors to be observed) of the people being studied.
3. Feasible: Each question is focused enough to address issues that can be answered within the time period and with the available resources.
4. Based on the literature: Previous studies and agency experiences that have focused on this or similar topics have been considered.
5. Client feedback: Some clients and family members of clients who are personally affected by the program have been consulted.
6. Clarity: The study questions are well written, clear, and succinct.

The next section introduces guidelines to help shape or define these study questions.

GUIDELINES FOR FOCUSING AN EVALUATION

A set of four guidelines can be followed to focus the evaluation or determine its purpose. These four guidelines are partially based on the work of others, especially that of Stecher and Davis (1987).

1. *Identify the stage of the program/practice area's development in which the evaluation is being emphasized (planning, implementation, or outcome).* Identifying the program/practice stage that reflects the evaluation concern is the first guideline. As an evaluator begins to focus an evaluation, the stage of interest is easy to identify. As was discussed in chapter 2, programs have developmental stages, and evaluations address important issues at all of these stages, including a planning or input stage, when the ideas

and vision for a new program/practice area emerge and are developed and detailed in a proposal; the implementation stage, by far the longest; and the outcome stage, when the program's impact on client outcomes is the major focus. As noted previously, these stages may not always occur in this order, and they sometimes overlap.

2. *Identify the program or practice elements.* The second guideline is to identify the program/practice elements that are the primary interest and focus of an evaluation. A program or practice element is a distinct entity that is critical to its functioning. Figure 5.1 provides a closer look at some of the most common elements at the various stages of the intervention. Can you identify other elements that are not in the figure? As figure 5.1 shows, each element or combination of elements could become the focus of an evaluation.

For example, if input elements are the evaluation focus during the conceptual and planning stages, they could include target goals or purposes of a program, the theoretical underpinnings of the program or practice approach, prospective client populations to be recruited, characteristics and professional training requirements of staff members to be hired, and a proposed operational budget for the program. The focus of the program's implementation stage is the program process elements, which may include components of the program as they are being implemented, the client population that is served, staff members and volunteers working in the program, staff training and educational needs and opportunities, available electronic technologies, and the record-keeping system. During the output/outcome

FIGURE 5.1   Examples of Program and Practice Elements at Different Stages of the Intervention's Development

Input Elements	Process Elements	Output Elements	Outcome Elements
• Purpose of a proposed intervention • Theoretical underpinnings of a proposed intervention • Identification of prospective clients and recruitment strategies • Descriptions of facilities and equipment needed • Costs	• Intervention components being implemented • Client population being served • Staff members and volunteers working in the program • Education and training of staff members • Records and record-keeping procedures	• Total number of clients served • Number of staff contact hours with clients • Number of clients completing program • Client dropouts	• Measures of client outcomes

stage, output elements and outcome elements are different. Output elements include statistics such as number of clients served and number of contact hours that staff members spend with clients. Outcome elements are the outcomes that measure clients' progress in reaching their goals.

3. *Formulate evaluation questions.* Once the stage and program element(s) are identified, study questions can be formulated about the element(s) of interest. Such questions are best identified through a brainstorming process that involves as many stakeholders as possible. At this stage, do not worry if the questions chosen seem realistic or not. Because this is a brainstorming step, a fairly open-ended, creative process can occur that yields several evaluation questions. Let's look at some examples of possible evaluation questions during each of the three program stages.

In the planning stage, prospective clients are a central element that requires more in-depth examination. Any number of questions could be asked about prospective clients, such as the following:

- What characteristics provide a pertinent client profile (e.g., age, ethnic group, socioeconomic status, evidence of particular problems, clinical diagnosis, specific medical condition)?
- Where could we find and recruit such prospective clients?
- Have we consulted them to find out more about their needs and views about the proposed program? Have we consulted a representative sample of such people?
- If there are more clients than the proposed program can serve, what characteristics and qualities of the client population will receive priority?
- What are some obstacles to reaching prospective clients who have, for example, a clinical diagnosis?

Given the needs of the prospective client group, it is important to explore other sets of elements as well, such as the types of direct-care staff that need to be hired; the qualifications of staff members who can provide the proposed services, and the recruiting and hiring of people with these credentials; and staff applicants' educational level, specialized degree or discipline, prior skills and experience, and various demographic characteristics. As figure 5.1 suggests, other elements of the planning stage could be the focus of an evaluation, including the facilities needed to house it, the technologies required to run it, and the costs described in a budget.

The implementation stage requires consideration of another set of elements, those that make up a program/practice area and move it forward. Such elements include the components of a program being implemented; the clients who are being served; their needs, problems, and diagnoses; current staff members; funding sources; an operating budget; necessary facilities; and technologies in use.

Any number of evaluation questions could be suggested for each of these elements. For example, several questions could be posed about existing staff members:

- Are professional staff members using best practices?
- Are the racial and ethnic characteristics of staff consistent with the affirmative action standards of the agency and the government? If not, how can we recruit and retain minority staff members?
- Are staff trained to effectively help clients with psychological, psychiatric, and other mental problems (e.g., helping people with developmental disabilities integrate socially in the community)?
- How do case managers use their time? How much time, on average, do they devote to direct contact with clients? To evaluation activities? To advocacy? To paperwork?
- Why is there such a high turnover rate of occupational therapists in the program?

Output elements are manifestations of such things as resources that have been used or the extent to which clients have participated in the program. For example, resource outputs could be such things as the number of staff or volunteer contact hours with clients, the costs of running the program, and the wear and tear on physical resources. Client outputs could be the number of clients who have attended at least some program sessions, the number who have successfully completed the program, and the number who have dropped out.

Many evaluation questions could be raised about each output element. Let's take the subgroup of clients completing the program as an example:

- What are the demographic (e.g., gender, socioeconomic group, ethnicity, age) characteristics of clients who completed the program?
- How long did it take for clients to complete the program? Which clients needed more time than others? How much professional staff time was needed to help them on average?
- What are the characteristics of those who dropped out of the program early? At what stages did they most frequently drop out? What factors could explain why they dropped out?

Outcome elements are a special type of output element that reflects the impact of the program/practice area on the clients after they completed it. These elements are usually client-focused and reflect a measure of progress or lack of progress in achieving their goals. Output and outcome elements are sometimes difficult to distinguish. For example, successful completion of a job-training program is more of an output element because it is not an actual indication of client progress in itself, whereas finding a job as a result of training is more of an outcome element. Similarly, completing rigorous drug rehabilitation counseling is a practice output but discontinued drug use is the ultimate desired outcome. When you think about it, completion of a counseling program is not an adequate justification for a program to continue, but making progress toward discontinuing drug use is.

Exercise on Outcome Elements

Formulation of outcome elements tends to require more effort and creativity than the formulation of output elements. The following questions pose examples of this. Try to answer each question:

- What would be a valuable measure of improved marital relations in a family agency beyond completing weekly sessions for three months?
- Beyond the initial physical placement, how can we know whether a foster-care agency was successful in placing children with disabilities in family home care?

Ultimately, evaluation questions focusing on outcome elements ask whether the clients who have completed a program function considerably better than they did when they first began receiving services. Statistical measures are often used to determine not only whether clients have made progress but also whether that progress is statistically significant. If evaluators decide that clinical significance is more important than statistical significance, the question is, did the clients meet the clinical criteria of success based on improving their outcome scores from pretest to posttest? In some agencies, it is important to determine both outputs and outcomes for staff members. For example, an agency may want to know what new skills a staff member learned from attending a particular training session or workshop. This can be an important question, especially if the skills are critical for providing services effectively to clients. Note that the learning of such skills could be either an output element or an outcome element. They are output elements in the context of the program that serves clients, but they are outcome elements if the training workshop is the sole focus of an evaluation.

4. *Identify supportive and resistant forces that need to be considered and addressed before conducting the evaluation.* The previous guideline is largely meant to be a creative, brainstorming step that does not allow feasibility issues to interfere with decisions. However, feasibility becomes an important consideration with this guideline. In addition, the contextual issues of the program and agency become more important. There are two

basic questions to ask about the larger context of the program: (1) what resources are available to support the evaluation? and (2) what factors do we need to consider that could cause resistance or interference in conducting the evaluation?

Identify the Potential Resources

Identifying resources to support the evaluation is often critical. Most evaluations will be feasible only if they have resources available to support them. In some settings, these resource factors may be referred to as strengths of the agency context. It is important to consciously and deliberately identify potential resources because supportive factors are often present but unrecognized. In the case that the resources are required, they can be more easily engaged if you know about them and have considered them from the beginning.

Possible examples of resources or strengths that support an evaluation can be any number of things. The subsequent partial list can help evaluators and stakeholders begin to consider such resources:

- Strong interest in conducting an evaluation among some or all stakeholders
- Prior agency experience in completing useful evaluations, especially successful ones
- Financial support for an evaluation
- Awareness among stakeholders of the problem (or concern) inherent in a program that is the focus of the evaluation
- An openness among stakeholders to examine a problem in greater depth rather than just on the surface
- Some understanding, expertise, and respect for evaluations among stakeholders
- Expressed interest in the evaluation by clients and their families
- Staff interest in helping with the evaluation
- Openness to an evaluator as a helpful resource and ally of the program/ practice area

Examine Factors Resistant to Conducting a Program Evaluation

Although it is important to examine the factors that can support an evaluation, resistant factors are also extremely important to consider, as they may determine the success or failure of the evaluation. They can also be decisive in determining whether to conduct the evaluation (e.g., the evaluation of staff morale described earlier in the chapter).

Once resistant factors are identified, it is critical to explore their impact on an evaluation and address them if warranted. In some cases, this involves discussions with resistant or misinformed stakeholders to listen to and respond to their views. In other instances, this may involve seeking an outside evaluator with more expertise or finding a qualified practitioner in the agency who can conduct the evaluation on a limited budget.

Examples of resistant factors, like resources, include any number of things. The following list can help evaluators and stakeholders begin to identify them:

- Are there time limitations that may preclude conducting an evaluation?
- Are the costs of conducting an evaluation so high that it is not affordable to do so?
- Is the payoff risky in terms of what the findings might suggest?
- Is the type of evaluation that we want so subjective that it may not be feasible or even acceptable to some stakeholders?
- Could the results of the evaluation suggest a need for a change that the agency is not prepared to consider?
- Are there limits to what we can change about the program, given the funding agency's requirements or limited resources?
- Are the special interests of various stakeholders and others likely to lead to counterproductive results or divisiveness?
- Does the agency lack the expertise to conduct such a study?
- If there is no need to justify such an evaluation to the funding agency, why rock the boat?
- Will there be problems in gaining access to client data?
- Do stakeholders and/or the collaborative team have the required creativity and flexibility to implement the evaluation?

A PRACTICAL TOOL

Stecher and Davis (1987) offer a practical way to begin focusing an evaluation on issues important to the agency. Their exercise begins by identifying the program or practice elements that are of concern, followed by writing general study questions, identifying potential resources to support the evaluation, identifying resistant factors, and finally considering specific evaluation procedures. This exercise is intended as a creative way to quickly focus an evaluation on one or more concerns.

Figure 5.2 can be used to explore two (or more) program or practice concerns of importance to an agency. Feel free to use it for that purpose. You may be surprised how quickly you can find a focus for your evaluation. After identifying two program or practice elements as a possible focus, work across the chart from left to right for each element. In the second column, identify one or more general study questions to explore for the element. For example, if a practice element is the high rate of client cancellations and no-shows for appointments with social workers, a general study question could be, why are there so many client cancellations and no-shows in this practice area? This is a good study question because it can lead to several specific questions:

- What percentage of the clients show up for the initially scheduled interview with the social worker? What reasons do clients give, if any, when they do not show up?
- Are the same clients missing appointments over time?
- Are these clients rescheduling canceled appointments?
- What are the characteristics of clients who are canceling or not showing up for appointments?
- Do people from particular ethnic, age, or gender groups cancel more often than members of other groups?
- Are the clients' illnesses preventing them from showing up for appointments?
- Do clients have adequate transportation to get to appointments?
- What is the average time that a client has to wait to see a social worker after an intake interview?

Next, in the third column of figure 5.2, identify potential available resources that are likely to be valuable in supporting a study that addresses each identified study question. Then do the same, but with constraints or resistant factors that could potentially work against such an evaluation. A final step in the far-right column is to begin considering overall evaluation procedures, such as a one-group pretest and posttest design, a needs assessment interview of prospective clients, or observations of worker-client relationships through a two-way mirror.

FIGURE 5.2   Exercise on How to Focus an Evaluation Plan

Program or practice element	General study questions	Resources	Resistant factors	Evaluation procedures
1)	a)	a)	a)	a)
	b)	b)	b)	b)
	c)	c)	c)	
2)	a)	a)	a)	a)
	b)	b)	b)	b)
	c)	c)	c)	

Examples of Questions Formulated by Students

This section offers several examples of how students in an MSW program used this exercise to develop a focus for the evaluations they conducted as part of a course assignment. Note that many of these general study questions focus on practice more than programs; they are also often quite specific.

Examples of Study Questions Focusing on Clients' Issues

Encouraging client diversity

- Why are there so few non-African American clients served in this program? Why are other racial groups not using agency services?
- To what extent is the Latino community being served?
- Is there sufficient and open communication between school social workers and Spanish-speaking parents? What are the potential communication problems between them?

Clients not actively participating in treatment

- Does a lack of day-care services prevent some parents from attending a program? Why isn't day care for clients' children available?
- When clients do not speak in group therapy, what are the likely reasons? Are they shy, resistant to change, not understanding the topics of discussion, or are there other reasons?
- Are eligible teens aware of this group service? Why are some not aware?
- Is the existing group designed to meet members' immediate needs?
- Who is and who is not benefiting from group therapy?

Meeting goals and objectives

- Are clients reaching their initially identified goals?
- Is the goal of getting newly pregnant women into prenatal care being reached?
- Why are some clients completing the program successfully and others are not?

Satisfaction with a program

- Are Latino clients satisfied with the pregnancy-testing program?
- What do clients find most helpful about the social worker's services? What could the social worker do to be more helpful?

Examples of Study Questions Focusing on Staff Members and Technology Issues

Staff hesitations or negligence in implementing particular interventions

- Do staff members make appropriate referrals? What do they do when clients initially choose not to follow through with a referral?
- Are intake staff members adequately trained to conduct comprehensive intake interviews?
- Are in-service training programs successful in preparing staff to do their jobs?
- Are staff members using evidence-based approaches? How can we find this out?
- Are staff members completing their client records in a timely way after each client contact?

Hiring and staff turnover concerns

- Are staff satisfied with their positions? What are they dissatisfied about?
- Why is there a high staff turnover among long-term-care workers?
- Is there a shortage of qualified staff available to fill existing employment openings?

Technology

- Are the family-skills videos appropriate and useful for existing clients?
- Are clients using the family-skills videos at home? If not, what are the reasons for not using them (e.g., need appropriate equipment [DVDs] to run the videos)?
- What are clients learning from viewing these videos?
- How satisfied are they with these videos?

The final step in the focusing exercise in figure 5.2 involves identifying possible evaluation procedures. This topic is covered in more depth in later chapters. Identifying evaluation procedures is an important consideration in the focusing exercise because the evaluation questions eventually selected must be realistic to answer. Put another way, a successful evaluation requires feasible evaluation procedures. Evaluation questions can address major concerns of a program that everyone wants to investigate, but there is no point in proceeding with an investigation without a realistic plan.

Example of Formulating a Feasible General Study Question

A substance abuse agency wanted to find out whether its clinical program was successful in bringing sobriety to its clients. This could be the ultimate type of question that any agency wants to ask: can the agency claim that the program is responsible for changing the lives of its clients related to the goals of the program? However, this is not a feasible question to answer unless the agency can do all of the following:

- Develop a valid measure of the outcome variable: sobriety
- Conduct an experimental design and randomly assign participants to a treatment or control group
- Find the funds and other resources to conduct such an evaluation
- Stay committed to the evaluation from beginning to end
- Conduct a follow-up evaluation to find out whether clients maintained sobriety over a reasonably long period of time

A more feasible evaluation question could be, are most clients making statistically significant improvements in their specific goals by the time they complete the program?

The next two chapters consider important topics of the planning stage, a needs assessment and crafting goals and objectives for a proposed intervention.

KEY TERMS

Formulating evaluation questions
General study questions
Program elements
Resistant factors working against an evaluation
Resources supporting an evaluation
Stages of program development

DISCUSSION QUESTIONS AND ASSIGNMENTS

1. Select a program element from the input stage, implementation stage, or outcome stage listed in figure 5.1 and identify three general study questions that could be investigated about the element.
2. Attempt to arrive at a focus for three different program elements in your agency using figure 5.2. Then choose one element that you would recommend be pursued. Consult your supervisor as you explore each of these steps so that your focus will be useful to the agency.

3. In the exercise described in question 2, identify one supportive force and one resistant force to conducting the evaluation you have proposed. How could the supportive force assist you in implementing your proposed evaluation? What steps could you take to address or counteract the resistant factor?
4. Two questions are posed in the "Exercise on Outcome Elements" box in the chapter. Select one of the questions and create a measurable outcome for it.

REFERENCE

Stecher, B. M., & Davis, W. A. (1987). *How to focus an evaluation*. Thousand Oaks, CA: Sage.

Part III

The Planning or Input Stage

Part III describes the evaluation tasks to be completed during the planning stage of a proposed intervention. Based on the three-stage approach, the planning stage comes prior to the implementation of the intervention. Several crucial tasks are to be completed during this stage relevant to an evaluation. They include designing the intervention, identifying funding sources, identifying and recruiting clients, and hiring staff members. Two additional tasks during the planning stage are considered evaluation activities: conducting a needs assessment and crafting goals and objectives for the proposed intervention. Chapter 6 discusses needs assessments and their importance in shaping an intervention. Chapter 7 delves into how to craft goals and objectives for a new intervention so that the clients' progress can be measured.

Chapter 6

Needs Assessments

How do we know that there is a need for the intervention?

Chapter 6 focuses primarily on issues related to step 1 (identify the problem or concern to be evaluated) and step 2 (identify and explore ways to involve stakeholders) of the Seven Evaluation Steps. A critically important task during the planning stage is determining whether or not there is a need for the proposed intervention. (See figure 6.1.) Typically, this involves conducting a needs assessment. It is important to become informed about a group of prospective clients before designing a new intervention to help them because valuable resources are to be committed. The planning stage is the primary period when this documentation is expected to be completed. During the planning stage, various stakeholders can identify, document, advocate, and debate the need for a new program or practice area. In other words, well-conceived, well-conceptualized programs and practice approaches are typically preceded by an important planning process that involves a variety of helpful inputs. It is also important to note that a needs assessment could be conducted again after a program is under way to confirm that the underlying needs of the client group are being monitored.

FIGURE 6.1 Documenting the Need for an Intervention

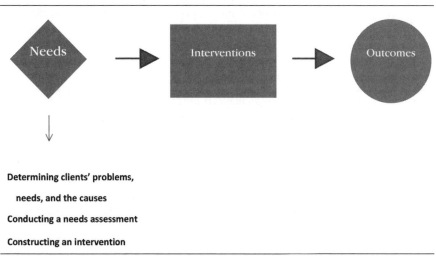

Determining clients' problems,

   needs, and the causes

Conducting a needs assessment

Constructing an intervention

Although rigorous planning makes sense before implementation of an intervention, such preparation is often ignored or underplayed for many debatable reasons. The agency provider may be rushed into getting a program under way prematurely because of deadlines imposed by a funding agency or an agency board. Or perhaps a needs assessment seems unnecessary because there is plenty of anecdotal data available in support of an intervention. Another frequent excuse is that there is no expectation to systematically document the need. Finally, program administrators sometimes are not well prepared for the necessary planning tasks before them. In this case, this chapter can provide administrators with major guidelines and tasks for planning a new program.

THE LOGIC MODEL

The logic model is both an organizing framework and a tool to theoretically analyze a program as it is being developed. It can also be used to analyze a practice approach. The logic model helps to highlight how the three stages and the tasks within these stages can be logically linked into an organic whole, beginning with the problems of prospective clients and culminating in anticipated client outcomes. In brief, the tasks especially pertinent to the logic model at each stage of program development are depicted in figure 6.2.

FIGURE 6.2   The Logic Model

Planning Stage

Determine the clients' problems →
Determine specific unmet needs →
Determine the causes of their problems →
Craft goals and objectives of an intervention to meet the clients' specific unmet needs →
Design an intervention to address these goals and objectives

↓

Implementation Stage

Implement and monitor intervention as proposed

↓

Output and Outcome Stage

Measure the extent to which the clients' goals and measurable objectives are reached. These outcomes are ideally measured for the short, intermediate, and long run.

The example that follows outlines some steps taken by one group in implementing the logic model in the design and implementation of a parenting education program for teenage mothers. In this example the outcomes are established at three different points in time: initial, intermediate, and long run, reflecting what is expected at the completion of the program and at two later points in time. A weakness of this example is that some pertinent information is missing, such as the policies defining this proposed program; also, the clients' problems, unmet needs, and underlying causes are not explicitly stated during the input steps and are not clearly understood in defining the intervention.

Example of a Description Using the Logic Model of a Parenting Education Program for Teenage Mothers

Input steps

- Agency and high school identify pregnant teens to participate in program.
- Agency provides appropriate teaching materials, staff, and so on.

Program activities implemented

- Program provides parenting classes on prenatal care, infant nutrition, safety, proper care, feeding, and so on, twice a week for one hour to teen mothers with a child from three months prior to birth to one year after delivery of child.

Output steps

- Pregnant teen mothers attend all sessions of the program.

Initial outcomes

- Teens are knowledgeable about prenatal care and nutrition.
- Teens are knowledgeable about proper care and feeding.

Intermediate outcomes

- Teens follow proper nutrition and safety guidelines.
- Teens deliver healthy babies.
- Teens provide proper care and feeding.

Long-term outcomes

- Babies achieve appropriate twelve-month milestones for physical, motor, verbal, and social development (Ross, Lipsey, & Freeman, 2004).

As discussed in chapter 1, the logic model is implemented within a larger context of policies, administrative leadership styles, communication patterns, financial issues, and other factors that inevitably have an influence. The influence of the policies of the proposed program is important to mention here. A helpful first step in using the logic model would be to identify the specific policies of the program that define the problem of interest and how it can be solved. These policies can then serve as a guide in walking through the steps in figure 6.2. For example, if the parenting education program for teenage mothers mentioned above is to help teenage mothers raise their babies in healthy ways, hopefully the policies of this program can be identified to help determine what specific problems and needs are to be addressed by the program. Then goals and objectives could be crafted that would be the basis for determining what program activities and teaching materials are needed by this particular group of teenage mothers. In short, devising an effective program to help them could be achieved by moving through the series of steps of the logic model beginning with the program's policies.

Introducing the logic model into the program-planning process has the potential to create fundamental changes in how a proposed program is shaped and implemented, especially when the effort is initiated in an early stage, such as during the conceptualization of a program. Aspects of the logic model are increasingly being built into funding agencies' requirements for most grant proposals. Grant proposals are expected to document such things as the links among clients' problems, needs, causes, and the program approach proposed to help them. This and later chapters describe some of the issues that are raised and addressed when the logic model is incorporated into the planning process, including:

- Identifying the links between pertinent client problems and specific needs
- Determining how these problems and needs relate to underlying causes
- Identifying the goals of the program based on the problems, needs, and underlying causes for this group of clients
- Crafting measurable objectives for these goals
- Logically linking these goals and objectives to a program approach that is evidence-based and can help these clients achieve their goals and objectives
- Anticipating that the introduction of the program approach will result in these clients progressing satisfactorily toward the goals and measurable objectives initially identified and crafted

THE LINK BETWEEN PROBLEMS AND NEEDS

The logic model is introduced during the program planning stage to stress the vital need to begin by identifying the clients' problems, needs, and their underlying causes. A note about the link between needs and problems is helpful here. The reference to a needs assessment may imply that problems are not pertinent. For example, why isn't this process referred to as a problem assessment? Although clients' problems and needs are similar, there are some important differences. Some prefer using the term *needs* over *problems* when referring to the nature of the help clients receive because it puts a more positive face on the focus and less on client deficits. Needs may also imply something that is manageable and capable of being changed, whereas a larger social problem may seem more insurmountable and unsolvable, at least in the immediate future. Needs also refers to some aspects of a problem that can be immediately addressed, while that may not be possible for other aspects of the problem.

DePoy and Gilson (2003) view needs as a systematic, evidence-based phenomenon linked to all or part of the problem. They suggest that identification of the need-related aspects of a problem helps specify the conditions and actions necessary to address the focus of the problem. For the purposes of this text, a revised version of DePoy and Gilson's definition of needs is used. Needs are considered only part of an overall problem that is identified by a client and selected because there is evidence that it can be overcome, alleviated, or ameliorated by an intervention (see table 6.1).

Note that the problems in the examples of table 6.1 are usually stated in broad terms that may fit many different client circumstances. In contrast, the needs linked to each problem are more specific and intended to fit some clients with these particular circumstances and not others. For example, truancy is a problem that could be related to any number of needs going unmet. In table 6.1, truant students face two types of needs: trying to cope with challenging family conflicts and needing more supervised time before and after school because parents are employed outside of the home during the day. In other instances, truancy could be related to a lack of preparedness for academic courses, a lack of interest in school, a substance abuse problem, interpersonal difficulties pertaining to acceptance at school, difficulty adapting as a recent immigrant, and so on.

TABLE 6.1 Examples of Connections between a Problem and a Need

Problem	Specific need
1. Inadequate housing	1. Housing needs plumbing repairs
2. Unemployed	2. Needing a job
3. Marital estrangement	3. Healthy marital communication
4. Truancy from school	4. Buffer from family conflicts and having something to do after school
5. Social isolation	5. Healthy social contact with peers

THE UNDERLYING CAUSES

So a need is an aspect of a larger problem identified by a client and per-ceived to be amenable to change. Meeting a set of needs, then, is the intended focus of a proposed program. However, before rushing too quickly into the design of such a program, another important question is, what are the underlying causes of the problem that prevent the need from being met? This is a critical question for stakeholders to explore if a proposed program or practice area is to be designed to directly confront underlying causes. Underlying causes partially reflect barriers and other resistant factors that prevent needs from being met. Therefore, identified needs are likely to be met only if the underlying causes are understood and confronted.

Let's return to the example of the five sets of problems and specific needs described in table 6.1. Once we identify the problems, needs, and underlying causes, as described in table 6.2, we discover that we have a more complete understanding of what a program has to be designed to do to be effective.

Let's look more closely at the first example in table 6.2 of inadequate housing as the problem and plumbing repairs as the specific need to be met. We might next ask why the plumbing (and other aspects of housing) has not been addressed. After all, most plumbing repairs seem fairly straightforward

TABLE 6.2   Examples of Connections among a Problem, Need, and the Underlying Causes

Problem	Need	Underlying causes
1. Inadequate housing	1. Housing needs plumbing repairs	1. Deteriorated housing con-ditions, limited funds for repairs, and no repair skills or repair resources available
2. Unemployed	2. Needing a job	2. Lacks training in a skilled job area and lacks hope and motivation
3. Marital estrangement	3. Healthy marital communi-cation	3. Lacks communication skills, no models for healthy marital relation-ships, and no incentives to stay married
4. Truancy from school	4. Protection from family conflicts and having some-thing to do after school lacking	4. Problems involving parental relationship and parental guidance
5. Social isolation	5. Healthy social contact	5. Lacks social skills and no groups or organizations available to offer positive social contacts

and relatively easy to make. Yet the example suggests that the group of clients with this housing problem have modest incomes, no funds available for major repairs, and no plumbing repair skills or resources available even if funds were found.

You may still wonder why it is so important to identify and distinguish problems, needs, and underlying causes. This will become more evident in later chapters when the focus is on developing an intervention that will succeed in meeting unmet needs. For now it is important to remember that an effective new program or practice approach must be linked to a clear sense of what the problem and needs are and how they can be solved. Let's look next at how needs assessments are important for developing programs.

INPUT STAGE AND PLANNING THE PROPOSED PROGRAM

The input stage of program development is when planning becomes the major focus. Several important tasks are completed in this stage, including identifying the prospective client population that is to be the focus of a new program and the problems of the clients that the proposed program is to address. Here is where the complex tasks of exploring the problem in more depth occur. The clients' problem, the specific needs that are part of the problem, and the underlying causes are all a focus of this task. Once the client population has been identified in general terms and the target problem has been examined in more depth, a decision needs to be made as to how to assess, in a systematic way, the clients' problems and needs. This is where a needs assessment becomes front and center.

Before delving into the mechanics of a needs assessment, it is important to emphasize that this is both a subjective and a political process. Meenaghan, Kilty, and McNutt (2004) identify some key overall social and political factors that can influence the implementation of a needs assessment. They recommend that evaluators and stakeholders be fully aware of the people and groups involved in each of the following activities:

- Who chooses what problems are to be examined?
- Who identifies what information is collected and why?
- Who analyzes and interprets the information that is collected?
- Who controls access to dissemination of the information collected?

These activities are critical to the shape that a needs assessment will take, how the data will be analyzed, the results that will be emphasized and ignored, who will have access to the results, and how the results will be disseminated. These points illustrate how the evaluation process is always a political process as well as a research undertaking, as mentioned in chapter 1. The specific stakeholders, in particular, can be crucial in influencing this process. Thus, it is important to identify all relevant parties who have a stake in the results and to get them involved as early as possible. It also means that the stakeholders should be as fully involved as possible in every step. The participant action approach and the empowerment approach, described in chapter 2, are good models to follow in this regard.

WHY CONDUCT A NEEDS ASSESSMENT?

Why conduct a needs assessment? A broad, systematic research effort like a needs assessment can be highly beneficial in addressing many community-wide needs and problems. Most important, such an assessment can provide valuable information for understanding a particular social problem that is troubling a local community. The alternatives—depending on hearsay or a few case examples as evidence, or having hunches about a problem—are not enough documentation to take the problem seriously (Marlow, 2011).

Needs assessments are particularly useful when considering a new policy or program initiative or when considering changes to or discontinuation of an existing program. Also, if outside funding sources (e.g., federal, state, or local government; private foundations; corporate support) are needed to support a program, the documentation from a needs assessment takes on even greater importance.

A needs assessment can answer several important questions. Consider the example of parenting children in a low-income neighborhood. Several questions could be asked about their parenting in this neighborhood:

- To what extent and how are the (biological, step, surrogate) parents actively involved in raising their children?
- To what extent and how are the parents economically able to provide for their children?
- What problems do mothers and fathers face in their roles as parents?
- What trends are evident in teen pregnancy, unmarried parenting, single parenting, and divorce? Are these family patterns increasing or decreasing?
- To what extent do services exist in the community to help parents with their parental roles?
- What are the demographic characteristics of the mothers and fathers who use existing services? What are the characteristics of those who do not use existing services?
- What barriers exist to access existing services?
- What service gaps are evident?
- What new policy initiatives could benefit these parents?

SOME PURPOSES OF NEEDS ASSESSMENTS

You may ask, "What good will a needs assessment do, anyway?" Of course, there are no guarantees, but many positive benefits can come from a needs assessment of a particular group of people. Further, the more stakeholders and potential stakeholders that are involved and committed to such an assessment and informed by it, the more likely it is that a genuine community-wide concern for a client group will emerge.

Although a needs assessment is particularly important in documenting the need for a new program, it has other important purposes:

- Determining the adequacy of existing programs
- Determining the adequacy of existing informal resources
- Assessing client accessibility
- Obtaining data for crafting goals and measurable objectives for a new program

New Programs

One purpose of a needs assessment is to explore in more depth whether a new program is needed. A key question in this exploration is whether there are enough prospective clients to warrant such an initiative. Specific questions could be asked about the activities or programs that the respondents would be interested in using, possible priorities for some activities over others, how important the activities are to clients, and the times when they would be most likely desired and used. Another set of questions can explore possible barriers that prevent some people from accessing any of the activities. Potential barriers could emerge related to decisions about particular times a program is offered; the location, costs, and need to charge any fees; and possible psychological issues related to such things as how welcomed clients would feel.

Adequacy of Existing Programs

A needs assessment can also be very useful in determining the extent to which programs are already available to meet the needs of a particular group. This line of questioning naturally precedes attempts to document the need for a new program, even though this may not be taken seriously because of competition among agencies. Assessing the existence of other programs similar in nature to a proposed program is desirable to determine whether the need is already being met. Such a task is important not only to avoid program duplication but also to explore and create complementary and collaborative relationships with relevant existing agencies and programs.

An assessment of programs that already exist begins with finding them. Next, the programs could be visited and evaluated in terms of their relevance to the needs of the particular group targeted for the proposed new program. The assessments should also explore the ability of existing programs to serve additional clients, particularly the targeted group that is the concern of the initiators of the needs assessment.

The sources of information for a needs assessment of existing programs may include the administrators and service-delivery staff members of the agencies that provide such services. Assessment tools can help obtain information on such topics as demographic characteristics of the people who use services, characteristics of those who tend not to use them, explorations of the nature of their services, and any indicators that the programs are effective. The barriers that keep some groups from accessing services could be explored and service gaps documented. In addition, the assessment process could explore the agencies' views on new program initiatives that would be beneficial to particular groups in the community.

Adequacy of Existing Informal Resources

Although it is important to assess whether existing agency programs are available to address a pressing need, it can be equally important to assess the adequacy of existing informal resources. Informal resources may include extended family; other family members not in the household; neighborhood clubs, centers, and civic groups; advocacy groups; churches, synagogues, mosques, and other religious groups; libraries, museums, and theatrical resources; and so on. Often informal resources are the first line of defense and the easiest resources for clients to approach.

Client Accessibility

There are many potential barriers that will inevitably discourage some people from using the services of a program, such as an unfriendly receptionist, a delay in returning a call, a misunderstanding of the purpose of a program, unawareness of the program, or a perceived insensitivity to a particular group's culture. Access issues are important to consider in the planning stage of program development. Serious consideration must be given to the various groups that are targeted as recipients and to the factors that could prevent any of them from using the program's services.

Chapter 8 describes several factors that could be sources of confusion or resistance that keep potential program recipients from using services. The most effective way to identify these access issues is to ask potential recipients to share their views on accessibility. Such questions can be included as a component of a needs-assessment questionnaire or as interviews with recipients. Stakeholders who are concerned about the recipients can also be enlisted to share their views. Also, access issues can be relevant to consider when selecting a particular program approach or deciding on what kinds of staff members to hire.

Crafting Goals and Objectives

An additional purpose of a needs assessment can be to gather data pertinent to the goals of a proposed program. Goals of proposed programs tend to be crafted from the providers' perspectives. To address this bias, a needs assessment could be used to obtain specific data from the perspectives of potential recipients. Most of the questions would be open-ended explorations. Questions can be designed to obtain information related to the proposed goals and objectives of the program by exploring the following:

- What do clients perceive as realistic goals for themselves?
- What do they perceive to be some measurable objectives? In other words, how might things be different once they reach their goals?
- How motivated are they to seek these goals?
- How important are the goals to others in their immediate circle of social support?

Example of Needs-Assessment Questions on Family Planning Asked of Potential Recipients

- Do you have an interest in planning the size of your family?
- Would you consider using any existing birth control methods that are available?
- Would you have an interest in discussing your family-planning needs and questions with a professional counselor if one were available?
- What are some questions about birth control that you would want to discuss with a counselor?
- Would you be open to possibly obtaining a birth-control method such as an IUD if a program was available to fit one for you?
- Do you currently have easy access to the birth-control methods you want to use?
- Would you be comfortable using a family-planning program if it existed?
- What would be your hesitations in using such a program, if any?

The next chapter is completely devoted to crafting goals and objectives for interventions.

METHODS OF CONDUCTING NEEDS ASSESSMENTS

A needs assessment is an organized, systematic effort to assess the need for something, in this case the need for a new program or practice area. Conducting a needs assessment of some or all of the prospective recipients of a program is wise to do because they are some of the people who will choose whether to use the program. The more that the program takes into account their specific needs, the more likely it is that they will find it relevant and use it. The specific methods for conducting a needs assessment can take many forms, including using existing data, constructing and administering a questionnaire, conducting interviews, conducting focus groups, arranging public forums, observing, or any combination of these.

Documenting Needs with Existing Data

Sometimes existing data is available to provide all or some of the documentation of the need for a new program. If so, this may be the place to start. Thus, the first recommended step in documenting the need for a new program is to explore whether relevant data already exists. This will be the least expensive way to conduct a needs assessment.

Steps for Reviewing Existing Data

DePoy and Gilson (2003) recommend a rigorous set of steps to effectively and efficiently review existing data for a needs assessment.

1. Determine the purpose of the review.
2. Set some search parameters.
3. Access relevant databases.
4. Obtain relevant information from the databases.
5. Organize the selected information.
6. Critically evaluate the information.
7. Prepare a report of the selected information.

Let's take a closer look at the numerous sources from which relevant existing data can be obtained (steps 3 and 4 in DePoy and Gilson's list). There are often several relevant choices: local studies, governmental studies, studies of research firms and academic units, secondary research, data available from social agencies, and mapping resources. Let's take a closer look at what each of these sources can offer.

Local studies. Local studies can be an excellent source of data because they may include the actual client populations considered for the proposed new program. Local studies also may have more credibility with some stakeholders, especially when sponsored by colleagues in the geographic area. Local agencies may include the local United Way office, a local governmental agency, or the local newspaper. All of these organizations are known to conduct such studies. A simple way to begin an investigation of local studies is to do a Google search of the name of your community, county government, university, or local agency, followed by the words *needs assess-*

ment. For example, a United Way agency in North Carolina (2011) conducted a needs assessment that focused on education; housing and poverty; and health and mental health.

Example of United Way Needs Assessment

The purpose of this study was to assess the most critical needs of the five-county Charlotte region and to identify the most significant and effective channels to address these needs. To accomplish this, the research team focused on United Way's three current funding areas: Children and Youth; Crisis, Housing and Stability; and Health and Mental Health. The components of the study included a review of previous community assessments, secondary data analysis, a survey of local human service agencies, and a series of four expert panels—one for each of the funding areas and a general panel.

Across the greatest needs of education, housing and poverty, and health/mental health, two intertwining themes pervaded—the need for preventive services and public awareness. Accordingly, this report makes several key recommendations to strengthen United Way's impact in the community. These include suggestions to fund programs that encourage prevention and campaigns that educate the public about the community's needs and available services; fund a broader range of programs than just direct service providers; and improve the funding process itself so that it is more focused and can make serious progress on specific causes instead of spreading funding thinly across the entire spectrum.

Governmental studies at the national and state levels. Governmental agencies at the national and state levels conduct studies of relevance to social service agencies. Two good sources are the U.S. Census (www.census.gov) and the National Center for Health Statistics (www.cdc.gov/nchs). The U.S. Census conducts not only a census of the entire U.S. population every ten years but also numerous smaller studies, known as Current Population Surveys, with nationally representative samples in between years. The surveys are conducted on numerous topics, have a good reputation for accuracy and reliability, and often are pertinent in documenting the needs of many subgroups in a population (e.g., elderly, families, and children).

Studies of nonprofit research firms, academic units, and professional journals. Many research firms and academic groups are also known to conduct and disseminate large-scale studies. Reports on some of these studies can be found on the Internet. Such firms often have large representative samples that can be generalized to even larger populations. A good example is Child Trends (www.childtrends.org), a nonprofit, nonpartisan research organization dedicated to improving the lives of children by conducting research and providing science-based information to improve the decisions, programs, and policies that affect children. Child Trends produces books, research briefs, and full research reports on such topics as child poverty, child welfare, health, marriage and family structure, teen sex and pregnancy, parenting, and family dynamics. They widely disseminate their reports, which arc oftcn frcc.

University-conducted studies can also be useful and are often reported on university websites and in professional journals. Several professional journals focus specifically on program and practice evaluations, including the following:

- *Evaluation: The International Journal of Theory, Research and Practice*
- *Evaluation Review: A Journal of Applied Social Research*
- *Evaluation and the Health Professions*
- *New Directions for Evaluation*
- *Evaluation and Program Planning: An International Journal*
- *American Journal of Evaluation*
- *Practical Assessment, Research and Evaluation*
- *Canadian Journal of Program Evaluation*

Evaluation reports can also be found in many other professional journals, such as *Social Work, Child Welfare*, and *Families in Society*.

Example of a Needs Assessment in a Professional Journal

Weinman, Buzi, and Smith (2005) focused on the risk factors, service needs, and mental health issues of 143 young fathers (aged sixteen to thirty-three) when they entered a fatherhood program. They found that almost 70 percent were unemployed, 42 percent had been in jail, and 39 percent were school dropouts. The most frequent mental health issues that the fathers identified included sadness and depression, nervousness and tension, helplessness, and aggression. Although the fathers identified these and other risk factors, they did not often request services to address them; the most frequently requested services were related to jobs and training. Because the results of this study were mostly problem-focused, the authors recommended that future assessments use a strengths perspective.

Secondary research. Another option to consider when relying on other studies is secondary research or data from a previous study. This option is pertinent only if a data set from a previous study exists and is available. Many research firms offer their data sets to interested parties for secondary analysis, and usually for a reasonable fee.

Example of a Study Using Secondary Analysis

John O'Donnell (1999) conducted a secondary analysis of data from an earlier federally funded research and demonstration project on casework practice in kinship foster care. Kinship foster care refers to the placement of children in the home of a relative approved by the agency as a foster parent. The data was collected in the prior study from caseworkers in two private child-welfare agencies. O'Donnell reported on a subset of the original data set that focused on the involvement of African American fathers. His findings documented the lack of fathers' involvement in the caseworkers' assessment and planning of foster-care services for their children. Although useful secondary data was available about several of these fathers, the data had limitations because it emphasized their problems, not their strengths. Further, the data did not explore some issues of importance to O'Donnell, such as why more fathers of children in paternal kinship homes participated in casework services than fathers of children in maternal kinship homes.

Agency data. Virtually every social agency, school, and institutional setting collects an enormous amount of data on their clients. Often these data have great potential as resources for a needs assessment. For example, the client records of these organizations can be valuable in providing information about the demographic and diagnostic characteristics of clients, numbers of clients with specific problems, different types of interventions that have been used to help them, the amount of time that clients have received services, and in some cases outcome data for current and former clients.

Example of Using Agency Data

A study by Faithfull, Cook, and Lucas (2005) investigated the need of patients with malignant brain tumors and their caregivers in a cancer and palliative care program for support services. The evaluators were interested in finding out which community support services clients were using. Data were drawn retrospectively from case notes and clinical records for a population of 1,254 patients referred to the palliative care program over one year. Data collected from the records included demographic characteristics, extent of palliative care service use, other health and social service use, symptoms experienced, and time from diagnosis to referral and death. This evaluation identified some important clinical needs and questions for this particular client group related to palliative care. A critical question recommended for investigation in a later study was what services the caregivers needed. A limitation of the study was that it was not known how accurate the case notes and records were.

In another instance, a study was conducted of runaway and homeless lesbian, gay, bisexual, transgender, and questioning youths in New York City (Nolan, 2006). The agency wanted to find out what happened to the youths after they left a transitional living program by using case files about them. The files included information on the youths discharged from the program over a five-year period. Information was taken from the files on demographic characteristics, pre- and post-housing status, pre- and post-educational status, foster-care history, abuse history, length of stay in the transitional living program, and reason for discharge. The case files had an abundance of helpful data. For example, in the area of abuse history, the study found that half the youth had reported experiencing physical abuse, and one-third had reported being sexually abused, mostly by family members, boyfriends, and family friends. Half had reported experiencing verbal or emotional abuse, including homophobic and transgender-phobic remarks.

Mapping resources.   Another recently developed approach uses computer and electronic files. Mapping visually locates specific groups or clusters of people or problems in a particular geographic area and helps users recognize where there are concentrations of problems. The concentrations can then be explored in terms of how they are associated with other characteristics, such as income level or ethnicity. For example, the U.S. Census tool American Factfinder can be used to select specific census data and map it across a geographic area of interest, such as a city or county. The tool, which allows for creating, viewing, printing, and downloading maps, is available online at www.factfinder.census.gov. The Reference Maps tool can be used to view boundaries of census geographies, such as counties, cities and towns, urban areas, congressional districts, census tracts, and census blocks. The Thematic Maps tool can be used to view geographic patterns in census data. Thematic maps are available for the 2000 Census, the 1990 Census, the Economic Census, and the Population Estimates program. The tutorial "Creating and Using Maps" is available for guidance.

Thematic maps may be particularly helpful when you want to compare statistical data of specific groups, such as median income, displayed in a map format. You can change the view of the thematic map by clicking on the area of the map you want to view in more detail or by selecting a new geography, theme, or data set. The Quick Tips command assists in navigating or customizing your map.

Example of Mapping as a Form of Assessment

A specific mapping program, referred to as a geographic information system (GIS) can help an evaluator gather more information about the characteristics of a local community, city, or county. The GIS can create maps for such things as the location of all senior centers, the degree to which neighborhoods are healthy, poverty levels in a community, locations of Medicaid users, crime rates, and particular agencies. More information can be found about the GIS program and its various features in the work of Hillier (2007).

Administer a Questionnaire

A questionnaire is a frequently chosen method to obtain relevant data for a needs assessment. A questionnaire can be an excellent way to inquire about the needs of a particular target group on a specific topic, such as family planning, housing improvements, or social activities for seniors. The questionnaire could be mailed to the intended audience, hand-delivered door-to-door, or handed out at a meeting or community gathering. An advantage of a questionnaire is that it can be distributed to a fairly large group of people without much effort. However, the questionnaire must be constructed so that it is completely self-explanatory and simple enough to fill out, as an interviewer will not be present to clarify anything.

Example of a Parks and Recreation Needs Assessment

Using a questionnaire mailed to every resident of the neighborhood, Line (2007) used a community needs assessment to explore neighbors' interest in several activity areas considered by an expanding community center. First, respondents selected from a list of activities the ones that they believed their family members would likely participate in, including baseball, T-ball, volleyball, tennis, after-school programs, nature and bike trails, tutoring, senior social clubs, educational seminars, and concerts. Next, respondents were asked about their interests in specific classes, such as karate, CPR and first aid, self-defense, arts and crafts, gardening, cooking, and safety. Then they were asked what methods they would prefer to receive information about upcoming park and recreation events. Options included monthly newsletters, flyers, public service announcements, e-mail, announcements in local newspapers, and information posted at the community center. Several questions followed about the best times for their availability, such as the best times for children's activities (e.g., mornings, midday, afternoons, evenings, weekdays, or weekends). In addition, respondents were asked how they felt about existing activities at the center. On a scale of 1 (very unsatisfied) to 5 (very satisfied), questions included how much they felt that various existing activities met their needs and how satisfied they were with the community center generally. Finally, they were asked about their readiness to participate in new activities if they were provided (e.g., "Would you come to the center to pre-register for these classes, and how much could you afford to pay for such classes?"). A final question asked if respondents wanted to be contacted about a particular program interest and, if so, to list the program and their name and phone number.

A disadvantage of questionnaires is that they almost always use quantitative methods and ask forced-response questions, because respondents are not likely to answer more than one or two open-ended questions. Another disadvantage is that questionnaires usually have low response rates. This problem could be addressed by administering the questionnaire to people attending a social event and encouraging them to fill it out at the event, which can work especially well if either the evaluator or the organization sponsoring the event are known and trusted by the people asked to participate.

Examples of Questions Used in a Domestic Violence Needs Assessment for the Victims

Stewart (2005) administered the following questionnaire:

1. How important is it for you to have information about domestic violence? (Circle 1 response.)
   Not important   Somewhat important   Very important

2. How important is it for you to have a safe place to stay if there is an emergency? (Circle 1 response.)
   Not important   Somewhat important   Very important

3. How important is it for you to attend an educational/support group? (Circle 1 response.)
   Not important   Somewhat important   Very important

4. How important is it for you to have help when you go to court? (Circle 1 response.)
   Not important   Somewhat important   Very important

5. How important is it for you to have individual counseling? (Circle 1 response.)
   Not important   Somewhat important   Very important

The example from Stewart (2005) uses a forced-response question format and identifies a few of the questions used by an MSW student to assess the needs of victims of domestic violence. Although the questions are effective for quickly finding out the degree to which respondents need each program area, qualitative questions could be added to gain insight into how the specific needs manifest and how respondents would use such a set of services if available.

Another way to structure a needs assessment in an agency that serves victims of domestic violence is to focus on victims' knowledge of what constitutes domestic violence and how it should be addressed. Examples of some of the types of questions that could be asked are the following (Women's Commission, 2005):

Multiple-choice questions

Domestic violence affects
(a) Only children who observe the violence in their home
(b) All children living in homes with domestic violence
(c) Only teenagers
(d) Only young children
(e) Does not affect children
[Correct answer is b]

True/false questions

Domestic violence only occurs in low-income families.
(a) True
(b) False
[Correct answer is false]
A batterer is never nice to his/her partner.
(a) True
(b) False
[Correct answer is false]

Questionnaires with informants could also be implemented, particularly if there are experts with special knowledge on a topic and who are well acquainted with the needs of the community. Informants can share their own and others' perspectives. Informants might be professionals or volunteers in counseling or advocacy programs, or teachers, administrators, and others who have frequent contact with a population of interest. Their expertise would be based largely on their familiarity with the population.

Example of Informant Interviews

Charla Williams (2006), an MSW student, conducted a needs-assessment inquiry of staff members of a crisis intervention unit of a family agency that provides shelter, case management, counseling, and advocacy services to victims of domestic violence or sexual assaults. The purpose was to find out from informants what additional programs they felt were needed for those experiencing domestic violence. The results of the questionnaire ranked support groups and transitional housing as the most important missing programs. The study also revealed that the family agency sponsoring the crisis intervention should advertise its services more, as many agencies were not familiar with them.

Conduct Interviews

Interviews are also a good choice for conducting needs assessments. An interview could be conducted with the target population, similar to using a questionnaire. Because an interview takes more time to administer than a questionnaire and requires training of the interviewer, interviews likely focus on a smaller group of respondents. Yet an advantage of interviews is that they can probe more deeply to elicit the views, attitudes, and needs of interviewees, which results in valuable qualitative data.

Informant interviews are a particular type of interviewing approach to consider, particularly if there are experts with special knowledge and who are well acquainted with the needs of the community. The informants can share not only their own perspectives but also those of others who may be more difficult to reach. Informants could be civic leaders, gang leaders or former leaders, representatives of advocacy groups, teachers with extensive experience in the community, volunteers and staff members of community agencies, and others.

Eliminating Health and Social Disparities: Some Interview Questions to Ask Agencies

- What role do you think your agency can play in community-based efforts to eliminate health and human service disparities?
- What does it take for agencies to be effective in eliminating disparities in the community?
- What other resources exist in the community aimed to eliminate disparities? How can these resources be strengthened?
- What goals do you think need to be measured in determining whether the community is making progress in increasing access to services and reducing health and social disparities?

Case studies and other in-depth interviews with a few people are another way to conduct a needs assessment. Case descriptions can be very useful in determining the need for a program by providing a fuller understanding of someone's circumstances and experiences or something of interest. By illuminating the complexities of the social circumstances faced by one or a few prospective clients or client families, for example, case studies can provide insights that may be relevant to understanding their struggles and resilience as well as how to help them.

The professional literature provides many examples of case studies that have focused on a few individuals or on a larger social system such as a cultural group, gang, or social system such as a mental institution or prison. These studies have often been enormously helpful in providing new insights into the lives of a particular group not previously understood or known in society and in discovering new ways to help effectively address unmet needs.

Goffman's book *Asylums* is a case study of a mental hospital in the 1950s. In this case, his study was a catalyst for beginning the de-institutionalization movement of the 1960s, which led to the creation of a whole new system of community-based residential and vocational programs for people with mental illness and mental retardation intended to replace programs that had been provided in institutional settings.

Example of a Case Study

Erving Goffman (1961) conducted a two-year participant-observation study of a large state mental institution reported in a book titled *Asylums*. In *Asylums*, Goffman vividly depicts what life was like in this institution and how the patients were regimented into a rigid, imposed schedule. The case description was most effective in conveying how the institution was harmful and counterproductive to patients. The book was timely and served as a strong catalyst for the de-institutionalization movement initiated a few years later.

A case description of an undocumented family of immigrants from Mexico could also provide valuable insights about the numerous difficulties they face. Using an in-depth interview approach with one family, an interviewer could obtain information about the difficulties that recently arrived families face in the United States and programs that could be developed to help. Likely problems that could be more fully understood through a case study approach include how to receive adequate medical care, find adequate housing, enroll children in day care and public schools, find transportation, get help if exploited on the job, and obtain legal assistance.

In-depth interviews with a sample of staff members and volunteers of local agencies that provide similar programs or help similar clients are another way to proceed with a needs assessment. Often social workers and others on the front line have a wealth of information from their daily contact with clients. Tapping into this wealth of information is another valuable data source for a needs assessment.

The number and variety of possibilities for conducting a needs assessment with either a questionnaire or an interview method are almost endless.

Examples of Other Needs Assessments

1. Residents of an older-adult assisted-living center were assessed on the basis of the importance of their spiritual beliefs and practices (Franco, 2004). A major intent of the study was to explore the need for additional programs to address residents' spiritual needs. Ten residents were interviewed with such questions as, Do you belong to an organized religious group? What spiritual practices do you use? How important is prayer or meditation to you? What do you think happens after death? How can the center provide more assistance to you in response to your spiritual needs?

2. In exploring the need for a new program for Latino children who had witnessed domestic violence, Wolochwianski (2005) administered a questionnaire for mothers who had been victims of domestic violence about their children. The simple questionnaire asked whether they had any children, their ages and sex, and whether they would be interested in their children receiving services for witnessing domestic violence. Further, mothers were asked about convenient locations, transportation, whether children could receive services while the mother was receiving counseling, and the best times for such services.

3. Caliento (2004), whose field placement was in a foster-care agency, assessed the need for a specific program for teen mothers in foster care. She asked the professionals serving the teens to fill out a structured questionnaire using a five-point Likert scale (strongly agree to strongly disagree). She asked them to rate the mothers on the basis of their needs for parenting-skills training, one-on-one in-home support, their ability to parent, education for preventing further pregnancies, child-care services for the baby, and several existing programs offered by the agency.

Conduct Focus Groups

Focus groups are a special form of group interview in which participants are invited to discuss a particular topic, for example, the needs of African

Americans for hospice care. Focus groups can be used to find out the views of several people on an issue of importance to a needs assessment. Members of focus groups are usually selected because they have personal knowledge about or expertise in a particular topic. The leader of a focus group facilitates a group discussion by asking members several general questions on the topic.

Example of a Needs Assessment Using Focus Groups

The United Way of Central Carolinas (2003) conducted a needs assessment focusing on eliminating disparities in social services. To "put its arms around" the complexity of the disparities issue, the group solicited input from the broader community. It convened thirteen "learning conversations" with community members and service providers to better understand disparities and to identify strategies in practice to eliminate them. They also facilitated four problem analysis sessions with community stakeholders to answer three basic questions: What are the precursors to disparities? What are the consequences of not addressing them? and Where can we, as a community, most appropriately intervene?

Arrange Community and Other Public Forums

Community forums are similar to focus groups in that a fairly open selection process is used to bring people together to discuss a topic of interest to all of them, such as new or improved housing or fighting crime. This open selection process can be a special invitation to selected members of the community or a more open invitation to the entire community with a public announcement informing people of the upcoming community forum and its purpose. Participants are likely to belong to the same community or neighborhood, and the topic is likely to focus on an issue that has broad implications that affect large numbers of people.

Example of a Community Forum on the Growing Mortgage Foreclosure Rate

The local newspaper wrote a series of articles on the growing rate of foreclosure among homeowners, particularly in lower-income neighborhoods. After that, a housing assistance agency decided to pursue this need further in one of these neighborhoods. It held a community forum to openly discuss the problem and to determine the extent to which it was a concern of residents. Along with a presentation of the results of the newspaper series and an open discussion of the problem, agency personnel handed out a confidential questionnaire on foreclosures for affected residents to fill out about themselves or close friends. Some of the questions asked were the following:

- What kinds of loans did you/they purchase?
- What were the interest rates and other charges in the mortgages?
- Did you/they feel that the rates were unusually high or unfair?
- How much down payment was required?
- What circumstances led to the foreclosures for individual families?
- What kinds of help do they want?

Observations

Observations are another approach for assessing the need for a program. Social workers regularly depend on their observational skills in practice, such as when visiting clients in their homes. The nonverbal communication of clients, in particular, is often considered as important as their verbal communication. Observational evaluations use all of the senses, particularly sight and hearing, to collect data about a program and the needs it intends to address. Observations focus on what can be seen or heard, especially the behaviors of people. Behavior includes any number of things, such as a verbal comment or nonverbal expression, a conversation between two or more people, body movements, and physical contact between people.

Windshield surveys are one form of observation in which an individual new to a neighborhood drives through it to gain information (Shuster & Goeppinger, 1996). A windshield survey is usually structured such that the observers know what they are looking for. Usually these observations focus on the physical aspects of a neighborhood, such as types of housing, physical conditions of housing, street conditions, commercial entities, people who are out and their activities, and other observable characteristics.

Some Guidelines for a Windshield Tour of an Agency's Neighborhood

Kelly Koney (consultant to Council for Children's Rights, Charlotte, NC, personal communication, 2002) provides the following guidelines for a windshield tour:

1. Keep your observations objective.
2. Observe what can influence how a client uses the agency's services.

   - Is there a nearby bus stop?
   - Is there an easily accessible parking lot?
   - How safe is it to walk around?
   - Is this an affluent neighborhood that may intimidate some lower-income people?

3. Is the agency located in a residential neighborhood? Are there mostly houses, apartments, or businesses? What are the conditions of the buildings, streets, sidewalks?
4. What types of people are out? What are they doing? What are their facial expressions toward you and others?

An important variation in observation studies is whether the evaluator participates in the activities or events being observed. Sometimes participant observation is used, which is unstructured observation involving the evaluator as a participant. A participant-observer role helps the evaluator become more of an insider who observes people and their social context without drawing excessive attention to his or her presence. Participant observers are likely to use fairly unstructured interviewing methods and unstructured observations in their data collection (e.g., Patton, 1987).

Example of a Needs Assessment Using Participant Observation

An MSW student (Jordan, 2005) wanted to evaluate the extent to which collaboration occurred in decision making of teams of collaborative agencies meeting at a child advocacy center. She used the participant-observation method to collect data on the leadership styles of team leaders and the activities evident in the team meetings. She chose to observe a random sample of client cases discussed by the teams at each meeting. Leadership style was defined and measured as of four fairly distinct types: telling, selling, participating, and delegating (Hersey & Blanchard, 1977). Participating and delegating styles reflected a more collaborative leadership style. Jordan's thesis was that the leadership styles were related to such activities as number of information disclosures, number of team agreements toward action steps, and number of team recommendations.

An example of how one evaluator took on the participant-observation role in a needs assessment of the stigma problems of people with mental retardation was partially revealed in several activities that he participated in with these participants once they informed him of their comfort with his presence (Dudley, 1983). The activities provided firsthand exposure to some stigma problems embedded in social situations and facilitated more open sharing of reports of stigma problems:

- Dancing with the people being studied
- Eating with them at restaurants
- Riding public transportation with them
- Joining them for visits at their home
- Sitting with them at their workstation at a sheltered workshop

- Double-dating
- Talking with them or listening to their conversations at various social occasions

An important caveat for the participant is to minimize or avoid any interference with the behaviors being observed. This requires a balance between being able to participate enough to become an insider but not too much so as to create unnecessary reactivity. A drawback to participant observation is that it takes a much greater amount of time to build rapport and to gain acceptance from those being observed before fully concentrating on data collection. This initial period is a time in which such things as informed consent issues and the evaluator's role can be clarified and supported. This method also usually takes additional time during the data collection period to obtain a saturation of types of behaviors that reflect the many possible variations that could be key to a special area of need. In the example on stigma, it is evident that observations occurred during a variety of activities to obtain a saturation of various types of stigma expressed with a wide range of familiar people and strangers in several different social situations.

Using a Combination of Approaches

Many needs assessments use multiple methods of data collection to capture a picture of a community from several different perspectives and formats. Actually, multi-method needs assessments are the best approach for producing the most accurate assessment. For example, two or more data sources can be compared or a source of qualitative data can supplement a quantitative source. Considering the variety of approaches described previously, a comprehensive needs assessment could, for example, involve obtaining demographic data from the U.S. Census or from a local health department, administering a questionnaire to the population of interest or informant interviews with key neighborhood leaders, observing discussions at neighborhood meetings, and carrying out informal interviews with professionals from social agencies in the area.

Example of a Multi-Method Needs Assessment

Hymans (2000) reported on a multi-method study in which BSW and nursing students joined together to complete a comprehensive community-wide assessment of a local neighborhood as part of a macro practice course. The goals of the project included understanding community assessment, assessing how a community functions, developing a broader understanding of social work practice, and providing a service to a community. The students used several data collection methods, including interviews with key informants, observations of neighborhood meetings, gathering existing demographic data, reviewing official documents, using mapping tools, conversations with political and religious leaders, and networking with professionals in the area.

PRACTICE AREAS AND NEEDS ASSESSMENTS

Although needs assessments are commonly used to plan new programs, they are much less frequently considered in planning new or expanded practice approaches. Yet needs assessments at the practice level can have some of the same purposes as programs. For example, needs assessments can help in planning new practice areas or approaches by providing information on clients' needs, their perceptions of their needs and prior experiences in addressing them, and their thoughts on how helpful a proposed practice approach appears to be.

Needs-assessment information can also be helpful in investigating any accessibility barriers for a new practice approach. A most effective way to learn more about accessibility barriers is to explore this issue with prospective clients. Psychological and cultural accessibility may be the largest accessibility areas to confront. In this regard, a needs assessment can uncover whether a new practice approach comprises goals, techniques, and lines of questioning that are sensitive to and compatible with particular cultural beliefs of some groups. For example, a practice approach intended to help clients gain new insights into their problems may not be as practical or even relevant to some groups as a training approach that stresses learning new skills.

Similarly, a needs assessment can be a vehicle for learning more about how to craft goals and objectives for a new or expanded practice area. Goals crafted from the provider's perspective may need to be cross-checked by the perspectives of potential recipients. Asking recipients questions about proposed goals and objectives of a practice approach such as the following may help:

1. What do you perceive as realistic goals for yourself?
2. What might be some measurable indicators that your goals are being reached?
3. How important are these goals to you and others in your circles of social support?

Assessments conducted in practice areas, like those conducted for new programs, have several methodological options at their disposal. They can be qualitative or quantitative. Qualitative methods can include in-depth interviews with clients, minimally structured observations, and brief questionnaires with open-ended questions. Pertinent qualitative data for a needs assessment can also be drawn from existing client records and client journals. Family genograms and ecomaps can also be used as assessment tools and can provide visual descriptions of family relationships and complicated connections to external social systems.

Quantitative needs assessments are also frequently used in developing practice areas. Standardized scales are one form of assessment. These scales are used to assess a wide range of needs and issues, such as self-esteem, depression, addictions, family well-being, and other complex and multi-dimensional variables. Several sources of standardized scales are available in social work and related fields (e.g., Fischer & Corcoran, 1994; Ginsberg, 2001; Jordan & Franklin, 2003; Royse, Thyer, Padgett, & Logan, 2006). These scales should have strong validity and reliability. Questionnaires and interviews developed by experienced practitioners are other quantitative tools that can be used.

Example of a Standardized Scale Used in Assessments of Practice

One agency used an anger evaluation scale as a needs-assessment tool in developing a new group approach. This scale helped adolescent clients focus on discussing goals and objectives in this problem area of their behavior (Patrick & Rich, 2004). The individual items of the scale were used to facilitate discussions with clients about the many ramifications and variations in expressions of dysfunctional anger. They also used the scale as a baseline measure of the clients' dysfunctional anger and as an ongoing measure of their anger at different points in their work together. The anger evaluation scale consisted of ten statements on anger using a five-point Likert scale (strongly agree to strongly disagree). Examples of scale items are the following:

- I often get angrier than necessary.
- I usually stay angry for hours.
- As a result of my anger, I use threatening language or gestures.
- I use alcohol or drugs to calm my rage.

STEPS IN CONDUCTING A NEEDS ASSESSMENT

A needs assessment should not be planned and executed in a vacuum so that its results will be well received by all stakeholders. Several steps are important to consider that focus primarily on involving stakeholders from the beginning and incorporating them into each step to the extent possible. Keep in mind the participatory action approach, described in chapter 2, as one guide. Other resources provide additional information on these steps (e.g., Meenaghan, Kilty, & McNutt, 2004).

1. Create a broad-based committee or team to sponsor the assessment. Attempt to include all actual and potential stakeholders. Make sure

that they represent the varying views of their constituencies, including different views and experiences on how the program or practice area should look.

2. Have an extensive discussion with the committee about the pertinent agency policies and the general intent of a proposed program or practice area. General intent can include identifying target groups of clients that you wish to help, general goals for helping them and their families, and initial assumptions about the causes of their problems and possible solutions.

Example of Data Gathering from Different Types of Fathers

A coalition of several local agencies prepared to conduct an assessment of the needs of uninvolved and minimally active fathers and existing services to fathers in the county. Fortunately, a nearby foundation was willing to provide a small grant to complete the study. A strategic-planning firm was enlisted to assist. The coalition proposed to conduct a needs assessment of four subgroups of fathers using multiple methods: fathers living with their very young children, nonresidential fathers who pay child support, nonresidential teen fathers, and fathers with children with special needs. Fathers of special needs children were selected because of the coalition's previous commitment to such children. The other three groups represented fathers perceived to have special needs that could be realistically met by the coalition's effort. Five methods were identified: (1) a series of focus groups with representatives of the four targeted subgroups of fathers, (2) one-on-one interviews with fathers, (3) key informant interviews with pertinent professionals, (4) an assessment of existing agency services to fathers, and (5) further examination of existing U.S. Census data on fathers in their county.

3. Explore funding support for your project and incorporate the ideas of potential funding agencies in your continued articulation of the problem and goals of your project. Also, begin articulating a proposal for obtaining funds. Possible funding supports could be identified earlier in the process in a more general way.

4. Decide on the methods that you will use to conduct your own needs assessment. This is often a firsthand, in-depth study of the community. Possible methods to consider are focus groups, informant interviews, interviews of a sample of prospective recipients, and interviews with existing agency resources and services. Decide whether you need either a professional firm or an individual consultant to help develop your research methodologies.

5. Conduct your needs assessment and compile an easy-to-read report of your findings for your stakeholder committee.
6. Involve all stakeholders in your committee in articulating a proposal for a new program or practice area. Develop the proposal by supplementing and revising any earlier versions of your problem definition and goals on the basis of your needs-assessment results. Then develop a set of general strategies and specific program/practice components that you could implement to achieve your goals.
7. Be sure to consider program/practice interventions at various levels in your general strategies. These could include individual and family services to prospective recipients, group services, community education efforts, advocacy, and new agency policy initiatives that would directly or indirectly support your new program.

The preceding steps are designed especially for a needs assessment of an at-risk group in a city or county. This general outline has been used to conduct a needs assessment with one at-risk group and could be used with other at-risk populations as well, such as teenage mothers with their first baby, recent immigrants from Mexico or Central America, cancer survivors, homeless people without access to adequate housing, and socially isolated elderly lesbian women.

Steps in a Needs Assessment of Caregivers

An evaluation group conducting a needs assessment of family caregivers of older adults defined its own steps for conducting a needs assessment (Kietzman, Scharlach, & Dal Santo, 2004).

1. Describe the current population of caregivers by compiling a descriptive profile.
2. Determine the existing and unmet needs of caregivers by obtaining input from professionals, consumers, and advocates.
3. Inventory existing caregiver resources and services by identifying all programs and services already serving caregivers.
4. Identify service gaps including existing barriers to equitable access to caregiver resources and services by assessing what the gaps and barriers are.
5. Prioritize the identified service needs of caregivers by synthesizing information gathered and ranking the needs.
6. Design a plan for the delivery of caregiver services that reduces identified barriers to access, supplements existing services, and creates new services where none exist, in the most effective and efficient manner possible by implementing a decision-making process that results in a plan of action.

As an exercise, compare the steps of Kietzman, Scharlach, and Dal Santo (2004) to the steps in conducting a needs assessment described just before them in this section. Who might be some of the stakeholders in Kietzman and colleagues' project? How do you think their stakeholders could become more involved in conducting their needs assessment? What would be some of the advantages and disadvantages of adding the participatory action research steps to their needs assessment?

The next chapter considers another important evaluation topic during the planning stage: crafting goals and measurable objectives. It is important to carefully craft goals and objectives before implementing a new program or practice area.

KEY TERMS

Community forums
Conducting interviews
Constructing questionnaires
Data available in social agencies
Focus groups
Governmental studies
Local studies
Logic model
Mapping
Needs assessments
Observations
Participant-observation
Purposes of a needs assessment
Role of policy in informing needs assessments
Secondary research
Steps in conducting a needs assessment
Studies in professional journals and on the Internet
Studies of nonprofit organizations
Using existing data

DISCUSSION QUESTIONS AND ASSIGNMENTS

1. Use the logic model to design a program for older adults who have lost their spouses and are socially isolated, have some chronic medical problems affecting their mobility, and live in multicultural neighborhoods. Begin by finding a needs assessment article or report that identifies some of the needs for this population. Then brainstorm with classmates or other colleagues to identify some ways to meet these interpersonal and mobility needs. Describe a proposed program that addresses many of the needs so that the

adults can maintain their independence and natural supports in their neighborhoods.

2. This is a project for two or more students to complete. Focus on assessing the needs of families in a community context. Conduct an informal, multifaceted needs assessment of families in the community and the resources that already exist to help them. This assignment is partially intended to help you integrate work at several different system levels, especially family and community assessments. Specific suggestions for carrying out this assignment are as follows:

- Attempt to talk with a variety of parents and other adult family members in the community, asking them what they think are the critical needs and problems that families and family members face. Ask for their opinions on how these needs can be met. What types of resources and services are needed, and how can social workers help them overcome the problems they identify? Be sure to explain to them your purpose and your intention to keep all information that they share confidential.

- Consider observing what is happening with the family members (e.g., parents, grandparents, children, teenagers, and babies) that you see. What are they doing, what does their affect seem to communicate, what strengths do they appear to have, and what problems and needs seem evident through your observations?

- If you have difficulty talking with parents and other adult family members because they are unwilling or hesitant, identify and talk with advocates of families in the community, such as community leaders, volunteers, teachers, agency personnel, and other informal leaders.

- Look at the findings of any recently conducted local studies that might reveal something about the needs of families. Consider newspaper articles and community hearings. Explore citywide and countywide studies and the U.S. Census if they offer data that pertain to your particular community.

- Think about and share other ways to learn about the needs of families in the community. Thinking outside of the box is often overlooked in doing an assessment like this.

- After assessing the needs of families, identify and locate social agencies, community centers, churches, schools, day-care centers, businesses, and other organizations in the community and find out how they are attempting to help families or individual family members.

3. Using data from the U.S. Census, investigate the needs of children younger than five years of age in your community. This can be done online at www.census.gov. Select one report and describe what you learn about their needs.

4. Conduct a windshield tour of the neighborhood surrounding your agency or another neighborhood in which a large concentration of your clients live. Use the suggestions in this chapter to help you conduct the assessment. Then share what you learned with the class or agency colleagues.

5. Conduct a needs assessment using the American Factfinder mapping tool available at the U.S. Census website (www.factfinder.census.gov). Use the Thematic Maps tool to view some of the geographic patterns in the census data. Select a city or county of interest to you, identify a data set of the census, and create a map that visually displays data for the city or county.

6. Work in small groups of three to five to complete this project (which can be carried out in conjunction with a policy course and is a variation of an exercise that appeared on the Baccalaureate Social Work Program Directors discussion list).

- Select a community and identify a policy question that highlights an apparent unaddressed need (e.g., Do children need somewhere to go after school? Do teens need something to keep them off the street? Is a domestic violence hotline needed in the community?). You may want to seek assistance in identifying your policy issue from local agencies or funding agencies.

- Once you have identified a policy question, conduct a needs assessment of the local community that provides data to tentatively confirm or refute your initial policy question. One of the questions of your needs assessment can be the policy question that you identified. Other questions can be used to document the suspected need(s) that you have identified.

- Write a policy change proposal that can address the need that you have begun to document. Your proposal should include the following:

  (a) What is the unmet policy reform that is needed?
  (b) How did you discover and document it?
  (c) What do you propose to do to meet this need?
  (d) How can it lead to advocacy for social justice issues?
  (e) Where will you get funding?
  (f) How will you secure other resources (e.g., space, materials)?
  (g) Who will be your staff and volunteers? How will they be paid?
  (h) How will they be recruited and trained?
  (i) What will be your budget?
  (j) What are the limitations or obstacles to implementing your plan? How might these obstacles be overcome?

- A reaction paper of one or two pages can also be requested from each group member reflecting on such questions as, what was difficult? What was fun? What did you learn about the field of policy reform and community-based social work?

REFERENCES

Caliento, K. (2004). Needs assessment for adolescent parents in foster care: Program development. Unpublished manuscript, University of North Carolina at Charlotte.

DePoy, E., & Gilson, S. F. (2003). *Evaluation practice: Thinking and action principles for social work practice.* Pacific Grove, CA: Brooks/Cole-Thomson Learning.

Dudley, J. (1983). *Living with stigma: The plight of the people who we label mentally retarded.* Springfield, IL: Charles Thomas.

Faithfull, S., Cook, K., & Lucas, C. (2005). Palliative care of patients with a primary malignant brain tumor: Case review of service use and support provided. *Palliative Medicine, 19,* 545–550.

Fischer, J., & Corcoran, K. (1994). *Measures for clinical practice: A sourcebook.* New York: Free Press.

Franco, S. (2004). Spirituality among residents at Presbyterian Wesley Care Center. Unpublished manuscript, University of North Carolina at Charlotte.

Ginsberg, L. (2001). *Social work evaluation: Principles and methods.* Boston: Allyn & Bacon.

Goffman, E. (1961). *Asylums: Essays on the social situation of mental patients and other inmates.* Garden City, NY: Anchor Books.

Hersey, P., & Blanchard, K. H. (1977). *The management of organizational behavior.* Upper Saddle River, NJ: Prentice Hall.

Hillier, A. (2007). Why social work needs mapping. *Journal of Social Work Education, 43*(2), 205–221.

Hymans, D. J. (2000). Teaching BSW students community practice using an interdisciplinary neighborhood needs assessment project. *Journal of Baccalaureate Social Work, 5*(2), 81–92.

Jordan, A. M. (2005). Development of a multidisciplinary team assessment tool for a child advocacy center. Unpublished manuscript, University of North Carolina at Charlotte.

Jordan, C., & Franklin, C. (Eds.). (2003). *Clinical assessment for social workers: Quantitative and qualitative methods* (2nd ed.). Chicago: Lyceum Books.

Kietzman, K. G., Scharlach, A. E., & Dal Santo, T. S. (2004). Local needs assessment and planning efforts for family caregivers: Findings and recommendations. *Journal of Gerontological Social Work, 42*(3/4), 39–60.

Line, S. (2007). Harrisburg parks and recreation. Harrisburg, NC: Harrisburg Parks and Recreation.

Marlow, C. R. (2011). *Research methods for generalist social work* (5th ed.). Belmont, CA: Brooks/Cole.

Meenaghan, T. M., Kilty, K. M., & McNutt, J. G. (2004). *Social policy analysis and practice.* Chicago: Lyceum Books.

Nolan, T. C. (2006). Outcomes for a transitional living program serving LGBTQ youth in New York City. *Child Welfare, 85*(2), 385–405.

O'Donnell, J. (1999). Involvement of African American fathers in kinship foster care services. *Social Work, 44*(5), 428–441.

Patrick, J., & Rich, C. (2004). Anger management taught to adolescents with an experiential object relations approach. *Child and Adolescent Social Work Journal, 21*(1), 85–100.

Patton, M. (1987). *How to use evaluative methods in evaluation.* Newbury Park, CA: Sage.

Ross, P. H., Lipsey, M. W., & Freeman, H. E. (2004). *Evaluation: A systematic approach* (7th ed.). Thousands Oaks, CA: Sage.

Royse, D., Thyer, B., Padgett, D., & Logan, T. (2006). *Program evaluation: An introduction* (4th ed.). Belmont CA: Brooks/Cole.

Shuster, G. F., & Goeppinger, J. (1996). Community as client: Using the nursing process to promote health. In M. Stanhope & J. Lancaster (Eds.), *Community health nursing: Promoting health of aggregates, families and individuals* (pp. 289–314). St. Louis: Mosby.

Stewart, B. (2005). Domestic violence needs assessment. Unpublished manuscript, University of North Carolina at Charlotte.

United Way of Central Carolinas. (2003). Retrieved December 12, 2012, from http://ui .uncc.edu/sites/default/files/pdf/2011_UW_Needs_Assessment_Full_Report.pdf.

Weinman, M. L., Buzi, R. S., & Smith, R. B. (2005). Addressing risk behaviors, service needs, and mental health issues in programs for young fathers. *Families in Society, 86*(2), 261–266.

Williams, C. (2006). A crisis intervention needs assessment. Unpublished manuscript, University of North Carolina at Charlotte.

Wolochwianski, J. (2005). A needs assessment for a new program for Hispanic child witnesses of domestic violence in Mecklenburg County. Unpublished manuscript, University of North Carolina at Charlotte.

Women's Commission. (2005). Adult domestic violence pretest/posttest. Charlotte, NC: Author.

Chapter 7

Crafting Goals and Objectives

The ultimate question of importance is, what is the intervention intended to accomplish?

Frequently, planning a new program or practice area involves preparing a grant proposal for funding, and this proposal can be an important exercise in describing what the intervention is supposed to look like. The proposal includes many elements of relevance to an evaluation, including the following:

- Program goals and objectives
- Services and technologies for helping clients reach goals
- A budget
- An evaluation plan to determine whether the program is effective

An evaluation plan, the last component mentioned, is typically required in most grant proposals. Unfortunately, such a plan is often largely incidental to the program construction process of many proposals. What often happens is that it tends to be an add-on prepared by someone in tune with research methods who is not directly involved in the construction of the program; the primary motivation for preparing the evaluation plan is to satisfy the funding agency.

In any event, evaluation considerations are extremely important to think about and plan for while a program is in the development stage. The logic model helps explain why. As described in chapter 6, the logic model recommends that the input, implementation, output, and outcome elements be logically connected. These stages and their respective elements need to be carefully thought out in relation to one another, and this all needs to begin in the planning stage. This chapter examines two critical components of program and practice interventions: goals and objectives. Goals and measurable objectives are formulated during the planning or input stage, when a program or practice area is under construction. Goals and objectives provide a central anchor or reference point for conducting most evaluations.

The goals and objectives of a new intervention need focused attention. Some pertinent questions are the following:

- What are the goals of the intervention?
- What are the measurable objectives crafted for each of these goals?
- Are the goals and objectives logically linked to clients' problems, unmet needs, and underlying causes?

• Is there a logical link between the goals and objectives and how the intervention is implemented to reach these goals?

Helping an Agency Develop a New Program with an Evaluation Infrastructure

A graduate student devised the following set of questions to guide her while helping her agency integrate an evaluation component into a new proposed program:

1. What is the problem that you want to solve or tackle? What do you believe are the causes of this problem?
2. Who are the people experiencing this problem that you want to help?
3. What are your overall goals for solving this problem? How long will it take to reach each goal?
4. What intervention strategy do you plan to use to meet your goals? Describe your intervention plan. How will it contribute to meeting goals?
5. Identify the specific indicators (measurable objectives) that will tell you that you have reached your goals. List as many as possible.
6. What resources do you have that will help you conduct an evaluation?
7. What constraints may hinder you in conducting an evaluation?

GOALS FOR PROGRAM AND PRACTICE INTERVENTIONS

Every program and practice intervention should have a set of goals that provide direction and an end result to pursue for clients. Basic questions about goals are the following: Where is this program/practice area going? What do we want to accomplish? How feasible is it to have success in achieving this goal? What approaches are known to work in helping clients reach these goals?

Although having goals is something that every agency intervention should have, most staff members and some agency administrators may not be well versed in them. This can result in the interventions spinning their wheels, going in unproductive directions, and wasting valuable resources. In other instances, agency interventions may have goals, but goals that are too vague to provide any direction or benchmarks for measuring progress. Examples of some vague goals that are used in helping clients are the following:

• Becoming more independent
• Resolving conflicts in a parent-child relationship

- Becoming an empowered family
- Being discharged from the hospital
- Increasing positive social behaviors
- Reducing antisocial behaviors
- Improving performance in school
- Successfully working in a competitive job
- Keeping the youth safe
- Alleviating crises
- Reuniting a client with her or his family

Example of a Frequently Ignored Program Goal

During the past several decades, sheltered workshops have been considered an essential type of vocational program in the array of program offerings available for people with mental retardation. This has been the case in both community-based and institutional systems. A major goal for most sheltered workshops is to prepare people for the competitive workforce. Sheltered workshops are protected work sites for people with disabilities that employ them in assembling consumer goods like the airplane headsets used for watching movies or small hardware items like small bolts sealed in a plastic bag and sold in hardware stores. Yet these programs are often, in reality, driven by two implicit goals that are in direct tension with the major goal. The implicit goals are to find contracts of any kind to occupy the clients in the workshops and to provide a safe environment for them during the daytime hours. Because the implicit goals are important, sheltered workshops seldom succeed in accomplishing the major goal of preparing participants for competitive employment (e.g., Dudley & Schatz, 1985).

CHARACTERISTICS OF GOALS

Measurable goals are critical to any successful program or individual practice intervention. They are important because they provide an intervention with a direction to pursue and an outcome to reach. Without goals, an intervention could be an aimless effort that does not seem to go anywhere important. Goals have many other characteristics that are important to understand as well. Goals are needed at all system levels. Goals are oriented to a time period. They are expected to be relevant to the intervention to which they are linked, and they should be responsive to the needs of the clients whom they serve. They can have one dimension or be considered in combination with other related goals. Some focus on program implementation while others focus on the outcomes of clients.

All System Levels

Social work has the potential to operate at all system levels, including the individual, family, group, community, organization, and policy. Primary and secondary prevention are preferred to tertiary prevention, because problems that can be avoided or headed off at an early stage will bring less harm and cost less to achieve. Yet most programs and practice interventions that governmental agencies are willing to fund focus on tertiary issues or treatment. Treatment interventions usually provide help once a problem is fully evident and has obvious adverse effects on clients' lives. Unfortunately, government agencies tend to be unwilling to invest in funding or sponsoring interventions until clients reach this tertiary stage. Nevertheless, goals can be formulated at all system levels, even though goals at macro levels such as community and policy need to be given much greater consideration in most social work circumstances.

Time-Oriented

Goals are oriented to a time period, for the short run, middle run, or long run. Short-term goals can be helpful as stepping-stones to mid-range goals, and mid-range goals are intended to lead to long-term ones. Although short-term goals are important, long-term goals are ultimately most important because they reflect the outcomes expected of successfully functioning people. For example, a short-term goal for a client with an addiction problem may be to no longer desire drugs while attending a drug treatment program, a mid-range goal may be to live drug free in a halfway house for six months, and the long-term goal may be total withdrawal from drug use and drug culture. Similarly, a short-term goal for an ex-offender may be to stay out of trouble and regularly report on his or her activities to a probation officer during the probation period, while the long-term goal is to discontinue committing crimes altogether. Later in the book, we will discuss how agency evaluations tend to give primary emphasis to short-term goals and overlook the mid-range and long-term ones.

Linked to the Intervention

The goals of an intervention should be a logical outgrowth of the intervention. After having a reasonably thorough description of the intervention, one should have a good grasp of what it intends to accomplish. The goals of the program should logically and realistically reflect this. For example, if a program involves counseling, its goals are likely to reflect some form of psychological or interpersonal improvement in the client, whereas a program designed to refer clients to other agencies is likely to have goals related to connecting clients with the referral agencies and using their services.

Responsive to the Clients' Needs

Social workers always advocate for clients in some form or another. We want our interventions to make a difference in our clients' lives and prefer to involve them to the greatest extent possible in the decisions that will help that to happen. While program and practice interventions need to be responsive to client needs, so does an evaluation. A bold way to increase client participation is to involve them in the evaluation as it progresses. For example, the participatory action approach, described in chapter 2, is designed to do this.

Interrelated with Other Goals

Programs and practice interventions can have one central goal or several interrelated ones. It often depends on what the problem is, what policies are being addressed, the expectations of the agency provider, and the resources available. Interrelated goals are important because some goals cannot be effectively addressed without considering their interdependence with other goals. For example, a welfare reform program may emphasize one goal: clients' obtaining of jobs. Or the program could be more comprehensive, giving fairly equal emphasis to two or three interrelated goals, such as obtaining a decent-paying job, securing day care for the client's children, and securing a safe home for the family. A program that has a set of interrelated goals often tends to be more effective in helping clients than one with a single goal.

Focused on Either Programs or Client Outcomes

Goals can focus on any number of things, including clients, staff members, and others. Posavac and Carey (1997) identify three types of goals: setting up a program, implementing a program, and determining whether the program is successful in helping the clients meet their goals or outcomes. All three types of goals are interdependent. Outcome goals for clients are the ultimate reason for having a program. However, outcome goals depend on prior success with implementation goals and planning goals.

Example of Types of Goals (Posavac & Carey, 1997)

Planning goals: Goals that are involved in setting up a program (e.g., locating a satellite facility site for the program, hiring a team of five clinical supervisors). These goals are carried out by service providers.

Intermediate or implementation goals: Goals involved in executing or carrying out the program (e.g., admitting twenty-five qualified clients, providing weekly supervision of each direct-care worker). These goals are also carried out by service providers.

Outcome goals: Goals for clients to achieve as they complete the program (e.g., learn communication skills that help express anger verbally). Outcome goals are primarily carried out by clients.

LIMITATIONS OF GOALS

Some efforts to craft goals for interventions have challenges that should be noted. These challenges overlap in some ways. They are not always easy to measure, they can be too theoretical or global, and they can be unobservable. Also, some goals are only discovered after a program has been implemented.

Not Easy to Measure

Many goals do not easily convert into measurable forms without losing some of their properties or meaning. A severe case of anxiety, for example, is a complex psychiatric condition to diagnose and measure. This is particularly the case when overcoming anxiety becomes a goal of a clinical program. In this instance, we often want to know not just whether the client has an anxiety disorder but also the severity of the anxiety and what constitutes improvement or decline. In practice, changes in a severe anxiety disorder can be most easily detected by a clinical social worker who uses qualitative questions individualized to a particular client's sources of anxiety and other circumstances. Obtaining a standardized quantitative measure of improvement in an anxiety disorder appears to be more challenging. However, existing standardized scales with established properties of validity and reliability may be another way to measure whether such a goal has been reached, even though the scales may miss some subtle but important properties of this psychiatric condition.

Other goals may be fairly easy to convert into measurable forms but difficult to measure practically. In this case, methodologies are sometimes lacking for obtaining valid data, such as when reliance depends on a client's self-reporting. Many types of behaviors that are considered personal and private can be intentionally distorted. Clients typically underreport alcohol and drug consumption. Reporting of abuse by perpetrators and victims is also challenging to measure, as is accurate disclosure of safe sexual practices like condom use and number of sexual partners.

Too Theoretical

Many program and practice interventions are constructed from an abstract model that begins with theoretical notions of goals. Such theoretical goals are difficult to measure empirically. For example, many mentoring programs for young African American teenage males offer a surrogate father for a parent who is missing or unavailable in the biological family. These programs typically choose outcome goals for the teenagers such as developing a healthy male identity, preparing to become an active father, and contributing to the well-being of the African American community. Although several overt indicators of the theoretical notions may come to mind, measuring them as they were intended in their theoretical form becomes more challenging.

Too Global

Other goals of interventions begin as global outcomes that are expected in the larger community or society, such as reducing the number of homicides or drug trafficking. One small program may be able to address these larger social problems in very limited terms, but many other causal factors beyond the reach of the program are difficult to influence. In other words, a global goal may be very difficult to link to one small program focused on a small number of people and their immediate social circumstances.

An example of a global goal for a community program is reducing the number of divorces in a community of 75,000 people. The community group First Things First, in Gastonia, North Carolina, established a premarital group-counseling program for couples sponsored by local churches, synagogues, and mosques. The hope was that the program would have an impact, however small, on the divorce rate. However, they needed help in considering less global goals, such as participants staying together, particularly during the challenging years of early marriage. Reducing the number of divorces in their community, while relevant and noble, is something that the group had to admit was much bigger than anything it could tackle on its own. The group came to realize that the divorce rate has multiple causes, many of which were beyond its influence and ability to change.

Unobservable

Many goals that are important for programs to influence are internal aspects of human functioning, including people's attitudes toward themselves and others, their feelings, and their cognitive mental processes. Take racial attitudes, for example. A program may be set up to improve its members' attitudes toward one another in a culturally diverse community. Such a community could have, for example, African American, Latino, and white members who have lived there for several years, along with recent immigrants from Mexico, Central America, and Iran. In this case, positive racial and ethnic attitudes could be a crucial ingredient in helping such a community function well. Racial attitudes have been measured numerous times in the past, primarily using surveys. Yet we know that such surveys have many limitations: they often do not elicit totally honest reporting of attitudes, particularly deep-seated attitudes that are difficult for a person to express when faced with self-perceived racial conflicts or threats. A challenge for such programs is to find more accurate, in-depth ways to uncover these deeply seated and distorted thought processes and how they can change over time.

Unintended Goals

Without question, it is essential to identify the goals of a program during the planning stage. This often takes place as part of a larger effort to describe the purpose of a program and the expected outcomes. Nevertheless, unanticipated or unintended goals can also emerge once a program is implemented and may become as important as the initial goals. When this occurs, which can be often, it is recommended that the new goals, if relevant, be added to the existing ones but not replace them. In this case, measurable objectives should be quickly crafted for them and evaluation data collected as part of an overall evaluation plan.

Identifying unintended goals during program implementation is helpful. Program providers can then address them by adding a new program component or giving new emphasis to collaboration and referrals to other agencies. For example, adding a special referral component to a program is important if an unanticipated client problem is identified that is related to the existing goals but that falls outside of the program's focus and resources.

Unanticipated goals can easily emerge as staff members become more familiar with their clients and their needs. For example, conversations with some teen parents in a family-planning program revealed that some teen mothers viewed pregnancy as a "prize" if the father was popular or a well-known athlete (Dudley, 2007). This was considered a prize regardless of whether they were dating him. Such a discovery by a program could result in expanding its attention to this faulty teen viewpoint and to the importance of the father's responsibilities; it could also result in the program targeting such popular guys for counseling and education.

CRAFTING MEASURABLE OBJECTIVES

As indicated at the beginning of the chapter, every intervention should have a set of goals to provide it with direction and an end result. A second principle naturally follows this one: goals should be accompanied by specific measures or indicators that can inform whether they are being reached. These specific indicators are measurable objectives. The educator Mager (1997) describes a concise and entertaining way to learn how to develop measurable objectives within educational settings; his writings are primarily concerned with measuring students' performance in the classroom. With some modifications, Mager's conceptual material has been applied by the author to evaluations in the human services.

Defining Measurable Objectives

Measurable objectives are statements that identify indicators of whether a goal is reached by one client or a set of clients. Let's first look at measurable objectives for clients at the practice level. Typically, each goal has several measurable objectives, as each objective may reflect only one small aspect of the broader goal. A social worker developing measurable objectives should begin by selecting a specific time in the future (e.g., two weeks, six months) and imagining what would be expected of a client at that time and how it will be manifested in measurable objective terms. For example, the social worker might determine that the goal is to improve a client's parenting skills. In this case, the goal can be that the client will have improved parenting skills with a particular child six months from now. Next the social worker and client can think of several indicators of improved parenting skills six months in the future. They may come up with such items as verbally (not physically) expressing anger toward the child nine out of ten times, or setting a time limit when permitting the child to go out to play.

A Goal and Five Measurable Objectives for Mr. Lopez

Goal: Mr. Lopez, a frail elderly adult, will remain as independent as possible in a minimally supervised living facility in his community.

Measurable objectives in eight months: Mr. Lopez will

- Wash his own clothes once a week
- Attend all of his meals in the dining hall
- After reminders, take his required medications in the morning, at noon, and before retiring
- Attend one or more social events offered by the facility each week
- Attend the religious services of his church in the community at least twice a month if a volunteer is available to drive him to the church

As you can see in the example of Mr. Lopez, the goal to remain as independent as possible is rather vague and impossible to accurately measure as stated. In this case, Mr. Lopez is living in a minimally supervised living facility and must remain fairly independent to avoid placement in a living facility for more dependent older adults. Remaining independent would mean different things to different people, so this goal needs specificity that is most relevant to Mr. Lopez's functioning at the facility. As the five measurable objectives indicate, independence for Mr. Lopez refers mostly to taking care of his clothes, eating in a dining hall, taking his medications, having some social contact, and participating in the religious life of his church.

Macro Goals

Goals can focus on larger systems and macro practice as well. Two goals that focus on the impact of community-level interventions are described next. The first focuses on cleaning up a neighborhood and the second attempts to promote better cross-cultural relationships. Each of these goals has three measurable objectives.

Goal: Neighborhood Volunteers Will Improve the Appearance of a Neighborhood

Measurable objectives:

1. Neighborhood volunteers will clean at least twelve empty lots.
2. Neighborhood volunteers will remove at least twenty-five abandoned cars from the neighborhood within six months.
3. Ten neighborhood volunteers will sweep targeted areas of the neighborhood on one Saturday morning in February.

Goal: Southeast Asian and African American Neighbors Will Improve Their Relationships with Each Other in the Logan Neighborhood.

Measurable objectives:

1. The Logan neighborhood will increase the number of requests for the Human Relations Council to become involved in resolving neighborhood conflicts in February over January.
2. The Logan neighborhood will decrease the number of police calls resulting from neighborhood conflicts in February so that they are less than January.
3. After electing co-leaders (one African American and the other Southeast Asian) for a neighborhood block, the Logan neighborhood will sponsor (gather) neighbors for one block party on a Saturday that involves at least 25 percent attendance from each racial group.

Writing measurable objectives is known as "crafting." Crafting suggests that this task is as much an art as a science. Essentially, there is not one perfect way to craft objectives. Each set of measurable objectives crafted for a goal can be uniquely applied to a particular client or group of clients. Several different outcomes may be considered and the wording can vary widely. Ideally, objectives are formulated after extensive discussion between the social worker and the client about what the client wants to achieve and what seems realistic. The worker is primarily a guide in helping clients articulate what makes sense to them and, at times, suggesting various ways to state the objective.

Example of Measurable Client Objectives in a Palliative Care Facility

Needham and Newbury (2004) conducted a study in a hospice agency of explicit goals (or measurable objectives) crafted by the patients, caregivers, and staff members as part of a clinical audit. Over six months, 79 percent of the patients set goals, along with 63 percent of the caregivers and 98 percent of the admissions staff. Examples of patient goals include being able to eat properly, being able to get out of bed, being able to be well, not having to take drugs. Of the ninety-seven patients who set goals, one-third were completed directly by the patients and two-thirds required assistance from staff members.

Objectives for Clients, Not Staff Members

Sometimes students and others mistakenly uses the term *measurable objective* to measure outcomes for service providers, such as, "The social worker will provide a psychoeducational group service for ten sessions to clients," or "The social worker will help the client find a job." These are examples of measurable objectives that focus on staff interventions instead of client outcomes. The problem with this is that both the clients' goals and measurable objectives should ultimately depend upon the clients' own actions, not the staff members'. Staff members may have activities to carry out in assisting the clients with these objectives but they should not replace them.

Let's return to the example of Mr. Lopez, the frail elderly adult mentioned earlier who wanted to remain as independent as he could in a minimally supervised community facility. His goal was to remain as independent as he could and the measurable objectives or indicators that he had reached his goal included washing his own clothes once a week, attending all of his meals in the dining hall, and attending the religious services of his church in the community. All of these are measurable objectives that involve Mr. Lopez as the subject. Mr. Lopez would have to do these things himself if he was to meet his goal of remaining independent.

It is true that staff assistance is often necessary before clients can do their part. For example, Mr. Lopez could not wash his clothes unless a washing machine and dryer were available to him and possibly a staff member would need to teach him how to use these machines. Likewise, Mr. Lopez would not be able to attend meals in the dining hall if the dining hall was not physically accessible or if he needed a walker to get there and none was available. Similarly, attending religious services was ultimately up to Mr. Lopez to do. He would have to get up on time, bathe and dress himself, and be ready for a ride to the church, but he would also need a volunteer from his church to provide him with the ride.

Some principles to remember in correctly crafting measurable objectives for clients:

- Both goals and measurable objectives of clients involve the client as the subject who is to carry out the activity.
- The only difference between goals and objectives is that goals are general and cannot be measured; measurable objectives are specific and are, as indicated, measurable.
- While activities of staff members are sometimes needed, they are not the recipients of services; they are only there in an assistance role to the clients.
- It is true that if the staff members do not fulfill their obligations, clients may not be able to fulfill theirs. In this case, it would become a staff problem that needs to be addressed, not a client problem.

Three Properties: Performance, Conditions, and Criteria

Measurable objectives have three properties (Mager, 1997): performance, conditions, and criteria. A performance is always necessary to have in an objective, while conditions and criteria are often helpful but not required. Usually, conditions and criteria provide details that are helpful in understanding the objective.

Three Properties in a Measurable Objective

Performance: what a person is expected to do

Conditions: prior circumstances or conditions needed before performance can be expected

Criteria: standards of acceptable performance reflected in such things as speed, accuracy, or quality

Performance. A performance is an action that a client is expected to take. The performance is required in every measurable objective because it describes the outcome that is sought. It should be an overt, observable action word, rather than an abstract or covert word.

For practice, attempt to identify the words in the following list that are observable or overt:

- Write
- Count
- Understand
- Ask
- Accept
- Attend

You were correct if you selected write, count, ask, and attend because each is an overt "action" word that you can observe. Any of these words could be selected as the performance in a measurable objective because they can be observed as happening or not. In contrast, the word *understand* is not overt or readily measurable. How do we know when our client understands something? Usually we have to ask a question and the answer can reveal understanding. So we could replace the word *understand* with *correctly answer* as the performance. In this case, we would be able to either hear or observe on a questionnaire whether the client gives the correct answer. *Accept* is another abstract word that social workers often use, and while it is an important term for social work, it can be easily misunderstood because it can mean different things to different people. Can you come up with another word that is like *accept* but overt or observable?

Some Suggested Performance Words to Use in Measurable Objectives

Choose	Find	Quote
Distinguish	Identify	Repeat
List	Recite	Spell
Read	Speak	Give
Restate	Tell	Match
Separate	Summarize	Select
Sort	Name	State
Write	Eat	Use
Attend	Ask	Call

Sometimes, a performance needs an overt indicator, a word or phrase that is added after a performance to help make it more observable. For example, "comply with instructions" is the performance in the measurable objective "The child will comply with instructions given by her mother." This performance may not be clear to some people, so an overt indicator can help. In this example, adding the overt indicator "follow them" helps. The objective can now read, "The child will comply with instructions (follow them) given by her mother."

"Provide documentation" is another example of a performance needing an overt indicator in the objective "The client will provide documentation of his citizenship (show his social security card) to receive food stamps." In this case, "show his social security card" is the overt indicator that indicates the documentation that he will provide.

Condition.   A condition is the second important factor to consider in crafting measurable objectives. A condition refers to a prior observable circumstance that takes place before a performance can occur. Conditions often begin with words such as if, after, as, during, when, while, with, or unless. For example, a measurable objective for a student enrolled in an evaluation course could be, "After identifying an agency's program goal, a student will write three objectives that will measure whether the goal has been reached." In this example, the condition that needs to occur before a performance is expected is "after identifying an agency's program goal." Now let's go further with this objective. What is the performance? You are correct if you decide the performance is "write." When you think about it, it makes sense that a goal has to be identified before you can write objectives for it. You could also say that the performance is "write three objectives." However, the word *three* is actually a criterion for the performance. So you would more correctly say that the performance is "write" or "write objectives."

Sometimes conditions are located in a measurable objective statement after rather than before the performance. For example, in the measurable objective "The client will say 'please' when asking for anything to be passed to him while eating dinner," can you identify the condition in this case? The performance?

You are correct if you identified the condition as "when asking for anything to be passed to him." Another condition is "while eating dinner." Both conditions make sense with this objective, as it would not make sense for the client to say "please" without asking for something to be passed or if he is not eating.

Criteria.   The third property often included in a measurable objective is criteria. Like conditions, criteria are not required in an objective but usually can add helpful details to define the objective. A criterion is a standard of acceptable performance, and is sometimes referred to as a quality that is expected in the performance. For example, an objective may be crafted for a client such as, "The client will attend Alcoholics Anonymous meetings." A criterion can be added to this objective to give it more detail and clarity: "The client will attend AA meetings weekly for twelve months." In this example, the criterion "weekly for twelve months" is added to the expanded version of the objective.

Criteria can describe any of the following qualities of the performance:

- Duration (e.g., six months)
- Frequency (e.g., five job interviews)
- Repetition (e.g., eight of ten times)
- Degree of accuracy or progress (e.g., 70 percent or more correct answers)
- Speed (e.g., complete the assignment in ten minutes)

Examples of Performance, Condition, and Criteria

The subsequent goal for clients has three measurable objectives and was crafted for several clients receiving services in a mental health outpatient program. Can you identify the performance, condition, and criteria in each measurable objective? (The answers are in appendix C.)

Goal: Clients will increase compliance with medication appointments.

Objective A: If clients wish to remember the dates and times of medication appointments, they will write the time of their next appointment on a calendar.

Objective B: If transportation is needed to appointments, clients will call to arrange for it at least two days prior to the appointment.

Objective C: If clients are ill or otherwise cannot come to their medication appointment, they will call and reschedule their appointment more than twenty-four hours before the missed appointment.

Although the chapter has thoroughly covered how to craft goals and measurable objectives, it has not considered how to involve stakeholders. Martin and Kettner (1996) offer a simple three-step approach to include stakeholders:

Step 1: A focus group representing the stakeholders is convened and informed about the most recent, widely accepted research and conceptual frameworks, theories, evaluations, and practice experiences pertinent to a proposed program. In addition, the social problem to be addressed by the program and assumptions about this social problem are made explicit and discussed.

Step 2: The focus group is asked to identify, discuss, and consider as many goals and measurable objectives for the proposed program as it can.

Step 3: The group arrives at a consensus on the best goals and measurable objectives.

Exercise: Involving Clients in Crafting Measurable Objectives

Create a fictitious client with a presenting problem and role-play a social worker and the client exchanging ideas about what to do about this problem. After the problem has been identified and thoroughly assessed, have the social worker help the client identify a goal and two measurable objectives in the client's own words. The worker's role is to ask questions that will help the client identify his or her goal and measurable objectives in his or her own words. Some helpful questions to possibly ask the client are:

1) What will it look like when you have reached your goal?
2) How will you know that the goal has been reached?
3) What will you be able to do or what will you be able to see when you have reached your goal?

SUMMARY OF PRINCIPLES

In brief, measurable objectives are statements that usually have four elements: conditions, subject, performance, and criteria. The subject and performance are necessary in every objective, while conditions and criteria are not required but are usually preferred. The subject is the client in most cases. The performance is the action verb describing what the client will be expected to do at the point in time when the goal is reached. Conditions, such as interventions by the social worker, are necessary to implement before the performance or action verb can occur. The criteria provide a standard of acceptable performance and could take the form of one of the standards introduced earlier (e.g., duration, frequency, degree of accuracy).

Several principles about goals and measurable objectives have been discussed that are important in crafting a measurable objective:

- Goals and objectives should be useful and have meaning to both the client and the agency.
- Objectives, like goals, are outcomes, not means.
- Crafting objectives is partially an art; there is no one perfect way to craft them.
- An overt indicator is a word or phrase added to the statement in parentheses after a performance to help make the performance more observable.
- Conditions typically are located in a measurable objective statement before the performance, though they can be located after the performance.

- Criteria are often needed in addition to the performance to indicate the level of quality of the performance expected.
- Criteria refer to a special quality of the performance (e.g., duration, accuracy, speed).

Exercise Regarding a Short-Term Goal and Its Measurable Objectives

Identify the performance, conditions, and criteria in each of the following measurable objectives crafted for survivors of domestic violence (Fenske, 2006) (answers are in appendix C):

Goal: Clients will decrease their depressive symptoms.

Measurable Objective A: When feeling depressed, clients journal their feelings, thoughts, and behavior 80 percent of the time.
Measurable Objective B: At the outset of depressive feelings, clients demonstrate (carry out) one positive coping skill one out of three times.

Additional suggestions can help craft a measurable objective statement:

- List only one objective in each statement or sentence.
- Clients are usually the subject of the statement, unless the focus is on staff members.
- Think of the performance as the action word and not the words that follow it.
- Leave out of the measurable objective the intervention used by the staff member to reach the goal; it only tends to clutter it.
- A condition can sometimes be confused with either criteria or the subject. Therefore, it is a good idea to list the condition prior to the subject and performance.

Exercise

What's wrong with each of the following measurable objectives? (The answers are in appendix C.)

1. Clients will meet with their counselor and take their meds.
2. The social worker will meet with the client for five counseling sessions to help the client express his or her anger verbally.
3. The father will spend nurturing time with his three-year-old son.

DIFFERENCES BETWEEN PROGRAM AND PRACTICE OBJECTIVES

Often it is difficult to distinguish measurable objectives of program and practice. As indicated previously, a measurable objective statement typically has the following elements in this order: conditions, subject, performance, and criteria. Typically, both program and practice objectives will have all these elements. Then how are they different? Practice objectives are usually more detailed and unique to a particular client, whereas program objectives are stated in more general terms to reflect the circumstances of all or some clients who are recipients of services.

The subjects of programs are all or some clients in the program and may be referred to simply as "the clients"; the subject of a practice objective would be one particular client or client system who could even be named in the objective. Performance words could also be more specific for practice objectives because they can focus in on a specific action that possibly only one client would be expected to perform by a particular time. Likewise, conditions and criteria can be tailored more to the needs of one client in practice than to a group of clients in a program.

For example, an individual client with a substance abuse problem might identify a specific behavior such as "state something positive about myself in front of my family" or "go out to see a movie if I stay drug free for a week," but this specificity may not be possible in an objective of a program. A program objective for a group of clients with similar circumstances will likely be more general, such as "attend a fun activity outside the home once a week" without identifying further specifics.

Goals Promoted by the Council on Quality and Leadership in Supports for People with Disabilities

The Council (1997), an accreditation organization, emphasizes the importance of personal goals for people who have developmental disabilities by taking the position that these people should define their own outcomes from their perspective and experiences. The Council emphasizes that there are no standard definitions of personal outcomes, as no two people will define them in the same manner. Instead, personal outcomes reinforce differences and diversity. The authors go on to say that helping clients develop their own personal goals provides three types of opportunities. First, it offers a way of getting further acquainted with the client; second, it provides a focus for organizing resources and coordinating supports to facilitate goals; third, the goals are the actual outcomes to be used to determine whether the client ultimately achieved what the agency intended.

The accreditation organization, the Council, emphasizes the importance of personal goals that are truly those of the clients, even if the clients have severe cognitive disabilities. This is a good example to close on not only because it places significant emphasis on personal goals for this organization but also because it expresses the value that clients should be empowered to craft their own goals.

The next chapter describes evaluations during the second stage, the implementation stage. A range of types of evaluations can be conducted during the implementation of the program, the longest and most varied stage for evaluation activities.

KEY TERMS

Characteristics of goals
Conditions in a measurable objective
Crafting objectives
Criteria in a measurable objective
Goals
Limitations of goals
Measurable objectives
Overt indicator in a measurable objective
Performance in a measurable objective
Program versus practice objectives
Subject in a measurable objective

DISCUSSION QUESTIONS AND ASSIGNMENTS

Answers are found in appendix C.

1. What is needed to improve these measurable objectives?

    - The clients will be monitored by the appropriate staff while at the group home at all times.
    - After ten to twelve therapy sessions, the client will engage in negative self-talk only 10 percent of the time.
    - When arriving for her appointment, the client will wait less than fifteen minutes to see the doctor 90 percent of the time.
    - During the school year, my client will turn in a progress report completed by teachers every week.
    - While at X agency, the mother will spend nurturing time reading to her child 100 percent of the time.

2. Identify a policy-level goal. Then craft three measurable objectives for the goal.

3. Identify the performance, conditions, and criteria in measurable objectives A and B:

   Goal: Clients with a mental retardation label will strengthen their socialization skills.
   Measurable Objective A: When introduced to new people, the client will shake their hands nine out of ten times.
   Measurable Objective B: After breakfast, the client will make his bed before leaving for work.

4. Identify the performance, conditions, and criteria in measurable objectives A, B, and C (Guy, 2006):

   Goal: Mental health clients will achieve optimum mental health.
   Measurable Objective A: If prescribed, clients will take (swallow) the correct amounts of medication daily for six months.
   Measurable Objective B: After ten to twelve sessions, clients will state four out of five techniques to control anxiety taught in sessions.
   Measurable Objective C: When experiencing thoughts of self-harm, clients will ask for help from their identified support system within twenty-four hours.

5. Identify the performance, conditions, and criteria in measurable objectives A, B, and C (Guy, 2006):

   Goal: John Doe will have stronger interpersonal skills.
   Measurable Objective A: John will say, "Good morning" to six out of ten coworkers when arriving at work each morning.
   Measurable Objective B: After six sessions, John will talk for ten minutes to one or two coworkers each week.
   Measurable Objective C: When talking to others, John will look at the person's face 75 percent of the time.

6. Identify the performance, conditions, and criteria in measurable objectives A, B, and C (Hawkins, 2006):

   Goal: Clients will develop assertiveness skills in a group on assertiveness.
   Measurable Objective A: After three group sessions, the clients will circle assertive comments and cross out aggressive comments on a worksheet and be correct eight out of ten times.
   Measurable Objective B: After five group sessions, the clients will write two ways they were assertive.
   Measurable Objective C: At the conclusion of treatment, clients will tell the social worker two things they liked and two things they did not like about group therapy without raising their voices.

REFERENCES

Council on Quality and Leadership in Supports for People with Disabilities. (1997). *Personal outcome measures*. Towson, MD: Author.

Dudley, J. (2007). Procreative consciousness and procreative responsibility of teenage parents. Unpublished data, University of North Carolina at Charlotte.

Dudley, J., & Schatz, M. (1985). The missing link in evaluating sheltered workshop programs: The clients' input. *Mental Retardation, 23*(5), 235–240.

Fenske, M. (2006). Crafting measurable objectives. Unpublished paper for a program evaluation course, University of North Carolina at Charlotte.

Guy, P. (2006). Crafting measurable objectives. Unpublished paper for a program evaluation course, University of North Carolina at Charlotte.

Hawkins, K. (2006). Crafting measurable objectives. Unpublished paper for a program evaluation course, University of North Carolina at Charlotte.

Mager, R. (1997). *Preparing instructional objectives* (2nd ed.). Atlanta: Center for Effective Performance.

Martin, L. L., & Kettner, P. M. (1996). *Measuring the performance of human service programs*. Thousand Oaks, CA: Sage.

Needham, P. R., & Newbury, J. (2004). Goal setting as a measure of outcome in palliative care. *Palliative Medicine, 18*, 444–451.

Posavac, E. J., & Carey, R. G. (1997). *Program evaluation: Methods and case studies* (5th ed.). Upper Saddle River, NJ: Prentice Hall.

Part IV

The Implementation Stage

Chapter 8

Improving How Programs and Practice Work

Robert Herman-Smith and James R. Dudley

How is the intervention supposed to be implemented?
How is it actually implemented?

This chapter addresses these implementation questions and others. It does this by focusing on some of the issues of implementation studies during step 4 (plan the evaluation) of the Seven Evaluation Steps. Documenting and monitoring how an intervention is implemented are vital areas of evaluation and essential for program integrity. During the implementation stage, many questions are asked and answered that revolve around the theme of how well the program or practice approach is working. (See figure 8.1.)

Implementation refers to the intentional application of interventions and strategies to solve problems in real-world settings (Mitchell, 2011). Implementation evaluation is primarily concerned with and investigates the procedures and processes established to carry out the program. In other

FIGURE 8.1   Evaluation of the Intervention

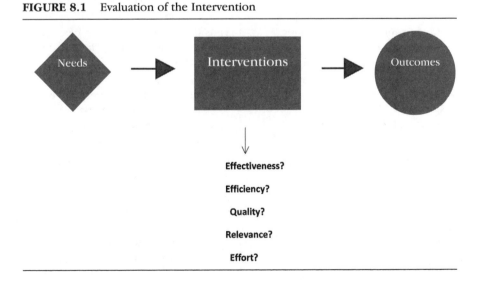

words, how well have agencies followed procedures to support a new intervention and how have these changes impacted clients?

The implementation stage of an intervention is an opportune time to conduct a variety of evaluations. These evaluations can raise numerous important, if not essential, questions about the integrity of a program or practice approach. For example, are all the required components of a program implemented as planned? What program components seem to work and which ones do not? Has a team of qualified and competent staff members and volunteers been hired to provide the designated services? Are the key parties (e.g., administrators, staff, volunteers, and clients) communicating adequately? Many of the types of implementation evaluations covered in the chapter are identified in table 8.1, along with some general evaluation questions that they raise. Although this is not intended to be an exhaustive list of evaluations of implementation, it offers numerous examples of what is important.

LINKING THE INTERVENTION TO THE CLIENTS' PROBLEMS

During the input or planning stage, major attention is focused on the problems and needs of prospective clients. As stated in chapter 6, a need is an aspect of a larger problem identified by a client that is perceived to be

TABLE 8.1　Types of Implementation Evaluations

Types of implementation evaluations	Some overall questions asked
1) Linking the intervention to the clients' problems	1) Does the intervention address the causes of the clients' problems that are the addressed concern?
2) Implementing the intervention as proposed	2) Is the actual intervention being implemented as it was intended or proposed?
3) Adopting and promoting evidence-based interventions	3) Is there evidence from manuals, evaluations, and/or clinical practice that an intervention works?
4) Focus on staff members	4) How are staff members selected, trained, involved, etc.?
5) Accessibility of the intervention	5) How accessible is the intervention to all of the intended target groups?
6) Program quality	6) Is the level of quality of the intervention high enough to satisfy the stakeholders?
7) Client satisfaction	7) How satisfied are the clients with the intervention?

amenable to change. Meeting a set of needs is the intended focus of a proposed program. Another issue is also important to explore: what are the underlying causes that prevent the need from being met? This is a critical question because the proposed program is expected to address the underlying causes.

An example of the logical link between the causes of a problem and the approach used by a program to address it is briefly illustrated in table 8.2 for the problem of child abuse. Several known causes of child abuse have been identified, including intergenerational transmission (abuse being taught from generation to generation), inadequate parenting skills, stresses associated with poverty, and isolation from important social supports. Each cause suggests a different program response. The example is somewhat simplistic because it infers that a complex problem such as child abuse has a single cause. Yet the example makes an important point. An intervention should be logically linked to the underlying causes of a problem. Each of the causes of child abuse suggests a response that will address it. As the example suggests, child abuse perpetrated by parents who were abused as children will not be reversed if it does not include some type of increased awareness and recognition of these intergenerational behaviors as part of the intervention. Similarly, some form of parenting skills training is absolutely essential if the problem is inadequate parental skills since abuse signals that parents need alternative disciplinary techniques. The link between child abuse and poverty can be addressed by preparing parents for a higher-paying job. Likewise, if social isolation is one underlying cause of abuse, teaching social skills and linking to healthy social contacts are logical responses.

As discussed in the last three chapters, the logic model provides an important organizing framework for understanding evaluations. Introducing the logic model at the implementation stage provides a framework for considering many ways to improve an intervention, to correct its course if needed, and to maintain its quality. The logic model helps focus on the sequence of steps that link the implementation of the program back to the clients' unmet needs and forward to the clients' anticipated outcomes or

TABLE 8.2   Link between Causes of a Problem and a Logical Intervention

Identified cause of child abuse	*Logical program intervention*
A. Intergenerational cause (abusing parent was abused as a child)	A. Facilitation of insight into intergenerational link through therapy
B. Lack of parenting knowledge and skill	B. Training in parenting skills
C. Economic stress from a low-income job	C. Increase in income through new job training and/or job change
D. Stress from social isolation	D. Peer support group of parents

accomplishments. In this regard, interventions should address the problems and needs of their recipients and the underlying causes. Further, the implementation of an intervention should result in the clients achieving their anticipated outcomes.

For many years, agencies have been adopting the reasoning behind the logic model in requirements for most grant proposals. Grant writers are expected to document such things as the links between clients' problems and the program approach they propose to implement. In brief, a convincing explanation needs to be mounted to the funding agency for how a proposed program can help clients resolve the problems of concern. For this reason, implementation evaluation is most concerned with the "program and practice activities" section of the logic model.

Some important implementation questions are raised as a result of the logic model. Does the program's approach seem to be directly linked to clients' problems? Furthermore, is there evidence that the approach can provide solutions to these problems? According to Pawson and Tilley (1997), an evaluation of the links between the causes of a problem and the program approach answers three key questions:

1. What are the mechanisms for change triggered by a program?
2. How do these mechanisms counteract the existing social processes?
3. What is the evidence that these mechanisms actually are effective?

Alcoholics Anonymous (AA) offers an example of an approach to a social problem—substance abuse. Implementation evaluations are interested in how programs actually work; for example, what are the mechanisms of an AA support group that helps people overcome the addictive tendencies of alcohol? Is it, as the philosophy of AA suggests, the spiritual ideology and message of the twelve steps? Is it the support that comes from others going through the same struggles? Is it a combination of spiritual ideology and social support from others struggling with substance abuse? Or is it something else? Evidence of what makes AA work for so many people could partially be found in the answers to these questions from an evaluation of a representative sample of some of the thousands of AA programs that meet regularly across the country.

Evaluation studies also have to answer the question about the social and cultural conditions necessary for change to occur among program recipients. In other words, how are the sociocultural factors recognized and addressed within a program? A new mentoring program for young African American men who did not have an adequate father figure for bonding provides an example. Several sociocultural questions could be asked of an agency sponsoring such a program. For example, to what extent and how does this program recognize the sociocultural factors? Are older African American men available to serve as mentors? Are the mentors capable of providing some of the missing pieces in well-being that these teenagers need? Do the mentors have any training or other preparation in male bonding based on an evidence-based curriculum?

One evaluation identified the essential elements of a program for preventing crimes in a housing complex for low-income residents. The evaluation team identified ten key elements of a crime prevention housing program that would be needed based on evidence of prior programs with a similar purpose that were effective.

Example of an Evaluation of the Essential Elements of a Housing Program

Foster and Hope (1993) wanted to identify the essential elements for preventing crime within a housing complex. Their evaluation focused on identifying a list of key elements found to be essential in the effectiveness of prior programs of a similar nature. They concluded that ten elements were essential:

1. A local housing office for the program
2. A local repair team
3. Locally controlled procedures for signing on and terminating tenants in housing units
4. Local control of rent collection and arrears
5. Tenants assume responsibility for caretaking and cleaning of the open space around units with the assistance of a locally supervised staff team
6. An active tenant advisory group with a liaison to the management of the program
7. Resources available for any possible small-scale capital improvements
8. Well-trained staff that delegate authority
9. A project manager as the key figure to be accountable for management of the program
10. A locally controlled budget for management and maintenance

---

In the housing example, the evaluators accumulated substantial evidence that the successful housing complexes in preventing crime in their city had ten essential elements. Housing complexes that were not totally effective were without all, some, or even one of the elements. As the elements suggest, some common themes included a housing management team with some local control, realistic expectations of the tenants, availability of important resources, an active tenant advisory council, and a collaborative relationship between the council and the management team.

IMPLEMENTING THE INTERVENTION AS PROPOSED?

Other types of questions address whether the intervention is actually implemented as proposed or intended. How an intervention is supposed to function may relate back to an initial grant proposal or other early planning documents. Implementation as intended could also be based on more current reports describing the policies and practices of programs that have been running for some time. Provision of a detailed description of an intervention as it is supposed to be implemented is a first step in this kind of evaluation.

A clear description of the intervention is needed prior to monitoring how it is implemented. Therefore, it is often a good idea to begin with an accurate, written description of the intervention, whether articulated in an initial grant proposal or somewhere else. It is wise to describe an intervention in enough detail so that it can be replicated. An example of a program description is in a report about a visitation program for non-custodial parents (Fischer, 2002). The purposes of the program are to assist parents in establishing an access agreement with the custodial parent and in pursuing their legal rights and responsibilities as parents. The article documents the process of establishing and maintaining visitation agreements and identifies the principal barriers to establishing visitation. It includes a description of the policy and legal context for the program, a review of the pertinent literature, a description of a pilot program, a pilot process assessment, and a pilot outcome assessment. Data are also included on the factors associated with successful visitation. The program description came from several sources, such as case files, administrative records, and results of the pilot assessments.

Some further questions in attempting to find out whether a program is implemented as intended include the following:

- Are the clients being served the ones proposed or intended to be served?
- Are current staff members adequately qualified and trained to provide the proposed services at the required level of specialty and quality?
- Are the program's goals and objectives evident or identifiable in the way in which the program is implemented?
- What happens on a typical day in a program (e.g., a daily routine study)?
- How do staff from different disciplines collaborate or work together?
- How are the roles of BSW and MSW staff members differentiated and complementary?

Weinbach (2005) points out that new programs may need to ask different questions than older programs when it comes to how the intervention is being implemented. Newer programs may need to ask:

- Is the program at its anticipated stage of development?
- How many clients have been served to date?

- Is the program fully staffed with qualified people?
- How well known is the program in the community?
- How well have sources of client referrals been developed?
- In what ways is the program supported and in what ways is it being questioned within the agency and community?

According to Weinbach (2005), programs that have been implemented for a few years or more and are considered more mature may ask another set of questions:

- Do the services and programs appear to have the potential to achieve their objectives?
- Are the services and other activities of the program consistent with the program model?
- Is the program serving the clients for whom it was intended? If not, why?
- Is the program visible and respected in the professional and consumer community?
- How much attrition has there been among clients and staff?
- Do staff members perceive that administrative support is adequate?
- How satisfied are clients with the program?

Often interventions are not implemented as they were intended or proposed, or they may have gone adrift of their intended course. This can occur for several reasons. Perhaps a program approach or model was not adequately articulated and discussed. Perhaps the program goals and objectives were not fully developed, were crafted as unrealistic, or were displaced for some changing circumstances. Also, a program could decide to change course because of the changing needs or understanding about the client population. Finally, the people in charge of implementing an intervention could be different from those who proposed and planned it. In this case, if close collaboration did not occur between the two sets of people, a lack of continuity from the planning stage to the implementation stage is likely. Also, if all or most stakeholders are not involved at least in an advisory way in both stages, there may not be enough accountability to ensure that the planning decisions are implemented at a later time.

Example of an Overlooked Target Group

A Head Start program was established in a local community that had an important stakeholder group, a neighborhood civic organization. The organization was very concerned with the needs of local children. This group wanted to make sure that families with the least available resources and the least ability to find an alternative program for their preschool children were given top priority. Once the Head Start program fully enrolled its cohort of children, the civic group decided to find out the social circumstances of the children and their families. To the surprise of some, they discovered that almost all the children were from very resourceful families with modest incomes that were likely to have access to comparable alternative programs. Therefore, the civic group raised its concern with the Head Start organization. When it received an unfavorable response, it pursued a lawsuit against the Head Start organization demanding that because the neediest families were the mandated target group they must be served. This lawsuit eventually ended up as a class action suit that resulted in a ruling that all Head Start programs in that city had to reserve a percentage of their openings for this neediest group of families.

Gardner (2000) offers an example of one way to create a description of a program involving a team of stakeholders. This program was developed using the logic model. One purpose of this exercise was to provide a clear program description; another was to more fully orient staff toward the program and its workings. At one point, some general questions were raised and discussed among all staff members, including "How would you describe how you go about working with clients?" and "What would be the important elements in the process of working with families?" Gradually, a diagram developed consisting of a series of boxes, each of which described a step in the process. Stage 1 described how families were encouraged to request services from this program. Stage 2 included helping families assess their strengths and the constraints they faced. Stage 3 involved goal setting. Stage 4 involved matching resources to family goals. How the family and staff worked to reach the goals was the focus of Stage 6, and Stage 7 involved completing the contract. The program description was then tested by asking some of the families, staff members, and other agencies how they perceived that the program actually worked using their experiences with it. Although the results of the interviews largely validated the proposed stages and principles that had been identified, the results also suggested the need to qualify and further refine some principles.

Monitoring an intervention's implementation can be done in several different ways. Sometimes agencies conduct staff activity studies using a list of prescribed activities, such as direct contact with clients, contact with other programs on behalf of clients, phone contact with clients, record keeping, staff meetings, and so on. In some instances, the studies may be interested in finding out whether too much time is spent on one type of activity, such as record-keeping; in other instances, the interest may be in finding ways to increase time spent in direct contact with clients. These studies tend to be largely quantitative in nature (e.g., staff members tally the number of hours and minutes in each activity, each day, for a week or so).

Other evaluations attempt to find out more about the intricacies of the practice interventions provided to clients. The evaluations can be open-ended qualitative studies that identify what the social worker is actually doing on the basis of observations, videotapes, or analyzing journal entries recorded by the practitioners that describe what they are doing. Or the evaluations can be more deductive and quantitative by examining the extent to which prescribed activities reflecting a particular practice theory or practice model are implemented.

Exploration of the intricacies of a practitioner approach can be developed by prescribing an intervention protocol. For example, a protocol can be encouraged for medical social workers of a home-health program when clients manifest different types of problems. A frequently encountered problem in home-health settings are clients who are socially isolated, lack contact with friends and family, and are alone most of the time. In this case, a protocol could be to implement some or all of the following interventions:

- Provide a list of resources available to the clients that can reduce their social isolation.
- If clients are interested, assist with referral to a support group relevant to their interests and needs.
- Encourage activities appropriate to their medical condition.
- Explore and facilitate the clients' expression of interests in particular activities.
- Help clients express their feelings about themselves, their sense of satisfaction with their lifestyle, and any desire to change it.
- Help clients explore and resolve feelings related to social isolation, such as grief from loss, a recent loss of a previous health status, or an unresolved, conflicted relationship.

Once these and other activities are implemented, efforts can be made to document any evidence that the client has progressed toward specific outcomes, such as additional supports from other agencies, increased contact with others, and less time alone.

ADOPTING AND PROMOTING EVIDENCE-BASED INTERVENTIONS

A needs assessment should result in general agreement among stakeholders about a service gap that is contributing to a social problem. However, once the need is identified, stakeholders must also come to consensus about various strategies or interventions they will use to address the identified need. This happens during the adoption phase of the intervention. As an example, a suburban community might be concerned about increasing juvenile crime. A needs assessment determines that most juvenile crime is taking place on weekdays between the hours of 2 p.m., when high school is dismissed for the day, and 6 p.m. when most parents in the community arrive home from work; therefore, more community or school-sponsored after-school programs for juveniles might result in reduced juvenile crime. The basic need (more after-school programs) has been identified. However, the type of program needed to address the problem might not be a settled matter for stakeholders. Some stakeholders could believe adolescents in the community need more self-discipline. They might favor competitive sports programs or military-type programs. Other stakeholders could believe adolescents need better role models and more individual attention. They might prefer more mentoring programs. Consensus on the type of program needed is often difficult to achieve, but key stakeholders must come to agreement about the type of program they believe is acceptable for addressing the problem.

A central issue to be addressed in adopting an intervention is whether the intervention is evidence-based. As was reported in earlier chapters, evidence that an intervention works can take many forms and can have varying degrees of validity or accuracy. It also varies in terms of its efficacy from one client population to another. The best evidence is based on evaluation studies using all of the characteristics of evaluations described in chapter 1. A definition of evidence-based interventions was given in chapter 2 stating that evidence comes mostly from both research studies using quasi-experimental or experimental designs and clinical practice. It is also important that evidence-based sources are consistent with the values and expectations of the clients who receive such interventions. Evidence indicating that an intervention is effective needs to be pursued and promoted whenever possible. Three general ways to promote evidence when adopting an intervention are shared next. They are using evidence-based manuals and tool kits, generating clinically based evidence, and critically consuming evaluation reports. All three have the common thread of exploring the association between the introduction of an intervention and the client outcomes that are desired.

Evidence-Based Manuals

For the past several years, funding sources have begun requiring community programs to adopt evidence-based practices, which are intervention models with demonstrated efficacy in random controlled clinical trials (Hallfors & Cho, 2007). Most evidence-based interventions have a highly prescriptive treatment protocol, that is, they expect practitioners to carry out a set of activities with clients in a particular sequence. Treatment manuals and tool kits are more likely to be used in health and mental health services than in other types of social work services. Part of the appeal of evidence-based manuals is that they have a body of evidence that supports their ability to create client change.

However, a growing body of health and mental health services research has shown that efficacious interventions (those that yield positive outcomes when delivered under optimum conditions in research clinics) might not be as effective (produce desired outcomes for their target populations) in "real world" settings (Fixsen, Naoom, Blase, Friedman, & Wallace, 2005; Hallfors & Cho, 2007; Proctor, Silmere, Raghavan, Hovmand, Aarons, et al., 2010). Furthermore, some practices can be difficult to implement, especially when dealing with client populations that are transient or dealing with major life stressors associated with poverty, or such things as unreliable transportation, or problems locating trustworthy child care. There are at least three major concerns about the adoption of evidence-based practices available in manuals.

First, many program directors and practitioners have been reluctant to embrace these evidence-based practice manuals. One reason for their reluctance is the perception that evidence-based practices interfere with the freedom to do their jobs as they see fit. In other words, some practitioners believe that externally driven evidence-based practices do not value their clinical judgment. This can be problematic since mental health practitioners, like workers in other fields, resist practices they believe have been imposed on them (Brodkin, 1997; Glisson & Green, 2006).

Second, many funders demand that programs use evidence-based practices without an appreciation for the investment of time and resources required to make them work as intended. There is a large body of literature showing that implementing evidence-based practices takes at least two years, often longer (Durlak & DuPre, 2008). Funders must be willing to give programs the time, funding, and other resources needed to hire the right staff with the kinds of degrees, certification, and experience to perform skills required by the practice, as well as time to integrate new practices into the agencies where they are delivered. Programs must also devote considerable resources to training their staff to implement evidence-based programs if they expect them to be effective.

Third, evidence-based practices must be a good match for the problem and the client population for which they are implemented. A clinic-based nutrition program for pregnant teens delivered in public health clinics might be highly effective in an urban or suburban area. Urban and suburban clinics are likely to run a number of clinic sites, and potential clients might be able to rely on a well-developed public transportation system to get them to visits. The same program might fail in poor, rural areas since it requires teenagers to visit health clinics that are spread out across large geographic areas. Reliable transportation might not be available in these areas. In brief, adopting an evidence-based intervention using a manual is not a guarantee of success. An intervention's success ultimately rests on whether the right intervention was adopted for the right population at the right time and in the right context (Fixsen et al., 2005). Even under the best of circumstances, implementing a new intervention takes a considerable amount of support from the stakeholders. Yet, use of evidence-based manuals in combination with other initiatives such as obtaining clinically based evidence and critically consuming other evaluations is definitely a worthy effort in promoting evidence-based interventions.

Implementing an Evidence-Based Manual in a Domestic Violence Intervention Program

A domestic violence prevention and intervention program called Safe Families operated in a mid-size city for a number of years. Safe Families completed a needs assessment and found that no other agency in the region was providing services to very young children exposed to domestic violence. After securing funding for services, Safe Families decided to adopt an intervention called child parent psychotherapy (CPP), an evidence-based mental health intervention that addresses emotional and behavioral problems experienced by children younger than six years old who have witnessed domestic violence (Lieberman & Van Horn, 2004). Treatment involves up to thirty one-hour sessions including both the parent and child. The model's efficacy has been supported by two random controlled clinical trials (Lieberman & Van Horn, 2008; Lieberman, Van Horn, & Ippen, 2005). However, implementing CPP provoked a number of unanswered concerns among staff. CPP assumes that participants are no longer experiencing violence in the home, but staff, based on many years of experience with victims of domestic violence, knew that relationships between perpetrators and victims are often "on again, off again." CPP also assumes that mothers are emotionally ready to process past violence and to accept that their children were affected by the violence, but staff knew that mothers enter services at different levels of readiness to process this type of information. They might require more individual treatment before they can properly understand how violence has affected their children. This example illustrates that it is often important for a program evaluator who introduces an evidence-based manual to have a prior dialogue with agency staff, acknowledge their questions about evidence-based interventions, and learn more about how staff members have addressed their concerns in the past. What are some questions you would want to ask staff to help you contextualize their implementation of CPP?

Generating Clinically Based Evidence

Clinically based practice can be another important source of evidence that an intervention works. Of course, clinically based evidence depends upon an agency provider being committed to evaluating their intervention as it is being implemented. Anecdotal "evidence" with little or no effort to explore causal connections between an intervention and client outcomes cannot be taken as serious evidence. Nevertheless, anecdotal evidence that clients are benefiting from an intervention can be a starting point in attempting to introduce an evaluation process.

Clinical practice can be an important source of evidence, especially when it is accompanied by an evaluation component. This evaluation component should have all or most of the following features. First, an intervention that is being introduced should be described and recorded in as much detail as possible. One test of enough detail is whether it can be replicated by another agency or even another practitioner in the same agency. Adequately describing an intervention is not an easy task. It presumes the input and consensus of the varied stakeholders that it is worth implementing. Further, for replication purposes, an intervention needs a description thorough enough that it takes into account the varied ways in which it needs to be implemented with different clients. These variabilities and nuances in implementation are important to capture and articulate. For example, an intervention may need to be implemented for at least five sessions with clients having one set of circumstances, but at least ten sessions for another group. As another example, if the intervention is flexible enough to be implemented with different systems, then these variations also need to be explained. For example, how is the intervention introduced differently to an individual as opposed to members of a small group? Other circumstances that affect how the intervention needs to be described are also important such as whether the client is voluntary versus mandated to receive the intervention.

Another related consideration is how the individual characteristics of different client systems (e.g., ability, age, culture) are likely to respond to the varied ways that the intervention is implemented. For example, are clients with greater intellectual attributes more likely to respond well to an intervention than those without a strong intellect? Also, are racial or ethnic characteristics and the gender of clients likely to respond better to one variation of the intervention than another? Do recent immigrants need a prior emphasis in some areas such as resolving personal documentation issues or addressing fears of deportation before benefiting adequately from the intervention?

Most important, the components of a research design (i.e., group design) are important to utilize when an intervention is being implemented. The clinical practitioner should pay attention to sampling issues such as who was selected to receive the intervention and who was not, and what is the rationale for this sampling decision? The clients' goals or outcomes are also very important to measure both before and after the intervention is implemented. It also makes sense to measure these outcomes periodically while the intervention is being implemented. Another important factor is to find ways to manage the influences outside the realm of the intervention by having a comparison group or using a single-system design that captures the impact of extraneous influences over time.

Critically Consuming Evaluation Reports

Everyone in the human services, including students and faculty in professional programs and employees in social agencies, has a role to play in promoting evidence-based practice. One important way to do this is to regularly read and keep abreast of evaluations and other relevant material in professional journals, books, and unpublished reports. Several professional journals are mentioned in chapter 6 that have an exclusive focus on evaluations. Professionals working in a particular field such as mental health or child welfare should obtain access to journals in their fields for a similar purpose. Agency sponsors should subscribe to these journals, use them in workshops, and make them available to staff members to read.

A primary purpose of many evaluation reports is to provide evidence supporting an intervention's effectiveness. Strictly speaking, this evidence applies to the clients in the report who received the intervention. From there, a critical consumer of the report has the skills to determine the extent to which these findings may also be applicable to other client groups, always with some caution and skepticism. Reading an evaluation report in an attempt to understand evidence-based information can be challenging. Critical consumer skills are definitely needed. These skills include being able to identify and comprehend all of the sections of an evaluation report, including the problem definition and literature review sections, the purpose of the evaluation, the research design, the findings, and the recommendations. In addition, a critical consumer must detect the weaknesses, flaws, and biases of the evaluation, whether identified by the author or not. Not an easy task, and it is one that takes a lot of practice.

The findings and recommendations provide the most important information in a report because this is where the consumers determine whether the report can be useful to them. In other words, can the findings be relevant to the consumers' work with their clients? This is a bigger question that boils down to several smaller questions like: how are the clients in the report similar and different from the clients of the consumers; how is the intervention that is being evaluated relevant to the one used by the consumers; are the findings in the report pertinent to consumers' clients and their goals; and how can these findings be applied, cautiously, with the consumers' clients?

Chapter 12 focuses entirely on the critical consumer skills needed to evaluate an evaluation report. These skills are reviewed using the Seven Evaluation Steps as an organizing framework. Chapter 12 looks closely at each of these steps, their importance to stakeholders, how they should be described in a report, and what they reveal of interest to a critical consumer.

An evaluation report published in a social work journal is used to illustrate how critical consumption can occur.

FOCUS ON STAFF MEMBERS

There are several components of implementation within any program or practice area that could be evaluated (Fixsen et al., 2005). We will address many of the most commonly examined areas of focus in implementation evaluations that pertain to staff members. They include staff selection, staff orientation and training, ongoing consultation and coaching, staff adherence to the protocol of an intervention, diversity, efficiency, and staff working conditions.

Staff Selection

Hiring the ideal candidate is not always possible. Fluctuations in the labor market, accessibility of training programs in a particular area, interest in the type of position offered, and the pay scale for the position are just a few of the issues that affect hiring. Still, programs should devote considerable resources to hiring the right person.

An implementation evaluator should look for evidence of a hiring plan. There should be evidence that a written recruitment plan was developed before hiring began. This should include a basic job description, salary range, minimum qualifications, and preferred qualifications. Staff involved in hiring should agree on the kinds of skills the new hire should possess. If the agency is determined to diversify its staff, these efforts should be documented. Sometimes, this takes the form of special outreach programs such as advertising the position in non-English-language media or participating in a jobs fair that attracts potential applicants from cultural minority backgrounds.

Staff selection involves staff recruitment for the new program. Many staff positions have minimum educational and licensing requirements that applicants must meet to be considered for the job. For example, trauma-focused cognitive behavioral therapy (TF-CBT) is an evidence-based, manualized intervention for children aged 3 through 18 who have experienced trauma (Cohen & Mannarino, 2008). This intervention has specific implementation guidelines for how it should be implemented. Only practitioners who have gone through the training can practice TF-CBT. Consequently, a program using TF-CBT must (1) hire someone who is certified to practice it, or (2) obtain training for hires that are not yet certified.

Program planners might prioritize hiring someone with certain characteristics if there is reason to believe doing so will facilitate client participation and engagement. For example, if many clients who will be receiving services under the program do not speak English, hiring someone who speaks that population's first language would be important. Doing so would save the agency money since it would not require money to pay for interpreting services. People who need the services might also be more willing to participate if some staff members can speak their native language.

A New Hire That Was Not a Good Fit

One of the authors (Herman-Smith) has a background in early childhood mental health. A highly regarded social worker accepted a position in an agency where he worked. She had over twenty years of experience performing mental health evaluations with children aged five through twelve. Part of the responsibilities in her new job was to complete mental health evaluations with children ages two through five. This social worker wanted to work with younger children but did not have much professional experience with them. During her initial work with younger children, she insisted that the children stay seated for most of the session without a break. She refused to sit on the floor with them and insisted they remain in a chair. She was annoyed that so many of the children "displayed poor boundaries" by reaching for and pulling on the very nice bracelets and necklaces she liked to wear. After three months, she quit the job. She could not adapt to the natural impulsiveness, shifting interests, and need for frequent movement that is common in younger children. Transferring skills from one setting and population and using them with another can be challenging. In this case, the agency could have provided more training and support to help the new employee adapt to the new work environment.

Staff Orientation and Training

Staff selection is only the first step. Orientation and training are critical to the staff's success in a new program. New hires require orientation. Orientation refers to the process of teaching new hires the formal rules of the organization, from employee benefits to safety protocols in the agency to the agency's chain of command. Orientation to the work environment is critical in helping new hires do their jobs safely and effectively. Implementation evaluators should look for evidence of a formal, written orientation plan.

Training refers to assistance with the more technical aspects of the new job. During training, employees are familiarized with the history, theory, and rationale for an intervention. In human service agencies particularly, training focuses on the how, when, and where of interacting with clients. Orientation usually refers to new hires only. Training involves teaching both new hires and existing staff who have taken a new position how to work effectively in their work roles. Training is needed, even if hires have several years of experience doing similar work in the past, since their skill sets will probably be used in new ways in their new jobs.

Ongoing Consultation and Coaching

Perhaps too often, job skill development has been conceived as something that happens shortly after a person is hired. A person is hired, goes through orientation, gets training for some specified period of time, and then does the job he or she was hired to do. There are two reasons this perspective on skill development is limited. First, social workers and other human service providers engage in work requiring them to make quick judgments in ambiguous situations. The "right" answer is not always obvious and, in many cases, whether the social worker made the right call with a particular client at a particular time remains a matter of debate. Good clinical supervision, the support of peers, and program administrators are critical, especially for new social workers. Second, the traditional didactic training approach, one in which a trainer does most of the talking during a time-limited lecture in a classroom, has a limited impact on professional skill development (Dixon et al., 1999; Proctor et al., 2007). Training introduces employees to the basic structures of intervention, but they need ongoing support to carry out their daily, on-the-job tasks as they were designed.

Ongoing consultation and coaching that provide skill demonstrations from supervisors, opportunities to practice these skills, and immediate feedback are more likely to result in improved professional skills than training and workshops (Joyce & Showers, 2002; Schectman, Schroth, Verme & Voss, 2003). Spouse (2001) defines coaching as having four components: on-the-job teaching, immediate assessment and feedback, supervision, and emotional support. Skill transfer for human services staff happens in much the same way as it does for children learning a sport (Fixsen et al., 2005). A coach instructs and guides the novice in the nuances of a new activity while rules are being applied and tested (on-the-job teaching). As the novice becomes more adept at the activity, the coach assesses performance and gives advice on ways to enhance the skills needed to improve (immediate assessment and feedback). Basic rules of the game are then reexplained, reinforced, and applied to new situations as they arise (supervision). All of these activities are provided in the context of an emotionally supportive relationship that considers individual staff's needs and assets.

As in any teaching activity, coaching is often more effective if the coach/ supervisor has a good working knowledge of the intervention that supervisees perform with their clients. Ideally, the supervisor has experience carrying out the specific intervention modality. A clinical supervisor might have years of experience assisting children who have experienced trauma. If the supervisee is required to implement, for example, trauma-focused cognitive behavioral therapy, an evidence-based, manualized intervention with strict guidance on how it should be implemented (Cohen & Mannarino, 2008), and the coach/supervisor has limited experience with this approach, the quality and effectiveness of coaching may be limited.

Implementation evaluations should focus on the method and frequency of staff education. There is nothing wrong with off-site training and workshops for the purposes of raising awareness of practice issues, meeting basic continuing education requirements, exploring new practice models, or reinforcing ethical practices. If training is primarily defined as off-site workshops, with no on-site opportunities for immediate feedback and practice, the likelihood that practices will be implemented as intended is relatively small (Brownson, Colditz, & Proctor, 2012). Implementation evaluators should look at the basic structure of training, supervision, and feedback. In addition to off-site continuing education opportunities, ideally there should be evidence of a supervision plan that includes direct observation of staff's interaction on at least a semi-regular basis. There should also be evidence that supervisors have given concrete feedback to staff and provided opportunities to practice skills improvement.

Staff Adherence to Intervention Protocol

Implementation evaluation is not directly concerned about performance evaluations of individual staff. Instead, implementation evaluation is concerned with staff adherence and competence in carrying out a *specific* treatment protocol. Adherence is the extent to which individuals implementing the intervention conform to the intervention protocol (Hogue et al., 2008). Measurements of adherence focus on the quantity or presence of prescribed treatment activities defined in an intervention manual or other established protocols for an intervention. Competence is the skillfulness of intervention delivery (Forgatch, Patterson, & DeGarmo, 2005; Stein, Sargent, & Rafaels, 2007) and also includes qualities related to interpersonal communication, mastery of technical aspects of intervention, and skills in responding to individual clients. These qualities are not routinely a part of staff evaluation, but they can have a large impact on whether interventions are effective with clients. As with ongoing consultation and coaching, implementation evaluations look for evidence of a supervision plan that includes direct observation of staff's interaction on at least a semi-regular basis. There should also be evidence that supervisors have given concrete feedback to staff and provided opportunities to practice skills improvement.

Adherence and Competence in Parent-Child Interaction Therapy

Adherence is the extent to which staff complies with an established protocol. Parent-child interaction therapy (PCIT; Eyberg, Boggs, & Algina, 1995) includes a number of features that promote adherence to a protocol. PCIT is an evidence-supported clinical intervention for children three years through eight years of age with disruptive behavior problems. Training for PCIT is extensive and therapists must adhere closely to the treatment manual. Much of the work involves working with parents. Each session has a list of activities to be completed; for example, the therapist modeling behavior, parents practicing behaviors, and discussion of homework to be completed before the next treatment session. At the end of the session, the therapist completes a checklist of all the activities required to verify that each has been addressed for the session. In addition, the parent completes a checklist with the same activities to verify they took place, such as "The therapist explained my homework assignment for this week," or "The therapist talked to me about how to give commands to my child." Practitioners can adhere closely to protocol but still lack competency. Competence refers to the skillfulness of delivery. Practitioners with high levels of competence successfully convey warmth, empathy, and authenticity that is foundational to social work practice (Hepworth, Rooney, Rooney, Strom-Gottfried & Larsen, 2009; Murphy & Dillon, 2008). In the context of PCIT, for example, is the therapist approachable? Does she greet the family warmly when they arrive for a session? If the parent wants to discuss issues in her personal life other than parenting in a particular session, does the therapist cut her off or skillfully redirect the conversation? Is the therapist aware of other services that can help the family and assist with referrals as needed?

Staff Diversity

Agencies should take a closer look at the demographic characteristics of their staff members and volunteers to determine whether they are similar to the demographic characteristics of the client population. In addition, it is a good idea to determine whether these characteristics take into account projected changes in the client population over the next five to ten years. Having a diverse staff that roughly approximates the demographic characteristics of the client population is a meaningful ideal to pursue. Equal employment strategies can be helpful in reaching this ideal. The more genuine and rigorous the effort that goes into implementing equal opportunity standards in recruitment, hiring, and retention, the more likely it is that the agency will recruit diverse staff members and volunteers. Demographic characteristics of importance should include race, gender, ethnicity, social class, religious affiliation, age, regional background, marital status, having children or not, sexual orientation, and other characteristics related to the needs of specific populations. This type of evaluation is not necessarily intended to support the notion of pairing clients and social workers on the basis of similar background characteristics (e.g., African American clients paired with African American staff); however, staff diversity can provide a signal to many of minority status that they belong there or are welcomed as program participants and recipients. In general, the more varied the backgrounds of staff members and volunteers overall, the greater their capacity will be to plan and implement a culturally sensitive and effective program.

Staffing Efficiency

Staff members' use of their time can be another focus of an evaluation. Administrators sometimes wonder how their employees spend their time. For example, how much time in a week, on average, are staff scheduled to spend in direct contact with clients, in meetings, in collaborating both with other in-house staff and staff of other agencies, in record-keeping, and so on. Often staff members are thought to see too few clients, and there may be a question about how they could use their time differently. Agencies should schedule staff and volunteer time efficiently, particularly in a human services environment with limited resources. Efficiency in itself tends to increase the outputs and outcomes for programs. Keep in mind the distinction between staff evaluation and use of staff time. Staff evaluation refers to how efficiently staff members use their assigned schedules to accomplish tasks assigned by the agency. Staffing efficiency refers to whether management has structured staff time in such a way that they can accomplish the tasks they have been assigned efficiently. Staff members should not be held accountable for inefficient program design of staff efficiency by management.

Staff Working Conditions

How satisfied are staff members with their working conditions? This is an important question that many agencies downplay. The rationale for minimizing its importance can vary. Some administrators may say that staff are paid to provide their services, so why emphasize their satisfaction? Other administrators may think that seeking to satisfy staff members could weaken their own authority. This rationale may be especially important to a top-down administrator who does not encourage staff participation in major decisions of the agency.

Nevertheless, studies have found a strong correlation between staff contentment with their working conditions and their productivity and retention. Agencies with low staff morale are usually among those with high staff turnovers. Mor Barak, Nissly, and Levin (2001) conducted a meta-analysis of twenty-five studies on retention and turnover of staff and their antecedents. The studies reported a range of staff turnover in the agencies studied of 30 percent to 60 percent in a typical year. Among the contributors to staff turnover were burnout, job stress, a lack of support from coworkers and supervisors, and other organizational conditions. Therefore, paying close attention to staff satisfaction with work conditions can be important, and staff satisfaction evaluations are among the ways to investigate such issues.

Some of the issues revolving around working conditions and morale that make sense to periodically investigate include salaries and annual salary raises, availability of medical coverage for employees and family members, retirement benefits, workload issues (e.g., size of caseload), availability and quality of their supervision, opportunities for advancement, support for professional licensing, openness of administrators to staff members' views on programs and personnel matters, availability of useful in-service and outsourced training opportunities, reasonable vacation and sick-leave policies, other family-friendly policies, and incentives and rewards for doing exemplary work. At least one study also found that the challenges imposed by some client groups, such as clients with mental illness, also affect job satisfaction (Acker, 1999).

ACCESSIBILITY OF THE INTERVENTION

As discussed previously, a major focus of implementation evaluation is how program and practice processes affect clients. Events and processes around implementation can impact interventions in ways that ultimately determine their effectiveness. How accessible is the program for clients and potential clients who are intended to be recipients? Access is a problem if the clients from the target group originally intended as the recipients are underrepresented or tend to drop out. Access is also an issue if a particular racial, ethnic, or cultural group that needs the program's services is underrepresented among the group of recipients.

Outreach to Diverse Populations

Accessibility of programs is, in part, a diversity issue. Programs may be used primarily by people of one demographic characteristic, such as white and middle class, and used only minimally by other groups, such as Latinos or low-income earners. Over time, this demographic profile can become institutionalized and come to be viewed inadvertently by agency staff and the wider community as the norm. In other words, people begin to assume falsely that the program must have been designed for this particular group. As a result, other groups may not even consider using this program.

Sometimes, programs are sensitive to diversity issues but fail to reach out to the target community. A large body of research documents health and mental health disparities between groups related to race, ethnicity, and socioeconomic status. People who are poor or racial/ethnic minorities are less likely to receive health and mental health services, and the quality of services they receive is often inadequate. Implementation evaluation should examine the degree to which new programs reach diverse populations. This includes a written plan that defines diverse populations. Diversity can reflect race, ethnicity, income, geography, gender, sexual orientation, or other areas of difference that might affect program referrals, access, or engagement. Programs should be aware of the history of intergroup conflict in the communities in which they practice and be aware of how this history might affect some community residents' interactions with the program. One way to reach out to oppressed groups is advertising services in neighborhoods where they predominate. Another way is to align oneself with someone who is a trusted leader or advocate for their community.

Adults with Developmental Disabilities

A community group wanted to serve adults with developmental disabilities with little or no social contact beyond their immediate families. They were people who simply spent all of their free time in their family homes. The impetus for creating this program was that it would be uniquely available to isolated individuals in the city. The program would fit their special needs because there would be a cohort of professional staff members available trained to help them and an agency van to transport them to and from the program. However, the sponsor of this program, a group of parents with developmentally disabled members, made very little effort to channel their resources into special marketing, recruiting, and other forms of outreach. As a result, the new program was quickly inundated by other people with disabilities who were higher functioning and more independent. Once these people found out about the program, they adopted it as their own, and the staff members took the path of least resistance and went along with organizing their efforts around creating social opportunities for them. The original target group was forgotten largely because it did not have a vocal advocate.

If comprehensive client records are kept, it can be fairly easy to determine whether some groups are accessing the program and others are not, or if some use the program more than others. A first step in determining whether there are accessibility problems is to identify the types of people that the program has decided to serve. Next, determine the characteristics of the clients actually being served or those most likely to continue in the program beyond the initial session or stage. Finding the discrepancies between the characteristics of the two groups can begin to reveal the characteristics of client groups that are underrepresented.

Physical Access

Physical access is evident in different physical structures within which a program is located. Since the Americans with Disabilities Act (ADA) was signed in 1990, federal law has required most buildings to be accessible to citizens regardless of physical ability. Even when buildings are ADA-compliant, physical space can present problems for some clients. For example, a center-based program for people with early stage Alzheimer's and their families might serve fewer clients if they are located in a large building or if parking is far from the building because this increases the chances they will become lost, confused, or agitated. Program planners cannot anticipate all the special circumstances that clients might require to overcome physical barriers; however, the program should be located in facilities that minimize physical barriers and have resources available to accommodate as many people as possible, regardless of ability.

Geographic Access

Geographic access refers to a program's location. Geographic access plays an important role in program success. A program that is not on a well-known, easily accessible, and safe street poses obvious barriers. Further, the absence of common public transportation routes that travel to and from the program site are barriers. Any program located outside a downtown area or outside the main section of a town can be fraught with barriers for many people. This is a particular challenge for clients without access to a car, public transportation, or reliable transportation from friends or family. In some cases, well-known business and shopping centers may be the most accessible sites.

Psychological Access

Psychological access refers to the environmental tone set by a program, that is, its sense of welcoming. Psychological access is often difficult to assess because staff behavior is interpreted subjectively. Some behaviors can be observed, for example, staff rudeness or a warm greeting to clients. An agency that does not return phone calls can deter potential clients. Other behaviors can be difficult to observe unless one is highly sensitized to the client's perspective. Gay and lesbian people, for example, may be sensitive to subtle messages that appear judgmental or unwelcoming. An example would be asking a child with two parents of the same sex for the child's mother's name and father's name. The absence of employees of the same racial or ethnic group is another possible barrier for some. A program brochure might seem exclusive if it does not mention that a particular group is among those who are eligible for services. For example, would a family service agency provide counseling to a divorced couple involved in shared custody or to a gay couple? It is important for the agency to mention in brochures and other marketing materials that they are inclusive, if in fact they are.

Psychological access is evident in many programs that focus on mental health issues or are identified as mental health agencies. Many people have misunderstandings about mental illness that make them reluctant to admit they or their family members have a need for mental health services. Often a program sponsor that attempts to reach people with such sensitivities may consider locating the program in a school, community center, or house of worship to ward off this possibility.

Cultural Access

Cultural access issues are similar to psychological access issues. They can be subjective, subtle, and difficult to detect. However, as our society becomes more diverse, program sponsors are increasingly challenged to make special efforts to be sensitive to the cultural aspects of clients and potential clients. If a program wants to be inclusive in this regard, special considerations must be given to preparation for work with African Americans, Latinos, low-income clients of all ethnicities, and recent immigrants from around the world. Each of these groups and subgroups has cultural beliefs, practices, rituals, and sensitivities that are important to consider in planning and carrying out a program.

Access Issues for African Americans' Use of Hospice

In chapter 2, a study was described that investigated why African Americans did not use hospice services proportionate to their numbers in a particular city (Reese, Ahern, Nair, O'Faire, & Warren, 1999). The researchers' activities began with a small qualitative study of African American pastors. This pilot study was followed by a larger quantitative study of African American hospice patients that documented their access barriers to hospice. Findings revealed that African Americans in this city had a preference for life-sustaining treatment (e.g., chemotherapy, resuscitation, life support) over palliative care. The respondents were also opposed to accepting terminality, planning for it, or discussing it with others. The findings of the studies were used to facilitate a social action effort to increase alternative services that reflected the priorities of the community.

A group service, for example, that emphasizes open sharing, self-disclosure, equality, and participation by all will likely find resistance from some cultural groups. The hesitation from various groups will come because of their emphasis on patriarchal families, hesitations to self-disclosure, varying beliefs about how anger should be expressed, how animated they can be in a lively discussion, how much they can confront others, how they perceive authority figures, and what they choose to talk about (Reid, 1997).

Barriers to Using a School Program

Child Trends (Kennedy, Wilson, Valladares, & Bronte-Tinkew, 2007) conducted a study of barriers to low-income children and adolescents using after-school programs. They identified five types of barriers:

1. Safety, transportation, and cost: Unsafe neighborhoods, the cost of after-school programs, and problems getting to and from a program are persistent barriers that limit participation for many children.
2. Family responsibilities: Many adolescents have other responsibilities, such as babysitting younger siblings, preparing meals, or taking care of household chores that prevent them from participating.
3. Desire or need to work: Many older youths take on part-time or even full-time after-school jobs.
4. Lack of identification with staff members: Trusting relationships between youth participants and staff members are a central feature of these programs. Children and youths often prefer staff members who are similar to themselves in race, gender, and experience, but the most important consideration is that staff care about children and youths and can connect with participants.
5. Lack of interest in organized activities: Adolescents, more so than children, often have little or no interest in activities offered through after-school programs. Adolescents frequently cite boredom, a desire to relax and hang out with friends, and dissatisfaction with program activities as reasons that they would rather not participate.

Cultural access is important to consider in almost every program. Issues could include such things as a lack of knowledge about the services provided by a program. In this regard, how well does an agency brochure or flyer explain the purpose of a program in a language that can be understood by client groups? Is the program material provided in languages other than English in communities in which there are groups of people who speak English as a second language? A lack of diversity among the staff members and volunteers could be another factor that discourages some people from seeking out a program's services. A face that is similar to your own may be synonymous with being a friendly face. Any of these factors could be barriers; one way to determine how problematic they are is to openly discuss them with people of these cultures.

Accessibility barriers can go beyond the factors described here. They could be any of several things that we might suspect but cannot identify from those who hesitate to use services. In many instances, we do not know what the barriers are that keep some people from using a program or service. Yet we know that some people who need a program do not use that program. Further, we always need to be sensitive to and vigilant in seeking to learn what might get in the way of people engaging with and fully using a program. In summary, several issues pertaining to client access may need to be evaluated.

PROGRAM QUALITY

Although virtually all implementation evaluations are interested in improving the quality of a program or practice approach to some degree, some are especially known for their interest in program quality. When standards of quality are clearly defined and measurable, it is fairly easy to measure the performance of a program or practice approach against these standards. In some cases, however, clearly defined, minimal performance standards are not defined or do not even exist. Also, quality evaluations primarily use qualitative methodologies, and measures tend to be subjective. Thus, quality evaluations are not as exact and predictable as one would hope.

An Exercise in Evaluating Practice Quality

Social work practice classes at the MSW level often can get into discussions about how to implement a particular practice theory or approach, such as the solution-focused or person-centered approach. An often fruitful way to explore such a question is to select a specific client case, real or made up, that one group could role-play (after preparation) using the solution-focused approach and another group using the person-centered approach. Other classmates could observe the role-plays and attempt to identify specific techniques and behaviors that reflected the respective approaches and those that did not. Afterward, the entire class could summarize the salient elements in each approach that manifested in the role-plays.

Some of the common models of quality evaluations described in chapter 4 included accreditation studies of programs and quality assurance evaluations. A fuller discussion of these types of evaluations will help illustrate the complexities of evaluating a program's quality.

Accrediting a professional program.   The process of accrediting a professional academic program, such as professional social work, is one form of quality control. The accrediting agencies propagate professional standards that academic programs are expected to adopt and implement. Member agencies typically are expected to prepare lengthy reports, referred to as "self-studies," to document how they meet these standards in their programs and in their administration. The self-study report is submitted to the accrediting agency, which assigns a team of accreditation officials to carefully review the self-study and conduct a site visit of the program. Site visits are used to find multiple sources of evidence that the member agencies are actually doing what they report in the self-study. Multiple sources of evidence include random samples of student records; informal observations; data on outcomes for graduates; and eliciting of the views of administrators, staff and faculty members, field instructors, and students. The standards of an accrediting agency tend to be broad and subjective.

Example of the Accreditation Process

The Council on Social Work Education expects all professional programs at both the BSW and the MSW level to prepare their students with content on social and economic justice. Programs are expected to show how they do this in the self-study and in each syllabus through lectures, outside speakers, assigned readings, assignments, and other methods. As long as the self-study and each individual syllabus shows how and where social justice content is covered and how students are expected to demonstrate that they understand and apply it in their practice, the standard is essentially met. However, this form of quality control is quite subjective and leaves open the possibility of many unanswered questions. For example, what types of social justice are acceptable? How does the accreditation agency know that the content has actually been covered in every section of a particular course? How can faculty determine that students have embraced a belief system that supports this content? How can they know that graduates will actually use the content in their work once they have graduated?

Quality assurance. Quality assurance programs exemplify a focus on quality evaluations. Some agencies also sometimes refer to quality assurance as quality improvement or quality control. Quality assurance activities focus on a sampling of events and records that provide a snapshot of how the program and its staff members work. The key to quality assurance is determining whether an acceptable level of quality is reached. In a practical sense, the results of quality assurance data collection efforts can be immediately used to improve or fill omissions in a program. A case example was given in chapter 4 of a quality assurance evaluation protocol of an agency providing residential programs for youths in foster homes. The example described the specific procedures that the agency used to conduct the evaluation.

Social agencies that have a quality assurance evaluation typically take a close look at several aspects of a program using multiple methods of data collection. These methods include staff peer reviews of a random sampling of client cases, a close-up review of some client records, inquiries into client perceptions and satisfaction, and observations of a few services. Quality assurance is usually conducted by a team of staff members, not agency administrators, who are employed either by the agency being evaluated or by another agency. Because the process involves staff members, there is likely a strong tendency that reviewers are supportive of staff members and possibly biased in favor of their viewpoints and practices.

Best practices. Once a theoretical approach and all its dimensions or components are defined, along with procedures for implementing them, standards can be set to ensure that the approach is implemented in a professionally acceptable way. Best practices are pertinent here. Best practices is a concept that represents the highest standards of quality for a specific area of professional practice. Best practices are partially established by evidence-based research demonstrating that a practice approach is effective in helping specific client populations. An important way to establish best practices is through peer-reviewed professional journal articles published and disseminated by researchers and practitioners.

CLIENT SATISFACTION

Client satisfaction studies investigate how satisfied clients are with the services they receive. Such studies are extremely important to conduct. They reveal clients' perceptions of the services they are receiving, what they feel works, and what may be problematic. These studies can help pinpoint what was helpful to clients, where there might be a breakdown in services, and where improvements may need to be considered. Client satisfaction questions also offer a fuller picture of the interface between the clients and their service provider. They help agencies determine how each party (client and social worker) perceives what is happening and any discrepancies between the two. In this case, a concurrent study of the social worker's perceptions would also need to be conducted using the same or similar questions.

There is often a close correlation between whether clients are satisfied with a program and whether the program is effective in helping them. This is likely to be the case because if clients are not satisfied with the services they receive, one of several possibilities is likely. Dissatisfied clients may not trust their providers or the services they are offering, and therefore they may not fully engage in using them. Dissatisfied clients may throw out various obstacles to receiving services, such as withholding information, minimizing participation, avoiding in-depth interventions, sporadic attendance, or even discontinuing use of the program.

In addition, client satisfaction studies can reveal, in part, how effective programs are, if client satisfaction is viewed as a necessary though not sufficient condition for claiming program effectiveness. It is the authors' view that if there is an absence or low level of client satisfaction generally, it is difficult to conclude that a program has been effective in helping them. Involuntary clients may be an exception, in that their lack of satisfaction is likely to be related to their involuntary status. In this case, a report of program dissatisfaction presumably relates more to their status than to any of their accomplishments or progress. In some studies, client satisfaction scores are even viewed as an outcome measure of success. In summary, the client's perceptions are always important to consider, even though they are a subjective viewpoint that is influenced by their perspectives and biases.

Satisfaction of Clients in an Inpatient Psychiatric Facility

Baker, Zucker, and Gross (1998) report that client satisfaction studies are rare among inpatient mental health patients. Their 770 clients had serious and persistent mental illness, and in most cases had schizophrenia and were involuntarily hospitalized. The authors explored, among other things, clients' perceptions about the different treatment modalities used, treatment goals, and the philosophy of treatment. The authors discussed several specific issues revolving around conducting client satisfaction surveys with this type of population, including considerations of what aspects of satisfaction should and can be measured, whether such surveys can reflect client stability in satisfaction, and whether the results can be used for program improvement.

Although client satisfaction studies are important to have as a component of virtually every program, they do have their weaknesses. As already indicated, clients' perceptions are bound to be subjective and perhaps biased. They can also be difficult to interpret. If you were to ask ten clients,

"How satisfied are you with social work services?" what would it mean to each client? One person may associate "satisfaction" with one image, while another associates it with something altogether different. For example, satisfaction or lack of satisfaction in a social worker's help could mean any number of things:

- Liking or disliking some characteristic of the social worker
- Being unhappy with the initial waiting period
- Feeling angry or disappointed about what the social worker said during a recent session
- Being disrupted by a change to a new social worker
- Being grateful that the social worker helped them to find a resource
- Being pleased that the current social worker is not judgmental like the previous one
- Being comforted that the social worker listens intently

The list of possible interpretations can be almost limitless, which suggests that we may never know what clients mean when they check a particular response category of a satisfaction survey.

A related example of a weakness in client satisfaction studies revolves around interpreting what the word *satisfaction* means to the clients who fill out a survey. Because the term is ambiguous, it will likely need to be defined. It could be interpreted in various ways, for example, as "no major complaints," "being acceptable," or "being preferred over similar services of competing agencies." Satisfaction to some may mean a program or service that meets a very high standard overall, such as being exceptionally well delivered, having almost every aspect done well, being reasonable in cost, and being offered at the best time and at a convenient location for the client. In contrast, to others the standard of satisfaction may be very low, such as simply being pleased to receive an opening in the program and being treated in a friendly way. Again, a client satisfaction study may never uncover what standard of satisfaction the respondents use.

Of course, one could respond to the point about the ambiguity of satisfaction by saying that it does not matter what the standard is. It is all about perception and the perceiver. If the client perceives the program or service as satisfying, then that is all that counts, particularly if satisfaction means they will continue to use the program and continue to engage the provider in the helping process.

Options for Determining What Satisfaction Means

Keep in mind that there are options for exploring a client's satisfaction in more detail or depth. One option is to use a questionnaire format that asks forced-response satisfaction questions for each of several aspects or dimensions of the program and its services. It is up to the evaluator to decide which program dimensions are most important to include in the study. Examples of program dimensions include asking whether clients are satisfied with the agency's fee schedule, the extent of the waiting period, the psychological accessibility of the agency, whether services are available at convenient times, the friendliness of the receptionist, the social worker's ability to listen, and the social worker's ability to help them find solutions to their problems. When analyzing the responses to these questions, the evaluator can zero in on the dimensions of the program that are more and less satisfying by comparing them. Further, if one or two dimensions are particularly troubling for clients, they can be singled out and addressed in this type of instrument, which may lessen the impact that the troubling feelings have on their responses to questions about the other program dimensions.

The Dimensions of Satisfaction Used by a Nursing Home Admissions Department

Family members were asked five questions about their satisfaction with admissions when admitting their loved one to a nursing home (Huntersville Oaks Nursing Home, 2005). These five questions addressed the following five dimensions of admissions:

1. Support provided
2. Information regarding financial issues
3. The orientation to the nursing home
4. The amount of information provided
5. Overall assistance given

A five-point Likert scale (excellent, very good, good, fair, poor) was used to frame the questions.

Typically, a client satisfaction questionnaire with forced-response questions has one or two open-ended questions at the end of the instrument. The questions provide an opportunity for the respondent to comment on something that other questions did not address. The open-ended questions could be simply stated as, "Please share any additional comments," or "What are you satisfied with the most?" and "What are you least satisfied with?"

Example of Another Way to Explore Client Satisfaction

In the case of one client satisfaction study (Dansky, Colbert, & Irwin, 1996), two additional questions were asked: "Would you recommend this program to a friend" (yes, not sure, no), and "Would you return to this agency in the future if the need arose" (yes, not sure, no). Both questions get at client satisfaction with respect to telling others and returning in the future.

Another option is to use an unstructured interview format with open-ended questions about satisfaction. In this case, clients would be encouraged to respond to the questions in their own words as naturally as possible. Probing would be added as needed when clients' responses were not fully clear or needed elaboration. A qualitative interview may take a fair amount of time, perhaps an uninterrupted period of an hour, in a place that feels hospitable to clients. An interviewer could be someone known by the clients or a stranger. Both choices have advantages and disadvantages. A person who is known to clients and identified with the agency sponsor would be able to establish rapport more quickly and possibly ask questions within the context of the specific helping process. A disadvantage of using a familiar interviewer is that clients may be hesitant to share negative responses for fear of jeopardizing their standing as clients. A stranger may have more challenges establishing rapport because he or she would be unfamiliar to the clients; a stranger, though, may also have advantages eliciting an honest set of responses if clients are assured that their responses will be kept confidential.

Occasionally, a qualitative questionnaire has been used to determine satisfaction. In one study, forty children of divorced parents were asked to share their perceptions of a family-in-transition program in which they participated (Oliphant, Brown, Cambron, & Yankeelov, 2002). They were asked to respond to open-ended questions about the usefulness of the program in helping them cope; their feelings, experiences, and ideas about the program; and additional topics that they would have liked to have covered. They were also asked to list specific things that helped them. A qualitative questionnaire, while relevant with many types of clients and in a variety of circumstances, may also be too open-ended, time-consuming, and challenging to complete. A lower response rate may also result. Another option, of course, is to combine two or more methods. Possibly the structured questionnaire could be administered first, followed by an unstructured interview.

The decision about which type of instrument to use depends on whom is being studied, the costs, and time available. For example, the best fit for a satisfaction study of people who are unable to read would be an interview rather than a questionnaire, whereas a phone interview or a mailed questionnaire may be the best fit for a regional study of clients who live some distance from the evaluator.

Example of a Client Satisfaction Interview for Children

Prior, Lynch, and Glaser (1999) reported on a client satisfaction interview with children who were in a child sexual abuse program. The interview schedule used included both quantitative and qualitative questions. The children were asked to rate the social work services on several dimensions (listening and talking, providing information and explanation, social worker's attitude and demeanor, continuity and accessibility, and special occasions) using a three-point scale of positive, neutral, and negative. In each of these cases, the children were asked to elaborate on their answers. For example, one thirteen-year-old girl elaborated on her positive response about the social worker listening by saying, "If I didn't want to answer, which I sort of had to, she wouldn't force me to, she'd just go on to the next question, she wouldn't ask me to think."

Administering and Collecting a Client Satisfaction Instrument

It is often wise to alert clients that a client satisfaction survey is coming before it is actually handed out. Some agencies send a note or a postcard out to a client informing them of the study, explaining the purpose of the survey, stating how important clients' feedback is in evaluating the program's effectiveness, emphasizing confidentiality, and thanking them ahead of time. One agency even offered to give clients a small gift the next time that they came to the agency as an incentive for filling out the survey. Such gestures often may be important in maximizing clients' interest in participating. Further, such preparatory steps are often viewed as signs of courtesy and recognition of the value of clients' time.

Example of Multiple Use of Satisfaction Surveys

An agency providing group homes to people with developmental disabilities regularly uses several satisfaction surveys to obtain feedback on how the agency is doing and how it can improve its programs (Lori Gougeon, executive director of Residential Support Services, Charlotte, NC, personal communication, Jan. 21, 2005). This agency has a client satisfaction interview that is conducted with every client annually, using students and volunteers as interviewers. They also have a satisfaction questionnaire administered voluntarily to staff members and another questionnaire administered to all family members of clients. Finally, the agency conducts an annual satisfaction interview with several key community representatives who are familiar with the agency. The community representatives vary each year and have included representatives of other agencies, landlords and employers of clients, regular volunteers, leaders of civic associations, church members, and store clerks.

How the client satisfaction study is administered is also important to consider in order for the evaluator to have valid and reliable data. The person administering the questionnaire or interview needs to be well prepared and trained. In this regard, the person assigned to hand out a questionnaire to the clients is often not directly involved in the evaluation process for practical reasons. Usually it is not realistic for the evaluators or their assistants to be available to give it out to every client. Those assigned to hand it out could simply be asked to hand out the survey and remind the client to fill it out and return it. They could be a receptionist, secretary, a volunteer, another staff member, or even a manager who is uninformed about it.

In one example one of the authors (Dudley) encountered, a receptionist at a medical clinic handed him a patient satisfaction questionnaire and asked him to fill it out before he even saw his physician. The receptionist apparently did not know what the questionnaire was all about. So the author filled it out imagining what the visit with the physician would be like. He did not contest this inappropriate request so as not to avoid any delay in seeing the physician.

Other examples of mistakes and overt biases that have been evident in administering client satisfaction surveys include identifying clients to fill out a survey only after they have communicated a favorable verbal impression of the program provider, failing to adequately explain the purpose of the satisfaction survey, placing completed surveys in an open pile that violates privacy rights, requiring clients to fill out the survey rather than giving them the choice to participate, and looking over the results of clients' surveys in their presence.

What Students Learned from Conducting a Satisfaction Interview

Four graduate students conducted client satisfaction interviews with several people with mental retardation who lived in group homes. Afterward, they shared their experiences and what they learned with their class. Among the things that they learned were the following:

- Open- and closed-ended questions elicited very different, sometimes contradictory responses.
- Probe questions following interview questions can easily influence the nature of client responses, suggesting that probes should be standardized.
- Meeting in private is important because some of the questions were about their daily lives on a very personal level.
- The location of the interview in group homes made a big difference in responses (choices were the living room, the person's bedroom, and the office where the staff member usually works).
- Sometimes it was difficult understanding the respondent's speech, so a staff person assisted. In these instances, it became quite evident how much the staff member became an

"interpreter" by speaking for the respondent, interfering with what he or she said, and having an influence merely by being present.
• Some questions such as "What makes you happy?" brought more meaningful responses than most other questions.

Maximizing the chances of a high response rate by clients is another factor to consider. Because interviews are conducted with an interviewer present, their response rates are usually much higher than when using a questionnaire. How a questionnaire is introduced is critical. In terms of informed consent, all the necessary aspects of informed consent (e.g., purpose of the survey, confidentiality or anonymity, option to not participate, explanation of how results will be used, any potential harm or benefits from participation) should be shared, as both an introduction stated on the questionnaire and verbally by the person who administers it. Having a relatively quiet and private location for filling out the questionnaire is also important.

Another issue is how the survey is to be returned. Is it to be returned by mail? If so, it is necessary to include a self-addressed, stamped return envelope, with a reminder in large print to return it within a specific time, not to exceed seven to ten days from receipt. Furthermore, a follow-up reminder card or call helps increase response rate in many cases. If the questionnaires are to be completed at the agency site, allowing time to fill them out and having someone designated to collect them are necessities.

EVALUATING PRACTICE PROCESSES: SOME ADDITIONAL THOUGHTS

Many of the preceding types of evaluations could naturally focus on either programs or practice, even though the discussion so far has been mostly on programs. For example, linking client problems with the practice approach is relevant, as some practitioners may apply the same rigid approach with every client rather than varying their practice to clients' individualized needs. In this regard, one purpose of a practice evaluation might be to explore variations in the implementation of a practice approach and how variations may be linked to different types of client needs. It may well be that many staff members decide to use a specific practice theory without modifying it to what clients need. For example, one client may benefit from an approach that helps them gain insight into their problems using a cognitive behavioral approach, while another may need more emphasis on support rather than insight. More information on evaluating the implementation of practice approaches is presented next related to monitoring practice, accessing practice, and client satisfaction with practice.

Monitoring Practice

Practice quality is closely related to program quality, as the quality of an overall program depends on the quality of each service component, usually the services of individual staff members. Monitoring practice is a discipline that can help practitioners improve what they do. Social work practitioners often monitor the quality of their practice; some of their efforts may not even be considered evaluations.

Process recordings are an example of monitoring practice. Supervisors and practice teachers often request process recordings of new staff members and field students to find out what happens in their interviews. The recordings are then carefully reviewed in a supervisory session to explore the appropriateness of the social worker's responses to the client's comments. Often the recordings are helpful for revealing missed opportunities for the worker to respond to the subtle messages and emotional reactions of clients. The supervisory discussions can be very useful in helping new workers and students become more disciplined in how they use themselves in practice situations and in providing supervisors with enough information to be satisfied that clients receive satisfactory help.

Direct observations of practice through a two-way mirror or by videotaping and audio taping interviews are other ways to evaluate practice interventions through the supervisor-worker relationship. Other devices such as case summaries and personal logs of staff members can also be used to help practitioners monitor their own practice and receive helpful feedback from a supervisor. Discussion of case summaries of sessions can lead to planning future interviews and to modifications in a worker's approach.

Case managers carry a specific role that emphasizes monitoring the practice of other providers of service to a client (Frankel & Gelman, 2012). Social workers at the BSW level are especially equipped in their education to fill these positions. Case managers typically locate services for their clients, negotiate and facilitate contracts with agencies offering services, and monitor the range of services provided to the clients to ensure that they are appropriate to their needs and provided in a high-quality way.

Practice Accessibility

Problems of practice accessibility are inherent in an individual's practice, as they are in programs. Practitioners frequently face no-shows and early dropouts among their clients, which often points to accessibility barriers that need addressing. For example, prospective clients may explore the services of a practitioner by phone and agree to come to an initial interview. Yet they may neither show up nor call in to explain. Often clients come to an initial interview or the first session of a group but do not return again. Unless these no-shows and early dropouts are followed up in an attempt to find out what happened to them, practitioners cannot know whether accessibility barriers existed that could be overcome.

The Wrong Motives for Dealing with "No-Shows"

One mental health agency decided to address its high number of no-shows with two strategies. First, clinicians were encouraged to double-schedule appointments in hope that at least one of the two clients scheduled for each time slot would show up. If both clients showed up, the program director promised to find someone to meet with the second client. The other strategy was to employ a decision committee, which a client who had missed three or more appointments had to talk to before being scheduled for another session. The decision committee was used to stress clients' responsibility to attend all appointments and to inform clients that additional sessions would not be offered if they missed another session. The decision committee was not used to seriously explore the clients' reasons for no-shows. Both strategies were motivated by an administrative need to generate a maximum number of client reimbursements for the private-for-profit agency.

No-shows and dropouts can result from accessibility barriers, which should be carefully considered and addressed. Otherwise, the circumstances that cause or exacerbate the barriers could easily continue for prospective clients in the future. Some types of clients may easily use the services of a practitioner or program (e.g., a middle-class, married client, experienced in using a multitude of services, and who generally copes well with and manages personal issues). Others, possibly racial or ethnic minorities, low-income families, recent immigrants, single mothers, unmarried and inactive fathers, older lesbians, people with AIDS, people with chronic mental illness, and people with numerous other challenging characteristics are known to have been excluded or discouraged from using services. Studies have shown, for example, that no-show behavior can be correlated with low income (e.g., Allan, 1988), lower socioeconomic status (e.g., Lefebrve, Sommerauer, Cohen, Waldron, & Perry, 1983), age (e.g., Carpenter, Morrow, Del Guadio, & Ritzler, 1981), and substance abuse (e.g., Paolillo & Moore, 1984), among other factors.

Concluding that clients and prospective clients are simply resistant or unmotivated to use services is a frequently given excuse and a superficial way to ignore some of the more complicated and valid explanations. Some more valid explanations can be explored by considering the types of barriers described previously (e.g., physical, psychological, cultural, geographic, institutional).

Practitioners are encouraged to devise a plan to address accessibility barriers when they face a considerable number of no-shows or dropouts. Meyer (2001) offers some suggestions. One barrier may be the wait time before a first visit, as the longer the wait time to obtain a first appointment, the less likely a client is to keep the next appointment. Thus, workers should minimize any wait time initially or before any session. Another barrier could be the expectation of employers that clients accomplish speedy outcomes as a result of the growing pressures that assistance be short-term and address only immediate problems.

Another concern, according to Meyer (2001), may be that the client's problems with service providers in the past were barriers because former providers may have been unresponsive or unhelpful. In this case, special efforts may be in order to help clients openly talk about their negative past experiences, and they may need to be reassured that such experiences will not be repeated. Another suggestion is that the practitioner demonstrate the qualities of the therapeutic relationship from the very first contact, whether by phone or in person; these qualities include reliability, trustworthiness, calmness, respect, good listening, warmth, empathic responses, and not rushing. Well-thought-out and sensitive follow-up efforts are also encouraged when a client does not show up for an appointment. Such inquiries could include asking a client in a direct but nonjudgmental and caring way why he or she missed the appointment and exploring how the client wants to proceed.

Staudt, Bates, Blake, and Shoffner (2004) offer further suggestions for preventing no-shows. Besides emphasizing with clients such central practice qualities as conveying a nonjudgmental attitude and clearly explaining the confidentiality policy, they suggest some helpful practice notions that could enhance the possibility that clients will return for their second and later interviews. These practice techniques include contracting for a set number of sessions, eliciting what the client wants to get out of treatment, asking clients what might prevent them from returning, and educating clients about their role and the role of the social worker.

Client Satisfaction with Practice

Obtaining feedback from clients on their satisfaction is important to consider not only in monitoring programs but also in practice. Social workers can be encouraged to periodically have informal discussions with clients or ask them to fill out questionnaires to elicit their feedback on how helpful the services have been and what can be done to improve them. A social worker can ask clients several basic questions, such as the following:

• How satisfied are you with the services that you have been receiving?
• Are you feeling satisfied generally? In what ways?

- How might you be feeling dissatisfied or disappointed? In what specific areas?
- What am I doing that is helpful to you? How is it helpful?
- What additionally would you like me to do?
- What am I doing that is not helpful to you?
- How am I helping you reach your goals?
- How do you feel about the session today (a good overall question at the end of each session)?

Client Satisfaction Using a Focus Group

A graduate student (Borys, 2006) decided to conduct a client satisfaction study with her clients to find out what the aftercare residents of a substance abuse agency for women thought were the strengths and weaknesses of their program. She used a focus group format and asked the following questions:

1. What do you feel are the strengths of the program?
2. What do you see as some areas that need to be improved?
3. What part of the program have you struggled with the most?
4. If you could change anything about the program, what would it be?

In brief, a general consensus was reached about bringing back a residential program that had been discontinued; providing more advocacy for housing, jobs, and day care; having a supportive staff; and involving board members more with the residents, including being more of an advocate for them.

Client satisfaction is especially important to explore at the time that a client is terminating services. Yet it is strongly advised that client satisfaction explorations also occur periodically while services are still being offered. In this way, changes can be incorporated into a worker's practice during sessions that follow. In addition, periodic client satisfaction conversations can create greater bonding with clients because clients feel they are being heard and that their voice is important.

KEY TERMS

Best practices
Client satisfaction
Cultural barriers
Evidence-based practice
Geographic barriers

Implementation evaluations
Institutional barriers
Link between client problems and the intervention
Monitoring practice
Physical barriers
Practice accessibility
Program accessibility
Program implementation
Program quality
Psychological barriers
Quality assurance
Quality control
Quality improvement
Staff morale and satisfaction

DISCUSSION QUESTIONS AND ASSIGNMENTS

1. Identify the key elements of a program at your field agency that are necessary for it to be effective in addressing the causes of clients' problems. Then ask three different staff members to identify how these elements are present and operable in the program.
2. Review the factors of the larger context of a program in chapter 1. In your opinion, which factors are essential for the effective functioning of a program? Which are optional? Give reasons for your answers. Which factors are essential for accountability? Which are important in responding to the sociocultural characteristics of a program? Give examples.
3. Assume that you work for a child welfare agency that previously provided protective services in instances of child neglect. Now the agency is preparing to provide secondary prevention services to families who may be most prone to neglecting their children as a result of a range of problems. Identify a list of questions that you can ask families to determine which families would be most qualified to be clients of this secondary prevention program.
4. You plan an education symposium on preventing strokes for the older adults in your community and hold the symposium at the local hospital. You are pleased that the symposium has a good turnout of older and middle-aged adults but as you look around the room you see almost no African American adults present. You know that African Americans have a higher incidence of stroke than other ethnic groups. Design a plan for another community education program that will reach this underrepresented group of older adults.
5. Review the two strategies to address no-shows in "The Wrong Motives for Dealing with No-Shows." What is ethically wrong with

these strategies? How, if at all, could either strategy be modified in some way to make it ethical and possibly effective?

6. a) Conduct a role-play of a client satisfaction exploration between a social worker and a client after meeting for five sessions. You can use some of the questions found in the chapter or the following questions in the interview.

    a. Generally, how are we doing?

    b. How am I doing?

    c. What's helpful?

    d. What's not so helpful?

    e. What would you like to have that you are not getting?

  b) Now add the following variations in separate interviews:

    a. A client is Asian American and tends to defer to the person in authority.

    b. A client is from the Southern region of the United States and tends not to want to directly question the person in authority; the client tends to be less direct and less open but has some complaints to share.

    c. Vary the client's age (e.g., young adult, older adult).

    d. A client is the victim of domestic violence.

    e. A client is a perpetrator of domestic violence in an involuntary setting.

REFERENCES

Acker, G. M. (1999). The impact of clients' mental illness on social workers' job satisfaction and burnout. *Health and Social Work, 24*(2), 112–119.

Allan, A. T. (1988). No-shows at a community mental health center: A pilot study. *The International Journal of Social Psychiatry, 34*(1), 40–46.

Americans with Disabilities Act of 1990. Pub. L. 110-325.

Baker, L., Zucker, P., & Gross, M. (1998). Using client satisfaction surveys to evaluate and improve services in locked and unlocked adult inpatient facilities. *Journal of Behavioral Health Services Research, 25*(1), 51–68.

Borys, L. (2006). Focus group assignment for a program evaluation course. Unpublished manuscript, University of North Carolina at Charlotte.

Brodkin, E. Z. (1997). Inside the welfare contract: Discretion and accountability in state welfare administration. *Social Service Review, 71*(1), 1–33.

Brownson, R. C., Colditz, G. A., & Proctor, E. K. (2012). *Dissemination and implementation research in health: Translating science to practice.* New York: Oxford University Press.

Carpenter, P., Morrow, G., Del Guadio, A., & Ritzler, B. A. (1981). Who keeps the first outpatient appointment? *American Journal of Psychiatry, 138*, 102–105.

Cohen, J. A., & Mannarino, A. P. (2008). Trauma-focused cognitive behavioral therapy for children and parents. *Child and Adolescent Mental Health, 13*, 158–162.

Dansky, K. H., Colbert, C. J., & Irwin, P. (1996). Developing and using a patient satisfaction survey: A case study. *Clinical and Program Notes, 45*, 83–88.

Dixon, L., Lyles, A., Scott, J., Lehman, A., Postrado, L., Goldman, H., et al. (1999). Services to families of adults with schizophrenia: From treatment recommendations to dissemination. *Psychiatric Services, 50*(2), 233–238.

Durlak, J. A., & DuPre, E. P. (2008). Implementation matters: A review of research on the influence of implementation on program outcomes and the factors affecting implementation. *American Journal of Community Psychology, 41,* 327–350.

Eyberg, S. M., Boggs, S., & Algina, J. (1995). Parent Child Interaction Therapy: A psychosocial model for the treatment of young children with conduct problem behavior and their families. *Psychopharmacology Bulletin, 31,* 83–91.

Fischer, R. L. (2002). Gaining access to one's children: An evaluation of a visitation program for noncustodial parents. *Families in Society, 83*(2), 163–174.

Fixsen, D. L., Naoom, S. F., Blase, K. A., Friedman, R. M., & Wallace, F. (2005). *Implementation research: A synthesis of the literature.* Tampa, FL: University of South Florida, Louis de la Parte Florida Mental Health Institute, The National Implementation Research Network (FMHI Publication #231). Available at http://nirn.fmhi.usf.edu.

Forgatch, M. S., Patterson, G. R., & DeGarmo, D. S. (2005). Evaluating fidelity: Predictive validity for a measure of competent adherence to the Oregon model of parent management training. *Behavior Therapy, 36,* 3–13.

Foster, J., & Hope, T. (1993). *Housing, community and crime: The impact of the Priority Estates Project.* London: HMSO.

Frankel, A. J., & Gelman, S. R. (2012). *Case management: An introduction to concepts and skills* (3rd ed.). Chicago: Lyceum Books.

Gardner, F. (2000). Design evaluation: Illuminating social work practice for better outcomes. *Social Work, 45*(2), 176–182.

Glisson, C., & Green, P. (2006). The effects of organizational culture and climate on the access to mental health care in child welfare and juvenile justice systems. *Administration and Policy in Mental Health and Mental Health Services Research, 33*(4), 443–448.

Hallfors, D., & Cho, H. (2007). Moving behavioral science from efficacy to effectiveness. *International Journal of Behavioral Consultation and Therapy, 3*(2), 236–249.

Hepworth, D. H., Rooney, R. H., Rooney, G. D., Strom-Gottfried, K., & Larsen, J. H. (2009). *Direct social work practice: Theory and skills* (8th ed.). Belmont, CA: Brooks/Cole.

Hogue, A., Henderson, C. E., Dauber, S., Barajas, P. C., Fried, A., & Liddle, H. A. (2008). Treatment adherence, competence, and outcome in individual and family therapy for adolescent behavior problems. *Journal of Consulting and Clinical Psychology, 4*(4), 544–555.

Huntersville Oaks Nursing Home. (2005). Nursing home admissions satisfaction survey. Huntersville, NC: Author.

Joyce, B., & Showers, B. (2002). *Student achievement through staff development* (3rd ed.). Alexandria, VA: Association for Supervision and Curriculum Development.

Kennedy, E., Wilson, B., Valladares, S., & Bronte-Tinkew, J. (2007). Improving attendance and retention in out-of-school time programs. *Child Trends,* Publication 2007-17.

Lefebrve, A., Sommerauer, J., Cohen, N., Waldron, S., & Perry, I. (1983). Where did all the "no-shows" go? *Canadian Journal of Psychiatry, 28,* 387–390.

Lieberman, A. F., & Van Horn, P. (2004). *Don't hit my mommy: A manual for child parent psychotherapy with young witnesses of family violence*. Washington, DC: Zero to Three.

Lieberman, A. F., & Van Horn, P. (2008). *Psychotherapy with infants and young children: Repairing the effects of stress and trauma on early attachment*. New York: Guilford.

Lieberman, A. F., Van Horn, P., & Ippen, C. (2005). Toward evidence-based treatment: Child Parent Psychotherapy with preschoolers exposed to marital violence. *Journal of the American Academy of Child and Adolescent Psychiatry, 44*(12), 1241–1248.

Meyer, W. S. (2001). Why they don't come back: A clinical perspective on the no-show client. *Clinical Social Work Journal, 29*(4), 325–339.

Mitchell, P. F. (2011). Evidence-based practice in real-world services for young people with complex needs: New opportunities suggested by recent implementation science. *Children and Youth Services Review, 33*, 207–216.

Mor Barak, M. E., Nissly, J. A., & Levin, A. (2001). Antecedents to retention and turnover among child welfare, social work, and other human service employees: What can we learn from past research? A review and metanalysis. *Social Service Review, 75*(4), 625–661.

Murphy, B. C., & Dillon, C. (2008). *Interviewing in action in a multicultural world* (3rd ed.). Belmont, CA: Brooks/Cole.

Oliphant, E., Brown, J. H., Cambron, M. L., & Yankeelov, P. (2002). Measuring children's perceptions of the 'Families in Transition' Program (FIT): A qualitative evaluation. *Journal of Divorce and Remarriage, 37*(4), 157–164.

Paolillo, J. G., & Moore, T. W. (1984). Appointment compliance behavior of community mental health patients: A discriminant analysis. *Community Mental Health Journal, 20*(2), 103–108.

Pawson, R., & Tilley, N. (1997). *Realistic evaluation*. Thousand Oaks, CA: Sage.

Prior, V., Lynch, M. A., & Glaser, D. (1999). Responding to child sexual abuse: An evaluation of social work by children and carers. *Child and Family Social Work, 4*, 131–143.

Proctor, E., Knudsen, K., Fedoravicius, N., Hovmand, P., Rosen, A., & Perron, B. (2007). Implementation of evidence-based practice in community behavioral health: Agency director perspectives. *Administration and Policy in Mental Health, 34*, 479–488.

Proctor, E., Silmere, H., Raghavan, R., Hovmand, P., Aarons, G., Bunger, A., Griffey, R., & Hensley, M. (2010). Outcomes for implementation research: Conceptual distinctions, measurement challenges, and research agenda. *Administration and Policy in Mental Health and Mental Health Services Research, 38*, 65–76.

Reese, D., Ahern, R., Nair, S., O'Faire, J., & Warren, C. (1999). Hospice access and use by African Americans: Addressing cultural and institutional barriers through participatory action research. *Social Work, 44*(6), 549–559.

Reid, K. E. (1997). *Social work practice with groups: A clinical perspective* (2nd ed.). Belmont, CA: Thomson Learning–Brooks/Cole.

Schectman, J. M., Schroth, W. S., Verme, D., & Voss, J. D. (2003). Randomized controlled trial of education and feedback for implementation of guidelines for acute low back pain. *Journal of General Internal Medicine, 18*(10), 773–780.

Spouse, J. (2001). Bridging theory and practice in the supervisory relationship: A sociocultural perspective. *Journal of Advanced Nursing, 33*(4), 512–522.

Staudt, M. M., Bates, D., Blake, G. H., & Shoffner, J. S. (2004). Practice evaluation: Moving beyond single system designs. *Arete, 27*(2), 71–78.

Stein, K. F., Sargent, J. T., & Rafaels, N. (2007) Intervention research: Establishing fidelity of the independent variable in nursing clinical trials. *Nursing Research, 56*(1), 54–62.

Weinbach, R. W. (2005). *Evaluating social work services and programs.* Boston: Allyn & Bacon.

Part V

The Outcome Stage

Chapter 9

Is the Intervention Effective?

A critical question to ask at this stage is, how do we know that our program really helps clients?

This chapter addresses this outcome question. It does this by focusing on some of the issues of outcome studies during step 4 (plan the evaluation) of the Seven Evaluation Steps. To many people, the evaluation of programs and practice essentially means evaluating whether the intervention resulted in positive outcomes for clients. Outcome questions have a familiar ring to them: Did the clients reach their goals? Did they make significant progress? Is there evidence that the program made a difference in their functioning?

Although outcome studies are presented as one of three general types of evaluations in this text (i.e., planning, implementation, and outcome), it must be said that they are ultimately the most important type. If progress on clients' goals is not evident after the completion of a program, a provider will have difficulty justifying the program's continuation. This is the case no matter how well the program was planned, how qualified the staff members are who provide services, and even if the program's quality is superior. This is also true for practice interventions. If practice interventions do not lead to substantial gains for clients in the intended areas, then the intervention needs major modifications or should be discontinued and replaced with another approach.

This chapter describes the critical ingredients in outcome evaluations, including two basic elements: a clearly defined intervention and measurable client outcomes. Several types of evaluation designs used in outcome evaluations are presented. The advantages and limitations of each design and what each can claim are described, with examples of outcome evaluations given to help illustrate the relevant concepts. (See figure 9.1.)

Based on the logic model, outcomes for clients are directly linked back to activities completed in the planning stage. During that stage, clients' problems, needs, and the causes of their problems were identified and assessed. Goals and measurable objectives were crafted next, reflecting how these problems could be resolved. An intervention came next, developed particularly to help clients reach these goals. Finally, we now come to the outcome stage when we focus on measuring of these goals to determine if they have been achieved.

FIGURE 9.1   Evaluation of the Intervention

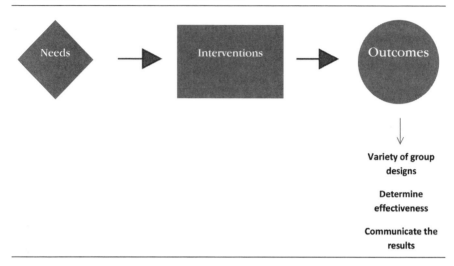

THE NATURE OF OUTCOMES

Program and practice outcomes can focus on many things. Outcome measures may be identified for staff members' performance, material resources, recruiting of more clients, or other concerns. Ultimately, however, the outcomes for clients are the focus of human service outcome evaluations. Outcomes typically are the goals of clients and measure whether the goals have been reached. Chapter 7 described how to identify, describe, and measure goals.

Outcomes Are Not Outputs

The outcomes of clients, which are the ultimate interest of a program or practice evaluation, have several distinct characteristics. Unfortunately, most agencies focus almost exclusively on outputs rather than outcomes in their performance reports that are available to the public. For example, an agency report may focus on the number of staff hours of counseling provided, the number of clients who use services, or the costs of a particular program.

Excerpts from an Annual Report of a County Government

The following statistics are from the annual report of the Cabarrus County government (2007):

- 322,000 people visited county-operated parks.
- 14,706 people participated in athletics, competitions, and other recreational events held in county parks.

- 7,801 calls and personal contacts came into the Veterans' Services office.
- 976,939 miles were driven by county vans.
- 81,847 rides were provided to disabled and/or elderly residents by the county transportation service.
- 35,335 individuals visited the Department of Social Services for services or assistance.
- 5,085 families in a crisis situation received assistance through the Department of Social Services.
- 3,885 children were protected from abuse, neglect, or dependency through provision of child protective services.

Note that all of these indicators are outputs, even though some may be misrepresented as outcomes. The last output in the preceding example, "children were protected from abuse, neglect, or dependency," is incorrectly stated and should be phrased "children were provided with child protective services." The agency did not have any evidence from a follow-up inquiry to conclude that the children were protected.

Outcomes Ultimately Focus on the Clients, Not Staff Interventions

A frequent problem for many who are new at crafting outcomes for clients is confusing client outcomes with outcomes for the staff that are helping them. For example, "The client will be referred to X agency for assistance whenever the program cannot help her." Note that this statement refers more to what a staff member will do than to what the client does. Many stakeholders may think that the goals of the staff members are outcomes. In a sense they are, but outcomes for staff activities are more appropriately referred to as the means of achieving goals.

Articulating and documenting outcomes for staff activities can be helpful, especially because client outcomes usually depend on the success of staff in reaching their goals. Outcomes for staff members can be viewed as an appropriate evaluation focus at the process stage, such as when we ask whether staff members use evidenced-based practice theories or provide quality services. Nevertheless, these outcomes are not the end results sought for clients.

Quiz: Are These Outcomes for Clients or Staff Members?

Try to pick out which of the following outcomes or goals are the clients' and which are the staff members'.

1. The clients will be transported to the grocery store in the agency van every Monday.
2. The clients will purchase groceries for the evening meal.

3. The client will have access to a planned meal written out on a piece of paper.
4. The client will pay for the groceries using the money available for shopping.
5. The clients will have enough money to buy the groceries.

The correct answers to the outcomes in the preceding quiz are that nos. 2 and 4 focus on clients and the others focus on staff members. The fifth outcome could be intended either for the clients or for staff, depending on who has control over the funds for shopping; unfortunately, it is presented in an ambiguous way. Overall, the five examples show how dependent client outcomes are on staff outcomes.

Outcomes Are Directly Linked to the Interventions

It is important that the link between outcome measures and the intervention used to influence them be readily evident according to the logic model. This should be the case both conceptually and practically. Often, having a commonsense approach to understand the intervention helps in the crafting of realistic outcome measures. For example, the community organization mentioned in chapter 7 that wanted to reduce the number of divorces in the community within the first few years of marriage decided to offer a premarital weekend retreat format at several different houses of worship to help couples become better prepared for their marriages. The retreat curriculum included five major components: communication between the couple, having realistic expectations of a partner, finances, health issues, and sexuality and intimacy. The sponsoring organization recruited speakers who had expertise in each topical area to lead the components. On the basis of this information, the evaluator devised a pretest-posttest measure of outcomes for the retreat based on what could be realistically expected from participation in each retreat component. Specific questions were devised on the basis of the specific objectives of each speaker. For example, the topic of having realistic expectations of your partner included questions such as, "Do you know what your spouse expects of you?" "Do you and your partner know how to resolve conflicts when they arise?" and "Do you know how to meet your partner's needs?" The response categories were "yes," "sometimes," and "no." The sponsors finally realized that reducing the number of divorces was not a realistic goal for their program even though it was obviously relevant.

Outcomes Are Determined at Different Points in Time

The point in time to measure a client outcome is an important factor to consider. For example, outcomes can be measured when a client completes a program or at some future time. Outcomes can be short-term (e.g., when a client completes the program), intermediate (e.g., three months later), or long-term (e.g., twelve months later). The time selected and the specific outcome expected depend on the amount of time realistically needed for the program to have such an impact.

Example of Outcomes at Different Points in Time

A crisis center for transient youths decided to use short-, intermediate-, and long-term outcomes for the youths they sheltered. Their outcome measures were as follows:

Short term: reduction in runaway behavior, physically aggressive behavior, and serious physically aggressive threats while residing at the crisis center.

Intermediate term: residence in a safe, least restrictive environment for two months after discharge and increased family access to community services.

Long term: residence in a safe, least restrictive environment for six months after discharge, increased school attendance, and reduction in involvement with the juvenile justice system.

Unfortunately, most evaluations are set up to measure client outcomes only when clients complete the program or otherwise terminate from the agency. This is an important time to measure outcomes, as it provides a measure of how much change occurred while the client was in the program. Yet this single short-term outcome measure usually reveals little, if anything, about the long-term effects of a program. Inpatient programs for drug-addicted clients, for example, are often criticized for not providing a long-lasting impact on recovery. Clients who leave a program may be drug free, but the true test of their success is likely determined over time, once they return to their community and reconnect with their social supports, both previous and new. Unfortunately, many substance abuse programs do not conduct a follow-up evaluation to determine whether their services led to long-term recovery or a return to addiction and a lifestyle that supports addiction.

VARIED WAYS TO MEASURE OUTCOMES

Martin and Kettner (1996) identify what they perceive as four kinds of outcome or performance measures: numeric counts, standardized measures, scales of level of client functioning, and client satisfaction indicators. Numeric counts are generally used to measure client conditions, status, and behaviors. Examples include attendance at school, frequency of drinking alcohol, and numbers of violent and other antisocial behaviors. Standardized measures usually measure such things as client feelings, attitudes, and perceptions. Examples of such scales include self-esteem, clinical anxiety, hope, and happiness. Level-of-functioning scales measure client and family functioning. Examples include scales of adaptive behavior, employment behavior, wellness, and social integration. Martin and Kettner (1996) also refer to client satisfaction as an outcome; however, they view client perceptions of the services received as only an intermediate outcome, not a final one.

Child Welfare Outcomes Document on the Internet

The U.S. Department of Health and Human Services' Children's Bureau (2009) includes child welfare outcomes as part of its annual report to Congress. The report also provides data on states' performance in meeting the needs of children and families who come into contact with the child-welfare system. Federal data-reporting systems are used to gather data on seven outcomes: reduced recurrence of child abuse and neglect, reduced child abuse and neglect in foster care, increased permanency for children in foster care, reduced time in foster care to reunification, reduced time in foster care to adoption, increased placement stability, and reduced placement of young children in group homes and institutions. The executive report and additional information can be found on http://www.acf.hhs.gov/sites/default/files/cb/executive06_09.pdf.

Practical Measures of Outcomes

Ideally, virtually every agency has identified client outcomes that they are helping clients accomplish. Because the outcomes are the ultimate reason for the agency's existence, it makes sense to keep them at the forefront of their work, their conversations with clients, their sources of referrals, and their education of the general public. One agency, for example, does just that. Community Choices Inc. (2006) helps pregnant women addicted to alcohol and/or drugs by offering group treatment. The outcomes of the agency are evident in much of its material, including the brochure handed out to prospective clients and referral agencies. Outcomes that they highlight for clients are becoming drug free; maintaining or regaining custody of children; having a healthy, drug-free baby; becoming self-sufficient; finding a job; finding permanent housing; improving parenting skills; and feeling better about themselves. The open and direct communication about the outcomes has many benefits, including helping the women identify what they want or need, self-selecting the agency as a result of desired outcomes, and communicating the agency's purpose and intentions to the general public.

Outcome Indicators Used for Clients in a Domestic Violence Agency

The following indicators are from White (2005):

- Homicide rate (chosen by the county government)
- Perceived degree of safety
- Knowledge of a safety plan that could be used in an emergency
- Acknowledgment of a broad definition of domestic violence
- Favorable responses to client satisfaction questions
- Referral contact rate (when client follows through and contacts another agency he or she is referred to)
- Recidivism rate (returning to agency a second time or more)

Litzelfelner (2001) gives another example of a need for practical outcomes when the overall goal of a program is not measurable. She points out that the goal of child protective services to protect children from abuse is not usually measurable. Abuse and re-abuse of children are often undiscovered or unreported. She offers what she views as practical alternative measures in a set of four general areas related to child abuse: child safety, child permanency, preserving families, and child health and development. For each area, she identifies several measurable objectives and activities to reach the objectives. For example, for child safety, she suggests two objectives as examples: (1) 90 percent of children served will not reenter the system within two years following their initial discharge (based on reports of the agency's home visit and case management services), and (2) each quarter, 85 percent of caregivers participating in the parent education program will demonstrate three nonphysical behavior management techniques during the agency's home visits. As an exercise, identify the weaknesses in this approach to measuring child abuse. Then develop an alternative approach that could be another way to measure child abuse.

Outcomes can also be measured by qualitative methods. One student who was working with a group of emotionally disturbed children in a public school decided to use journaling to measure progress on their personal goals related to self-esteem (McLean, 2007). She encouraged her group members to keep an ongoing journal of their impressions discussed in the group. They were given ten minutes at the end of each session to write about their impressions. During most sessions, members were asked to journal on the topics that had been discussed, such as, what are the benefits of self-esteem? or how can mistakes be opportunities for growth? Journaling during the first and last sessions was used to evaluate their progress in working on their personal goals. During the first session, members were asked to journal on their goals and expectations for the group. The topic for them to focus on was, what do I want to get out of this group? The final session was used to journal on the topic, how has the group changed my self-esteem? Quantitative ratings were also used to evaluate their progress on goals during the last session.

CRITERIA FOR CHOOSING OUTCOME MEASURES

What determines whether an outcome measure is adequate or acceptable? Martin and Kettner (1996) offer seven criteria: the outcome measure's usefulness, validity, reliability, precision, feasibility, cost, and unit costs.

Usefulness

First, the measure needs to be useful and relevant to stakeholders. This is a commonsense criterion that raises an important question: How will the outcome measure be useful? Will it offer helpful information to stakeholders to support the program or assist them in improving, expanding, or even reducing it?

Validity

Is the outcome measure valid? Validity is one of the two psychometric standards for determining whether a measure is satisfactory. Validity refers to whether the outcome measure reflects what it is supposed to measure and whether it does so accurately. Accuracy is the key issue. The more valid that a measure is, the better it is. For example, an outcome measure for father involvement should include several different functions or activities, not just one. Some will involve direct contact with their child (e.g., how many direct contact hours in an average week, quality of the specific activities), and other functions may involve no contact but direct responsibilities (e.g., attending a parent-teacher conference, arranging a dental appointment for the child). From this example, it is clear how complex outcomes like father involvement are and the enormous challenges they pose for creating accurate measures. Father involvement requires at the very least a certain amount of contact; and the quality of that contact, whether direct contact or indirect responsibilities, is also important to consider.

Reliability

The third criterion for choosing an outcome measure is reliability. Reliability is a second key psychometric standard in determining whether a measure is satisfactory. Reliability refers to the internal consistency of the measure. It asks two questions: whether the measure of the outcome consistently measures it from one time to another and whether the measure is consistently applied among different people (e.g., do different clients consistently understand the measure in the same way?). Reliability is weak if the questions asked in a measurement instrument are ambiguous, with words likely to be understood and interpreted differently at different times or by different respondents. For example, satisfaction with a program can be interpreted in many ways.

Precision

Precision is the fourth criterion. Precision refers to how well the outcome measure captures the incremental changes in clients' condition, either quantitatively or qualitatively. Quantitative measures are at the interval, ordinal, or nominal levels. Qualitative measures are at the prenominal level. For example, incremental quantitative measures are the number of times truant children attend school (interval level) and their average letter grade (ordinal). An example of an incremental qualitative measure is the subtle variations in how a parent uses nonviolent strategies in disciplining their children.

Feasibility

A fifth criterion in deciding on outcome measures is their feasibility. Is the measure viewed as practical and acceptable to all stakeholders? Some may be opposed to a measure because it is at odds with their cultural values or ethics. For example, a measure of assertiveness needs to take into account the ways that various cultural groups view confrontation with authority. Feasibility may also be a problem if it is likely to demand a lot of the attention and time of staff members in explaining or administering it.

Cost

The cost of an outcome measure is another criterion. Does the measure require some major start-up or maintenance costs? Another possible cost factor is the purchase of any standardized scales owned by other people or organizations.

Unit Cost Reporting

Unit cost reporting is the final criterion. Can the measure be described as a cost per unit of outcome? For example, the cost of a client graduating from a program could be used as a cost per unit of outcome. Numeric counts lend themselves to this type of cost more than other measures, such as standardized scales.

OUTCOMES AND PROGRAM COSTS

Sometimes outcome studies are conducted that focus directly on costs. Some refer to these evaluations as cost-benefit or cost-effectiveness evaluations. Cost-related evaluations are increasingly important to consider, given the diminishing funds for human service programs and the increasing call for financial accountability. One ethical dilemma with cost-benefit studies is that it is too difficult to directly translate the benefits of a program, such as reduced child abuse or treating and managing severe mental illness, into financial savings. Although immediate financial savings are evident in such things as fewer health-care visits and avoiding legal costs in a court case, the benefits of protecting a child from harm go well beyond material factors and may have implications for the life of the child and for the child's offspring. In brief, although fiscal matters have obvious value, their value is limited and should be subordinate to the value of basic human needs.

Cost-effectiveness evaluations, similar to cost-benefit studies, may have more utility in human service programs than cost-benefit studies. In this case, the client outcomes resulting from a program can be analyzed according to cost. The cost, for example, of obtaining adoptions, on average, for special needs children could be considered in terms of costs. The costs could then be compared to the costs of such an outcome in the previous year, or two different programs could be compared on the basis of the costs incurred in completing a successful adoption.

It is complicated but possible to calculate costs in a human services program. For example, one could categorize costs into direct (e.g., staff salary) and indirect (e.g., secretarial salary, telephone bills). Costs could also be divided into fixed (e.g., building maintenance) and variable (e.g., salaries), and recurring (e.g., rent) and nonrecurring (e.g., equipment). Determining the costs of providing services to an average client must take all of these costs into account, which sometimes becomes a real challenge to figure out. For example, in the 1970s, with de-institutionalization of people with mental retardation, some legislators wanted to argue in favor of either community-based services or institutional services which had lower per capita costs. This exercise led to the discovery that it was easier to calculate the per capita costs of community-based services because they were discrete (e.g., residential, vocational, recreational). In contrast, the cost of institutional services, encumbered by extensive capital costs such as maintenance of buildings and grounds, was more difficult to calculate accurately.

EVIDENCE-BASED INTERVENTIONS

Once the outcome measures have been carefully selected for an evaluation, another challenging task is to demonstrate that the measures are logically and empirically linked to the intervention that will be used. Interventions that are empirically linked to important outcome measures are evidence-based interventions. This raises a critical point about evidence-based interventions—they are interventions that have, to some degree, a demonstrated causal relationship to particular client outcomes.

Evidence-based interventions were defined in chapter 2 as integrating individual practice expertise, the best-available external evidence from practice research, and the values and expectations of clients (Gambrill, 1999, p. 346). This definition suggests that evidence-based should not be either defined simply by one criterion or based on solely one source. Instead, the interventions should have multiple factors in common. One such factor, a necessary one, is that evidence-based interventions have the best evidence available that they are effective in helping clients, and strong evidence is available to support the claim in the measures of client outcomes. Thus, we can say that evidence-based interventions should be grounded one way or another in outcome evaluations of some form.

O'Hare (2005) describes four important characteristics of evidence-based practices: they use critical-thinking skills, obtain scientifically credible evidence, seek multiple sources of evidence whenever possible, and seek diversity-sensitive evidence.

Critical-Thinking Skills

Critical-thinking skills are used to determine whether an intervention is evidence-based. Critical thinkers are natural skeptics about how well an evaluation is conducted, whether someone else's evaluation or one's own. Critical thinkers are also skeptical about whether their interventions actually work. As mentioned in chapter 1, Gibbs and Gambrill (1996) identify several types of problems that evaluators experience when they fail to be critical thinkers, including the selection of weak or inappropriate interventions.

Scientifically Credible Evidence

Evidence-based interventions must have documentation that is scientifically credible. This means, in part, that there is scientific evidence of a causal relationship between the intervention and clients' outcomes. Such evidence for programs is most likely to come from group designs, especially experimental and quasi-experimental designs, which are known to be superior to other evaluation strategies (Cook & Campbell, 1979). Evidence for practice interventions is most likely to come from a version of a single-system design, especially a design that controls for as many extraneous influences as possible.

Scientifically credible evidence and critical thinking share many common values. Both approaches involve skepticism. Both carefully distinguish between questions of fact and questions of value. Both use caution when inferring what may have caused improvement in the client outcomes and when to make generalizations to other client groups, and both emphasize the need for measurement in the identification of clients' needs, interventions, and outcomes. Finally, both perspectives are likely to continually ask, does this intervention work?

Seeking Multiple Sources of Evidence

Triangulation, a process of using multiple methods to measure something, is also important to evidence-based interventions. Evaluators who obtain two or more measures of an outcome for comparison triangulate the findings. The process also adds confidence that the two measures are valid because of their similarity. The more sources available that document that the intervention has a causal relationship to client outcomes, the better. An example is to find out the frequency of a nonresidential father's contact with his children in an average week by seeking a report from two or more sources (e.g., the father, the children's mother, the father's current partner).

Criterion-related validity is another way to triangulate the findings of an evaluation. Criterion-related validity is a means of determining whether the scores of an outcome measure are valid by correlating the scores with those of another measure of the same construct (Babbie, 2001). The other measures of the same construct are external criteria. For example, an external criterion could be a behavioral indicator that correlates with a verbal response of a client to an interview question. If a short-term outcome measure of an evaluation is regular attendance at a drug treatment program, the evaluator could compare the client's report of his or her attendance with a report of attendance obtained from the drug treatment agency. In another example, the outcome measure could be a depression scale developed by an agency, and the scores could be correlated with the scores of the same clients using a well-established measure like the Beck Depression Scale (Beck, Steer, & Brown, 1996).

Evidence Is Diversity Sensitive

If there is evidence that a program or practice intervention is effective with one group of people, it is extremely important not to automatically conclude that it will be effective with other groups. This is a fallacy that has resulted from the misuse of previous findings, especially evidence that a particular approach helps white, middle-class men and generalization of its effectiveness to people of other races and social classes, as well as white women. Evidence must be obtained skeptically for each group before arrival at such a conclusion. The issue of generalizing the results of a group design to other people is the external validity of the group design.

Thyer and Meyers (2003) recommend that the most realistic way to generalize the results of a group design to other client groups is to use the process of replication. Replication involves repeating a group design with different client groups and at various times. If the results of a group design reveal that an intervention works for one client group, the intervention could be tried with a different client group that has similar characteristics. If the same result occurs, a claim that the intervention is effective would be somewhat strengthened. This could be followed by further replication, such as with similar clients in another agency or by other evaluators with similar clients in other geographic areas. Also, if the results of the group design indicate that an intervention is effective with a group of men, the intervention could be tried with a group of women. Or if an intervention works for young-adult clients, it could be tested with middle-aged adults. Repeated replication of a group design can be extremely valuable in exploring the extent to which an intervention can be generalized to others. Such replication can also be used to determine the limitations of an intervention and the characteristics of clients with whom it may not work and with client circumstances that are contraindicated.

Example of Setting Standards for Evidence-Based Practice

Harding and Higginson (2003), in a systematic review of articles from relevant professional journals, found twenty-two interventions for helping cancer and palliative care patients and their caregivers. They analyzed the twenty-two interventions on the basis of the type of patient and caregiver populations, the evaluation design used, and findings. They graded the evaluations as follows:

Grade I   (strong evidence): randomized control trials

Grade II   (fairly strong evidence): group designs with a comparison group

Grade III (weaker evidence): retrospective or observational studies

Grade IV (weak evidence): cross-sectional studies, Delphi exercises, consensus of experts

They concluded that there was a lack of outcome evaluation designs used to evaluate the effectiveness of the interventions. Instead, most articles contributed more to understanding feasibility and acceptability issues than to effectiveness. The authors encouraged programs to conduct more experimental and quasi-experimental designs to determine whether interventions effectively helped cancer patients and their caregivers.

Decisions on the sources of evidence for social work evaluations are important. Evidence can come from the reports and experiences of administrators, staff members, and faculty; clients' records; observations that document evidence; interviews and questionnaires that document perceptions of evidence; case examples of clients; other types of recordings; and scientific studies. Sources will vary in relevance and importance depending on their purposes. Evaluation has been conceptualized in this book as occurring at the input, implementation, and outcome stages of program and practice development. Using this framework, the types of sources of evidence used in the various stages will differ. Evidence-based interventions that follow are concerned with interventions in which there is scientifically credible evidence of a causal relationship between the intervention and clients' outcomes.

DETERMINING A CAUSAL RELATIONSHIP

How do we know whether the program or practice intervention was the cause of the progress in client outcomes? The answer to this question is complicated. Three conditions must be met before a causal relationship can be claimed. The first condition is that the program (or practice) intervention must precede clients' improved outcomes. This condition makes sense: a provider could not ethically claim responsibility for clients' progress if the progress occurred prior to the introduction of the program.

The second condition needed to claim a causal relationship is that an association is found between the introduction of the intervention and the client's improvement in his or her outcome measures. An association means that the client's improvement becomes evident after the intervention is implemented. To be able to determine whether improvement occurs in the outcome measure during the period of implementation, we need to obtain a measure of the outcome both before (i.e., pretest measure, or baseline measure) and after (i.e., posttest measure) the intervention is introduced.

An association between the intervention and clients' outcomes can be determined through one of two methods: a test of statistical significance or an established standard of clinical significance. Statistical significance can be calculated by applying a statistical test, which determines whether the probability of an association is high enough to claim significance. Usually, a probability of 95 percent is expected, with the likelihood of error at 5 percent.

Clinical significance is defined by clinical criteria established by a professional group or agency. In this case, the amount of improvement in client outcomes is satisfactory when it meets the established clinical criteria. Clinical significance may be preferred over statistical significance in many circumstances, as it is based on clinical judgment, not mathematical probability. However, statistical significance is usually expected in summative evaluations when evidence of a program's impact is expected to be based on scientific principles.

To illustrate these points, consider the example of a recovery group of clients with alcohol abuse problems. The group has as its desired outcome reduced alcohol consumption. Assume that the recovery group is a weekly treatment group that emphasizes cognitive behavioral therapy and a modified version of the twelve-step program of Alcoholics Anonymous. The blood-alcohol level of group members is the measure used to determine whether there is improvement. If statistical significance is the standard to be used, then there has to be a statistically significant difference between pretest and posttest scores of the average blood-alcohol level of group members. A statistical test, such as a t-test, can tell us whether the two measures were significantly different according to probability theory. The various types of t-tests and other statistical tests that can be used to determine statistical significance are discussed in the next chapter.

Let's determine whether group members improved significantly according to clinical criteria. The agency sponsoring the group intervention has a clinical standard based on the definition of satisfactory improvement reported in the professional literature. The agency has found studies that have reported that an intervention is not fully successful until a person totally withdraws from alcohol. Therefore, the agency decided that clinical significance would not be fully achieved until the group members totally withdrew from drinking; in other words, the members would not show enough improvement if they fell short of this high standard.

The ultimate condition for claiming the intervention is the cause of the client's improvements is the most difficult to achieve. This condition is the claim that the improvement occurring in the clients' outcome measure is due, at least in part, to the program intervention. We need to consider that many other factors, such as a change in family circumstances or joining an Alcoholics Anonymous support group, have an influence on the outcome as well. Usually, an intervention is not expected to be totally responsible for clients' improvement. If we are interested in determining how much of the improvement is due to the intervention, we would have to use an experimental design. A less dependable method is a multiple regression test, which is discussed in the next chapter.

Using the example of the recovery group mentioned earlier in the chapter, an experimental design could be used that includes an experimental group (i.e., clients in the recovery group) and a control group (i.e., another group randomly selected and assigned to receive traditional individual services). If the outcome scores of the experimental group members (their average blood-alcohol level) changed significantly from pretest to posttest and the outcome measure of the control group members changed less or not at all, then it can be claimed that the intervention provided to clients had a causal influence. The amount of influence that it had on the recovery group members is determined in two steps. First, the change in the members' outcome score from the pretest to posttest is calculated as the amount of change that occurred in the group. This change would then need to be reduced by the amount of change, if any, that occurred in the outcome measures for the control group.

Quasi-experimental and pre-experimental designs can also be used to explore whether a social work intervention has a causal influence on changes in client outcomes. In such cases, only tentative conclusions can be made about the intervention's influence or impact. However, in most cases, an experimental design cannot be realistically used for ethical reasons, as field-based evaluations are not amenable to the controls that an experimental study requires. Quasi-experimental, pre-experimental, and experimental designs are reviewed next for program interventions.

GROUP DESIGNS FOR PROGRAMS

Several group research designs are available for conducting outcome evaluations of programs. These designs are known as group designs because they measure the impact of an intervention on a group of clients, not on one client. Two overall categories of designs are possible in an evaluation study: cross-sectional and longitudinal. A cross-sectional design collects data from participants at one time only, and a longitudinal design collects data from research participants at two or more times. Longitudinal designs provide the most powerful evidence of a causal relationship between a program intervention and client outcomes.

Internal and external validity are important standards to use when evaluating the strength of a group design. Internal validity addresses whether the intervention and no other factors are responsible for improvement in the client outcome variable. Several extraneous variables could be responsible for improved outcome in addition to or instead of the intervention. For internal validity to be strong, for example, factors independent of the intervention present in clients' lives (e.g., receiving services from another professional agency, joining a self-help group) could be responsible for improvement in the outcome measure in addition to or instead of the intervention.

External validity addresses the issue of generalizing the results of a group design to other people. In this case, if the participants in the group design were randomly selected from a large population (e.g., a client group of one hundred or more), generalizations to the larger group are possible. However, if participants selected for the group design were drawn from a smaller population or were selected using non-probability sampling, generalizations are not advisable.

Experimental designs, quasi-experimental designs, and some pre-experimental designs are longitudinal designs that can be used to explore a causal relationship between a program and its impact on client outcomes. Several group designs are described in Campbell and Stanley (1963). Six designs are highlighted here because they are among the most practical ones for outcome evaluations of programs in human service agencies:

Pre-Experimental Designs

1. One-group posttest-only design
2. One-group pretest/posttest design

Quasi-Experimental Designs

3. One-group pretest/posttest design with a comparison group
4. Time-series design

Experimental Designs

5. One-group pretest/posttest design with a control group
6. Posttest-only control group design

All of these group designs can be used to explore the impact of a program on a group of clients, whether the intervention focuses on individual, family, small group, or community systems. All of these designs require that there be a clearly defined program intervention that can be replicated and at least one client outcome measure. These are the central elements of any group design. Other elements are included in some of these designs and not others.

Concepts Relevant to Group Designs

Clients' outcomes: outcome measures of what clients are to achieve

Program intervention: an intervention defined clearly enough to be replicated

Pretest or baseline measure: a measure of an outcome for clients prior to the intervention

Posttest measure: a measure of an outcome for clients after implementation of the intervention

Comparison group: a group of clients in a group design similar but not identical to the group receiving the program intervention; the group does not receive the program intervention

Control group: a group of clients in a group design considered identical to the group receiving the program intervention, based on either random selection and assignment or matching; the group does not receive the program intervention

Let's look at each of the six group designs and the concepts incorporated into each one. Diagrams of each design are also included in table 9.1 (where X symbolizes the program intervention, O represents a measure of the client outcome, and R indicates that the two groups were randomly selected and randomly assigned).

TABLE 9.1   Pre-Experimental, Quasi-Experimental, and Experimental Designs

Diagram	Description
X O_1	1. *One-group posttest-only design*: intervention followed by a posttest measure of client outcome
O_1 X O_2	2. *One-group pretest/posttest design*: intervention preceded by a pretest measure and followed by a posttest measure of client outcome
O_1 X O_2 O_3 O_4	3. *Pretest/posttest design with a comparison group*: pretest/posttest design with a comparison group that does not receive intervention
O_1 O_2 O_3 X O_4 O_5 O_6	4. *Time-series design*: multiple measures of client outcome before and after the intervention
R- O_1 X O_2 R- O_3 O_4	5. *Pretest/posttest design with a control group*: pretest/posttest design with a control group that does not receive intervention
R- X O_1 R- O_2	6. *Posttest-only control group design*: a posttest-only design with a control group that does not receive the intervention

One-Group Posttest-Only Design

Pre-experimental designs are often important to consider initially because they are easy to implement and take less time than stronger designs. This design involves collecting data at only one point in time after implementation of the intervention. Thus, this is a cross-sectional rather than a longitudinal design. During time 1 the intervention is introduced, and during time 2 the posttest measure of client outcome occurs.

This design is a good one for a beginning exploration of program impact, and it can simply answer the question of whether it is possible that the program had an impact. A one-group posttest-only design has several weaknesses. Most important, there is no pretest measure to determine whether any improvement occurred during the time of the intervention. Furthermore, none of the extraneous influences (e.g., environmental changes) are controlled for. An important conclusion derived from this design if the client outcome measure is not positive or favorable is that the intervention does not work.

One-Group Pretest-Posttest Design

The pretest-posttest design builds on the previous design by adding a pretest measure before the initiation of the intervention. This design, like the first one, is pre-experimental. However, it is longitudinal because data are collected from the clients at two different times—before and after the introduction of an intervention. The design is helpful in revealing how much improvement occurred between the pretest and the posttest. During time 1, the pretest score of the outcome variable is measured, during time 2 the intervention is introduced, and during time 3 the posttest score of the outcome variable is measured.

An example of a pretest-posttest design was described earlier in this chapter. The community organization that sponsored the premarital weekend retreat to reduce the number of divorces in the community was essentially interested in determining whether participants made progress between the time that the retreat began and ended. The pretest-posttest design served that purpose and helped them further refine the curriculum offered.

With this design, we can only determine whether improvement occurred during the time that the program was introduced, not whether the program was necessarily responsible for any change in the client outcome measure. The most important weakness of this design is that it does not have a comparison or control group to control for extraneous influences.

Example of an Evaluation with a One-Group Pretest-Posttest Design and a Qualitative Component

The purpose of an evaluation conducted by Lynch (2007) was to explore the impact of an independent-living skills-training program on the resilience, social support, and life skills of sixteen ethnically diverse foster-care teenagers. The teenagers' scores on standardized measures of resilience, social support, and life skills were compared before and after they participated in the training program. The improvements in scores from pretest to posttest were found to be statistically significant for social support but not for resilience and life skills.

Pretest-Posttest Design with a Comparison Group

The pretest-posttest design with a comparison group builds on the two previous designs. It is longitudinal in nature, as data are collected of the client outcome measure both as a pretest and as a posttest. However, another group similar to the first group is organized as a comparison group that does not receive the intervention. This design compares the progress of both groups during the intervention period. As table 9.1 indicates, the design is diagrammed with two different groups: one that receives the program intervention and the other that does not. At time 1 a pretest score of the outcome variable is measured for both groups, and during time 2 the intervention is introduced for the group assigned to receive it and nothing happens for the comparison group. The comparison group could receive services that are usually available as an alternative to nothing. At time 3 a posttest score of the outcome variable is measured for both groups.

Example of Pretest-Posttest Comparison Group Design

Engagement services during the intake period were introduced to female clients in a substance abuse treatment program as a motivational strategy to draw them into treatment (Comfort, Loverro, & Kaltenbach, 2000). An evaluation was conducted to determine whether the engagement services resulted in an increased use of treatment services. The evaluation used a pretest-posttest design with a comparison group. The engagement services involved an engagement specialist offering van transportation to the agency and child care during intake interviews, and making telephone calls to remind clients of intake appointments. Although transportation and child care were always offered to the group, members infrequently used child care in particular. Nevertheless, the results revealed that clients receiving engagement services were more likely than those in the comparison group to use treatment services.

A comparison group can be drawn from a larger pool of clients, such as those on a waiting list or clients who are receiving traditional services during the time of the study. This type of design can reveal with more confidence than the previous ones herein whether the program had a causal influence on client outcomes. The most important weakness of the design, though, is that the clients selected to be in the program and those selected for the comparison groups are likely to have many differences that the design does not control for. Such differences are likely to have a considerable influence over the measures of client outcomes. This design also creates a potential ethical problem that needs to be addressed, as one could convincingly argue that the clients in the comparison group should receive the program intervention as well. They may, for example, have as great a need for the intervention as does the group receiving the intervention.

A comparison group should be as similar as possible to the intervention group, particularly with variables or characteristics important to a study. For example, both groups should have similar demographic characteristics (e.g., age, gender, ethnicity), and both groups should be similar in terms of the important variables of the evaluation, such as their mental illness diagnosis or the problems that the program addresses. Comparison group studies should report on these characteristics and indicate when the two groups are significantly different according to specific characteristics. This reporting helps the reader take into account whether any of the differences in characteristics could have influenced their respective client outcome scores.

Example of Determining Similarity between Treatment and Comparison Groups

Waites (2000) assessed the generalist problem-solving skills of two groups of students, those beginning and those graduating from a BSW program. This can be thought of as a pretest-posttest comparison group design, with the graduates as the group receiving the intervention (successful completion of the BSW program) and the beginning students as a comparison group. Waites wanted to find out whether the comparison group was similar to the graduating group given several important characteristics: gender, ethnicity, age, grade point average, extent of volunteer experience, and number of social work courses completed. She found that the two groups were not significantly different on the basis of gender, ethnicity, age, or grade point average. They were different on the basis of volunteer experience and number of social work courses taken; these differences were expected given the group members' different status in the BSW program.

Time-Series Design

A time-series design is another type of quasi-experimental design. This design has many of the features of the previous designs and is also different from the other designs in that it has several pretest and posttest outcome measures, not one. The design involves obtaining several client outcome measures before the introduction of an intervention and several additional measures after the intervention has been implemented. Table 9.1 diagrams a time-series design.

A major advantage of a time-series design is that it overcomes some of the ethical problems of the designs that use comparison and control groups, as it has neither. An important feature of the multiple pretest and posttest measures of this design are the data trends that can help determine the extent to which the intervention, as opposed to other factors external to it, is the causal agent. Stated another way, its multiple measures of client outcomes provide more opportunities to determine whether extraneous influences exist.

Pretest-Posttest Design with a Control Group

The fifth design, a pretest-posttest design with a control group, is the classical experimental design. It is the most powerful design for determining causality. It is similar to the pretest-posttest design with a comparison group with one exception. Clients are first randomly selected from a larger pool of prospective clients and then randomly assigned to either the intervention or the control group. Because of the two steps of random selection and assignment, the two groups of clients can be treated as statistically identical because the random selection and assignment tend to balance out the extraneous differences between the two groups. With this design, pretest and posttest measures are obtained from both groups before and after the intervention group receives the intervention.

This design is diagrammed in table 9.1. Prior to time 1, clients are randomly selected and assigned to either receive the services of the program or to a control group. During time 1 a pretest score of the outcome variable is measured for both groups. During time 2 the intervention is introduced for the group assigned to receive it and either nothing happens for the control group or it could continue to receive existing agency services. During time 3 a posttest measure of the client outcome variable is obtained for both groups.

Example of a Pretest-Posttest Control Group Design

Ciffone (2007) evaluated whether a curriculum-based suicide prevention program was instrumental in changing unwanted attitudes and in reducing students' reluctance to seek mental health treatment among groups of students in two demographically diverse high schools. He used a pretest-posttest control group design. Students were randomly assigned to treatment and control groups by the classes that they were assigned. Those in the treatment group were provided a three-day presentation by the school social workers who spoke in their health classes. Those in the control classes had no outside speakers in their health classes during the same period. The pretest and posttest instrument consisted of eight questions. The attitudes toward suicide were measured partially by the item, "Most teens who killed themselves were probably suffering from mental illness." Students' responses to the item in the intervention group changed from "no" to "yes" when their attitudes improved. Two other items measured help-seeking attitudes or reluctance to seek mental health treatment: "If suicidal thoughts crossed my mind regularly, I would seek out and talk to a friend about these thoughts," and "If I was very upset and suicidal thoughts crossed my mind, I would be willing to talk with a professional counselor about these thoughts." Higher percentages of students in the intervention group were favorable to these statements in the posttest than in the pretest.

This design is quite powerful in determining whether the program intervention influences the outcome measure for the client group in the program because it controls for all extraneous influences. Nevertheless, the design poses even more serious ethical challenges than any of the other designs. It can be viewed as unethical to randomly select and assign clients to receive or not receive an intervention, particularly without their consent. Most likely, if agency resources are able to provide a program intervention for all clients, the decision to select some clients should be made on the basis of professional criteria, not mathematical probability. This dilemma could be worked out by randomly selecting clients from a waiting list and then randomly assigning one group to receive the intervention and the other group to continue to wait for services offered at a later time. However, it would be important to explain this arrangement to clients in an informed consent protocol. Also, other unanticipated consequences must be considered, such as exposing the vulnerabilities of clients in the control group to life-threatening crises during a waiting period.

Posttest-Only Control-Group Design

The sixth design, a posttest-only design with a control group, is the same as the experimental design except that it does not have a pretest for either group. The design depends completely on the initial random selection and assignment steps to ensure that participants in the two groups are identical, which is particularly important because there are no pretest measures to determine whether the two groups begin essentially at the same point in their outcome measures.

This design is preferred over the pretest-posttest design with a control group if there is concern that administering a pretest measure could influence the outcome. For example, a test about a knowledge area used as a pretest measure may also be used as a posttest measure to determine how much the clients learned during the intervention phase. An intervention could be safe-sex training and the outcome measure could be a test that measures how well clients understand safe sexual practices. The problem here is that the test could be discussed informally among clients during the intervention phase to determine the correct answers and the clients could then report these answers in the posttest phase. In this case, testing factors rather than actual learning from the intervention could be responsible for any improvement in the test from pretest to posttest.

In other instances, this design could also be preferred over the pretest-posttest design with a control group if the pretest seemed unnecessary or undesirable. It may be undesirable or not logistically possible to implement, or an evaluator may find it too costly to administer a pretest measure because it would involve time and effort of the staff members to interview clients or administer a questionnaire as a pretest.

Table 9.1 diagrams the posttest-only control-group design. Prior to time 1, clients are randomly selected and are either assigned to receive the program's services or assigned to a control group. During time 1 a pretest score of the outcome variable is not measured for either group. During time 2 the intervention is introduced for the group assigned to receive it and either nothing happens for the control group or it continues to receive existing agency services. During time 3 a posttest measure of the client outcome variable is obtained for both groups.

This design, like the classic experimental design, is quite powerful in determining whether the program intervention influences the outcome measure for the client group in the program because it controls for all extraneous influences. However, this design also poses serious ethical challenges for the same reasons that it does for the classic experimental design. The clients could be randomly selected from a large waiting list and then randomly assigned either to receive the intervention or to wait for services to be offered later. However, it would be important to explain this arrangement to clients in an informed consent protocol, and a plan to address unanticipated consequences must be considered, such as the control-group clients' vulnerability to a life-threatening crisis during the waiting period.

It is important to note that all group designs have another major limitation if they only measure client outcomes immediately after clients complete a program. Such outcome measures, as mentioned earlier, are usually only short-term outcomes. Therefore, programs are encouraged to consider one or more additional outcome measures at later points in time (e.g., three and six months later) to determine whether clients' progress from participating in a program is sustained over time.

OUTCOME EVALUATIONS FOR PRACTICE

The outcome evaluations described previously are generally available for practice evaluations as well. Some of the variations in how outcome evaluations for practice and programs may differ are presented next, with an emphasis on how to implement outcome evaluations in an individual worker's practice.

Client Satisfaction and Effectiveness

It is important that practitioners hold themselves accountable for the effectiveness of their interventions even when others may not do so. This is an ethical obligation mandated by the NASW's Code of Ethics (see chapter 3). The code points out that practitioners are to "monitor and evaluate policies, the implementation of programs, and our practice interventions" (NASW 1999, section 5.02[a]).

There are some basic questions that practitioners can periodically ask clients, such as the following:

- Are my interventions helping you? In what ways?
- Are my interventions helping you in the areas in which you are seeking help (e.g., related to presenting problems, identified needs, solutions desired, expressed hopes)?

- Are my interventions helping you meet your goals identified in our initial work together?
- How would you describe your progress so far in achieving your goals? How have my interventions played a part in helping you or in hindering you?

The specifics of how clients communicate that the practitioner's interventions have helped (or have not helped) can be especially important. For example, did they respond to the practitioner's questions or did they spontaneously offer comments? Spontaneous comments may be more authentic and more likely to be valid indicators of their views.

These and similar questions are considered client satisfaction questions to most people, but they are also quite relevant to the question of effectiveness. These types of questions focus on client outcomes and their connection to our intervention. They ask, in essence, did the intervention have a role in bringing about any positive changes to clients' goals or outcomes? In some instances, clients' responses to the previous questions may be the only available information. In this regard, they have limitations, especially because they are subjective and not necessarily reflective of actual outcomes. For example, clients could report accomplishments that did not actually happen (e.g., discontinued drug use) or overestimate what actually happened (e.g., reporting completion of homework every day, when it may be sporadic). That is why objective measures of outcomes are also extremely important to obtain, such as checking whether drug use is evident in a client's urine or obtaining an independent report of the client's drug use from a spouse or another reliable source.

As discussed in chapter 8, however, it could be argued that clients' reports on their outcomes and how the interventions have affected them are a necessary but not sufficient indication of intervention effectiveness. Conversely, obtaining an objective measure of a client's outcomes without some verification or concurrence from the client can be viewed as overlooking the clients' role in having some awareness and control over their change.

Single-System Designs

Practice evaluations of outcomes can be conducted in several ways, and many of them revolve around variations of a single-system design. A single-system design is a variation of a time-series design on a practice level in that it involves several measures of the outcome variable both before and while an intervention is being introduced. A single-system design (SSD) is a practice evaluation tool that measures whether there is a causal relationship between the practitioner's intervention and a client's outcome measure. This design is typically used with one client system at a time whether it is an individual, family, or group. The SSD uses a graph as a tool to visualize the clients' progress, and it is intended to be used by both the client and the social worker in determining whether any progress has been made. The graph helps simplify the explanation for how much progress has been made and it does not require a statistical test for explanation, although one can be used.

An SSD graph consists of two or more phases. A baseline phase (phase A) is always needed as well as one or more intervention phases (e.g., phases B, C, and D). The client outcome measure is plotted along the vertical axis, and a timeline for recording measures of the outcome measure is identified along the horizontal axis (e.g., daily, weekly). Figure 9.2 illustrates an ABC design with three phases: a baseline phase, a phase when the first intervention is introduced, and a phase when the second intervention is introduced.

An SSD can be conducted using a variety of designs, including AB, ABC, ABAB, and BAB. The simplest design is an AB design, which consists of a baseline phase and one intervention phase. In this case, the client outcome measure is obtained along a standardized timeline, such as weekly or daily intervals during both phase A (baseline) and phase B (intervention phase). For example, a woman with clinical depression wants to develop new friendships but is resistant to getting out and meeting people. The social worker attempts to help her by providing supportive services, as support has been missing in the client's life and is thought to be what she needs to begin attending social occasions in her church and local community center. The frequency of attending these social occasions each week was the client outcome indicator, measured every week while the client was in contact with the social worker's agency. The social worker's intervention, introduced during phase B, is the support service. This AB design requires measurement of the frequency of the client's attendance each week for a few weeks to obtain a baseline measure that is stable or does not fluctuate highly. This outcome indicator continues to be measured weekly during

FIGURE 9.2   The ABC Design

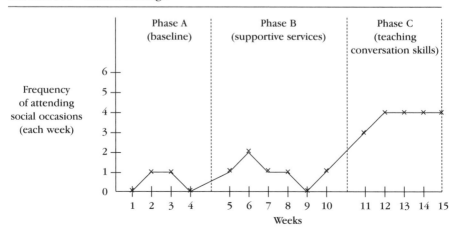

phase B, when the social worker's intervention is introduced. The intent of the AB design is to discover whether the client attends more social occasions after the intervention is introduced than she did before.

Another single-system design is the ABC design, illustrated in figure 9.2. This design begins with a baseline phase (phase A) followed by the first intervention phase (phase B), and then followed by another intervention phase (phase C). The ABC design is particularly useful when the first intervention does not have sufficient impact by itself. A second intervention can then be introduced in phase C to either replace or supplement the first intervention. Often the combination of the two interventions can have a significant impact when neither intervention can have an impact by itself.

Using the same example of the woman with severe depression, providing support services weekly could be the first intervention to encourage more social contacts (phase B). If this intervention does not succeed, teaching the client conversation skills could be added as a second intervention (phase C). The ABC design can plot the client's attendance at social occasions during phases A, B, and C to determine whether attendance increases during implementation of both the first and the second intervention. In figure 9.2, combining the two interventions, support services and teaching conversation skills, visibly documents greater social contact for this client.

Another variation is the ABAB design, which consists of a baseline phase followed by an intervention phase, then another baseline phase when the intervention is removed, and finally the reintroduction of the intervention phase (figure 9.3). This design has a special additional feature of withdrawing the intervention after phase B to find out whether other factors (e.g., a self-help group, a new friend, joining a new church or synagogue) may be responsible for any continuation of client progress evident in phase B. If progress on the client goal declines during the reintroduction of phase A, this provides further evidence that the intervention and improvement are linked. Finally, the intervention can be reintroduced in the second phase B to find out whether progress reappears.

FIGURE 9.3 An ABAB Design

Phase A	Phase B	Phase A	Phase B

Although the ABAB design can, in some ways, be an alternative to having a comparison or control group, it can also pose ethical problems if the intervention is withdrawn while the client still needs it. Similarly, it would also be unethical to withdraw the intervention if a client wishes to continue it or if withdrawal could cause harm. However, temporary withdrawal of the intervention may be less of an ethical concern if the social worker or client became unavailable because of a vacation or a visit to a sick relative. Withdrawal may also be less of a concern if the intervention is mandated and if the client wants a temporary break from services.

An ABAB design has another limitation in that it works only when the outcome measure can be reversed. If a client is taught a new set of behaviors, once he or she has learned the behaviors, they may not be reversed in many cases. For example, if a parent is taught new assertiveness skills in phase B, withdrawal of the intervention is not likely to lead to an immediate reversal of the newly developed skills.

Sometimes a BAB design is relevant if the social worker cannot begin with a baseline phase. This may be the case particularly when it is urgent to introduce the intervention during the first contact with the client. With this design, the baseline phase can be introduced after the intervention has been implemented for a while, and the intervention can be reintroduced in a third phase. However, like the ABAB design, withdrawal of the intervention could pose ethical problems and may not work with irreversible outcome measures.

Goal Attainment Scale

A goal attainment scale (GAS) is a versatile evaluation tool that can be used to measure client outcomes. It is quite useful in evaluating the extent to which the worker's interventions affect clients' goals or outcomes in a favorable way. The GAS works well as an outcome measure with any of the SSD designs described previously. As table 9.2 indicates, a GAS is a five-point scale ranging from the most unfavorable to the most favorable outcome

TABLE 9.2 Goal Attainment Scale (GAS)

Levels of predicted attainment	Scale
Most unfavorable outcome thought likely (−2)	
Less success than expected (−1)	
Expected level of success (0)	
More success than expected (+1)	
Most favorable outcome (unlikely but still plausible) (+2)	

thought likely at a future follow-up time. The middle point on the scale is considered the expected level of success. The client and social worker use the right-hand column to fill in qualitative descriptors of each of the five points on the scale, with the expected level of success usually determined first.

A GAS has many advantages as an outcome tool. It is an incremental scale that can be used to measure degrees of progress. It can be individualized to a client's particular or unique circumstances. And it is used most effectively when the client and worker collaborate in the development and use of the scale. When the tool is used in this way, it can be a great motivator in getting clients to work on their goals. The scale can also become a useful discussion topic when discrepancies become evident between what the worker and client perceive as the client's level of success. It can also become the focal point of an informal or formal contract between the worker and client.

Table 9.3 illustrates the use of a GAS in a parent-training program in which several parenting skills were introduced and practiced in small groups for parents who had been abusing their children. This is a building-block approach that begins with reading; learning comes next, followed by using or applying a parenting skill. Note that the scale reflects a decision to set an expected level of success for these parents after three months of simply learning one parenting skill. Although this may not seem like a far-reaching level of success, this program documented evidence that learning one skill would realistically take this long to internalize.

Cox and Amsters (2001) effectively used the GAS as a multidisciplinary measure of client outcomes for rural and remote health services. They found several principles to be important in using a GAS. The goals need to remain realistic and relevant to both the clients' capacity or potential and the agencies' resources. In addition, the levels must be mutually exclusive and measurable. They found that the GAS had limitations as well; most important, it was not effective if staff were not fully trained in its use.

TABLE 9.3 GAS with Goal of Improving Parenting Skills

Levels of predicted attainment	Scale
Most unfavorable outcome thought likely (−2)	Ignore parenting skills altogether
Less success than expected (−1)	Read a book on parenting skills
Expected level of success (0)	Learn one new parenting skill
More success than expected (+1)	Use one new parenting skill with children
Most favorable outcome (unlikely but still plausible) (+2)	Use two new parenting skills with children

Notes: Date and rating at construction: January 5; Date and rating at follow-up or evaluation time: April 5.

A GAS can be developed as either a qualitative or quantitative measure or a combination of the two. The scale in table 9.3 uses both types of measures; for example, it measures the number of parenting skills learned and takes into account four different behaviors that overlap: ignoring, reading, learning, and using. The scale can also include more than one variable at each level.

A GAS can be implemented with the following principles and sequential steps kept in mind (Dudley, 2011):

1. Consider whether the GAS is the most appropriate design to use with a particular client. Among other considerations, a GAS depends on clients meeting with a worker for more than one session and having measurable goals.
2. Make sure that you cover and that the client understands all the pertinent issues of informed consent, including the purpose of the selected tool, how it works, how the client can benefit, and the other aspects of informed consent.
3. Help the client identify the problem.
4. Identify a goal that can resolve this problem agreeable to the worker and client.
5. Set a realistic date for the goal to be achieved, referred to as an evaluation time.
6. Then work together to construct specific predictions for a series of five levels of reaching the goal (most unfavorable, less than expected, expected level of success, more than expected, and best anticipated success) by recording them on the scale. Usually the easiest way to do this is to first identify the expected level of success, followed by the outer limits of the most unfavorable and most favorable outcome. Finally, identify the less-than-expected and more-than-expected levels.
7. Now the GAS is ready to be used by measuring the client's actual level of attainment in reaching the goal during the first session as a baseline measure.
8. Finally, the client's actual level of attainment in reaching the goal can be measured during an evaluation session or during the last session. At this time, discuss the progress that has been made and how the GAS was helpful in measuring this progress.

Target Problem Scale

The GAS has limitations. For example, some problems may not easily translate into goals, or clients may not be either willing or able to identify goals to work on. Also, a GAS does not work well if a client is seen for only one session. An alternative outcome scale that can be used is a target problem scale (TPS). In brief, a TPS helps clients identify their problem(s), apply an intervention to overcome or cope with them, and then periodically rate the problem to measure any deteriorations or improvements. A TPS is helpful, for example, if the client remains preoccupied or overwhelmed with multiple problems and is not prepared to immediately pursue goals to overcome the problems.

Like a GAS, the TPS is an incremental scale. It measures the degree of severity of the problem, and the scale is individualized to a client's particular circumstances. Figure 9.4 describes a TPS (Marlow, 2011). In this scale, target problems are identified in the far-left column. This form provides space for up to five problems. Each problem is then assessed in terms of its degree of severity for each of six sessions. The five-point severity scale measures problems from "no problem" to "extremely severe." The next column to the right is the improvement scale used to calculate the degree to which a problem has changed for better or worse. Finally, an overall improvement scale can be used to determine the extent to which improvement has occurred.

FIGURE 9.4   Target Problem Scale (TPS)

Target Problems								Overall Improvement*
			Degree of Severity Session #					Degree of Change
	1	2	3	4	5	6	(1 to 5 scale)	
1.								
2.								
3.								
4.								
5.								

Severity Scale	**Improvement Scale**
NP = no problem	1 = Worse
NVS = not very severe	2 = No change
S = severe	3 = A little better
VS = very severe	4 = Somewhat better
ES = extremely severe	5 = A lot better

*The **Overall Improvement Rating** is the total of the degree of change, divided by number of target problems, which results in a number that reflects the client's overall improvement on all problems.

The overall improvement rating is obtained by totaling the degree of change scores and dividing by the number of target problems. This results in a number that reflects clients' overall improvement on all problems.

An example of a TPS used with parents who were lacking strong parenting skills is described in figure 9.5. As the figure indicates, the parents had multiple problems, including overlooking their parental neglect, getting to appointments late, spending too little time with their child, getting the child to bed late, and yelling at each other. Figure 9.5 summarizes the clients' progress or lack of it after six sessions. In brief, the TPS indicates that their difficulty in facing parental neglect improved from "extremely severe" in the first two sessions to somewhat better or "not very severe" by the sixth session. Overall, most of their progress on other problems over six sessions was in getting to counseling sessions on time and in spending more time with their child. A little improvement was evident in not yelling at each other so often.

FIGURE 9.5 TPS for a Family

Target Problems							Overall Improvement*
	Degree of Severity Session #						Degree of Change
	1	2	3	4	5	6	(1 to 5 scale)
(Examples)							
1. Overlook parental neglect as a problem	ES	ES	S	S	NVS	NVS	4
2. Come late to appointments	S	S	S	NP	NP	NP	5
3. Ignore their child's need to spend time with parents	ES	NVS	NVS	NVS	NVS	NVS	4
4. Get child to bed late	ES	ES	ES	VS	ES	ES	2
5. Parents yell at each other	S	S	S	S	S	NVS	3
							18/5 = 3.6

Severity Scale	**Improvement Scale**
NP = no problem	1 = Worse
NVS = not very severe	2 = No change
S = severe	3 = A little better
VS = very severe	4 = Somewhat better
ES = extremely severe	5 = A lot better

*The Overall Improvement Rating is the total of the degree-of-change scores, divided by the number of target problems, which results in a number that reflects the client's overall improvement on all problems.

Sequencing Blocks

Other means of evaluating a client's outcomes, positive or negative, are also available, even though they may not be readily known or used. For example, sequencing blocks are a qualitative exercise that can help clients explore the causal relationships among prior behaviors that resulted in a positive or negative outcome. In this case, the outcome behavior is known and the behavior that caused it is to be discovered. Sequencing blocks can be used to help clients gain insight into prior behaviors and interactions that could trigger a current problem behavior that is being addressed (Laura Kroll, graduate student placed at Alexander Youth Network, Charlotte, NC, personal communication, April 15, 2006). This is an exercise that can use narrative from the discussions between a worker and client about a problem behavior, such as cursing out a teacher or getting angry and walking off a job. The discussion typically begins with the current problem behavior and its larger context. Then the discussion can work its way in reverse, going

FIGURE 9.6   Sequencing Blocks

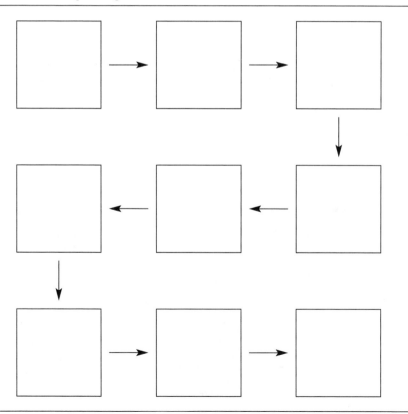

back to what happened just before the problem behavior occurred, and then what happened before that. The conversation eventually can get back to the initial set of behaviors or incidents in the overall episode. Figure 9.6 portrays typical sequencing blocks. As the discussion between the social worker and client proceed, individual behaviors and interactions are written into the blocks in the order that they occurred.

Figure 9.7 describes an example of a teenager who was expelled from school for cursing out his teacher. In this case, the teenager, John, was meet-

FIGURE 9.7 Sequencing Blocks for a Teenager

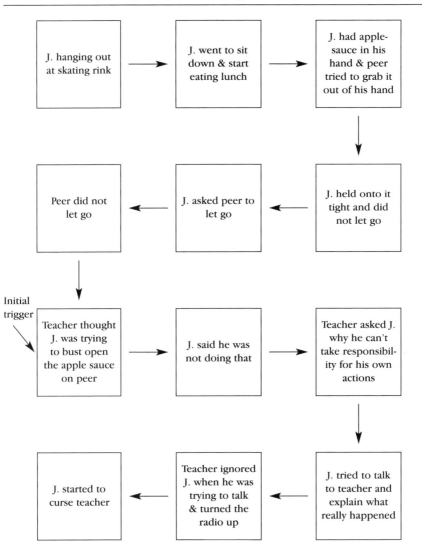

ing with a school social worker about the incident upon returning to school from a suspension. The sequencing blocks were used to help him gain insight into the earlier triggers and the precipitating factors contributing to the problem. The discussion began with the problem behavior and worked its way back one behavior and interaction at a time. It eventually got back to a trigger in which the teacher perceived, incorrectly, that John had initiated a conflict with a peer around opening a container of applesauce at lunch on a field trip. The sequencing block exercise helped John understand not only that his teacher had misperceived the cause of the conflict but also how he could have avoided the interchange with the teacher until after calming down and how he may have been able to avoid the incident in the first place, by avoiding sitting with the peer who got him into trouble.

Sequencing blocks can also be used to identify prior behaviors or decisions that result in positive outcomes for a client. For example, consider a client with a disability who has difficulty meeting women but who is interested in a friendship and had an unusually positive experience one night in meeting a new acquaintance. The client initially explained this discovery as a "miracle." The worker and client used this positive outcome to look back at prior behaviors and decisions made by the client that may have been positive triggers that could be tried again.

KEY TERMS

> Clinical significance
> Experimental designs
> Goal attainment scale
> Longitudinal study
> Measurable client goal
> Posttest
> Pre-experimental designs
> Pretest
> Quasi-experimental designs
> Sequence blocks
> Single-system design
> Statistical significance
> Target problem scale

DISCUSSION QUESTIONS AND ASSIGNMENTS

1. Review the six group designs summarized in this chapter and then answer the following questions (appendix C has answers):

   • Which design seems ideal? Why do you think so?
   • Which design is the easiest and least expensive? What can be concluded from this design?

- Why are multiple measures of the client outcome variable obtained when conducting a time-series design? What are the benefits of the multiple measures?
- Which design may be the most practical for determining whether the program intervention was responsible for positive changes in the outcome variables? Why?
- What is useful about a pretest/posttest design?
- Under what circumstances would you consider a posttest-only control-group design?

2. This is an assignment that can be completed in class or as an assignment to tape and bring to class.

   A. Role-play a worker/client relationship using a goal attainment scale (GAS). Conduct a first session when the GAS is introduced. Identify a goal that you and your client want to work on. Make sure that you both mutually agree on the goal. Also identify a goal that both you and your client agree is measurable. Explain the GAS to the client so that it can be readily understood. Consider using a simpler version that fits your particular client: maybe a three-point scale, simpler words, modified wording (e.g., vision of the future or dreams rather than goals).

   B. Later, conduct a session in which the worker and client assess how well the client did in reaching the defined goal. Have your client rate her or his progress along with your rating, and then discuss why your ratings may be different. Finally, explore what the specific benefits of the evaluation tool are to the client.

3. Design a program or practice intervention and a set of outcome measures for a group of clients by following three steps:

   A. Select a group to focus on (e.g., teen fathers, teen mothers, teens who are not parents).
   B. Identify two outcome measures for the group.
   C. Design a program or practice intervention to help the group reach the outcomes.

4. Critique White's (2005) choices of outcome indicators (in a box earlier in the chapter). Which ones do you think are most useful and why?

5. Assume that you are working in an agency serving people with a dual diagnosis of depression and alcohol abuse. Identify three outcome indicators for clients that could be used to measure the impact of a program on depression, and then identify three outcome indicators indicating that the alcohol abuse problem is reduced.

6. This is a policy-related assignment. Set up two teams of students: one assigned the task of identifying and arguing for the advantages of keeping welfare recipients on the welfare rolls and the other on removing them from the welfare rolls. Each team should begin by identifying three to four desired outcomes of maintaining or reducing, respectively, the number of welfare recipients. For example, a possible outcome for reducing the rolls could be savings to the taxpayer, while an outcome for maintaining recipients on welfare could be to provide skilled job training or to provide medical assistance to families.

7. This is a major class assignment. Carry out the following steps in completing this assignment.

   A. Identify a need for a practice evaluation in your field agency and a client system that can benefit from an evaluation. Inform the client system about the evaluation and encourage them to participate.

   B. Select the type of evaluation and specific tool that most readily fits your client situation. Feasibility is one important consideration in your selection. For example, consider the number of sessions that you will likely see your client, the overall amount of time that your agency will serve the client, and any difficulty you may have in identifying a measurable goal(s) for the client. Choose a tool from the following: a single-system design, a goal attainment scale, a target problem scale, or sequencing blocks.

   C. Discuss the assignment thoroughly with your field instructor to make sure that she or he understands the assignment and the evaluation tool that you will use.

   D. Obtain informed consent either in written or oral form. Make sure that all of the pertinent issues of informed consent are covered and understood by the client (e.g., purpose of the selected tool; how it works; how the client, worker, and agency can benefit; expectations that you have for the client's participation; informing the client that this is a class assignment to be turned in; ensuring confidentiality; reminding the client of the option to say no or withdraw after the evaluation begins). Whenever your field agency has a protocol for obtaining informed consent, use it to complete this assignment.

   E. Formulate and implement your practice evaluation.

   F. Finally, describe what you have learned about evaluating your practice from doing this assignment and what advantages and limitations you see in using this tool.

   G. Turn in a paper or give a presentation that includes a description of how you implemented each of the above steps. Also, include the instruments that you used.

REFERENCES

Babbie, E. (2001). *The practice of social research* (9th ed.). Belmont, CA: Wadsworth/ Thomson Learning.

Beck, A. T., Steer, R. A., & Brown, G. K. (1996). *Manual for the Beck Depression Inventory* (2nd ed.). San Antonio, TX: Psychological Corporation.

Cabarrus County. (2007). Performance report 2006. Concord, NC: Author.

Campbell, D., & Stanley, J. (1963). *Experimental and quasi-experimental designs for research.* Chicago: Rand McNally.

Ciffone, J. (2007). Suicide prevention: An analysis and replication of a curriculum-based high school program. *Social Work, 52*(1), 41–49.

Comfort, M., Loverro, J., & Kaltenbach, K. (2000). A search for strategies to engage women in substance abuse treatment. *Social Work in Health Care, 31*(4), 59–70.

Community Choices Inc. (2006). *Helping mothers have healthy babies and families.* Charlotte, NC: Author.

Cook, T. D., & Campbell, D. T. (1979). *Quasi-experimentation: Design and analysis issues for field settings.* Skokie, IL: Rand McNally.

Cox, R., & Amsters, D. (2001). Goal attainment scaling: An effective outcome measure for rural and remote health services. *Australian Journal of Rural Health, 10,* 256–261.

Dudley, J. R. (2011). *Research methods for social work: Being producers and consumers of research* (updated 2nd ed.). Boston: Pearson.

Gambrill, E. (1999). Evidence-based practice: An alternative to authority-based practice. *Families in Society, 80,* 341–350.

Gibbs, L., & Gambrill, E. (1996). *Critical thinking for social workers: A workbook.* Thousand Oaks, CA: Pine Forge Press.

Harding, R., & Higginson, I. J. (2003). What is the best way to help caregivers in cancer and palliative care? A systematic literature review of interventions and their effectiveness. *Palliative Medicine, 17,* 63–74.

Litzelfelner, P. (2001). Demystifying client outcomes. *Professional Development, 4*(2), 25–31.

Lynch, C. J. (2007). Exploring the implementation of a transitional services program for adolescents in the Texas Foster Care System. Unpublished doctoral dissertation, University of Texas at Austin.

Marlow, C. (2011). *Research methods for generalist social work* (5th ed.). Stamford, CT: Thomson Learning.

Martin, L. L., & Kettner, P. M. (1996). *Measuring performance of human service programs.* Thousand Oaks, CA: Sage.

McLean, T. (2007). Evaluating progress on personal goals of a children's group using journaling: Proposal for the formation of a new group. Unpublished manuscript. University of North Carolina at Charlotte.

National Association of Social Workers. (1999). Code of ethics of the National Association of Social Workers. Washington, DC: Author.

O'Hare, T. (2005). *Evidence-based practice for social workers: An interdisciplinary approach.* Chicago: Lyceum Books.

Thyer, B., & Meyers, L. (2003). Linking assessment to outcome evaluation using single system and group research design. In C. Jordan & C. Franklin (Eds.), *Clinical assessment for social workers: Quantitative and qualitative methods* (2nd ed., pp. 385–405). Chicago: Lyceum Books.

U.S. Department of Health and Human Services (2009). Child welfare outcomes 2006–2009: Report to Congress. Executive Summary. Retrieved on February 6, 2013 from http://www.acf.hhs.gov/sites/default/files/cb/executive06_09.pdf.

Waites, C. (2000). Assessing generalist problem-solving skills: An outcome measure. *The Journal of Baccalaureate Social Work, 6*(1), 67–79.

White, M. (2005, March 16). A demonstration of evaluation as a central aspect of social work practice at the Women's Commission. Presentation to a social work research class, University of North Carolina, Charlotte.

Part VI

Final Steps in Completing an Evaluation

Evaluations are not complete until two additional major areas are addressed. Chapter 10 describes the process of analyzing the data obtained from an evaluation. This is part of step 5 of the Seven Evaluation Steps (implement the evaluation). Data analysis is discussed for quantitative and qualitative findings. This chapter also addresses data analysis when both quantitative and qualitative findings are collected. The final area of an evaluation is covered in chapter 11 and involves preparing and disseminating a report of the findings. This involves step 6 and 7 of the Seven Evaluation Steps.

Chapter 10

Analyzing Evaluation Data

Jeffrey Shears and James R. Dudley

How do we transform data collected in an evaluation into useful information?

The analysis of evaluation data comes next in the evaluation process. Analyzing the data is an aspect of step 5 (implement the evaluation) that continues into step 6 (prepare a written or oral report) of the Seven Evaluation Steps. In step 5, once quantitative data are collected, they are coded and entered into a computer program such as SPSS (Statistical Package for the Social Sciences) and prepared for analysis. Qualitative data are usually prepared for analysis in narrative form. In step 6 the data are analyzed and transformed into useful findings that are then interpreted in an understandable way for gatekeepers.

Although the basic principles of data analysis are virtually the same for evaluations and other kinds of research, differences are evident in emphasis and use. Such differences are the primary focus of this chapter. Data analysis is also closely linked to the topic of the next chapter, writing a report and disseminating the findings. In actuality, the choice of which data analysis tools to use depends on the kind of report and dissemination strategy that are most helpful to the stakeholders and other people.

FORMATIVE OR SUMMATIVE EVALUATIONS

Evaluations depend on both quantitative and qualitative research methods as well as mixed methods. As discussed frequently in previous chapters, the methods used depend on the evaluation's purpose and the stage of program or practice development in which they occur. One way to decide whether to use quantitative or qualitative data analysis is to ask whether the evaluation is formative or summative.

Formative Evaluations

As mentioned in chapter 2, formative evaluations mostly focus on planning for a program or improving the implementation or delivery of services. The evaluations tend to be exploratory in nature and may need either qualitative or quantitative methods, or both, depending on their purposes.

Formative evaluations are typically conducted by the agency administering the intervention, which allows for considerable flexibility in choosing the methods of data collection and analysis. Formative evaluations do not require one particular type of procedure, as they can be conducted to identify small glitches in programs, breakdowns in delivering services, or an unanticipated drifting away from the original program design. These evaluations can take on many different forms. Examples include a needs assessment questionnaire with forced-response and open-ended questions, a standardized scale, an open-ended journal format, or observations that are either unstructured or structured.

Formative evaluations may examine the interactions between clients and practitioners, management strategies, practice philosophies, or costs associated with a program. For example, an agency wants to understand why a program for eating disorders for teenage girls has not been successful in having participants complete the twelve-week program; only one-fourth of participants participated long enough to complete the treatment. A formative evaluation could provide some meaningful information to fine-tune this program. Here exploring questions that are critical of the program could be beneficial in identifying glitches in the delivery of services. Conducting a more in-depth evaluation of the clients and their needs, and obtaining a profile of those who are successful and those who fail to complete the program are also important examples of a formative evaluation.

Summative Evaluations

Summative evaluations focus on the outcomes of programs and practice areas and attempt to answer the ultimate question: did the intervention reach its goals? These evaluations have a finality to them because they attempt to measure whether an intervention was effective. Summative evaluations are also typically conducted by an external agent, such as an independent evaluator or a governmental agency, to ensure that they are objective. Further, they primarily depend on choosing from a more limited set of research design options, such as a quasi-experimental or experimental design. These designs work best when they use quantitative measurement instruments with strong psychometric properties.

If an evaluator's question is to determine whether an intervention is effective, then this is considered a summative evaluation and thus draws from quantitative research methods. Summative evaluations seek to explain how the independent variable, a program intervention, influences the dependent variables, the desired client outcomes. For example, does participation in a program influence parental attitudes? Does group therapy improve marital stability? Do parental education classes significantly improve parents' ability to support early infant development?

STAGES OF PROGRAM AND PRACTICE DEVELOPMENT AND DATA ANALYSIS

The stage of development of a program or practice area, whether planning, implementation, or outcome, also provides some clarity about what data collection and analysis methods are used and whether quantitative and/or qualitative data analyses are preferred.

The Planning or Input Stage

One area in which data analysis is needed is the input or needs assessment stage of a program. Needs assessments, as discussed in chapter 6, are usually proposed when there is a concern that a new intervention may be important to consider for a specific target population. During this stage, various evaluation strategies, such as handing out questionnaires or analyzing secondary data, might be used to examine the specific needs of a community. Evaluators could also conduct focus groups or individual interviews with community members, or consult other local experts to clarify where services are needed and how to better allocate resources. For example, a needs assessment of a new target population to be served by a county's mental health system might involve interviewing prospective clients, giving out questionnaires to staff members who work with mental health clients, or conducting focus groups with other stakeholders who have a vested interest in an issue. These strategies can be qualitative or quantitative in nature. In general, it is wise to combine different strategies. Royse, Thyer, and Padgett (2009) discuss the importance of triangulation, or seeking multiple sources and comparing them. For example, interviews with people who are homeless, those who work with the homeless, and other key informants could all be initiated and compared to discover their similarities and differences.

Because of the varied nature of needs assessments, there are a number of types of data analyses that can be used to answer questions about the perceived needs of a community. Using focus groups with stakeholders, for example, could involve tape recording their responses to a few open-ended questions and analyzing the responses through a content analysis of the words that are used. Another possibility is to organize their responses into themes at a more abstract level to discover possible links among these themes. Berg (2004) and others present other impressionistic approaches that can be used to evaluate qualitative data collected from evaluations.

In other instances, strategies for assessing the needs in a community can be quantitative in nature. The data resulting from a questionnaire with forced-response questions or existing secondary data collected from a previous evaluation are examples. Let's assume that there is a concern that more public housing is needed for homeless people in a local area and that existing shelters keep detailed records on these people. An evaluator might be able to complete a needs assessment by developing a descriptive account or profile of the homeless population. The descriptive analysis could give some insight into the severity of the issue. The descriptive statistics could include simply calculating mean (average) scores along with standard deviations and ranges; or frequency distributions of such variables as age, gender, income, family structure, and length of time being homeless. This information would be informative to stakeholders, as it provides concrete data for making informed decisions about the needs of homeless people in the community.

Another possibility for data analysis is to compare the quantitative responses of two different groups of interviewed people. In this case, bivariate analysis would be used to help determine whether the responses of the two groups are significantly different and the amount of difference that is evident. Given the previous example of a needs assessment of prospective mental health clients, you may find that groups of prospective clients and mental health workers agree that particular types of services are needed in a satellite office somewhere in the county, but they may disagree about where the location should be. Using this information, the evaluator can report on how much consensus and difference exists in the responses of the two stakeholder groups.

Implementation Stage

Another point in time in which data analysis is needed is the implementation stage of an intervention. This is the stage in which the most varied types of evaluations can occur, as described in chapter 8. A range of evaluation activities can be considered that are similar in some ways to those mentioned for the input stage. Evaluators could conduct focus groups, interviews, administer questionnaires, conduct observations, or undertake a combination of these activities. However, the intent of these evaluations is very different from those conducted during the input stage. Evaluations during the implementation stage are intended to find out whether an intervention works as planned; how well it works; and whether some components, such as a staffing issue, an intake glitch, or ambiguity in how a particular service is delivered, need to be changed or at least fine-tuned.

For example, an intake unit responsible for assessing and diagnosing clients' problems or needs in a mental health outpatient clinic may refer clients to various staff members and recommend different kinds of services, but the staff members may treat the recommendations differently. Some may ignore them, others interpret them one way, and still others interpret them another way. It appears that clarity and consistency are needed in how the intake referrals are prepared, received, and used.

Because of the varied nature of evaluations that occur during the implementation stage, there are several types of data analyses that can be used to answer questions about the intervention's implementation. In the example of intake services at a mental health clinic, interviews with intake workers and staff could include a set of open-ended questions to determine whether there are differences in their perspectives or understandings of procedures.

For example, an open-ended question is, "What do you see as the relationship between the recommendations provided by the intake workers and the decisions made by the treatment staff on how services are to be implemented?" Because these would be open-ended questions with qualitative responses, a content analysis could be conducted to categorize comments by key words. The categories could then be cross-tabulated by whether they were made by intake or treatment workers. If an examination of specific words failed to reveal important distinctions in comments, then themes could be teased out of the comments at a more abstract level of analysis and cross-tabulated.

Another possibility for data analysis is to compare the quantitative responses of two different groups of interviewed people. In the example of intake issues at a mental health clinic, a set of forced-response statements is possible. For example, "The intake workers' recommendations are optional to implement," and "The recommendations of intake workers are usually not feasible." Response categories for such statements could include: strongly agree, agree, disagree, and strongly disagree. In this case, bivariate analysis would help determine whether the responses of the two groups are different and, if so, by how much. Using this information, the evaluator can report on how much consensus or difference exists in the responses of the two stakeholder groups on the intake workers' recommendations.

Outcome Stage

Outcome evaluations emphasize different kinds of data analysis than those used during the planning and implementation stages. Outcome studies focus on the relationships between the intervention and the desired client outcomes. This focus is used not only to determine whether there is an association between the intervention and outcome but also to go a step further and determine whether the intervention caused the outcome measure to change favorably.

For example, in a substance abuse agency, interventions might be group treatment. The evaluator wants to conduct an outcome evaluation to find out whether the intervention is responsible for any progress in clients' short- and long-term decreased substance use. An association will need to be found between the two entities, as well as an evident causal relationship. Several types of controls are needed to determine whether there is a causal relationship between group treatment and progress made to discontinue substance use. This could include being able to rule out other environmental events in clients' lives and other changes beyond external events. As was discussed in chapter 9, a quasi-experimental or experimental group design would need to be used to take into account extraneous influences.

Data analysis strategies used in the outcome stage are the most complex, and several are reviewed subsequently to highlight when to use each strategy and what each strategy can accomplish. Each strategy has limitations; thus, the limitations are also described. For example, some statistical strategies can be used to find out whether there is an association between an intervention and client outcome. Other strategies can be used to determine whether a causal relationship exists and to what extent a causal relationship is evident.

SUMMARY OF PERTINENT TOOLS FOR QUALITATIVE DATA ANALYSIS

As reported earlier in this chapter, many evaluations are qualitative in nature or at least have qualitative components. They may collect data using open-ended questions, in-depth interviews, focus groups, unstructured observations, or existing data sources. Three qualitative data analysis strategies are especially relevant for such evaluations: case studies, condensed responses to general categories, and theme analysis.

Case Studies

Case studies involve one or a few research participants, but they are intended to provide stakeholders with insights into an entire group of people that the case example tends to represent. Case studies are detailed portrayals of an individual that can illuminate how a larger group of people that the individual represents is functioning. Case studies are also possible with other social units such as a cultural group, a family, or neighborhood (Dudley, 2011). Case studies can be prepared using many different research strategies, such as in-depth interviews, participant observation, and existing documents. Case studies typically do not go beyond a descriptive state. A few examples of case studies follow.

A Mexican boy recently immigrated to the United States with his mother, who was an undocumented worker. The boy was having extreme difficulty adapting to his peers and teachers in the public school in his new community. He was finally suspended. He ended up in the juvenile court system after torturing and killing stray animals. A case study describing his difficulties in adapting to a U.S. school could provide valuable insights into the struggles that many immigrant children face as they attempt to adapt to a new environment in the United States.

A teenager living secretly with HIV was experiencing severe depression because she did not know what to do. She did not want to seek treatment from a health clinic because she was uninformed about the treatments that could be made available to her, and she did not want to disclose her condition to her family for fear of being disowned. To make things even worse, she had no one she could trust to talk to about what she was going through.

She began to have suicidal thoughts and contemplated running away. A case study described the challenges that this teenager faced and the obstacles associated with attempting to get help; it provided valuable insights into how teenagers with HIV or AIDS could be helped in the early stages of this disease.

Case studies can be an important approach to consider because they offer insights about what might be typical, challenging, or possibly misunderstood about particular types of clients who participate in a specific program. A case study could also illustrate how a client was especially successful in participating in and using the specific services of a program. Quality assurance evaluations use the case study approach to explore how a few randomly selected clients function in a program and interact with providers. Case studies also can be used in a needs assessment to gain a fuller understanding of the social circumstances of prospective clients. Case studies used to conduct a needs assessment are described in chapter 6.

The data analysis involved in preparing a case study begins with careful planning. A case or cases need to be selected and specific topics for exploration chosen. Such decisions are determined by carefully considering what the evaluator and other stakeholders want to accomplish and what is practically possible. Other issues are important once data has been collected. A case description should be prepared and organized to tell the story about an individual (or a family, a group, a neighborhood) in the most effective way. Constructing an outline of the story can help identify the most important topics and further questions to ask. Another task is to determine when enough data has been collected on each chosen topic or when additional data is needed to fill out the story. As a case study is prepared and all the data on topics are assembled, another consideration is to discover and describe how the topics may be related so that the story can reflect a more holistic account and perspective. It should be kept in mind that preparing a case study is an effort in creativity and art as well as science. The important thing to remember is to tell the story that needs to be told in the most creative, accurate, compelling, and comprehensive way.

Condense Responses into General Categories

Another strategy for analyzing qualitative data is to create a set of general categories (usually no more than ten) and assign responses to these categories. This option is mostly used with data collection strategies that elicit brief qualitative answers. Qualitative methods that lend themselves to brief answers include open-ended questions in interviews and questionnaires, some questions asked in focus groups, and some semi-structured observations. Condensing a large number of short responses into fewer general categories is useful for succinctly summarizing and organizing responses together that have similar meaning. For example, a client satisfaction study could have the question, what do you like about living here? asked of residents of a group home for people with developmental disabilities. The responses of a large sample would be too numerous to meaningfully grasp in their original form, so a smaller number of general categories can be used, such as "types of food or beverages," "social activities," and "hygiene activities."

In some ways, this strategy is similar to the manner in which a frequency distribution summarizes the quantitative responses to a forced-response question. The only difference is that the quantitative responses are already in categorical form, whereas the qualitative responses are assigned to general categories on the basis of their similarities (e.g., taking baths and brushing teeth fit into the "hygiene activities" category). The general categories created from this qualitative strategy are usually at the pre-nominal level of measurement and could be used as a set of response categories for a forced-response question in a later study.

The steps involved in condensing qualitative responses of an open-ended question into fewer general categories are as follows (Dudley, 2011):

1. Prepare the brief responses for analysis by listing them all together with other responses to the same question.
2. Review and become familiar with all responses to the question.
3. Code responses using the same code for all similar responses (e.g., symbols, such as a letter in the left margin, or different colors).
4. Group similar responses together into categories and give each category a label, which should clearly describe the category of responses (e.g., "hygiene activities" includes taking a bath, washing in warm water, brushing one's teeth).
5. Assign each of the brief responses to the category that fits best and count the number of responses that fall into each category.
6. Report the results in quantitative form (e.g., hygiene activities: 27; food or beverages: 22; social activities: 19).
7. Although general categories provide a useful summary of the responses, it may be helpful to include some specific responses for a category in parentheses as examples, which help emphasize the human side of data.

It is important to involve two evaluators who work independently in selecting the general categories and assigning responses to the categories. Two reviewers are used to ensure that there is inter-rater reliability.

Theme Analysis

A third qualitative data analysis strategy is to identify common themes or patterns that are prevalent in narrative data. Theme analysis is useful in analyzing lengthy narrative material from data collection strategies such as participant-observation, in-depth interviews, focus groups, and unstructured observations. This strategy can also be used to analyze existing data from sources such as journal articles, case records, and other agency material.

Example of a Theme Deriving from Focus Group Responses

A social work student (Leary, 2003) conducted a focus group study of volunteers of several churches that had been sponsoring shelters for homeless people in their churches on a weekly basis during the winter months. A theme resulting from the sessions was identified as a perceived need of homeless people to talk to someone at the church. When the volunteers began discussing the needs they witnessed from the homeless people, they identified the homeless people's need to talk to someone who could listen to them and provide compassion. An abbreviated version of four of the comments found in the narrative that reflected that theme were as follows:

- I think one of the big needs is just to listen to them, be compassionate, and be there for them. I remember one evaluation meeting . . . when you have the homeless at the meeting with you, and I remember one of the fellows saying, "Just don't feed us and leave us."
- I would have loved to have one of the clergy members, deacons, priests, whatever, come and say an opening prayer with our people as it can be a show of force that this whole congregation is behind this program. . . . I think that is a really important part, to have a show of force, that clergy and staff support the program 100 percent. I think the guests actually get a sense of being special when we are all present.
- During Lenten season, when we would have community meals on the same night as the shelter program, one of the things that was very interesting was that . . . they were much more likely to sit down with [one of the pastors]. Some of the issues that were shared . . . [included] offering the possibility of some counseling services and providing that there. I see that as caring, a very crucial kind of caring, to their situation, and also it's definitely a help.
- A lot of them have a lack of self-confidence; they don't believe in themselves anymore. Mainly they need someone to talk to, to reassure them they are still a human being and worth something.

Conducting a theme analysis usually takes more time, covers more data, and can be more intellectually demanding than the previous two strategies.

Like the strategy of reducing responses to fewer general categories, it is important to involve two independent evaluators in coding themes to ensure inter-rater reliability. If the two people disagree on a particular theme or how it is reflected in narrative, a third person can be involved to help reach a consensus.

The major stages involved in conducting a theme analysis include the following (Dudley, 2011):

1. Prepare narrative data for analysis by typing it into electronic files.
2. Carefully review and become familiar with all narrative data.
3. Assign a code (e.g., using symbols or magic markers) to each point in the narrative that reflects a specific theme.
4. Group the coded narrative reflecting each theme on the same page (e.g., copy and paste to move data around the file).
5. After carefully reviewing the narrative for each theme, give the theme an accurate label (e.g., a few words, a phrase, a sentence).

Theme analysis can involve additional steps, such as examining how the coded narrative of each theme might vary. For example, some of the narratives illustrating a theme may describe it in a positive way, while others describe it in negative terms. Identifying variations in how a theme is depicted can help further delineate what the theme actually means.

Example of Identifying Variations in a Theme

In one student's evaluation (Grantham, 2001) of the needs of patients in a hospice setting, several people identified the theme of legal issues related to finances, end-of-life care, or insurance. On further examination, she found that variations in the comments about legal issues seemed to refer to one of three things: financial problems, a legal will, or advanced directives.

Another step that can be taken in a theme analysis involves capturing how different themes may be related to one another according to what the narrative suggests for each respondent. Relationships among themes can be explored further in later evaluations as hypotheses.

SUMMARY OF PERTINENT TOOLS FOR QUANTITATIVE DATA ANALYSIS

Descriptive Analyses

It is important for evaluators to ask descriptive questions to understand more about the clients participating in a program, such as, how old are the clients in the program? What is the education level of those who complete the program? And what is the demographic profile of those who drop out of the program? Other descriptive questions might be, what is the level of stress of the clients? How many children attended the program? What is the educational level of participants who do not complete the program? And, how many sessions did both the fathers and mothers participate in together?

Descriptive analysis, or univariate analyses, is used to answer descriptive questions. The analyses are considered univariate because the descriptive question focuses on only one variable at a time. Univariate questions provide a way to describe something about the sample, such as its variability or range. The level of measurement of the variables in descriptive research will inform you about which univariate analyses to use. If the level of measurement of the variable is ordinal or nominal, for example, then percentages and frequency distributions are appropriate. If variables are at the interval/ratio level, then you can report the mean, range, and standard deviation. (See table 10.1.)

Levels of measurement. Nominal-level data are the simplest form in which numerical labels are used. Nominal data are categorical, and categories are distinct, mutually exclusive, and exhaustive of all possible circumstances (e.g., gender, race). The categories or scores in nominal level data cannot be ranked, ordered, or manipulated mathematically (e.g., addition, division, multiplication).

A higher, more sophisticated level of measurement is ordinal-level data. Ordinal data are ranked or ordered from lowest to highest, such as Likert scales that range from strongly disagree to strongly agree, which are ordinal-level measures. The limitation with ordinal-level data is that there is no way to determine the distance between the various levels. For example, it is not possible to calculate a numeric distance between strongly disagree and disagree.

TABLE 10.1 Review of Levels of Measurement

Levels	Examples	Measurement procedures	Mathematical operations permitted
Nominal	Gender, ethnicity, political affiliation	Categories	Counting the number in each category and comparing sizes of categories
Ordinal	Likert scales, social class, military rank	Categories and ranking with respect to one another	All of the above plus statements of *greater than* and *less than*
Interval/ratio	Age, years of education, household income	All of the above plus description of numerical distances between scores	All of the above plus all other mathematical operations

Although there are four levels of measurement, we do not usually differentiate between interval and ratio data. As a result, interval and ratio data are combined and presented together. Unlike nominal and ordinal measures, interval/ratio data permit classification, ranking, and signifying the exact distance between scores to be defined. Measures such as age in years, number of days on a job, or annual income are interval/ratio data.

Frequency distributions. A frequency distribution is a statistic that describes the number of times that each value of a variable is observed in a sample. For example, in a question using a Likert scale, a frequency distribution describes how many participants selected "very satisfied," "satisfied," "dissatisfied," and so on. Frequency distributions can be presented as actual frequencies or as percentages. Usually percentages are easier to grasp with the large samples. Often, however, frequency distributions list both frequencies and percentages. Frequency distributions are an appropriate statistic for use with categorical variables, including both nominal and ordinal variables. A frequency distribution could also be used with an interval/ratio variable if the responses are reduced to categories.

Measures of central tendency. Three types of measures of central tendency are possible to use in evaluations: mean, median, and mode. The mode is the easiest measure to use, as it is the most common or frequently occurring number. In addition, the mode can be used regardless of the level of data measurement. The median is the middle point, or the fiftieth percentile of the data, and can be used with ordinal, interval, or ratio data.

The most commonly reported measure of central tendency in research is the mean. Keep in mind that the mean score is an average and that its interpretation is limited, as it can be extremely sensitive to outliers. As a result, the mean score might not be very close to most scores in a sample. This can be problematic when the mean is reported by itself; for example, we often see the mean score reported for a standardized test, income, or housing prices. As a result, we should be mindful that stakeholders may need to be given an explanation of a mean score and its limitations. When using analyses on interval/ratio data, we should report not only the mean but also the range and standard deviation. This will give stakeholders an idea of how the data are distributed and will make the mean score more meaningful.

Measures of variability. The range of scores is important when presenting interval/ratio data, as the mean can be sensitive to extremes in scores. As a result, knowing the range of scores can indicate the distribution and help determine whether the mean actually reflects most people in the sample. For example, if the mean age of mothers in a support group is 30 years, but the range is from 19 to 65 years, the mean score may not indicate most women's age in the group, as a few 65-year-old women can greatly increase the mean age of the sample.

When you add the standard deviation to the mix it gives a clearer picture of the sample distribution. The standard deviation is the measure of variability that informs how scores relate to one another and to the mean. The standard deviation is useful in interpreting the percentage of scores that are close to the mean. In normally distributed data, 68 percent of scores fall within plus or minus 1 standard deviation from the mean. Further, 95 percent fall within two standard deviations of the mean, and 99 percent fall within three standard deviations. Returning to the age of mothers, if the data are normally distributed and the mean age is 30 and the standard deviation is 3, then you would expect that 68 percent of mothers are between the ages of 27 and 33 (30 ± 3, where 3 is one standard deviation). Similarly, 95 percent of mothers in the study are between 24 and 36 years old (30 ± 6, where 6 is two standard deviations). Further, you could conclude that 99 percent of mothers are between 21 and 39 years old. This interpretation could be trusted if data are normally distributed; in reality, though, much of the data are skewed and not normally distributed. In other words, if there are a few 65-year-old mothers in the sample, they do not indicate a normally distributed age of participants, with a standard deviation of 3.

Testing Hypotheses

Often program and practice evaluations are designed to test the hypothesized relationship between the intervention and progress on client outcomes. The intervention is considered the independent variable and the client outcome is the dependent variable.

Research Terms

A *hypothesis* is a hypothetical explanation describing the relationship between two variables.

An *independent variable* is the variable presumed to cause a change to occur in the dependent variable.

The *dependent variable* is the effect variable, or the variable changed by the independent variable.

Several different types of hypothesis testing are possible to determine whether there is a relationship between the intervention and client outcome. Each type of testing is determined by the type of quasi-experimental or experimental design used (see chapter 9). Table 10.2 summarizes the types of hypotheses that are possible, the level of measurement required for independent and dependent variables, and the statistical tests to be used.

TABLE 10.2   Types of Hypotheses

Type of hypotheses	Level of measurement of variables	An appropriate statistical test to use
Questions of association	Independent variable and dependent variable are nominal	Chi-square
Questions of association	Independent variable and dependent variable are interval/ratio	Pearson correlation
Questions of difference between two groups	Independent variable is nominal; dependent variable is interval/ratio	t-test
Questions of difference between three or more groups	Independent variable is nominal; dependent variable is interval/ratio	ANOVA
Questions of prediction	Independent and dependent variables are interval/ratio	Linear regression
Questions of prediction	Independent variables are interval/ratio; dependent variables are nominal	Logistic regression

Questions of association.   Many times hypothesis testing occurs only to explore an association between the intervention and outcome. When the intervention is introduced, the client outcome is expected to change. With questions of association, nothing more can be determined, such as whether the intervention had a causal influence or was responsible for the change in client outcome. Questions of association are explored in a one-group pretest-posttest design. This design is a pre-experimental design (see chapter 9).

Questions of association between the intervention and client outcome can be determined by applying a statistical test. The two most common statistical tests are chi-square and correlation. A chi-square test is used to determine whether the values of one variable are associated with the values of another variable. This test is also sometimes referred to as a cross-tabulation of variables. The chi-square test is used only when both the intervention and the outcome are measured at the nominal or ordinal level. In other words, both variables must be categorical. For example, the evaluation question could be, Does attending a psychoeducational group session about the high-risk factors associated with contracting AIDS result in more correct answers (to true/false questions on a test) after the session than before it?

A correlation test is the other statistical test frequently used to explore questions of association. It is also sometimes referred to as a Pearson correlation. This test not only answers the question of whether there is an association between the intervention and client outcome but also indicates how strong the association is. For example, the evaluation question might be, Is there a relationship between the number of group sessions attended and the number of fathering activities carried out? The assumption in a correlation test is that both variables are at the interval/ratio level. In this example, the intervention measured at the interval/ratio level could be how many group sessions members attended or for how many hours they attended group sessions. The client outcome variable is also at the interval/ratio level and can be how often a father participates in specific activities with his child over the duration of a week. The results of the correlation test may indicate that the variables are positively associated, negatively associated, or not associated.

The correlation test indicates the strength of the relationship between the intervention and client outcome and can range from −1.0 to 1.0 with a score of 1 or −1 indicating a perfect association, positive or negative, respectively. Evaluators are much more likely to find correlations between the intervention and client outcome to be less than ±0.6.

For example, we might say that a correlation score of 0.3 is a weak correlation, but we have to keep in mind that most correlation scores in evaluations are rarely greater than 0.6. A positive correlation generally occurs when large numbers for one variable are associated with large numbers of another variable, and a negative correlation generally occurs when large numbers of one variable are associated with small numbers of the other variable. For example, an evaluation that finds a negative association between family therapy and reduced marital stress could find that the number of counseling sessions increases as the level of marital stress decreases.

Questions of differences between groups.   A second type of hypothesis testing explores whether there is a difference between two or more groups, such as the group receiving the intervention and a comparison group that is not. A group design that is likely to rely on this type of analysis is the one-group pretest-posttest design with a comparison group. Two commonly used tests of differences between groups are the t-test and analysis of variance (ANOVA). T-tests examine differences across two groups, whereas ANOVA examines differences across three or more groups.

The requirements for using a t-test are that the independent variable (whether or not an intervention is introduced) must be dichotomous and nominal. The dependent variable (e.g., the client outcome) must be measurable at the interval/ratio level. The requirements for using an ANOVA are the same as for a t-test, except the independent variable is nominal and includes three or more categories. In an evaluation, this could mean comparing three different groups of participants (e.g., intervention group, group receiving traditional services, and group receiving no services).

There are some basic questions that the t-test can answer in evaluations. For example, a program evaluation question may ask whether there is a difference in parenting attitudes (the client outcome) between those who have completed a nine-week intervention on parenting and those who have had no intervention. In brief, a t-test can be used to determine whether the two groups are significantly different on the basis of their parenting-attitudes scores. What we attempt to determine is whether the mean score for one group differs significantly from the mean score for the other group, or whether the observed differences are too small and thus attributable to either sampling error or chance factors. If we cannot determine that the mean scores are significantly different, then we can conclude that the groups are the same, for purposes of analysis.

There are two types of t-tests that are often used in evaluations: paired samples and independent samples. The requirements for both tests are that the independent variable is nominal and the dependent variable is interval. The decision on which type of t-test to use in an evaluation is based solely on the makeup of the groups in an evaluation.

A *paired-samples t-test* is used if there is an interest in comparing a pretest score and a posttest score of the same group. This test is often used with a one-group pretest-posttest design. For example, the evaluation question may aim to determine whether a ten-week community center enrichment program decreased classroom disruptions in adolescent boys. The pretest measures indicate how many disruptions the teacher reported over the first semester of school before implementation of the program. During the second semester of the school year, the adolescents complete the program and the teacher records the number of classroom disruptions again. Let's presume that the pretest scores for the group were 11.5 disruptions per week during the first semester. The posttest scores indicate a drop to 9.2 disruptions after the program is completed. The question is, was there a significant difference in scores or are the differences attributable to chance or error? The t-test informs us whether the scores are statistically significantly different from one another, in which case we could reasonably say that the program effectively reduced classroom disruptions. If the scores are not found to be significantly different, then the pretest and posttest scores are basically the same, and the intervention did not significantly decrease classroom disruptions.

An *independent-samples t-test* is used to compare two different groups. This test is often used with a one-group pretest-posttest design with a comparison group. An example would be to compare the self-esteem scores of two groups of clients after the first group completed a special program and the comparison group received no intervention. We could compare the self-esteem posttest mean score of the first group with the posttest mean score of the second group.

ANOVA allows for expansion of the principles of the t-test to a statistical test that examines whether there are differences across three or more groups. The ANOVA and t-test assume that the independent variable is nominal and that the dependent variable is interval/ratio. In an ANOVA evaluation, for example, this could mean comparing three different groups of participants (e.g., an intervention group, a client group receiving traditional services, and a client group receiving no services). We would compare the mean posttest scores of the three groups to determine whether one made significantly more progress on the client outcome measure than the other two groups.

An ANOVA can also be used to determine whether there are significant differences in the interventions of three different subgroups. An ANOVA can be used if, for example, there are concerns that clients received different numbers of therapy sessions because of their geographic location. The research question might be, is there a difference in the number of therapy sessions because of clients' geographic location? In this case, location could be measured as urban, suburban, and rural. The independent variable is the three geographic locations (nominal) and the dependent variable is the number of therapy sessions (interval/ratio). Let's say that you conduct an evaluation and find out that urban clients received an average of twelve sessions per week, suburban clients received an average of sixteen sessions a week, and rural clients received an average of seventeen sessions a week. Your initial thought may be that urban clients receive significantly fewer therapy sessions than do suburban and rural clients. However, the ANOVA findings may indicate that there is not a statistically significant difference in the number of therapy sessions among these groups; thus, you conclude that the difference in number of therapy sessions is simply due to chance and there is really no difference in the number of therapy sessions in each group for purposes of analysis.

Questions of prediction.   Regression models are another statistical test that can be used in program evaluations. Several regression models or tests are available to predict a client outcome (dependent variable) from more than one intervention (independent variables). A regression model can investigate whether an intervention is more effective with men or women or with some age groups more than others. If participants have experienced a variety of interventions, then a regression model can show how the interventions, working together, predict the dependent variable. Consider an agency that serves families after a child dies. If the family members participate in group therapy, individual grief counseling, and a support group, then the regression can show how much variance or change in the client outcome (e.g., recovery from grief) is accounted for by the combination of all three interventions. In addition, the regression can show whether specific interventions, such as group therapy, are more effective than other interventions in improving the client outcome. If one intervention is found not to be a significant predictor of client outcome, then this is scientific evidence that this intervention may not be effective.

Two regression models that can be used in evaluations are linear regression and logistic regression. Both allow the research question to predict a dependent variable from a number of independent variables. The difference between the models is that the dependent variable is at the interval/ratio level in linear regression and at the nominal level in logistic regression. For more information on regression analysis, see Weinbach and Grinnell (2009) as a resource.

MIXED METHODS AND DATA ANALYSIS

Qualitative and quantitative data analyses have been described separately so far. This is not intended to mislead readers into thinking that the methods are unrelated; they often are related. Often evaluations use mixed methods, quantitative and qualitative. With mixed methods, each method enhances the other by its particular qualities. Sometimes one method is primary and the other secondary. Other times both quantitative and qualitative methods are equally valuable to an evaluation.

An illustration of an evaluation with both methods being equally important is Ellis, Marsh, and Craven (2009). Their mixed methods evaluation examined the effectiveness of a widely used peer support program designed to facilitate students' transition to adolescence and high school. The quantitative component was an experimental design involving seventh-grade students in three schools. This design determined that the peer support program enhanced the students' self-concept, school citizenship, connectedness, and resourcefulness during a two-year period. These four concepts were all measured by well-tested measurement instruments. The qualitative component of 90 percent of the experimental group responded to open-ended questionnaire items and focus group discussions. These findings gave the students opportunities to express their views about the benefits of the program, the effectiveness of the peer support leaders, and other issues not identified by the quantitative methods. Using two of the qualitative data analysis strategies described earlier in the chapter (theme analysis and condensing responses from open-ended questions to categories), these findings found benefits of the peer support program in several domains including connectedness, problem-solving ability, sense of self, optimistic thinking, school citizenship, and adjustment to high school. Many of the quantitative and qualitative findings reinforced each other while the qualitative findings also provided major insights into the personal perspectives of the students.

The combination of qualitative and quantitative methods in evaluations offers several advantages to evaluations, including complementarity, triangulation, and accountability.

Complementary Data

Quantitative and qualitative methods each provide distinct kinds of data that can be complementary to each other and useful in evaluations. Quantitative data are useful for purposes such as providing numeric measures of client satisfaction, client outcomes, and profiles of prospective clients. The numeric measures can also be used to make decisions about program effectiveness. In contrast, qualitative data provide a human side to quantitative measures, showing why quantitative measures are important and how they affect real people. These naturalistic data can provide a fuller picture of the concerns and encounters of people and bring greater identification with them, their plight, and the progress they make.

Triangulation

Qualitative and quantitative findings on the same topic can be helpful in triangulation of the findings. Use of both methods can provide two types of information sources on the same topic. For example, in one evaluation, clients with a dual diagnosis of developmental disability and mental illness were ask forced-response questions such as, "Do you like living here?" (Dudley, Calhoun, Ahlgrim-Delzell, & Conroy, 1998). They were also asked open-ended questions on the same topics to learn more about the meaning of their responses. Open-ended questions included, "What do you like about living here?" and "What do you not like about living here?" Sometimes there were inconsistencies in responses. For example, a few responded that they liked living where they were but then they focused on a long list of things that they did not like in responses to the open-ended questions. So, the combination of the two types of questions provided the evaluator with an opportunity to ask for clarification about any discrepancies between their responses. In other cases, open-ended questions clarified why many clients said that they liked where they lived, as several qualitative comments confirmed their positive responses (e.g., they liked having their own bedroom, being treated with respect, having more freedom than in the past).

Example of an Evaluation Using a Mixed Methods Approach

The purpose of an evaluation conducted by Lynch (2007) was to explore the impact of an independent-living skills-training program on the resilience, social support, and life skills of sixteen ethnically diverse foster-care teenagers. The teenagers' scores on standardized measures of resilience, social support, and life skills were compared before and after they participated in the training program. The improvements in scores from pretest to posttest were found to be statistically significant for social support but not for resilience and life skills. In a qualitative component of this mixed-methods study, the youths' descriptions of the same constructs of resilience, social support, and life skills were, in most cases, consistent with scores on standardized measures. For example, most of the youth had difficulty describing and recollecting life skills information, such as managing money and locating appropriate housing, which was consistent with scores suggesting that they "mastered" only about half of the life skills items.

Accountability in Giving Answers

A third advantage of using mixed methods in evaluation is that it holds participants accountable for their answers. When forced-response questions are asked, it is relatively easy for participants to answer them without revealing much, if any, information about their views or motives. In the previous example of clients with a dual diagnosis, a "yes" response to the question about whether they like where they live tells little about what they like. They may answer affirmatively because that is the normative response to give and they think a negative response could get them into trouble with providers. Therefore, qualitative responses on the same topic can hold participants accountable for their answers. If they do not like where they live, it will be more difficult for them to cover up their negative feelings in responses to open-ended questions. Further, qualitative responses provide useful information that can be addressed directly. Accountability in this case addresses validity and accuracy issues as well, for when a question is asked in two different ways, responses are likely to be closer to the truth or reality.

The chapter has highlighted many of the data analysis tools and strategies that can be used to analyze evaluation data. Quantitative, qualitative, and mixed methods strategies have been offered. This information can be supplemented by several specialized qualitative and quantitative data analysis texts that provide more detail on how to conduct an analysis. Some of these texts are identified in the chapter and listed as references. The next chapter addresses the last steps in conducting an evaluation, preparing a report and disseminating the findings to stakeholders and other interested parties. The findings incorporated into a presentation are determined, to a large extent, by the choices made in data analysis, so this chapter is an important resource to use in the final steps of preparing and disseminating a report.

KEY TERMS

ANOVA
Case studies
Chi-square
Correlation
Creating general categories

Descriptive statistics
Frequency distributions
Independent samples t-test
Measures of central tendency
Measures of variability
Mixed methods
Paired-samples t-test
Questions of association
Questions of differences in groups
Questions of prediction
Regression models
Theme analysis
t-test

DISCUSSION QUESTIONS AND ASSIGNMENTS

1. Select an evaluation report from a social work or evaluation journal. Critique the methods section of the evaluation by answering the following questions:

   • What data collection methods were used? Were the methods distinctly quantitative or qualitative? Or were mixed methods used?
   • How were the data analyzed? Which qualitative and quantitative data analysis tools described in the chapter were used?

2. Find and review an evaluation study that used mixed methods. Did the authors refer to the evaluation as a mixed-methods evaluation? How did the data analysis procedures connect the two different quantitative and qualitative data analyses? Describe the findings that made connections between the quantitative and qualitative findings. Explain whether you think such findings were helpful to the overall findings section. If you think these combined findings were not helpful, explain why not.

REFERENCES

Berg, B. (2004). *Qualitative research methods for the social sciences.* Boston: Pearson.

Dudley, J. R. (2011). *Research methods for social work: Being producers and consumers of research* (updated 2nd ed.). Boston: Pearson.

Dudley, J., Calhoun, M., Ahlgrim-Delzell, L., & Conroy, J. (1998). Measuring the consumer satisfaction of class members of a lawsuit. *Journal of Intellectual Disability Research, 42*(3), 199–207.

Ellis, L. A., Marsh, H. W., & Craven, R. G. (2009). Addressing the challenges faced by early adolescents: A mixed-method evaluation of the benefits of peer support. *American Journal of Community Psychology, 44*(1–2), 54–75.

Grantham, V. (2001). Theme analysis of client records. Unpublished student assignment, University of North Carolina at Charlotte.

Leary, A. (2003). Room in the inn: Exploring church involvement in serving the homeless. Unpublished student research project, University of North Carolina at Charlotte.

Lynch, C. J. (2007). Exploring the implementation of a transitional services program for adolescents in the Texas Foster Care System. Unpublished doctoral dissertation, University of Texas at Austin.

Royse, D., Thyer, B., & Padgett, D. (2009). *Program evaluation: An introduction* (5th ed.). Belmont CA: Wadsworth Cengage Learning.

Weinbach, R. W., & Grinnell, R. M. (2009). *Statistics for social workers* (8th ed.). Boston: Pearson.

Chapter 11

Preparing and Disseminating a Report of Findings

How do we prepare a report that is useful and optimizes the possibilities of positive changes for clients?

This chapter explores the final two steps of the Seven Evaluation Steps: step 6 (preparing a report of the findings) and step 7 (disseminating the findings to others). Once the data are gathered from an evaluation and analyzed, preparing a report naturally follows. Several different types of reports are possible, depending on the needs of various stakeholders. A report can be communicated orally, in written form, or both; comprehensively or in brief summary form; and the formatting options are almost unlimited. Reports can be technical, a formal presentation at a public meeting, a set of topics and questions covered at a staff workshop, a series of informal discussions, a brief written summary, a paragraph for state legislators, a manuscript, a press release, or other formats.

Once the report is completed, the findings are expected to be disseminated to all stakeholders and interested parties. This dissemination, of course, should occur in the most useful form possible. Ideally, findings are disseminated to several different types of stakeholders; some are obvious, such as funding agencies and agency administrators overseeing the program. Other important stakeholders can be easily overlooked or forgotten, such as clients, family members, and pertinent community groups.

Although different strategies are available to disseminate findings, they largely depend on the format chosen for the report. In other words, the two steps of preparing a report and disseminating findings are largely intertwined. The decision about a report's format determines how and even if it will be useful to some stakeholders. For example, a lengthy technical research report may be useful to a funding agency or a professional journal but not to other stakeholders, such as clients and their families. For this reason, it is best to begin by exploring the needs of each stakeholder, finding out what kinds of information and what format will be most helpful to them, and proceeding to select the most useful reports and means of distributing the findings.

CONSIDERING THE INPUT OF STAKEHOLDERS

Like all the previous steps of an evaluation, it is very important to spend an adequate amount of time thinking about and planning these final steps. Unfortunately, a poorly thought-out and written report can easily negate all the hard work up to this point. Likewise, neglecting to give enough time and serious thought to how to disseminate findings could deter what an evaluation was intended to achieve.

The best way to begin these two final steps is to consider who the stakeholders and other potential readers of the report will be (e.g., funding agencies, board members, advisory committee members, administrators, program service providers, legislators, current or prospective clients, community groups, advocacy groups, professionals, the public). Some stakeholders may be designated as primary and others secondary, which can help prioritize where more of the time and energy should be devoted to dissemination (Morris, Fitz-Gibbon, & Freeman, 1987). The evaluation sponsor and others who requested the evaluation are examples of primary stakeholders, and others could include a funding agency, the agency's board of directors, a chief executive officer, program directors, other key staff members, and any other decision makers. Secondary stakeholders are more likely community groups, other staff members, clients, other organizations interested in the program, the public, and legislators. Although the latter groups may be considered secondary, they should not be overlooked.

Each group is likely to have different needs related to a report, and the differences are usually reflected in how easy it is to understand the material and how relevant and useful the information is. Timing may also be important for stakeholders, as timing may be crucial to a decision-making timetable. Therefore, it is likely that different types of reports and strategies for dissemination are needed, especially to address a diverse audience of stakeholders.

It is usually wise to ask stakeholders several types of questions before you begin to write a report. Morris et al. (1987) suggest the following questions:

- What do you want to know about the evaluation and why? What expectations do you have for a report?
- Will you answer any important questions or make any decisions about policies, programs, or practice on the basis of the report's findings? If so, what are these questions?
- Are there any acceptable criteria that you have adopted to claim success or lack of it? For example, do you expect a minimum amount of increase in client scores from pretest to posttest or a minimally acceptable percentage of clients who are satisfied with services?
- Are there any ethical or political considerations that need to be carefully thought out before preparing the report? For example, are there controversial issues that need to be addressed cautiously and in a del-

icately balanced way? Is there any potential resistance to some of the findings that could come from particular groups?

- Should the findings of the study be made available to clients? If so, in what form?
- How can the clients benefit from the findings? What can be done to maximize client benefits?

FORMAT OF THE REPORT

Several communication formats are possible for sharing evaluation findings with stakeholders (Morris et al., 1987), including several written possibilities, such as a technical research report, an executive summary, a manuscript for a professional journal, a special report for clients, an agency brochure, a press release, or a one-page flyer or memo. Oral report options could include a curriculum for a staff workshop, a presentation before a public or community meeting, a poster session at a conference, personal discussions with some stakeholders, or a discussion that social workers can have with their clients in which they share some of the findings with them.

Technical Report

A technical report tends to be formal and lengthy. It is a comprehensive report that documents all of the steps in the evaluation process. It is the format that is most helpful for assessing whether the evaluation methods used reflect sound scientific principles, and it is the best format for demonstrating evidence-based research. A technical report uses a format similar to that of a formal research report. An outline of a typical technical report of a research study is likely to have all the following items:

- An abstract that summarizes the purpose of the study, the methods and sampling approach used, findings, and recommendations
- Background information on the research problem or topic, including a literature review, relevant viewpoints, and theories that help explain the topic
- The purposes of the study, including research questions and/or hypotheses
- A description of the sample characteristics and sampling approach used
- Description of the informed consent protocol
- Description of the data collection approach and specific measurement instruments
- A data analysis plan
- Findings, which can be an overall summary, highlights of the most important findings in tables and graphs, and results of data analysis

- Recommendations for how to use findings
- Limitations of the study (e.g., important questions that were not asked, poorly constructed questions, small sample size, an availability sampling approach, no baseline data collected, important uncontrolled extraneous variables)

Technical reports are usually most appropriate for summative evaluations. This type of report is often what funding agencies, program administrators, and others inclined to review the scientific aspects of an evaluation need. A technical report can also become a master copy of the evaluation process that can be reduced and modified to fit the needs of other smaller reports.

Executive Summary

An executive summary is short, often no more than one page. It usually contains a summary of a sentence or two for each section of a larger report. For example, an executive summary developed for a technical research report would summarize background information on the program concern, the purpose of the study, the research design, the findings, recommendations, limitations, and other implications. The summary is sometimes referred to as an abstract, particularly for journal submissions.

Executive summaries usually precede a technical report and help readers determine the contents of the technical report and whether it is worthwhile to read the full report or only sections. Executive summaries are useful for any stakeholders who may be interested in reading the technical report that it summarizes.

Journal Publication

Many times, an evaluation contributes something new in policy or practice that may be a breakthrough worthy of dissemination to a national or even international audience. Perhaps the program model that is evaluated is worth sharing with policy makers or other providers because it addresses a common or especially challenging problem area, or findings from the evaluation may be new evidence-based knowledge that a particular program model or practice theory has been effective in helping a particular client population. There are several excellent evaluation journals that publish manuscripts addressing these and other such policy and practice breakthroughs (see the list of journals in chapter 6).

Reports to Clients

Seldom do clients hear about the results of an evaluation relevant to them. Many times such reports can be shared, but they must fit the clients' particular needs and be presented in readily understandable language. A possibility is to share just one set of findings from an evaluation. For example, a university-conducted study on binge drinking to document the extent to which binge drinking was a problem among students found that more than 95 percent of student participants indicated that they did not binge drink. The university sponsor thought that this finding could encourage students to avoid binge drinking, so signs stating this finding were posted at various locations on campus. The finding was part of a larger effort by the university's dean of student services to overcome early signs that binge drinking was becoming a pattern among students.

Similarly, a finding on the success rate of clients completing a program could be publicized openly in an agency. For example, an evaluation might highlight the high rate of success of graduates of a program on key client outcome measures such as the following:

- Finding a job after participating in a job-training program
- Remaining in recovery after completing a residential program for substance abusers
- Lower divorce rate among graduates of a marital enrichment program than among non-graduates
- An increase in self-reported satisfaction of participants' parental role after attending a series of parent-training sessions

There are other creative ways to inform clients about findings. A simple flyer available at the front door of an agency or posted on a community bulletin board can highlight findings as well. These highlights should be prepared so that they are easily read and understood. Creativity is of utmost importance in preparing these reports, with graphics, photos, and personal testimonies among the resources to consider. It might be a good idea to attach a tear-off sheet to flyers for clients to give feedback or to make suggestions for follow-up actions.

Another way to share evaluation findings with clients is in the context of the worker-client relationship. In many instances, findings from an evaluation and the program or practice concerns that catalyzed the evaluation can be introduced into conversations with clients. Discrete findings that directly relate to what a client is working on can be quite helpful if timed well. Client satisfaction evaluations are a good illustration of this. The findings of a client satisfaction study can be introduced in a conversation between a social worker and client as follows:

Worker: We just completed our survey of client satisfaction. Do you remember filling it out?

Client: Yes, I did, but I am not expecting anything to come of it. These things are usually done to benefit the big people like the director of the agency.

Worker: Well, one finding revealed that a large percentage of the clients were not very satisfied with our group therapy program. They indicated that the topics that are covered and the discussions didn't really help clients solve the problems that they came here to solve in the first place.

Client: I could have told you that a long time ago. You didn't need a study to find that out. We [clients] often talk among ourselves about how we hate that group and wish we didn't have to attend it.

Worker: Do you want to know what we found were the reasons for dissatisfaction with the group therapy program? I have them here . . .

In these conversations, the findings should touch on issues of relevance to clients; in addition, an opportunity can be introduced for the client to react to the findings and to add his or her own interpretations and thoughts. Also, it is important to reassure clients that the agency is committed to doing something about client dissatisfaction because of the importance of their viewpoints. Some initial recommendations of the study could be mentioned in such conversations as well, with feedback sought from clients' perspectives. The feedback sessions should be documented and reported back to the evaluator and other stakeholders as a next step in resolving the identified problems.

Agency Public Relations Reports

The findings of a program evaluation can be a major news item for an agency when preparing its annual report or creating a brochure to inform other agencies and prospective clients about programs. Evaluations with positive findings are obvious materials for public relations promotions. A public child welfare program, for example, needed more positive press to highlight its success in finding adoptions for children. So it used some key findings from an evaluation to do so and included them in its annual report. The presentation, however, was similar to newspaper headlines rather than a technical report: "There has been an INCREASE in the number of foster children being adopted each year. From 895 in 1998/99 to 1,379 in 00/01," and "In 2002, the number of children in foster care has DROPPED for the FIRST TIME since 1990 to below 10,000 children."

Staff Workshops

Staff workshops and other types of staff gatherings are excellent venues for discussing most evaluation findings. Staff workshops are mentioned here because they usually focus on training, skills development, and information sharing. Staff members are key stakeholders who have direct contact with clients and firsthand exposure to their problems; they may also be the best-informed source on the functioning of programs and the conduct of practice.

Staff members are among the most important stakeholders of evaluations of programs and practice, whether they are recognized as stakeholders or not. When they are excluded from participating or from having a significant voice in an evaluation that affects them, it is quite possible that their exclusion will result in unnecessary complications, misunderstandings, and conflicts with agency administrators and the evaluators. Because staff cooperation is essential for most evaluations to occur optimally, evaluators will want these relationships to be cooperative and collaborative.

The findings of most evaluations are relevant for staff members to hear about and discuss. During the planning stage for a new program, the findings of a needs assessment can provide a range of information about prospective clients for the program. Staff members need this information for several reasons, such as to identify and recruit clients and assess their suitability for a program. During the implementation stage of a program, staff workshops could be used to discuss the findings of a staff morale study or a staff satisfaction study. It would also be useful for staff to become informed about findings on program accessibility, as they will need to implement many of the recommended strategies for reaching underserved groups.

Client satisfaction studies are directly relevant to staff and can provide helpful feedback on the interventions that need improvement. Program quality evaluations, as described in chapter 4, are designed to involve staff members as reviewers and peer evaluators. Evaluations that monitor their practice and involvement in programs are directly pertinent to them and can give them feedback on their interventions. Finally, outcome evaluations inform staff about whether their interventions effectively help clients. One evaluation that attempted to articulate a new model of practice illustrates how teams of social workers can become involved by responding to the findings of the evaluation (Gardner, 2000).

Presentations to the Public

In many instances, the findings of an evaluation should be communicated to the general public and to those who cannot be easily identified for invitation. The community surrounding agencies in particular may have a special stake in an evaluation's findings. Community residents could be invited to hear about an agency's plans. An agency that serves people with mental retardation by sponsoring group homes in the community, or a Head Start program located in a local church or settlement house are examples.

Sometimes public meetings are open to all and advertised as such; other times the meetings can be by invitation and a range of people may be invited to attend, such as civic leaders, volunteers, staff representatives of other agencies, local officials, and other active citizens. The format of the meeting can range from a formal presentation to an open discussion, but it is most important that the report of findings be prepared in a form that is pertinent and understandable to participants. These meetings could be opportune times to seek feedback from participants on recommendations before they are actually implemented.

Testifying at public hearings is another outlet for sharing evaluation findings. Sometimes the findings of an evaluation can document, in the public spotlight, the progress or lack of it for clients. For example, evaluation findings may support offenders in the criminal justice system that are on probation or parole and need verification of their progress or achievements. Data can be provided on the progress of individual clients as court testimony for their early release for good behavior. Evaluation findings can also be valuable for class action suits on behalf of groups of clients who need documentation that they are improving in their behavior from designated program interventions. An example of this kind of documentation is provided in a longitudinal evaluation by Dudley, Calhoun, and Ahlgrim-Delzell (2002).

Evaluation findings can also be publicized through a newspaper column or series, a radio talk show, or a television program. Stories of individual clients are the most effective way to portray to the public the plight of particular types of people and the possibilities of their overcoming such obstacles. A qualitative evaluation is typically a descriptive account of the lives of a group of clients and makes an excellent source for such a story. Such evaluations can illustrate how a group of clients learned to cope with their problems or were helped by a program to become more independent and satisfied with their lives. Informed consent procedures can be used to protect the identity of clients who are exposed in these stories by using fictitious names, making minor changes in their personal circumstances to prevent identification, and restricting access to narrative evaluation material.

Informal Exchanges of Information with Stakeholders

Another format for sharing findings with stakeholders is to arrange informal exchanges with particular stakeholders. In some instances, it may be important to provide handouts of findings as part of an informal oral report for special stakeholders such as board officers and advisory committees. These materials can be flexibly presented so that recipients can fully air their views and ideas for follow-up. Participants can also be consulted about the best venue for holding larger meetings of boards, advisory committees, and the community at large, as they may know best what aspects of the findings to share and how to do so most effectively.

STRATEGIES FOR PREPARING A REPORT

As was emphasized earlier in the chapter, reports can take many forms. They can be long or short, oral or written, and they can use many formats. Preparing the report may take considerable or little time, depending on its nature. Either way, however, it needs to be thoughtfully planned and executed. Four likely tasks to consider are highlighted next: clarifying the purpose of the report and its targeted audience, presenting helpful background information, organizing and presenting the findings, and making recommendations.

Clarifying the Purpose of the Report

The overall purpose of a report is to describe the findings and to offer recommendations to address the concerns about a program or practice area. However, as indicated earlier, a report can vary widely depending on who the stakeholders are. Before preparing the report, it is important to hold discussions with stakeholders to identify their needs. The specifics of the report can be determined from such discussions. Several specifics to consider are the findings to highlight and why. In addition, what recommendations are most important?

Equally important to selecting the specifics for the report are the strategies for disseminating them. An important question to ask about dissemination is, how can the report be presented to address the interest of the stakeholders and involve them in contributing to the implementation of the recommendations and any plans for follow-up?

Background Information

Most reports will need to include some background information on the evaluation before the findings. A technical report may do so in a lengthy and thorough way, whereas brief reports to other stakeholders may only mention helpful details in a few sentences, followed by questions. Most stakeholders will want to be reminded about the purpose of the evaluation, the evaluation questions, the types of people studied, and the methods. They may also want to be reminded of the concerns that led to initiation of the evaluation and the options currently available to address what to do about the program now.

Organizing and Presenting the Findings

Next, the findings of the evaluation need to be organized and presented so that they are readable, relevant, and useful. Organizing the findings is a very important task, which entails focusing the findings, ensuring their accuracy and clarity, and using visual aids when appropriate. Focusing the findings depends on the needs of stakeholders and on the initial evaluation questions. The evaluation questions can provide a focus and an organizing framework for the report, as the findings are supposed to answer the questions.

Example of Preparation of a Report for a Qualitative Study

A study (Leary, 2003) was conducted of several volunteers of an ecumenical program that offers overnight shelter to small groups of homeless people once every week during the winter months. Initially, the researcher identified three research questions to focus the study: (1) What are the needs of the homeless guests? (2) What efforts have the churches made to try to meet these needs? And (3) what efforts might churches try in the future? Although the evaluator explored all three questions in focus groups, participants gave much more attention to the third question, as the sponsoring organization and participants perceived it as the central set of findings. Therefore, it was decided that the major focus of the report would be on the third question.

It is also important to present findings accurately. Some of the questions to ask related to accuracy could be the following: Are the correct statistical tests used to analyze the data? Is there a balance of positive and negative findings when both exist? Are tables and graphs prepared accurately and are they easy to understand? Do the tables and graphs focus on the most important findings?

A report that includes only uninterrupted written or oral material can be boring and tedious. Therefore, in preparing a report, consider using tables, graphs, and other visual aids to creatively highlight and summarize important findings. The Statistical Package for the Social Sciences (SPSS), Microsoft Excel, and other computer programs can be used to prepare graphics. Tables are useful for consolidating several data points into a single visual presentation to highlight an important finding. For example, a table can highlight the characteristics of research participants, compare the outcomes of a treatment and comparison group, or compare the pretest and posttest measures of a one-group pretest-posttest design. Table 11.1 presents a summary of two subgroups of female teenage participants, those who were maltreated in childhood and those who were not, to highlight their differences. Note that the table reveals that the two subgroups were significantly different on the basis of family structure, race and ethnicity, and welfare status. Pie and bar charts are other ways to highlight findings. Bar charts can compare two or more groups of people on a particular measure. Pie charts are useful when a circular display communicates more effectively than a linear bar chart.

TABLE 11.1   Prevalence of Maltreatment in Female Teenagers, by Demographic
Characteristics

	Whether maltreated (%)		
Characteristics	*Yes*	*No*	*n*
Total sample	14	86	249
Welfare recipient*			
Yes	19	81	134
No	6	94	96
Parent education			
Not high school graduate	13	87	137
High school graduate	14	86	111
Family structure*			
Other	17	83	180
Both biological parents present	4	96	64
Race and ethnicity*			
White	33	67	16
Hispanic	5	95	33
African American	13	87	200

Source: Smith, 1996.
*$p < .05$, one-tailed.

Qualitative findings can be presented in several different ways, as case
studies to illustrate insightful issues or remarks about a pertinent topic, or
organized into general categories or themes.

Making Recommendations

Next, the findings are to be interpreted; interpretations in evaluation
studies often take the form of practical recommendations. The recommendations are an important section of a report which needs to be developed
carefully. Morris et al. (1987) suggest that recommendations are the most
important part of the report because stakeholders tend to turn to this section for guidance. Several guidelines can be helpful when preparing recommendations for a research report:

- Attempt to draw some general conclusions from the findings. What
  do they seem to say?
- List specific recommendations in such a way that they are relevant
  and useful to stakeholders.

Recommendations must be supported by the findings. Recommendations should not be a wish list or an excuse to promote a particular viewpoint unsupported by findings. A helpful exercise is to identify each recommendation in a report and then identify the specific findings of the
evaluation, if any, that support each recommendation. When there are no
findings to support a recommendation, it should be omitted.

Recommendations are usually stated tentatively, especially in formative studies, to permit the stakeholders to offer their own thoughts.

Recommendations should be practical and address such questions as whether the program should be continued, modified, expanded, or take another course. Good recommendations are stated in a way that is helpful to the agency and to clients. Sometimes, the more recommendations that are offered, the more helpful they are. For example, the evaluator may find out in an evaluation on staff morale that staff morale is low for several reasons, not one, and they are all supported by findings. Examples of recommendations from a staff morale study could include raising salaries, improving supervision, and/or reducing caseloads or workloads.

The discussion of a study's recommendations should also mention any limitations that need to be considered in implementing them. For example, an evaluation about the school adjustment of children born and raised in the United States may not have direct applicability for children who are recent immigrants. Examples of types of limitations that should be reported are a small sample, questions that were poorly formulated or not asked, a convenience sample or other non-probability sampling approach, a low response rate for a questionnaire, no baseline data collected, and uncontrolled important external variables.

STRATEGIES FOR DISSEMINATING REPORTS

A proactive strategy is needed to inform the stakeholders about the results of an evaluation. The information that stakeholders receive should be clear, thorough, and relevant to their needs. Because stakeholders have diverse needs, the information they receive should take into consideration such things as what to emphasize, how much material to report, and useful recommendations. Numerous strategies are available that reflect various ways to communicate findings. Oral options include presentations, informal discussions, conversations between practitioners and clients, staff workshops, and poster sessions in the community. Providing helpful written materials is equally important and can take the form of technical reports, summaries and sections of technical reports, published results in professional journals, memos and flyers, brochures and other educational materials, and more.

A report's preparation and dissemination are usually planned together. A dissemination strategy often naturally evolves from the format of a report. For example, a technical report is usually disseminated in written form and could be explained in a presentation. In contrast, findings of interest to clients are likely to be focused and shared informally through discussions and question-and-answer formats. Identification of a strategy begins with discussions with stakeholders about what they need and find useful. From there, an oral or written report is planned, as well as a strategy to share the report in meaningful ways with stakeholders.

Table 11.2 summarizes many options available for the range of stakeholders. Some types of stakeholders, such as funding agencies and agency board members, are likely to want to receive lengthy technical reports and summaries. These reports can be disseminated through informal discussions

TABLE 11.2   Options for Preparing and Disseminating Reports

Stakeholders	Primary formats for report	Possible dissemination strategies
Funding agencies	Technical report	Presentation at a meeting Giving out report
Board members	Technical report Executive summary	Presentation at a meeting Giving out report
Advisory committee members	Technical report Executive summary	Informal discussions Presentation at a meeting Giving out report
Administrators of program	Technical report	Informal discussions Giving out report
Legislators	Brief memo or executive summary	Mailing or e-mailing memo to all relevant legislators and providing access to more information
Current or prospective clients	One-page flyer Agency brochure	Informal discussions Conversation within worker/client relationships Giving helpful written material Radio announcements
Staff members and volunteers	Special reports	Staff workshop Presentation at other staff gatherings
Community groups	Special report One-page flyer Using helpful visual aids	Informal discussions Presentations at a community meeting
Public at large	Special report Press release One-page flyer or memo Using helpful visual aids	Presentation at a community meeting Personal discussions
Professional community	Manuscript for a journal Press release	Presentations at professional or community meetings Poster sessions at conferences Informal networking

and more formal presentations with question-and-answer formats. Other types of stakeholders (e.g., neighbors, representatives of other civic organizations and agencies, the public) may prefer special reports or brief summaries that can be presented and discussed in a more informal and spontaneous manner.

Why Invest in Dissemination?

There are several reasons to devote time, money, and energy to disseminating evaluation findings. The most practical reason is to involve stakeholders in any follow-up action for addressing a program or practice concern. Usually, evaluation reports include a list of recommendations to be considered, such as whether a program should be continued, expanded, changed, or discontinued after an evaluation is completed. One could easily reason that the more that stakeholders are involved in the decision-making process, the better the decisions will be because they will be based on a wide range of relevant perspectives.

In addition, many stakeholders will expect to hear about the results of an evaluation, especially if they participated in the earlier planning and execution steps. Leaving some stakeholders out of the final step could lead them to feel that they are not important participants. Staff members, clients, and community groups are among the stakeholders most often left out of this final step, with negative consequences not only for them but for the intervention as well. Staff members and clients in particular should become more active participants in the decision-making process, especially in an advisory capacity, and involving them and their feedback can enhance the functioning of interventions.

Another reason to give special attention to disseminating findings is that agencies usually want stakeholders to be ongoing participants in programs and practice areas, and many stakeholders want this as well. Viewing the findings can provide them with new information and insights about an intervention and the provider agency. It can help them become more informed in their roles as stakeholders, and they can discover the important role that evaluations play in enhancing programs and practice.

Ultimately, evaluation is an accountability measure. It addresses important questions such as the following:

- Is the program or practice intervention focusing on the target population with the greatest need?
- Is the intervention meeting the specified short- and long-term needs of the target population?
- Is the intervention being implemented with high standards?
- Are clients satisfied with the program?

- Is the intervention achieving its goals and objectives?
- Is it cost-effective?

These are questions that should not be left solely to evaluators and program administrators. Involving an active team of stakeholders, as advocated throughout the book, can optimize the likelihood that accountability will be real and substantive.

KEY TERMS

Agency public relations reports
Disseminating a report
Executive summary
Findings
Informal exchanges
Journal manuscript
Presentations to the public
Recommendations
Reports to clients
Staff workshops
Strategies for disseminating a report
Strategies for preparing a report
Technical evaluation report

DISCUSSION QUESTIONS AND ASSIGNMENTS

1. Select an evaluation report from a social work or evaluation journal. Critique the findings section by answering the following questions:

   - What are the major findings?
   - Were the findings presented clearly? If not, what was unclear? How could they be presented more clearly?
   - Were the tables easy to understand? If not, why not?
   - How are the findings useful to you as a practitioner?
   - Are the limitations of the study discussed? What are the limitations?

2. Using the same evaluation report used in question 1, determine how well the recommendations are supported by the findings by answering the following questions:

   - Identify each recommendation.
   - Identify the specific findings, if any, that support each recommendation.

- In your opinion, is each recommendation adequately supported by a specific finding. If not, why not?
- What recommendations were useful to you as a social worker?

REFERENCES

Dudley, J., Calhoun, M., & Ahlgrim-Delzell, L. (Eds.). (2002). *Lessons learned from a lawsuit: Creating services for people with mental illness and mental retardation.* Kingston, NY: National Association for the Dually Diagnosed Press.

Gardner, F. (2000). Design evaluation: Illuminating social work practice for better outcomes. *Social Work, 45*(2), 176–182.

Leary, A. (2003). Room in the inn: Exploring church involvement in serving the homeless. Unpublished student research project, University of North Carolina at Charlotte.

Morris, L. L., Fitz-Gibbon, C. T., & Freeman, M. (1987). *How to communicate evaluation findings.* Newbury Park, CA: Sage.

Part VII

Consuming Evaluation Reports

Chapter 12

Becoming Critical Consumers of Evaluations

Daniel Freedman and James R. Dudley

Increasingly sparse resources and finite amounts of reimbursable services are characteristics that seem to exemplify social work practices in the twenty-first century. As a result, social work practitioners must have the keen ability to implement effective interventions in a timely and efficient manner. As such, the ability to identify evidence-based practices from existing reported research is essential for the profession (Howard, McMillen, & Pollio, 2003). In consonance with this assumption, the accrediting body of social work education, the Council on Social Work Education (CSWE), requires curriculum content on research and evaluation methods. Similarly, the Code of Ethics promulgated by the National Association of Social Workers has an entire section on Evaluation and Research Standards (Bolin, Lee, Glenmaye, & Yoon, 2012; Staudt, 2007). One of the specific standards of the Code of Ethics directly supports critical consumption of research. It refers to social workers' obligation to "critically examine and keep current with emerging knowledge relevant to social work and fully use evaluation and research evidence in their professional practice" (National Association of Social Workers, 2008). Thus, the focus of this chapter is to highlight and illustrate how to be a critical consumer of evaluation reports. The sections that follow describe some of the key stakeholders that consume evaluation reports, followed by an examination of a recent evaluation report, and some thoughts on how to help stakeholders utilize information in evaluation reports. The Seven Evaluation Steps, introduced in chapter 1, are used to help organize this chapter.

Seven Evaluation Steps

Step 1: Identify the Problem or Concern to Be Evaluated
Step 2: Identify and Explore Ways to Involve Stakeholders
Step 3: Determine the Purpose of the Evaluation
Step 4: Plan the Evaluation
Step 5: Implement the Evaluation
Step 6: Prepare a Written or Oral Report
Step 7: Disseminate the Findings

STAKEHOLDERS WHO CONSUME EVALUATION REPORTS

Stakeholders who are interested in evaluation reports will have varying needs and capacities to consume these reports. Stakeholders of evaluations who have been discussed in previous chapters include a long list—students, administrators and practitioners working in agencies, board members, regulatory and funding agency personnel, clients, advisory groups, community groups, and others. This chapter briefly discusses the special needs of five of these groups—students, practitioners, administrators, reimbursement and regulatory entities, and clients of social services.

Social Work Students

As mentioned above, the Council on Social Work Education mandates that students of social work become critical consumers of research. Since 1981, the CSWE has required research methods courses for master's-level curriculum, and later this became a requirement at the baccalaureate level (Wodarski, Feit, & Green, 1995). Unfortunately, many students are sometimes fearful and weary of research methods. Plausible explanations for this discomfort are that most students have low levels of interest in research, some have problems developing research competencies, and sometimes they are unaware of the critical relevance of research to social work practice. Interestingly, studies reveal that experiential strategies of teaching have heightened students' interest and competencies in these courses (Harder, 2010; Lundahl, 2008). These strategies usually include students being actively involved in the design, implementation, and evaluation of a research project. Lundahl (2008) found that this type of involvement was not only meaningful, but also promoted a more thorough understanding of research.

On an academic level, developing a skill set for critically consuming evaluation reports is crucial. Accordingly, CSWE's most recent policy standards continue to support the "prominence" of research within social work education (Bolin et al., 2012). On the level of professional development, this skill set remains important as social work interns must be able to provide effective interventions to their client systems.

Practitioners

Having research skills may be equally, or perhaps even more important for practitioners. Professionals in social agencies are encouraged and sometimes expected to have an understanding of evaluation methods and to be advocates for the implementation of evidence-based practices (Gibbs, 2007). Many practitioners are using evaluations to inform their professional interventions, and to improve their ability to provide evidence-based practice to their client systems. Imagine the ill consequences that can emerge if they do not have these critical consumer skills. That is, consequences as significant as fatalities can materialize if evaluations are misinterpreted and ineffective practices are implemented with populations diagnosed with substance use, borderline personality, eating disorders, and other conditions.

In an ideal practice milieu, practitioners will apply the most effective interventions for empowering their client populations. Of course, this ideal is often not the reality due to multiple circumstances including lack of resources, training, and administrative support. Nonetheless, the professional development of social work practitioners includes identifying, critiquing, and accumulating knowledge of evidence-based practices, and the critical consumption of evaluation reports can be at the core of this endeavor. Practitioners with an advanced skill set in critically evaluating research may also be able to examine the strengths and weaknesses of psychometric instruments and data analysis strategies used to measure client outcomes.

Administrators

Administrators are a heterogeneous group that can consist of program and agency directors, quality assurance and human resource specialists, and members of leadership teams and boards of directors. As a group of stakeholders, administrators are a crucial cog in the process of making agency-level decisions, including the implementation of evidence-informed practice (Collins-Camargo & Millar, 2010). In an ideal organizational climate, the decision of which programs and practices to implement is based, in part, on determining best practices from the critical consumption of evaluation reports (Long, Tice, & Morrison, 2006). For administrators, this judgment is important; however, the reality of social service organizations is that administrators must also take into consideration the implications of budgets, personnel issues, agency mission and philosophy, and multiple political factors. In addition, Long and colleagues argue for the inclusion of clients and client systems in making organizational decisions. In other words, client inclusion can result in an empowerment-oriented infrastructure that can best meet the needs of its constituents. In theory, this inclusion of client input along with the critical consumption of evaluations can be used by administrators to make decisions based on a best practices inquiry (Petr & Walter, 2005).

Reimbursement and Regulatory Entities

Without a funding stream, the implementation of evidence-based programs and practices is a nonexistent consideration. Likewise, without having an accredited status, neither funding nor implementation issues have much bearing, as human service agencies will cease to exist. These salient issues arise through the functioning of reimbursement and regulatory entities. Examples of these systems include third-party payers such as Medicaid and Medicare, and accreditation organizations such as the Commission on

Accreditation of Rehabilitation Facilities (CARF) and the Joint Commission on Accreditation of Healthcare Organizations (JCAHO). Third-party payment systems will be interested in evaluation research inasmuch as it provides evidence of effectiveness that affects the reimbursement of programs and practices. What these entities have in common is that they are concerned about budgets or maintaining a profit margin. As such, evaluations that demonstrate short-term and less expensive interventions have a better chance of being reimbursed than services that are long-term and pricey.

In addition to these considerations, organizations such as JCAHO and CARF place more emphasis on whether agencies are maintaining practice standards that benefit clients and client systems. For instance, JCAHO is concerned about whether standards of health care assessment and treatment are being met, and whether clinical ethics and client rights are adequate. CARF focuses on similar components within health care settings with an emphasis on rehabilitation programs in mental health, substance abuse, retirement living, and multiple services offered in the community (Wilkerson, Migas, & Slaven, 2000). To the extent that evaluations address accreditation standards, regulatory entities will have vested stakes in consuming evaluation reports.

Clients

Clients are a heterogeneous population representing a diversity of races, social classes, ethnicities, educational levels, and income levels, as well as a wide range of psychosocial characteristics and intellect capabilities. Many are disenfranchised, vulnerable, and desperate for help. Some may be struggling with maintaining housing, others may be involved in situations of intimate partner violence, and still others may struggle with child care or parenting issues. The common denominator of most clients is that they are seeking assistance with navigating their social environment or relieving personal hardships and distress; they need interventions that will work for them in a most effective way!

Yet, it may seem unrealistic to expect that most clients of social services will be motivated to understand evaluation terminology and methodologies, let alone know how to locate relevant evaluation reports. Instead, it may seem more than enough to expect them to partake as fully as possible as recipients of services. Further, there may be the assumption of clients that professional providers will identify and implement empirically supported practices (Mildon & Shlonsky, 2011). Nevertheless, it seems plausible that clients of social services will have the most at stake in evaluation reports being critically consumed and used; as recipients of the interventions, they will want to know that they are effective. For fortunate clients, they may have support and assistance from family and friends, or special interest groups such as the National Alliance on Mental Illness, the ARC for People with Intellectual and Developmental Disabilities, and Parents, Families, & Friends of Lesbians and Gays. Generally, advocacy and client advisory groups, mentors, and coaches can be essential to assist them in assessing the effectiveness of the interventions they receive. Yet, in reality many clients will not have good working connections with such support groups or others having technical expertise. Overall, it is fair to state that recipients of social services have a tremendous stake in the evaluations of their interventions, and that much more advocacy is needed for bridging the gap among scholarship, practice, and client participation.

CRITICAL CONSUMPTION OF AN EVALUATION REPORT

As earlier chapters have pointed out, there are multiple types of evaluations of interest to social workers including needs assessments, program monitoring, client satisfaction studies, outcome studies, efficiency and cost-benefit analysis, program licensing, auditing, accreditation, and quality assurance. All of these evaluations have many characteristics in common, with the use of research methods being one of them. Research methodologies used in evaluations can vary widely, for instance, ranging from being exploratory as in an ethnographic case study to experimental designs. Evaluations also use a wide range of measures, both quantitative and qualitative, for determining the effectiveness of practitioners' interventions and programs alike.

The evaluation report selected as an example in this chapter is only one type of evaluation, but it reflects many of the characteristics of some of the more common reports that need to be consumed. The report, "Evaluation of a Spiritually Focused Intervention with Older Trauma Survivors," focused on evaluating the effectiveness of a spiritually oriented group intervention intended to lessen the physical and mental health symptoms of a group of older female trauma survivors (Bowland, Edmond, & Fallot, 2012). The research design that was used was an experimental design that tested the effectiveness of an eleven-session spiritual intervention based on similar interventions used in the past. In some ways, this evaluation is a template for testing evidence-based practice because it uses an experimental design. This evaluation report will hereafter be referred to as "the Bowland Report" in this chapter

The Bowland Report has several strengths. The methodology is a rigorously developed experimental design having strong implications for determining causal relationships. In addition, there are comprehensive details in many areas such as in its description of the intervention used and previous interventions that the intervention is based on. Further, it gives helpful details about the four client outcome measures that were used and the recruitment process involved in locating a sample of older women experiencing abuse and trauma in the past. Such details can be helpful to others who wish to replicate the evaluation in other settings. Yet, the report could be better organized and more concise and succinct in a few areas. Sometimes, material is not located in the sections where one would expect it to be. For example, the hypotheses that were tested were not located just before the method section. Thus some critical consumers may have difficulty finding them. Overall, this report is probably typical of most evaluation reports and reflects the kinds of strengths and limitations that are found in reports generally. In this chapter we will assume a critical consumer role and critique the Bowland Report. The Seven Evaluation Steps described in the book provide a framework for this critique. Some key comments will be made in introducing each step before delving into how Bowland and colleagues reported on them. Emphasis in this critique will be placed primarily on the concepts covered in earlier chapters of the book that can help the reader become a more critical consumer of evaluation reports. In other words, an exhaustive critique that covers all of the issues involved in each step is well beyond the purpose of this chapter.

A critical consumer can ask a number of good questions. For example, how well does the author(s) define the problem, goals, interventions, outcome measures, and other concepts? Does the author provide enough details about them and is the information succinct and fully relevant? Is the literature reviewed in the report helpful in elaborating on how others have viewed the problem? Does it appear that all of the appropriate groups of clients who could be recipients of the intervention are actually included? The reader is encouraged to attempt to answer these questions largely on his own and in small groups as these questions will only be addressed in general terms in the critique in this chapter. The reader is strongly suggested to obtain a copy of the evaluation report and read it before continuing in order to get the most benefit out of the chapter. A link to the abstract of the report is http://sw.oxfordjournals.org/content/57/1/73.short.

Step 1: Identify the Problem or Concern to Be Evaluated

Critiquing step 1 is a good time for a critical consumer to learn something about a problem or concern that is being addressed by an evaluator. A well-written report offers a problem definition that includes a literature review, an introduction of some theoretical concepts, and a perspective on how to solve this problem. Several sections in earlier chapters of the book address some of the issues related to defining the problem and finding solutions to solve it. Needs assessments are a major focus of chapter 6 and can be useful in defining the problem being addressed. In this regard, a good question to ask is whether a needs assessment was used to formulate the problem definition.

The concepts of problem, specific needs, and the causes of the problems are also discussed in chapter 6. The concept of specific needs is an

important concept because it refers to an aspect of the larger problem identified by the client and selected because it is perceived to be reasonable to
meet. These three elements (problem, specific needs, and causes) are all
linked together. In addition, the goals and objectives for addressing the
problem naturally follow next based on the logic model. The logic model is
a helpful framework to use in assessing how well an author has defined the
problem. For example, this model helps the critical consumer determine
how much of the larger problem faced by the clients in the study is reduced
to "specific needs" identified by them and viewed as something that can be
met. Also, it's important to figure out how much the authors of a report have
seriously considered the logic model.

Looking at the Bowland Report related to step 1, the literature review
about the problem itself tends to be brief, representing most of the first
page of the report. The problem is described as the long-term health and
physical problems of older women (45 years and older) resulting from
repeated and mostly earlier experiences of being sexually and physically
abused. Several references to specific literature provide documentation of
the problem and why older women have greater problems in these areas
than younger women or men; this is given as the reason why these women
were chosen for the study. This cited literature was largely published in the
1990s and early 2000s, raising a question of how up-to-date it is; for example, is more recent important literature available? The concepts of problems
and specific needs were not differentiated in this section and the causes of
the problems were briefly touched on. Child sexual and physical abuse, and
domestic violence, often continuing in these abusive relationships, were
among the causes identified. Overall, this section of the study could have
given more detailed attention to what the problem is, and a needs assessment could have been a helpful way of doing this.

Additionally in the introduction, other concepts are reported related to
addressing the problem of past abuse and trauma. The concept of spirituality, in particular, is defined and described as the key concept for overcoming current difficulties that these women were experiencing. Spirituality is
defined broadly and is viewed as including both strengths and possible
struggles of the past to address. Later in the article these spiritual strengths
and struggles are described in greater detail in the form of topics that were
covered in the eleven sessions of the intervention.

Step 2: Identify and Explore Ways to Involve Stakeholders

Critiquing step 2 is important to consider because it reminds the critical consumer that a political process actually occurred while an evaluation
was taking form and being implemented. Yet, unfortunately this "messy"
process is largely absent from evaluation reports. Because a report of an
evaluation does not usually describe who the stakeholders are, how they

may agree or disagree with each other, and how these differences are handled by the evaluator, we miss an important underlying process that needs to be re-created in our minds. Stakeholders of the evaluation process have been discussed in several previous chapters of the book. The emphasis on involving stakeholders distinguishes an evaluation report from other research studies that depend much less on them. Evaluators encourage the stakeholders to be involved in informing the purpose of an evaluation, improving its design, and disseminating it to others. This input can include recruiting clients as evaluation participants, contributing to the formulation of useful research questions, and identifying relevant outcomes. Moving to a broader context, an evaluation does not happen in a vacuum; instead it operates within the context of an ever-changing social environment, which includes stakeholder systems. Critical consumers of evaluation reports should be aware of how stakeholders' involvement may strengthen or possibly weaken the evaluation's efforts. Because the involvement of stakeholders is not often explicitly described in evaluation reports, critical consumers need to read between the lines and possibly speculate about whom the stakeholders were and how much each was involved and influenced the evaluation process.

The Bowland Report seems to follow this familiar pattern of not describing its stakeholder involvement. A senior newspaper and university hospital were the only organizations mentioned and they appeared to only play a role in advertising for research participants. The university sponsoring the evaluation approved of the ethical plan of the evaluation so it could also be considered a stakeholder. The Bowland Report addressed the needs of older women experiencing costly physical and mental health trauma. As such, the research team may have involved several types of stakeholders in the development of the evaluation, including mental health providers, spiritual leaders, and other groups specifically interested in the well-being of older adults. Clients of social services and survivors of traumas and abuse may also have been involved. The input of these groups, if consulted, would have significantly informed the evaluators about the needs of survivors of complex traumas, the interventions they required, outcome measures of importance, and other research components. Unfortunately, we do not know what the roles of stakeholders were and this could be considered a weakness of the report.

Step 3: Determine the Purpose of the Evaluation

Step 3 is possibly the most important step for the critical consumer to understand—what was the purpose of the evaluation? After reviewing the abstract of a report, a critical consumer would be wise to look for the overall purpose statement! The purpose of an evaluation is the pivotal section of a report that is most important to understand early on. If a critical consumer does not understand the evaluation's general purpose, the rest of the report becomes much more difficult to comprehend. The purpose of an evaluation can be either in the form of general questions to explore or hypotheses to test or both. When general questions are used, an evaluation tends to be more exploratory and tentative about what it finds, while the use of hypotheses suggests an explanatory study providing more definitive answers. The purpose statement is typically located just prior to the method section of a report; the method section then elaborates on how the purpose is to be implemented. A report needs to have clear and conceptually sound questions or hypotheses. These questions/hypotheses signal whether the evaluation will be relevant to a critical consumer's practice area and other interests.

The Bowland Report has four hypotheses that it tests. The hypotheses are somewhat ambiguously lumped together and could be misunderstood as one hypothesis. They are described as "a group intervention supporting the discussion of spiritual struggles and strengths and the development of new spiritual resources would reduce trauma-related posttraumatic stress, depression, anxiety, and somatic symptoms for older survivors of interpersonal trauma who indicated interest in such a group" (p. 74). It would be clearer to identify each hypothesis separately with the intervention being the independent variable and the client outcome being the dependent variable for each hypothesis. So, for example, the first hypothesis would be that the spiritual intervention will reduce the trauma-related post-traumatic stress of these women; the second hypothesis would be that the spiritual intervention will reduce their depression; and so on. The authors located the hypotheses well before the method section, which may confuse less experienced critical consumers in trying to find them.

The authors also discuss the concept of spirituality, citing several references. Perhaps they could have considered adding one or more client outcome variables measuring strengths and resiliencies as well as reducing mental symptoms. For example, they could have measured well-being, self-efficacy, happiness, and other concepts that approximate personal assets.

Step 4: Plan the Evaluation

Step 4 is a very technical step for a critical consumer to comprehend and absorb, and having some background in research methodologies would certainly help. A critical consumer's task in critiquing an evaluation plan or research design is quite challenging because it requires considerable technical knowledge about research methodologies. There are several aspects of a research design to critique including the intervention, client outcome measures, the group design used, sampling issues and characteristics of the sample, the data analysis plan, ethical concerns, and other issues. Chapters 6, 8, and 9 of the book describe different types of evaluations respectively, during the planning stage, implementation stage, and outcome stage. The Bowland Report that is the focus of this chapter uses an outcome evaluation. As chapter 9 indicates, the intervention and the client outcomes that are affected by it are the primary focus. An outcome evaluation is attempting to determine whether there is a causal relationship between an intervention and these outcomes—does the introduction of the intervention improve the client outcome measures? Several group designs are described in chapter 9 varying from a one-group posttest-only design to a pretest/posttest design with a control group. The latter design is the most effective one for determining whether the intervention has a causal effect. This design also creates ethical problems for those who are denied the intervention because some are selected randomly to a control group, not the treatment group. The sampling approach of this design is also important to examine to determine any biases in assigning clients to treatment and control groups. Measures of the outcome variables are also very important to examine in terms of evidence that they have validity and reliability. A further issue is whether the intervention is described in sufficient detail for replication by a reader.

Overall, Bowland and her colleagues did an excellent job describing the evaluation plan. The report reveals that they used an experimental design with a control group. Three points in time were designated for measuring the outcome variables—a pretest, eleven weeks later at the completion of the intervention as a posttest, and three months beyond the time they completed the intervention. Several things are important to include in describing such a design and the authors covered this material quite well. The intervention was described extensively. The definition of spirituality, a difficult one to obtain broad consensus on, was described with considerable detail. Spiritual strengths were highlighted as one of the areas of spirituality to be emphasized in the intervention, and some details were shared in the eleven-session curriculum about how spiritual strengths could help. The other major aspect of spirituality that was emphasized in the intervention was the difficulties that these older women may have had growing up with backgrounds involving patriarchal Christianity and the burdens it may have imposed.

The connection between the problems of these women and the proposed intervention is a most important question to ask. As was stated in chapter 8, what are the mechanisms for change inherent in the intervention that can help these women counteract their existing symptoms and their underlying problems? This is another way of asking whether the intervention can have a causal effect on the client outcomes of these women. According to the authors, their spiritual intervention was based on a previous spiritual model that had some evidence of reducing trauma-related mental health symptoms.

Client outcomes were also described clearly, including the four major ones: post-traumatic stress, depression, anxiety, and somatic symptoms. The measurement instruments for these outcomes were described in some detail and a table on "outcome and screening measures" was used to help the critical consumer visualize all of this material in one place. Many of the psychometric properties of these measures were reported while some measures may have lacked validity or reliability testing.

The authors described their extensive efforts to recruit older women with trauma and abuse in their background. As was mentioned earlier in the chapter, it would not be easy to find such research participants if they were not already known to an agency. Some recruitment and screening strategies were described that could be very helpful to know if one were planning to replicate this study. Steps were taken to create a pool of women who met the criteria of the evaluators. They were selected through convenience and purposive sampling, which limits the authors' ability to generalize the findings to others with similar characteristics with confidence.

The authors appropriately noted that the study was approved by the Human Research Protection Office of the sponsoring university. The ethics of using control groups and assigning some of the women to a control group on a random basis was partially addressed by offering participants assigned to control groups the opportunity to join the treatment group at a later time. However, the ethics of using control groups were not explicitly mentioned in terms of initially assigning some participants to control groups when they may have had an immediate need to benefit from the intervention. Also, only some of those in control groups later agreed to join a treatment group, leaving open the possibility that the experience of being in a control group may have discouraged them from seeking the treatment at a later time.

A very unusual and special strength of this design was a follow-up posttest three months after the intervention was completed. This second posttest measure gives the reader some evidence of whether or not the gains at the completion of treatment were still evident three months later. Unfortunately, follow-up measures several months after an intervention are seldom included in most evaluations.

A data analysis plan was described in the Bowland Report and seemed appropriate for a group design. It may be enough for a new critical consumer to merely be able to identify these tests and understand in general how they were used. While many of the statistical tests and analyses were complex and may be confusing to some critical consumers, the authors made a notable effort to explain them. Among the specific tests that were used were descriptive statistics (mean scores and standard deviations for each variable). The inferential statistics used to test the hypotheses were chi-square, ANOVA, MANOVA, and t-tests. The t-test was used to determine whether there was statistical significance in the changes in the client outcomes from pretest to posttest, while ANOVA and MANOVA were used to determine whether the changes were maintained at a three-month follow-up.

Step 5: Implement the Evaluation

Step 5, like step 2, is difficult for critical consumers to critique because most evaluation reports provide little if any information about implementation processes, at least in a technical report like the Bowland Report. Some of the questions about the implementation process raised in chapter 8 are important for critical consumers to consider here. Is the intervention actually being implemented as it was proposed? Also, is the quality of the intervention high enough to satisfy the stakeholders? These two questions can possibly begin to be answered by finding out if the implementation process was monitored. If it was not monitored, it would be highly unlikely that these questions could be answered. Some further questions could also be asked in attempting to find out whether a program is actually implemented as proposed. Are the program's goals and objectives evident or identifiable in the description of the way in which the intervention is implemented? Are the clients being served the ones who were intended to be served, and are existing staff members adequately qualified and trained to provide the proposed services?

Bowland and her colleagues reported on some of these implementation questions, which is a notable strength of their report. At least three instances of this are evident; (1) they report that they monitored how well the group leaders implemented the spirituality treatment model in their groups as it was designed, (2) whether the clients that were actually selected met the initial criteria, and (3) whether the data collectors were trained to do what was expected in measuring the client outcomes. First, to assess "leader fidelity" or the group leaders' ability to implement the spirituality treatment model as planned, an independent evaluator rated videotaped sessions randomly selected from each of the treatment and control groups (Bowland et al., p. 76, 2012). The mean adherence score for all sessions was 83.3 percent, which is above an existing ideal standard of leader fidelity of 80 percent.

Secondly, selection of the research participants was described to be carefully implemented. The research participants who were selected had to meet stringent criteria, including being older women who experienced interpersonal trauma, had an absence of cognitive or psychotic impairments, were not involved in psychotherapy, had a history of practicing the Christian tradition, and had no issues with being suicidal. The minimum age requirement was not specified but the youngest participant was 55 years old. Descriptions of how this screening was done were evident in the report using a phone screening protocol followed by an in-person clinical interview. As a final check, all of the participants in the sample were found to have more than one traumatic event and all but one of them reported multiple types of violence and abuse.

Third, data were gathered from the research participants on the outcome variables at three points in time, before and after the intervention, as

well as at a three-month follow-up. The authors indicated that the data collectors were five PhD students who were trained in the interview protocols,
and had clinical experience treating trauma survivors. To preclude the
potential for bias, the data collectors were not informed of the group assignments (treatment or control) of each research participant. In terms of the
reliability of the measurements of the four outcomes variables, all four
instrument measures had Cronbach's alphas, a reliability measure, at or
above .78 out of 1.00.

Step 6: Prepare a Written or Oral Report

Strategies in preparing a report are described in chapter 11. The data are
organized, analyzed, and finally interpreted. Critiquing step 6 involves examining the finding section, recommendations, limitations, and other issues.
Considerable thoughtful work is required in creating presentations of the
findings that will be understandable to those reading the report. Evaluation
reports usually tend to address the major questions of stakeholders reflected
in the initial purpose statements worked out in step 3. This report can be oral,
written, or both. Visual aids, such as tables and graphs, are often included in
the findings section to assist in highlighting the most important findings; thus,
tables and graphs are important for critical consumers to critique along with
the findings in text form. For example, are the tables clear and do they serve
a useful purpose in highlighting or elaborating on a set of findings?

The interpretations of the findings also require much thought and care
and should be developed in keeping with the needs of the various stakeholders. Interpretations usually begin with a summary of the most important findings followed by recommendations that are supported by the findings. These recommendations also need to be useful and practical to the
various stakeholders. Limitations in the interpretations should be acknowl-
edged based on limitations in the sampling procedures, some group
designs, and measurement instruments.

The findings of the Bowland Report are complicated because they use a
group design that involves many factors. With a group design, a critical consumer has to determine to what extent it can be claimed that the intervention and not something else has a positive impact on the outcome variables.
This is referred to as internal validity. Similarly, a critical consumer has to
also determine the extent to which the impact on the outcomes can be generalized to other client groups in other settings. This is referred to as external validity. Reading over the findings several times can help detect many of
these issues.

The Bowland Report reported their findings in steps. First they presented an analysis of the pretest scores of the participants' background characteristics and the four outcome variables for both the treatment and control groups; the results in table 2 indicated that these scores were not

significantly different and therefore they conclude that the groups were equivalent. This is an important step to take to determine if the differences in the participants in the two groups could be an extraneous factor influencing the intervention's effects on the outcome variables.

Second, a complex statistical analysis of the four hypotheses was presented, which indicated that the treatment groups made significant progress in reducing the scores of the four outcome variables. The women's scores for three of the outcomes (depression, anxiety, and physical health symptoms) in the treatment groups were reduced quite significantly, while they were not reduced in the control groups. This is displayed clearly in table 4 (p. 79). The intervention's impact on the post-traumatic stress symptoms of the women, the other outcome variable, was found to be significant but less so than the impact the intervention had on the other three outcome variables. This may explain why these scores are not included in table 4 but their absence is not explained.

The complexity of the statistical tests that were used was probably beyond what most critical consumers could fully understand, raising the question of whether this presentation could have been simplified. It is likely that the editorial board of the journal requested this degree of analysis. Yet, it would be wise to simplify the analysis for other stakeholders who may need less of this statistical evidence. This could easily be done by preparing a different report format for some stakeholders needing less emphasis on the statistical analysis. We will return to using multiple report formats later.

A central question for critical consumers that was not addressed is, to whom could these findings be generalized? This is a very important question for critical consumers who may wish to use these findings with their client populations. Generalizing to other groups should always be done with extreme caution even if a critical consumer's clients have characteristics similar to those in the sample. Among the reasons caution is important is because the initial participant pool was selected using non-probability sampling approaches and could have been skewed by a selection process that inevitably favored some women over others largely in unknown ways.

The discussion section followed the findings and involved four sets of recommendations. It is most important for critical consumers to first identify each recommendation and then determine what findings, if any, support each recommendation. The first recommendation was that trauma-informed services should be provided in both community-based agencies and long-term care facilities. The findings supporting this recommendation were that all four interpersonal trauma symptoms were significantly reduced by the spiritual intervention. The second recommendation stressed the value of practitioners seriously attending to clients' spiritual issues and resources to help them cope more effectively with the impact of trauma. This was supported by the finding that the intervention reducing these symptoms focused on spirituality issues.

The third recommendation was more in the form of a question to the critical consumers or readers. The question seemed to suggest that critical consumers can decide where group treatment models like their spiritual intervention could be offered. They asked, can these models be situated in assisted living centers in long-term care facilities or a church congregation? Stigma issues were mentioned as a reason to resist considering using mental health settings. Findings did not directly support this recommendation; it was not altogether clear why this is an important topic to raise without identifying some of the obstacles that the authors found in introducing their group model.

The fourth recommendation was also offered in the form of a question about whether social workers are qualified to address spiritual issues as a group leader or whether they may need to work collaboratively with clergy who presumably have this expertise. Growing numbers of social workers have been incorporating spirituality into their practice over the last thirty years and a growing body of social work knowledge in spirituality work could have been referenced here but was not. The authors did mention later in the conclusion that all of the facilitators in the study had training in theology and pastoral care. Possibly they could have suggested specific spirituality competencies or skills that would be important for those wanting to replicate their study; they did mention a feminist theological perspective.

Limitations were discussed in the discussion section. The authors identified a somewhat unusual one, namely the first author implemented the recruitment, screening, and intervention. Social desirability biases brought about by the direct involvement of the first author were identified as an issue but no further explanation was given for why these were a limitation. Other limitations that were briefly identified in the report were limited funds for advertising and having only one person directly involved; this was explained to make the point that the screening process took longer than desired. A small sample was mentioned as another limitation, and reliability was noted as missing in measuring the outcomes because only one evaluator was involved.

Other limitations were not mentioned. One important one could have been the ethical issues of using control groups. The authors explained that all of the participants in the control groups were later offered participation in a treatment group. However, possible ethical issues remained because the participants' access to the intervention was delayed and possibly inadvertently tainted by being forced to first participate in a control group. Another limitation that was indirectly noted related to the sample. Older women with interpersonal trauma are a difficult group to find just by virtue of the undesirability of having and sharing trauma experiences. The authors noted initial challenges in recruiting a broadly representative sample; most of the participants were self-selected as they volunteered because "they were interested in the project." Limitations in including only Christian participants and leaving out a measure of social support were mentioned as issues to address in future evaluations.

Step 7: Disseminate the Findings

Step 7, the last step of an evaluation, is to disseminate the findings to stakeholders and other interested people. Unfortunately, this step is often overlooked or minimized in importance, as explained in chapter 11. This is unfortunate because if the findings are not disseminated to stakeholders in several formats, they will inevitably be underutilized. Many stakeholders can only be effectively reached in brief written formats such as one-page summaries, brief bulletins, newsletter inserts, and timely handouts posted on bulletin boards. Many other stakeholders can only be reached with oral presentations in forums such as public hearings, informal conversations, workshops, perhaps a series of topical seminars, or other venues.

Some stakeholders could be overlooked in the dissemination of the findings based on a variety of questionable motives such as the following: that some stakeholders have nothing to offer, that they will only bring more questions and more headaches with them, that they will take too much time, or they will simply not understand the more "technical" issues. Unfortunately, clients, family members, and some community groups, in particular, are typically examples of those overlooked or viewed as irrelevant to the evaluation process.

THE NEED FOR MULTIPLE STRATEGIES

Ideally, a variety of evaluation reports need to be prepared and disseminated that are relevant to different stakeholders, rather than taking the position that one report "fits all." As indicated in chapter 11, stakeholders have widely varying needs and capacities as critical consumers. Different evaluation reports are usually prepared and tailored to the needs of funding agencies, administrators, staff members, agency boards, and clients. Technical reports are ideal for funding agencies, administrators of agencies sponsoring an intervention, and some key staff members. They are also ideal for most journal submissions. In contrast, technical reports are too lengthy and tend to be highly technical and challenging for others to understand. This usually includes most board members, most staff members, volunteers, clients, community groups, and others. Executive summaries of technical reports often work well for many legislators, board members, and others who may be interested in reading a succinct summary of the findings and recommendations of a technical report. These stakeholders usually do not have the time or sometimes the capacity to thoroughly understand a technical report. In these instances, specific sections of the report could also be provided on an as-needed basis. This could be handled informally and in an individualized manner.

Staff members are primarily interested in how the findings of a report will affect them and their roles as practitioners. In these cases, staff workshops, training sessions, informal presentations and dialogues, focused supervisory sessions, and other staff venues can be targeted to particular areas of the report that directly involve staff. Chapter 11 provides more information about the importance of informing staff about the findings of an evaluation and how this can be done. Reports for clients are usually different from all of the other stakeholders and will be discussed in the final section of this chapter.

The Bowland Report is clearly a technical report. It is similar to the technical report described in chapter 11 and includes a number of required content areas including a literature review, relevant theoretical concepts, research questions to be asked or hypotheses to be tested, the sampling approach and characteristics of the sample, the data collection approach, data analysis plan, findings, recommendations, and limitations of the study. The Bowland Report, when critiqued as a technical report, scores highly. It covers all of the sections of such a report and generally describes them well.

As has been mentioned earlier, consulting all of the important stakeholders is an important step to take prior to determining what reports can directly benefit each of them. Unfortunately, it is not possible to know how step 7 was taken by Bowland and colleagues based on what the report leaves out about dissemination. However, if Bowland and her colleagues only prepared the technical report published in the *Social Work* journal, they would probably have fallen short of preparing and disseminating the kinds of information needed by all of their important stakeholders.

In review, a technical report alone is not likely to be adequate in meeting the needs of all of the important stakeholders of an evaluation. Several of the steps in the Seven Evaluation Steps are left out of it or are downplayed. A description of step 2 (identify and explore ways to involve stakeholders) does not usually appear in a technical report even though the stakeholders can have a profound effect on an evaluation. While stakeholder participation involves a political process, there are ways to thoughtfully and appropriately disclose how stakeholders assisted in shaping an evaluation. Step 5 (implement the evaluation) is also largely left out of most technical reports and is an important aspect of a research design to disclose. Finally, step 7 (disseminate the findings) is largely ignored in technical reports.

HELPING CLIENTS BECOME CRITICAL CONSUMERS

Clients who are recipients of interventions are seldom seen as relevant stakeholders of an evaluation. Many reasons can be given for this, such as clients are viewed as incapable of being critical consumers, they have nothing to offer, involving them will take too much effort, and giving them a critical consumer role conflicts with their client role. Perhaps this kind of questionable reasoning is also based on the assumption that the technical report is the only "official" evaluation report. Needless to say, most clients would have enormous challenges understanding a technical report like the Bowland Report.

We have pointed out in both this chapter and chapter 11 that many types of reports and many dissemination strategies may be necessary to use if maximum benefits are to come from an evaluation. It is also important to stress that the clients who are the recipients of these interventions have special needs to be addressed as critical consumers that are unlike any other stakeholders. Let's review what some of these needs are, how we can help them become critical consumers, and what the benefits could be to agencies.

Evaluation reports can be simplified for various stakeholders without necessarily removing important meaning. As an example, the statistical analysis involved in an evaluation is necessary to complete and report on but it doesn't have to be displayed in all of its detail in the reports going to many of the stakeholders. Reports prepared for many of the stakeholders of an evaluation, especially clients, should, by necessity, be simplified. Many of the aspects of an evaluation, including the purpose, research design, data analysis, findings, and recommendations can be simplified and still retain sufficient meaning for clients and some other stakeholders. Here are some examples of explanations, in part using the Bowland Report:

> *A needs assessment:* A study that gathers accurate information about the needs of a group of people.
>
> *Example of a hypothesis:* Clients with trauma can be relieved of some of their trauma by participating in a spirituality treatment group.
>
> *Example of a finding:* The women's trauma symptoms were reduced by participating in the spirituality treatment group.
>
> *Example of a recommendation:* Services need to be provided in both community and institutional programs that help older women with past traumas.

Evaluators must be at least somewhat convinced that sharing the results of an evaluation with clients is beneficial. This would not necessarily mean that all clients would be expected to be such critical consumers. Perhaps, evaluators should start with clients who are higher functioning, seem to have more verbal skills and greater intellect, and, of course, a willingness to do this. Client volunteers could be sought by various means such as an open agency invitation to come to a social event where the findings of the evaluation will be presented. The event could include refreshments and other enticements.

Clients would also need to be convinced that they could benefit from taking on a critical consumer role. Also, they would need to have the confidence that they could understand the basics of an evaluation report including its purpose, research design, results, and recommendations. They may also need some technical assistance. The benefits to the agency of involving clients as critical consumers could be potentially enormous. One benefit would be that clients are given an opportunity to give feedback on whether the findings make sense to them. Further, the clients could be asked to give explanations for why some of the findings are unclear or ambiguous to stakeholders. For example, in the Bowland study, the post-traumatic stress symptoms were not found to be reduced as easily and as much as the other symptoms. Why would that be? Clients with these symptoms may have some possible explanations. Also, the spiritual intervention that the agency introduced, like any intervention, has strengths and weaknesses. What might the clients think were some of its strengths and weaknesses? How could it be improved? Empowering clients with a critical consumer role can strengthen the trust that clients have in the provider agency because they are being recognized as an important source of information. Also, many clients may feel better about themselves and their provider because they are being treated with greater dignity.

It may seem odd to some to end the book with a discussion of how clients can be encouraged to become more actively involved in the evaluation process. Yet, this is a very upbeat and relevant note to end with because we still have much to learn about how to involve clients. Indeed, evaluations are a dynamic and ever-changing enterprise. Evaluations will continue to grow in importance in the future as a tool for holding social programs accountable, and clients will likely be expected to be significant partners in this endeavor.

KEY TERMS

Administrators as critical consumers
Clients as critical consumers
Critical consumer role
Different evaluation report formats
Evaluation reports
Experimental designs
Practitioners as critical consumers
Reimbursement and regulatory entities as critical consumers
Seven Evaluation Steps
Students as critical consumers
Technical report

DISCUSSION QUESTIONS AND ASSIGNMENTS

1. Examine for yourself how the Bowland Report addresses each of the seven evaluation steps. Then answer how well you think these authors completed each of these steps. How did your answers compare to the answers given in this chapter?

2. Assume you are the authors or evaluators of the Bowland Report. Prepare a report of the evaluation that will be useful to staff members. First, choose a format for your presentation using one of the formats described in chapter 11. Next, prepare the actual presentation. It can either be done orally or in written form.

3. Assume that you have prepared an oral report of the findings pertaining to the four hypotheses in the Bowland Report for staff members. Now role-play this presentation with two people being the co-presenters and four or five people being staff members hearing and reacting to these findings for the first time. Discuss the implications for their practice.

4. In a role-play, select one of the hypotheses in the Bowland Report pertinent to a client who is an older woman experiencing costly physical and mental health trauma and discuss this hypothesis and the results of testing it with this client (or a client group). Help the client compare these results with what her situation is and facilitate a discussion that is helpful to the client.

REFERENCES

Bolin, B. B., Lee, K. H., Glenmaye, L. F., & Yoon, D. P. (2012). Impact of research orientation on attitudes toward research of social work students. *Journal of Social Work Education, 48*, 223–243.

Bowland, S., Edmond, T., & Fallot, R. D. (2012). Evaluation of a spiritually focused intervention with older trauma survivors. *Social Work, 57*, 73–82.

Collins-Camargo, C., & Millar, K. (2010). The potential for a more clinical approach to child welfare supervision to promote practice and case outcomes: A qualitative study in four states. *The Clinical Supervisor, 29*, 164–187.

Gibbs, L. (2007). Applying research to make life-affecting judgments and decisions. *Research on Social Work Practice, 17*, 143–150.

Harder, J. (2010). Overcoming MSW students' reluctance to engage in research. *Journal of Teaching in Social Work, 30*, 195–209.

Howard, M. O., McMillen, C. J., & Pollio, D. E. (2003). Teaching evidence-based practice: Toward a new paradigm for social work education. *Research on Social Work Education, 13*, 234–259.

Long, D. D., Tice, C. J., & Morrison, J. D. (2006). *Macro social work practice.* Belmont, CA: Brooks/Cole.

Lundahl, B. W. (2008). Teaching research methodology through active learning. *Journal of Teaching in Social Work, 28*, 273–288.

Mildon, R., & Shlonsky, A. (2011). Bridge over troubled water: Using implementation science to facilitate effective services in child welfare. *Child Abuse & Neglect, 35*, 753–756.

National Association of Social Workers. (2008). Code of ethics of the National Association of Social Workers (approved by the 1996 NASW Delegate Assembly and revised by the 2008 NASW Delegate Assembly). Washington, DC: Author.

Petr, C. G., & Walter, U. M. (2005). Best practices inquiry: A multidimensional, value-critical framework. *Journal of Social Work Education, 41*, 251–267.

Staudt, M. M. (2007). Two years later: Former students' perceptions of a clinical evaluation course and current evaluation practices. *Journal of Teaching in Research, 27*, 125–139.

Wilkerson, D., Migas, N., & Slaven, T. (2000). Outcome-oriented standards and performance indicators for substance dependency rehabilitation programs. *Substance Use & Misuse, 35*, 1679–1703.

Wodarski, J. S., Feit, M. D., & Green, R. K. (1995). Graduate social work education: A review of 2 decades of empirical research and considerations for the future. *Social Service Review, 1995*, 108–130.

Appendix A

The American Evaluation Association's Guiding Principles for Evaluators

A. Systematic Inquiry: Evaluators conduct systematic, data-based inquiries.
    1. To ensure the accuracy and credibility of the evaluative information they produce, evaluators should adhere to the highest technical standards appropriate to the methods they use.
    2. Evaluators should explore with the client the shortcomings and strengths both of the various evaluation questions and the various approaches that might be used for answering those questions.
    3. Evaluators should communicate their methods and approaches accurately and in sufficient detail to allow others to understand, interpret, and critique their work. They should make clear the limitations of an evaluation and its results. Evaluators should discuss in a contextually appropriate way those values, assumptions, theories, methods, results, and analyses significantly affecting the interpretation of the evaluative findings. These statements apply to all aspects of the evaluation, from its initial conceptualization to the eventual use of findings.
B. Competence: Evaluators provide competent performance to stakeholders.
    1. Evaluators should possess (or ensure that the evaluation team possesses) the education, abilities, skills, and experience appropriate to undertake the tasks proposed in the evaluation.
    2. To ensure recognition, accurate interpretation, and respect for diversity, evaluators should ensure that the members of the evaluation team collectively demonstrate cultural competence. Cultural competence would be reflected in evaluators seeking awareness of their own culturally based assumptions, their understanding of the worldviews of culturally different participants and stakeholders in the evaluation, and the use of appropriate evaluation strategies and skills in working with culturally different groups. Diversity may be in terms of race, ethnicity, gender, religion, socio-economics, or other factors pertinent to the evaluation context.

3. Evaluators should practice within the limits of their professional training and competence, and should decline to conduct evaluations that fall substantially outside those limits. When declining the commission or request is not feasible or appropriate, evaluators should make clear any significant limitations on the evaluation that might result. Evaluators should make every effort to gain the competence directly or through the assistance of others who possess the required expertise.

4. Evaluators should continually seek to maintain and improve their competencies, in order to provide the highest level of performance in their evaluations. This continuing professional development might include formal coursework and workshops, self-study, evaluations of one's own practice, and working with other evaluators to learn from their skills and expertise.

C. Integrity/Honesty: Evaluators display honesty and integrity in their own behavior, and attempt to ensure the honesty and integrity of the entire evaluation process.

1. Evaluators should negotiate honestly with clients and relevant stakeholders concerning the costs, tasks to be undertaken, limitations of methodology, scope of results likely to be obtained, and uses of data resulting from a specific evaluation. It is primarily the evaluator's responsibility to initiate discussion and clarification of these matters, not the client's.

2. Before accepting an evaluation assignment, evaluators should disclose any roles or relationships they have that might pose a conflict of interest (or appearance of a conflict) with their role as an evaluator. If they proceed with the evaluation, the conflict(s) should be clearly articulated in reports of the evaluation results.

3. Evaluators should record all changes made in the originally negotiated project plans, and the reasons why the changes were made. If those changes would significantly affect the scope and likely results of the evaluation, the evaluator should inform the client and other important stakeholders in a timely fashion (barring good reason to the contrary, before proceeding with further work) of the changes and their likely impact.

4. Evaluators should be explicit about their own, their clients', and other stakeholders' interests and values concerning the conduct and outcomes of an evaluation.

5. Evaluators should not misrepresent their procedures, data, or findings. Within reasonable limits, they should attempt to prevent or correct misuse of their work by others.

6. If evaluators determine that certain procedures or activities are likely to produce misleading evaluative information or conclusions, they have the responsibility to communicate their con-

cerns and the reasons for them. If discussions with the client do not resolve these concerns, the evaluator should decline to conduct the evaluation. If declining the assignment is unfeasible or inappropriate, the evaluator should consult colleagues or relevant stakeholders about other proper ways to proceed. (Options might include discussions at a higher level, a dissenting cover letter or appendix, or refusal to sign the final document.)

7. Evaluators should disclose all sources of financial support for an evaluation, and the source of the request for the evaluation.

D. Respect for People: Evaluators respect the security, dignity, and self-worth of respondents, program participants, clients, and other evaluation stakeholders.

1. Evaluators should seek a comprehensive understanding of the important contextual elements of the evaluation. Contextual factors that may influence the results of a study include geographic location, timing, political and social climate, economic conditions, and other relevant activities in progress at the same time.

2. Evaluators should abide by current professional ethics, standards, and regulations regarding risks, harms, and burdens that might befall those participating in the evaluation; regarding informed consent for participation in evaluation; and regarding informing participants and clients about the scope and limits of confidentiality.

3. Because justified negative or critical conclusions from an evaluation must be explicitly stated, evaluations sometimes produce results that harm client or stakeholder interests. Under this circumstance, evaluators should seek to maximize the benefits and reduce any unnecessary harms that might occur, provided this will not compromise the integrity of the evaluation findings. Evaluators should carefully judge when the benefits from doing the evaluation or in performing certain evaluation procedures should be foregone because of the risks or harms. To the extent possible, these issues should be anticipated during the negotiation of the evaluation.

4. Knowing that evaluations may negatively affect the interests of some stakeholders, evaluators should conduct the evaluation and communicate its results in a way that clearly respects the stakeholders' dignity and self-worth.

5. Where feasible, evaluators should attempt to foster social equity in evaluation, so that those who give to the evaluation may benefit in return. For example, evaluators should seek to ensure that those who bear the burdens of contributing data and incurring any risks do so willingly, and that they have full knowledge of and opportunity to obtain any benefits of the evaluation.

Program participants should be informed that their eligibility to receive services does not hinge on their participation in the evaluation.

6. Evaluators have the responsibility to understand and respect differences among participants, such as differences in their culture, religion, gender, disability, age, sexual orientation, and ethnicity, and to account for potential implications of these differences when planning, conducting, analyzing, and reporting evaluations.

E. Responsibilities for General and Public Welfare: Evaluators articulate and take into account the diversity of general and public interests and values that may be related to the evaluation.

1. When planning and reporting evaluations, evaluators should include relevant perspectives and interests of the full range of stakeholders.

2. Evaluators should consider not only the immediate operations and outcomes of whatever is being evaluated, but also its broad assumptions, implications, and potential side effects.

3. Freedom of information is essential in a democracy. Evaluators should allow all relevant stakeholders access to evaluative information in forms that respect people and honor promises of confidentiality. Evaluators should actively disseminate information to stakeholders as resources allow. Communications that are tailored to a given stakeholder should include all results that may bear on interests of that stakeholder and refer to any other tailored communications to other stakeholders. In all cases, evaluators should strive to present results clearly and simply so that clients and other stakeholders can easily understand the evaluation process and results.

4. Evaluators should maintain a balance between client needs and other needs. Evaluators necessarily have a special relationship with the client who funds or requests the evaluation. By virtue of that relationship, evaluators must strive to meet legitimate client needs whenever it is feasible and appropriate to do so. However, that relationship can also place evaluators in difficult dilemmas when client interests conflict with other interests, or when client interests conflict with the obligation of evaluators for systematic inquiry, competence, integrity, and respect for people. In these cases, evaluators should explicitly identify and discuss the conflicts with the client and relevant stakeholders, resolve them when possible, determine whether continued work on the evaluation is advisable if the conflicts cannot be resolved, and make clear any significant limitations on the evaluation that might result if the conflict is not resolved.

5. Evaluators have obligations that encompass the public interest and good. These obligations are especially important when evaluators are supported by publicly generated funds; but clear threats to the public good should never be ignored in any evaluation. Because the public interest and good are rarely the same as the interests of any particular group (including those of the client or funder), evaluators will usually have to go beyond analysis of particular stakeholder interests and consider the welfare of society as a whole.

Appendix B

Glossary

ANOVA (one-way analysis of variance) is a bivariate statistical test that is used to determine whether three or more groups are significantly different from one another with respect to a particular characteristic.

Assessments of client strengths (and weaknesses) are assessment tools in practice that include questions to explore clients' strengths and weaknesses; the assessment of clients' strengths is often an area that is otherwise overlooked in assessments.

Best practices are the "best" or most effective programs or practices known to help people overcome their problems. Evidence-based practices, in many ways, are synonymous with "best practices."

Biopsychosocial assessment tools are assessment tools in practice that identify questions and topical areas to explore with clients in three areas of their lives: biological, psychological, and social. Sometimes these tools also include assessment questions about the spiritual, mental, and cultural dimensions of a client.

Case managers monitor the range of services provided to their clients to ensure their quality and continued appropriateness. Case managers typically find services for clients, negotiate or facilitate contracts with agencies that offer services, monitor services to ensure that the agency actually delivers the contracted services, and advocate when necessary on behalf of clients.

Central tendency measures are statistics that summarize an entire set of scores by calculating a single representative number. Three types of measures of central tendency are available for use in evaluations: mean, median, and mode.

Chi-square test is a bivariate statistic used to determine whether the values of one variable are associated with the values of another variable. This test is also sometimes referred to as a "cross-tab," or cross-tabulation, of these variables.

Clinical significance is a way to determine whether enough improvement occurred in the client's outcome variable after implementation of the intervention. Clinical significance is based on clinical criteria established by a professional group or agency. In this case, the amount of improvement in the client's goal is enough if it meets the established clinical criteria.

Community forums are sessions in which several people come together to discuss a topic of interest to all of them. Participants are likely to belong to the same community or neighborhood, and the topic is likely to be an issue that has community-wide implications.

Condition is a property of a measurable objective that identifies prior circumstances or conditions required before a performance can be expected.

Correlation test is a bivariate statistical test used to determine whether there is a statistically significant association between two variables. A correlation test can be used only when both variables are at the interval/ratio level of measurement.

Criterion is a property of a measurable objective that is a standard of acceptable performance, reflected in such things as speed, accuracy, or quality.

Critical consumer role involves reading and evaluating research studies in a critical manner that identifies the strengths and limitations of studies. This role includes understanding a study, evaluating how well it was conducted and presented, and using the findings appropriately to improve social work practice.

Descriptive statistics are statistics used to summarize responses or scores for each variable. These statistics are also referred to as univariate statistics because they analyze one variable at a time.

Ecomaps are an assessment tool in practice that visually describe the client's person-in-environment constellation, including relationships with friends and family members who are significant to the client, agencies and schools that are involved, jobs, and other social supports.

Effectiveness refers to interventions being successful in bringing about the expected changes in clients' lives.

Efficiency refers to interventions concerned with channeling available resources to the intended target problem or concern without any waste.

Effort refers to what staff members, volunteers, and administrators put into a program or practice area when implementing an intervention.

Elements of programs and practice are distinct entities critical to their functioning. Several elements can exist in each of the stages. For example, input elements could be the target goals or purposes of a program/practice area. Process elements during the implementation stage could be the theoretical approach that is being used. Outcome elements can be the measures of client progress in reaching their goals.

Empowerment models refer to concepts, techniques, and findings that help specific oppressed groups or communities develop their self-determining ability and improve programs. Program participants are sometimes helped to conduct their own evaluations and use outside evaluators and other experts as coaches, facilitators, expert consultants, and critical friends.

Evaluation design is the plan for carrying out an evaluation. It includes a set of study questions and/or hypotheses to explore or test, a source from whom the data is gathered, a specific method of collecting the data, and a data analysis plan. A plan to protect human participants of the study is also an important component to complete and have approved.

Evidence-based interventions are interventions in which there is the best available external evidence that they are effective. Sources of evidence come mostly from research studies using quasi-experimental or experimental designs and practice experience. Evidence-based sources should also be consistent with the values and expectations of the clients receiving these interventions.

Experimental designs are longitudinal group designs that can be used to test whether there is a causal relationship between an intervention and a client outcome variable. These designs are the strongest designs for proving causality and have two groups, a group that receives the intervention and a control group that does not. Participants are selected and randomly assigned to the two groups. The control group is considered identical to the group receiving the intervention, except that it does not receive the intervention.

Experimental models are evaluation perspectives that posit that experimental and quasi-experimental designs are superior to other evaluation designs because they deliver scientifically credible evidence of the impact of programs on clients' welfare. The perspective posits that experimental designs and randomized samples are feasible and ethical, and the only way to rule out other influences such as other sources of help.

Family genograms are an assessment tool in practice that provide a visual display of a family across two or more generations and offer insights into and understanding of the patterns evident in the client's family.

Feminist perspectives on evaluation are defined both by the research methods that feminists prefer and the substantive areas they choose to study. Most feminist researchers prefer qualitative over quantitative methods because of the flexibility built into the method and the value it places on uncovering new knowledge at deeper levels of meaning. This evaluation focus tends to be concerned primarily with studying the relative positions and experiences of women in relation to men and the effects that gender issues have on both sexes, such as gender discrimination in hiring, the low representation of women in administrative and other leadership roles, and salary inequities based on gender.

Focus groups are a special type of group in which participants are invited to discuss a particular topic. Focus groups can be used to find out the views of several people on an issue of importance to a needs assessment. Members of focus groups are usually selected because they have personal knowledge on or expertise in a particular topic. The leader of a focus group facilitates a group discussion by asking members several general questions on the topic.

Formative evaluations focus on planning for a program and improving its delivery of services. Such evaluations are usually initiated and conducted by the agency sponsoring the program/practice area and are driven internally by staff of the agency and outside consultants whom they select.

Fourth-generation evaluations refer to a new approach for this millennium that strives to redress power imbalances and expand the repertoire of data gathering and analysis methods used in evaluations. Someone with this perspective distrusts all methods equally and can recognize and admit the situational limitations of the knower, whether based in science, literature, or another vantage point. This perspective particularly seeks to hear and value the often unheard indigenous voices of other societies in the world.

Frequency distribution is a statistic that describes the number and percentage of times that each of the values of a variable is observed in a sample.

General study questions for evaluations serve two purposes. First, they provide parameters for an evaluation, limiting what will be investigated. Second, they provide enough specificity to know what is to be explored in a specific sense. In other words, they are not too broad to be unrealistic and not too specific to be too restricting.

Goal is an end result intended for an intervention. Goals are important because they provide an intervention with a direction to pursue and an outcome to reach. Without goals, an intervention may be an aimless effort that does not seem to go anywhere important. Goals are often not in a measurable form and need measurable objectives.

Goal Attainment Scale (GAS) is a practice evaluation tool that can be used to evaluate the extent to which the worker's interventions affect the client's goals in a favorable way. It is an incremental scale that can be used to measure degrees of progress.

Implementation evaluations investigate the procedures and processes established to carry out a program. The overall questions are how well have agencies followed procedures to support a new intervention and how have these changes impacted clients?

Informed consent means that the participants of an evaluation are thoroughly informed about the study before they are expected to consent to participate.

Institutional review boards (IRBs) are a group of people at an agency or university who have been designated to promulgate ethical standards and to approve and monitor the ethical provisions of all studies sponsored by the institution. Evaluators and other researchers are required to submit a formal statement to their IRB that describes their study, its procedures, benefits, and how it protects research participants from risks of harm and invasion of privacy.

Logic model is a tool to theoretically analyze a program. The logic model helps highlight how the stages and elements of a program can be logically linked to one another in an organic whole. Using this model, the sequence of steps in a program's development are important to examine, beginning with the problems of prospective clients and culminating in anticipated client outcomes.

Mapping is a computerized approach that visually locates specific groups or clusters of people or problems in a particular geographic area. Mapping helps the user recognize where there are concentrations of problems and their association with other relevant factors.

Measurable objectives are statements that identify indicators of whether a client or group of clients reaches a goal. Usually each goal has more than one measurable objective.

Mixed methods are quantitative and qualitative methods of data collection and analysis that can be used in combination with each other in evaluations. Use of mixed methods offers several advantages, including use of the respective data to complement one another in evaluation findings and in triangulating the collected data.

Needs assessment is an organized and systematic effort to assess the need for something, in this case the need for a new program or practice area. Executing a needs assessment of some or all prospective recipients of a program is often the wisest way to conduct an assessment. The specific ways to conduct a needs assessment can take many forms, including use of existing data, construction and administration of a questionnaire, conducting of interviews or focus groups, arranging of public forums, observations, or a combination of these methods.

Overt indicator is a word or phrase added after a performance to help make the performance more observable in a measurable objective.

Performance is a property of a measurable objective that identifies what a person is expected to do.

Practice refers to the interventions of an individual social worker or human service worker. This is in contrast to a program that involves the interventions of all staff members in that program.

Practice evaluation is a study of one social worker's interventions with clients. Like a program evaluation, it uses the methods of research. However, in contrast to program evaluation, it focuses on how well an individual social worker implements his or her client interventions.

Pre-experimental designs are group designs that can be used to explore a causal relationship between an intervention and a client outcome variable. These designs have only an intervention group. They are the weakest group designs and have limited use, but they are often considered initially because they can be implemented more easily and take less time than experimental and quasi-experimental designs.

Program is an organizational entity in an agency that offers a set of goods and/or services with common goals. The goods and services are typically provided to a target population of clients who either seek them out or are selected to use them. A program typically employs more than one and usually several staff members.

Program evaluation is a study of a social program that uses the methods of scientific research. It concerns itself with the practical needs of an organization, not theoretical issues, and it focuses on how well an overall program implements its services.

Quality refers to a program and practice area being delivered as intended and being done very well at a very high standard.

Quality assurance is a set of evaluation activities implemented to gather information about the processes of programs. Its distinguishing characteristics include peer reviews, heavy reliance on client records, observation of small samples of the services, assurance that minimal standards are met, and immediate incorporation of useful results to improve the program. Quality assurance is also sometimes referred to as quality improvement or quality control.

Quasi-experimental designs are longitudinal group designs that can be used to explore a causal relationship between an intervention and a client outcome variable. These designs have features that control for some of the extraneous influences by using a comparison group or having multiple measures of the outcome variable.

Regression tests are statistical tests that can predict a client outcome from more than one intervention.

Relevance refers to an intervention meeting the clients' need and solving the larger social problem that clients are experiencing.

Results-oriented models are evaluation perspectives that focus on performance, outcomes, and accountability. Advocates of the results-oriented model believe that it is important to convince various stakeholders that the outcomes they achieve are the ultimate reason why they are in business.

Secondary research additionally analyzes data from a previous study. Many research firms offer their data sets to interested people for secondary analysis, often for a reasonable fee.

Sequencing blocks are an exercise that helps clients explore the causal relationships among prior behaviors that have resulted in a positive or negative outcome. In this case, the outcome behavior is known and the behavior that caused it is to be discovered.

Services are the activities offered by programs. Services focus mostly on the processes that help clients reach their program goals. Helping processes are the major focus of practice courses in social work programs and draw from a broad range of practice theories, such as cognitive behavioral, person-centered, and solution-focused therapies. In-service training programs are also valuable to prepare staff members and volunteers with the skills to assist in the helping processes that are the most effective.

Single-system design (SSD) is a practice evaluation tool that determines the impact of one or more interventions introduced by a social worker on a client system. An SSD uses a graph with the changes that a client makes plotted over time to observe whether the interventions are responsible for improvements in that behavior when they occur.

Stakeholders are the people invested in a program or practice intervention in some way. Examples include representatives of a funding agency, an agency board of directors, staff members, and clients. The success of these stakeholders is, in some way, likely to depend on the program's performance, so they have an obvious stake in what happens.

Statistical significance is a way to determine whether enough improvement occurred in the client's outcome variable after implementation of the intervention. Statistically significant associations can be calculated by applying a statistical test, which determines whether the probability of an association between the intervention and the outcome measure is high. Usually a claim of significance is made when the probability of being in error is less than 5 percent (expressed as $p < .05$).

Summative evaluations focus on the outcomes of programs and attempt to answer the ultimate question: did the intervention reach its goals? These evaluations have a finality to them in that they attempt to measure whether a program was effective. Summative evaluations are typically conducted by an external agent, such as an independent evaluator or a governmental agency, to ensure that they are objective. Funding and regulatory agencies are most interested in summative evaluations because they provide the kinds of information they need to make major decisions around future funding.

t-test is a bivariate statistical test used to determine whether two groups are significantly different on the basis of a particular characteristic. One variable in this statistical formula is the group variable (group 1 or group 2). The second variable is the characteristic being compared.

Target Problem Scale (TPS) is a practice evaluation tool that can be used particularly when client goals are difficult to identify. A TPS is helpful if clients remain focused on their problems and are not prepared to pursue goals beyond these problems.

Theme analysis is a type of qualitative data analysis that involves identifying common themes or patterns prevalent in several cases.

Variability measures are statistics that summarize how the responses to a question vary or disperse away from their central tendency. These statistics complement measures of central tendencies because they provide information about the variability of scores away from the clustering point(s). Two common statistics that measure the variability of scores are range and standard deviation. Both can be used with interval/ratio level variables only.

Appendix C

Answers to Exercises and Discussion Questions for Chapters 7 and 9

CHAPTER 7

"Example of Performance, Condition, and Criteria" (located in the text of chapter 7)

Can you identify the performance, condition, and criteria in each measurable objective?

Goal: Clients will increase compliance with medication appointments.

Objective A: If clients wish to remember the dates and times of medication appointments, they will write the time of their next appointment on a calendar. [**Answer**: Performance is "write the time," condition is "If clients wish to remember the dates and times of medication appointments," and criteria are "next appointment" and "on a calendar."]

Objective B: If transportation is needed to appointments, clients will call to arrange for it at least two days prior to the appointment. [**Answer**: Performance is "call," condition is "If transportation is needed to appointments," and criteria is "at least two days prior to the appointment."]

Objective C: If clients are ill or otherwise cannot come to their medication appointment, they will call and reschedule their appointment more than twenty-four hours before the missed appointment. [**Answer**: Performance is "call and reschedule," condition is "If clients are ill or otherwise cannot come to their medication appointment," and criteria is "more than twenty-four hours before the missed appointment."]

"Exercise Regarding a Short-Term Goal and Its Measurable Objectives" (located in the text of chapter 7)

Goal: Clients will decrease their depressive symptoms.

Measurable Objective A: When feeling depressed, clients journal their feelings, thoughts, and behavior 80 percent of the time. [**Answer**: Performance is "journal," condition is "When feeling depressed," and criteria are "feelings, thoughts, and behavior" and "80 percent of the time."]

Measurable Objective B: At the outset of depressive feelings, clients demonstrate (carry out) one positive coping skill one out of three times. [**Answer**: Performance is "demonstrate (carry out)," condition is "At the outset of depressive feelings," and criteria are "one positive coping skill" and "one out of three times."]

"Exercise" (located in the text of chapter 7)

What's wrong with each of the following measurable objectives?

1. Clients will meet with their counselor and take their meds. [**Answer**: There are two performances rather than one. Also, criteria describing how many times they will meet with their counselor and the specific meds and correct dosage need to be specified.]
2. The social worker will meet with the client for five counseling sessions to help the client express his or her anger verbally. [**Answer**: This measurable objective focuses on the social worker's performance, not the client's.]
3. The father will spend nurturing time with his three-year-old son. [**Answer**: Nurturing needs to be defined so that it is observable. Criteria are needed indicating how often he spends such time with his son.]

"Discussion Questions" (located at the end of chapter 7)

1. What is needed to improve these measurable objectives?
   A. The clients will be monitored by the appropriate staff while at the group home at all times. [**Improvements**: This objective focuses on staff behavior, not client behavior. It also needs an overt indicator for the performance ("will be monitored").]
   B. After ten to twelve therapy sessions, the client will engage in negative self-talk 10 percent of the time. [**Improvements**: After ten to twelve sessions, the client will engage in (state) positive self-talk nine out of ten times.]
   C. When arriving for her appointment, the client will wait fewer than fifteen minutes to see the doctor 90 percent of the time. [**Improvements**: This objective focuses on the doctor, not the client.]
   D. During the school year, my client will turn in a progress report completed by teachers every week. [**Improvements**: During the school year, my client will turn in every week a progress report with at least five of six items graded as As.]
   E. While at X agency, the mother will spend nurturing time reading to her child 100 percent of the time. [**Improvements**: While at X agency, the mother will spend thirty minutes each day reading to her child.]

3. **Identify the performance, conditions, and criteria in measurable objectives A and B:**

Goal: Clients with a mental retardation label will strengthen their socialization skills.

Measurable Objective A: When introduced to a new person, the client will shake hands nine out of ten times. [**Answers**: Performance is "shake hands," conditions are "When being introduced to a new person," and criteria are "nine out of ten times."]

Measurable Objective B: After breakfast, the client will make his bed before leaving for work. [Performance is "make his bed," conditions are "After breakfast" and "before leaving for work." There are no criteria.]

4. **Identify the performance, conditions, and criteria in measurable objectives A, B, and C:**

Goal: Mental health clients will achieve optimum mental health.

Measurable Objective A: If prescribed, clients will take (swallow) the correct amounts of medication daily for six months. [**Answer**: Performance is "swallow," conditions are "If prescribed," and criteria are "correct amounts" and "daily for six months."]

Measurable Objective B: After ten to twelve sessions, clients will state four out of five techniques to control anxiety taught in sessions. [**Answer**: Performance is "state," conditions are "After ten to twelve sessions," and criteria are "four out of five techniques."]

Measurable Objective C: When experiencing thoughts of self-harm, clients will ask for help from their identified support system within twenty-four hours. [**Answer**: Performance is "ask," conditions are "When experiencing thoughts of self-harm," and criteria are "from their identified support system" and "within twenty-four hours."]

5. **Identify the performance, conditions, and criteria in measurable objectives A, B, and C (Guy, 2006):**

Goal: John Doe will have stronger interpersonal skills.

Measurable Objective A: John will say "good morning" to six out of ten coworkers when arriving at work each morning. [**Answer**: Performance is "say 'good morning,' " conditions are "when arriving at work each morning," and criteria are "six out of ten coworkers."]

Measurable Objective B: After six sessions, John will talk for ten minutes to one or two coworkers each week. [**Answer**: Performance is "talk," conditions are "After six sessions," and criteria are "ten minutes to one or two coworkers each week."]

Measurable Objective C: When talking to others, John will look at the person's face 75 percent of the time. [**Answer**: Performance is "look at the person's face," conditions are "When talking to others," and criteria are "75 percent of the time."]

6. **Identify the performance, conditions, and criteria in measurable objectives A, B, and C:**

Goal: Clients will develop assertiveness skills in a group on assertiveness.

Measurable Objective A: After three group sessions, the clients will circle assertive comments and cross out aggressive comments on a worksheet and be correct eight out of ten times. [**Answer**: Performance is "circle assertive comments" and "cross out aggressive comments," conditions are "After three group sessions," and criteria are "on a worksheet" and "correct eight out of ten times."]

Measurable Objective B: After five group sessions, the clients will write two ways they were assertive. [**Answer**: Performance is "write," conditions are "After five group sessions," and criteria are "two ways they were assertive."]

Measurable Objective C: At the conclusion of treatment, the clients will tell the social worker two things they liked and two things they did not like about group therapy without raising their voices. [**Answer**: Performance is "tell the social worker," conditions are "At the conclusion of treatment," and criteria are "two things they liked and two things they did not like about therapy" and "without raising their voices."]

CHAPTER 9

1. **Review the six group designs summarized in chapter 9. Then answer all of the following questions:** (located at the end of chapter 9)

  • Which design seems ideal? Why do you think so? [**Answer**: Onegroup pretest/posttest design with a control group, because it controls for all extraneous variables.]
  • Which design is the easiest and least expensive to use? What can be concluded from this design? [**Answer**: One-group posttest-only design; the only conclusion that can be drawn from this design is that the intervention may have had an impact.]

- Why are multiple measures of the client outcome variable obtained when conducting a time-series design? What are the benefits of these multiple measures? [**Answer**: The multiple measures provide data trends that can help determine the extent to which the intervention rather than other factors external to it is the causal agent.]
- Which design may be the most practical for determining whether the program intervention was responsible for positive changes in the outcome variables? Why? [**Answers**: One-group pretest/posttest design with a comparison group or time-series design, because they do not involve the ethical dilemmas that the experimental designs impose and have features that control for extraneous variables.]
- What is useful about a pretest/posttest design? [**Answer**: The design can determine whether there was any change in the client outcome measure between the pretest and posttest.]
- Under what circumstances would you consider a posttest-only control group design? [**Answer**: This design is preferred over the pretest/posttest design with a control group if there is concern that administering a pretest measure could have an influence on the outcome.]

Index

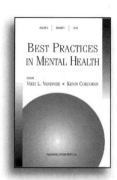

About the Author

James R. Dudley has extensive experience in both teaching and conducting program and practice evaluations. He has developed and taught program and practice evaluation courses in two different MSW programs over a fifteen-year period and has taught research methods courses at both the BSW and the MSW levels for more than twenty-five years. He has also taught BSW and MSW practice courses at all system levels (micro, mezzo, and macro) during the same period. Dudley has conducted evaluations large and small with a wide variety of topics, purposes, and methodologies; several of these are briefly described in various parts of the book as illustrations of concepts and methods. He has also supervised the evaluation projects of hundreds of graduate students that have been conducted in the students' field agencies as major course assignments, and he has conducted several evaluations involving students as assistants.